DIRE STRAITS

Dire Straits

Education Reforms, Ideology, Vested Interests, and Evidence

Montserrat Gomendio and
José Ignacio Wert

https://www.openbookpublishers.com

© 2023 Montserrat Gomendio and José Ignacio Wert

This work is licensed under an Attribution-NonCommercial 4.0 International (CC BY-NC 4.0). This license allows you to share, copy, distribute and transmit the text; to adapt the text for non-commercial purposes of the text providing attribution is made to the authors (but not in any way that suggests that they endorse you or your use of the work). Attribution should include the following information:

Montserrat Gomendio and José Ignacio Wert, *Dire Straits: Education Reforms, Ideology, Vested Interests, and Evidence*. Cambridge, UK: Open Book Publishers, 2023, https://doi.org/10.11647/OBP.0332

Further details about the CC BY-NC license are available at http://creativecommons.org/licenses/by-nc/4.0/

All external links were active at the time of publication unless otherwise stated and have been archived via the Internet Archive Wayback Machine at https://archive.org/web

Digital material and resources associated with this volume are available at https://doi.org/10.11647/OBP.0332#resources

ISBN Paperback: 978-1-80064-930-9
ISBN Hardback: 978-1-80064-931-6
ISBN Digital (PDF): 978-1-80064-932-3
ISBN Digital ebook (EPUB): 978-1-80064-933-0
ISBN Digital ebook (AZW3): 978-1-80064-934-7
ISBN XML: 978-1-80064-935-4
ISBN HTML: 978-1-80064-936-1
DOI: 10.11647/OBP.0332

Cover image: Kimberly Farmer, A collection of books (2017), https://unsplash.com/photos/lUaaKCUANVI. Cover design: Jeevanjot Kaur Nagpal.

Contents

About the Authors ix

Preface xi

1. The Functions and Role of Modern Education Systems:
A Brief Summary 1
   1.1 The Origins of Modern Education 1
   1.2 The Social Function of Modern Education 5
   1.3 To What Extent Do People Care about Education? .. 9
   1.4 The Goals of Education in the Knowledge Society ... 11
   1.5 Digitalisation: A Game Changer 13
   1.6 COVID-19: An Unexpected Disruption and an Accelerator of Change 16
   1.7 Why Are Reforms So Difficult? 18

2. Education and Ideology
(Or Is It the Other Way Around?) 19
   2.1. Ideology and Education: What Do We Mean? 19
   2.2 The Role of the State as an Education Provider 21
   2.3 Equity and the Function of Education:
Equaliser or Enabler? 31
   2.4 The Shape of Education: Architecture, Teachers, Curricula and Assessments 40
   2.5 Funding of Education and Ideology 63
   2.6 Conclusions 68

3. The Governance of Education Systems: How They Constrain or Facilitate the Implementation of Reforms 73
   3.1 Why Governance Matters 73
   3.2 The Power of Governments 74

3.3 The Dilemmas of Multi-Level States: When Power
Is Shared between Different Levels of Government   80
3.4 The Process of Decentralisation: A Bumpy Road   86
3.5 Funding. Who Raises the Money and
Who Spends it?   89
3.6 The Role of Stakeholders   96
3.7 A Special Case: Governance of VET Systems   106
3.8. Conclusions   114

4. ILSAs: Do They Count?   119
   4.1 What Do International Metrics Measure?   119
   4.2. ILSAs: What Do They Tell Us?   122
   Differences between and within Countries   122
   4.3. ILSAs: Trends Over Time   128
   4.4. Evidence from ILSAs on Effective Policies   134
   4.5. Conclusions   176

5. Does the Evidence Count?   187
   5.1. What Can We Learn from
Top-Performing Countries?   187
   5.2. What Can We Learn from Low Performers? The Latin
American Story   206
   5.3. What Have Countries Learned from the PISA Shock?   214
   5.4. What Can We Learn from Countries that
Improve in Europe?   222
   5.5. What Can We Learn from Countries where PISA Has
a Huge Media Impact but No Policy Reactions?   233
   5.6 Conclusions   237

6. Spain: An Inside Story   245
   6.1. A Rough Start   245
   6.2. Laws, Laws, Laws .... Are They Any Good?   248
   6.3. An Education Reform in the Middle of a Storm   253
   6.4. Aims, Policies and Impact of the Education Reform   257
   6.5. Back to the Future   264
   6.6. What Has Been the Role of PISA?   266

7. Education Reforms: The Interaction between Ideology,
Governance, Conflicts of Interest and Evidence 269
   7.1. Who Cares about Education and Why? 269
   7.2. Ideological Battles: What Are They About? 270
   7.3. Reform: Who Decides What, Who Funds, Who Has
   a Say, Who Has the Power to Block 274
   7.4. International Evidence versus Conflicts of Interest:
   Who is David and Who is Goliath? 279
   7.5. The Geography of Education Success 292
   7.6. Is the World a Better Place with Data? 296

References 299
Index 331

About the Authors

Montserrat Gomendio, a biologist by training, holds a BSc from Universidad Complutense (Madrid), a Ph.D. from Cambridge University (UK), and is currently a tenured Research Professor at the Spanish Research Council (CSIC). For many years, she combined her research work with leadership positions such as Director of the Spanish National Science Museum and Vice-President of the Spanish Research Council. In 2011 she was appointed Secretary of State for Education, Vocational Training and Universities in the Spanish Government. In 2015 she joined the OECD as Deputy Director of Education and in 2017 she became Head of the OECD Skills Centre. Since 2020 she has co-founded and co-chaired Skills WeGo, a consultancy on education, training and employment. Montserrat is a member of the Board of the International Baccalaureate. She has authored books and over 100 publications in peer-reviewed scientific journals.

José Ignacio Wert holds a law degree from Universidad Complutense (Madrid) and a master's degree in Political Sociology by Instituto de Estudios Políticos (Spain). He has been Deputy Director of the Centre for Sociological Research (a public research institution) and founder and CEO of Demoscopia, a leading polling firm in Spain, as well as serving in different managing capacities in other private ventures. From 2011 to 2015 he was Minister of Education, Culture and Sport in the Spanish Government and from 2015 to 2018 he was Spain's Ambassador to the OECD. Since 2020 he has co-founded and co-chaired Skills WeGo, a consultancy on education, training and employment. He is the author of four books and co-author of over two dozen others, plus several hundred articles in journals and magazines.

Preface

The aim of this book is to address the following question: why are education reforms so difficult to implement and so easy to reverse? We have had the privilege of looking at this fundamental problem from different perspectives: as academics, policymakers and advisors to governments all over the world, a vantage point which allows us to offer new insights.

Over ten years ago we started a conversation on education which is still ongoing and which remains our prime interest. During this time, education has been the focus of our professional careers and we have devoted all our efforts to this endeavour. Although we come from different backgrounds, we share the belief that education has the power to transform lives, economies and societies. We also share the view that education policies should be based on robust evidence, since we both have professional backgrounds (in academia and market and opinion research respectively) which are evidence-based and require an ability to analyse and interpret complex sets of data, draw solid conclusions and translate them into actionable measures.

We both joined the Spanish Government at the peak of the financial crisis (as Secretary of State and Minister), when levels of unemployment were dramatically high and the economy seemed on the verge of collapse. When we accepted the task of designing and implementing an education reform in Spain, we put a lot of effort into analysing both the international and national data in order to decide which policies should be implemented to overcome the many challenges facing the education system. However, we discovered that the evidence, which was so precious to us, was either misinterpreted or just ignored if it did not align with the interests of multiple stakeholders or with the ideological stances of different political parties. We also became aware that some of the conclusions and policy recommendations commonly drawn from international surveys did not apply to the Spanish context. This made the public debate around evidence-based policies confusing and easy to manipulate. Our education reform was approved in a context of intense political tensions and was the subject of a very polarised debate. As so often happens, when a different government came to power a new reform was approved which represented a complete reversal and which ignored the evidence about which policies had a positive impact.

After this experience as policymakers, we both joined the OECD (in different roles), where we learned how the surveys on levels of student performance, adult skills and teachers' practices are designed, the strengths and weaknesses of the data generated and the limitations of the conclusions and policy recommendations which have been so influential in the global debate on education policies. Unfortunately, we also discovered how little an impact this has on actual education reforms. One of us had the opportunity to visit many countries and discuss with governments and stakeholders the challenges that they faced, which policies had worked and which had failed, and the nature and magnitude of the political costs associated with different types of reforms. This experience made us aware of the extent to which the political costs of education policies is context-dependent. It also gave us a clear understanding of the geography of educational success: which countries and regions are high or low performers, and the reasons for such divergent outcomes.

This rather unique combination of professional experiences has provided us with a broad understanding of the dynamics of education reforms, as well as a wealth of information on the nature of the political battles, the impact of governance arrangements, the conflicts of interest which tend to remain hidden in the public debate, the disparate contexts faced by governments in different countries and the obstacles that derail most education reforms.

After this first-hand experience as policymakers and advisors to many governments, we needed to pause and make an effort to understand why education reforms are uniquely difficult to approve and implement, and why those which succeed are so easily reversed when a different political party wins the next election. In order to do this, we needed to rely on our academic training. This book is an attempt to understand why this is the case in the hope that our contribution will improve the chances that urgently needed education reforms will be implemented and successful policies will be preserved from political infighting or vested interests.

Our perspective is comparative education policy, with a clear focus on the interplay between ideological confrontations on the social purpose of education and the means to achieve different objectives, governance arrangements and the vested interests of an array of stakeholders in the education system. We also examine in detail the evidence provided by international surveys and investigate why it has failed to improve levels of student performance, despite its indisputable influence in shaping the narrative around good education policies. As we show, there is an intricate set of interactions between these factors that to a large extent explains why the political economy of education reforms is so complex.

First, we develop a comparative perspective on the politics of education which covers those factors that play a relevant role in facilitating or hindering reforms: ideology and governance. We explain what the ideological issues that are prominent for political parties on the right and left are, as well as the extent to which they are divisive and contribute to the polarisation of the political debate. When these ideological battles play a relevant role during elections, it becomes difficult for political parties to reach a consensus on issues which have generated deep cracks between voters.

Second, we analyse the impact of different governance arrangements on the nature of the obstacles facing education reforms. At the opposite ends of the spectrum, federal systems and centralised systems have a clear division of responsibilities, including decision-making power as well as raising and allocating the funding, so that either central government or regions are responsible for both. The recent trend to decentralise education among non-federal systems has led to a division of responsibilities between central government and regions, which is more complex and often less clear. Generally speaking, central government raises the funds through taxes which it then transfers to regions, and retains relevant decision-making power in terms of defining the architecture of the system, mechanisms to do with the selection and training of teachers, the basic content of the curriculum and national assessments. In turn, regions or local authorities are responsible for the management of their school networks and have some degree of responsibility over the curriculum and assessments depending on the precise level of autonomy that they enjoy. Decentralisation aims to make the education system more efficient and more responsive to local needs. However, in order to achieve this goal, capacity building must occur before any responsibilities are transferred and accountability mechanisms must be put in place so that the outcomes of the new arrangements can be assessed.

The complexity of *de facto* decentralised systems implies that many more actors have a relevant role to play in the approval and implementation of reforms. In countries where education is a polarised issue (since legislation tends to be approved by central government while regions are responsible for implementing the changes), when there are different political parties in power at different levels, coordination may be difficult. In addition, when the division of responsibilities is unclear this will lead to never-ending tensions between regions demanding more resources and more power, while central government implements accountability mechanisms to evaluate whether student outcomes are improving.

We also analyse the role of different stakeholders and their bargaining power. Education systems serve students (and their families) but parents are rarely organised in an effective way. Employers also benefit from a good-quality education system, but their role is normally limited to providing on-the-job training for vocational education and training students and apprentices. Since education systems invest huge amounts of funding, there are many stakeholders who obtain direct benefits from the education system and whose support or rejection of reforms will depend to a large extent on the impact that the latter have on the level of resources that they receive. Among education systems, most of the funding is allocated to paying teacher salaries; as a consequence, teachers have become organised as unions to defend their working conditions. Most unions defend job safety and similar salaries (unrelated to performance) for their members. In countries where unions are politically influential and have veto powers, they often block reforms which aim to introduce more demanding criteria to enter the profession, performance-related pay, or the dismissal of underperforming teachers.

Third, we analyse in detail the evidence provided by international large-scale assessments (ILSAs) to examine the extent to which there is robust evidence to support policy recommendations. We find that the strongest evidence there is about what does not work in education concerns investment. Contrary to the widespread assumption that levels of investment are directly related to levels of student performance, all analyses conclude that this is not the case when levels of investment are above a certain threshold. Since investment is the product of class size (which determines the number of teachers) and teacher salaries, none of these two variables has an impact on student outcomes.

The analyses show that there is another set of variables which is strongly context-dependent. The most influential is school autonomy, a policy recommendation which has been followed by many governments. However, for school autonomy to have a positive impact on student outcomes two conditions need to be met: it has to go hand-in-hand with accountability mechanisms and it only works among education systems which have already achieved high levels of quality.

The last group of variables represent different ways to measure a multifaceted dimension of the education system: equity. Unfortunately, our analyses conclude that no single variable can be used to measure levels of equity or progress over time. Furthermore, the seemingly arbitrary use of one or a few of these variables frequently leads to the wrong conclusions, a problem which is exacerbated by the fact that some of the most important aspects of equity are captured by variables which the international surveys neither measure nor take into account.

Finally, we examine the interplay between the evidence generated by international surveys, and the policy recommendations based on them, with ideology and governance. We conclude that the most robust evidence, i.e. lack of impact of greater levels of investment, decreases in class size and increases in teacher salaries, has had no influence whatsoever because it generates a head-on conflict with the vested interests of unions and most of the stakeholders that strongly oppose policies which lead to a decrease in the levels of resources that they receive. The evidence on variables which are strongly context-dependent (such as school autonomy) may be difficult for policymakers to interpret, since it requires a precise diagnosis of the state of maturity of the education system, which is often lacking. Furthermore, policy recommendations often ignore this fact and advocate such policies universally with dire consequences. Finally, the evidence concerning variables that attempt to measure equity is partial and non-conclusive, so the policy recommendations have been heavily influenced by ideology. This has led to a universal recommendation to apply comprehensive policies and avoid those that are regarded as "discriminatory" (such as ability grouping and early tracking). But the evidence shows that radical comprehensive policies lead to the worst outcomes in terms of equity among non-egalitarian societies. We argue that "policy borrowing" from egalitarian countries is based on the wrong assumption that inclusive education policies have led to high levels of equity. An alternative explanation is that among societies that are already equitable, the education system does not need to compensate for major inequalities and, therefore, inclusive policies work. The fact that such inclusive policies, when implemented in non-egalitarian countries, lead to bad outcomes suggests that other mechanisms are required in order to deal with the large degree of student heterogeneity present in societies with high levels of inequality.

Fourth, we look at the policies implemented by top- and low-performing systems and we examine which regions have succeeded in improving over time and which have failed. Countries in East Asia have transformed their education systems very fast over the last decades, allowing mostly illiterate societies to become the most successful systems in the world. The key to their success seems to be a trade-off between class size and teacher quality which has delivered excellent results. Substantial investment goes into selecting the best candidates, offering high-standard training, implementing demanding procedures to enter the profession and designing clear career pathways with high-quality professional development. In exchange, they have very large class sizes. Such countries do not have powerful unions which can veto these kinds of reforms and they all enjoy consistency for long-periods of time because their political systems are either semi-democracies, authoritarian, or full democracies which have adopted a very pragmatic, non-ideological approach to education. Latin America represents the opposite extreme since these countries have made huge efforts in terms of expanding access to higher levels of educational attainment (including university), but the returns are very poor because student performance remains very low compared to East Asia, and also to OECD countries. In this region the power of unions is unparalleled and they have played a major role by putting pressure on governments to decrease class size over time and by rejecting attempts to improve teacher quality and evaluate teachers or students. Thus, the trade-off has been exactly the opposite.

When we analyse the trends of countries positioned somewhere between these opposite poles (Europe, United Kingdom, North America, Australia and New Zealand), we find that most of them have not managed to improve their education systems during the last decades, despite major increases in levels of investment and many reforms. This clearly shows that the evidence provided by international surveys has not had the expected impact on the performance of education systems. We argue that this is partly because some policy recommendations are misleading, and partly because in certain political contexts solid evidence is not enough to overcome huge political costs, which tend to be the result of ideological battles and/or strong underlying conflicts of interest.

Despite this pessimistic conclusion, we remain convinced that the only way forward is to obtain robust evidence and, more importantly, to improve the policy recommendations so that they adapt more readily to the specific context experienced by each country. In countries where the magnitude of the political costs and underlying conflicts of interest are too great, the only way forward may be to start pilot projects rather than to implement systemic changes. If successful, such pilots may be expanded, but small steps like this will require time, and students may not have much time to spare since they need to face an uncertain, challenging and rapidly changing world.

1. The Functions and Role of Modern Education Systems

A Brief Summary

1.1 The Origins of Modern Education

This book is an attempt to understand why education reforms are uniquely difficult to approve and implement. In our view this is a crucial issue, since education allows individuals to have better jobs, to move up the social ladder, to adapt to changes and overcome challenges, to understand and integrate into their complex societies. At the aggregate level, good education systems allow economic growth and social prosperity. However, according to international surveys (in particular PISA), most countries suffer from "educational stagnation". By this we mean that, despite increases in funding and the availability of new data on good practices which could inform evidence-based education policies, student performance has not improved over the last decades in most countries. Thus, we believe that a profound analysis, which looks at this problem from different perspectives simultaneously, is required in order to contribute new insights which may help countries overcome the current educational emergency. We will start by describing briefly why and when governments became involved in building national education systems, the main stages that have taken place during their evolution, and why the demands for education systems to equip people with higher and wider levels of skills have increased over time. We will then examine why the pressures for education systems to improve are not being met in most countries. This is by no means a detailed historical review, but rather a brief introduction to the role that governments have played in modern times in order to situate the following chapters in the right context.

From a historical perspective, the involvement of governments in the funding, organisation and delivery of education systems is quite recent. In some countries, churches or private institutions became the first providers of education, but this was not done at the systemic level. Two main factors triggered state involvement in mass schooling, but these occurred at different points in time in different countries. One is fundamentally political, having to do with the processes of nation building and/or regime change. The other factor is related to the increasing needs of the labour market for skilled workers. These factors prompted state participation in the building of education systems which grew larger and larger over time until governments eventually became responsible for educating all of their citizens.

Mass schooling took place first in Europe, somewhat later in the US, and then expanded worldwide (Archer, 2013; Green, 2013). Although this process presents a number of national idiosyncratic elements linked to history and culture, there is considerable convergence across nations in the process of setting up and funding national education systems:

> During the late eighteen and nineteenth centuries, national states constructed mass schooling systems that eventually came to encompass their entire population of children. State authorization, sponsorship, funding, and control of mass education first developed in Western Europe [...] and later became a central feature of a highly institutionalized model of national development throughout the world. (Ramirez and Boli, 1987)

During this transition, the main debates focused on the role of the state versus other providers, and on how to define the aims of education. When governments became responsible for building education systems in their countries, there was an initial stage of expansion during which universal access to education was the main goal. Thus, schools were built and a growing number of teachers hired. Targets were mostly quantitative: enrolment rates, years of schooling or, at the most, rates of illiteracy. During the phase in which the education system was being built, the interests of governments, teachers, providers and stakeholders were well-aligned. A growing amount of public investment was reaching an increasing number of teachers and providers; thus, there were no major conflicts of interest, since almost everyone benefited from this expansion of access to education. Ideology did not play an important role since reaching more and more children was the shared and simple goal.

When this phase was over and universal access to education had been achieved, governments changed their focus from expansion of the education system in order to reach every child, to ensuring an efficient system which delivered a quality education. It is at this point (which was reached by different countries at different times) that conflicts of interest begin to emerge and ideology starts to play a major role. A system which distributes huge amounts of funding between many stakeholders generates tensions as soon as it ceases to grow, because expectations about future increases in resources are no longer met. Furthermore, since most education reforms are likely to affect how resources are distributed between teachers and the many stakeholders, changes that are perceived as a threat to the resources that they receive, their privileges or the balance of power, are likely to elicit opposition (Grindle, 2004; Moe, 2011; Moe and Wiborg, 2017).

In addition, while enhancements in efficiency and quality benefit students, major efforts are required to increase the quality of the existing teaching force and those who wish to join it. Achieving this goal may create conflicts as the education system becomes more demanding towards its own constituents and enhanced transparency results in a loss of power for many stakeholders. In particular, in countries where teachers have not achieved high standards, teacher unions (who no longer benefit from a growing teaching force) may oppose accountability and performance-related incentives to defend the interests of their membership. Teacher unions were created to defend the interests of their members, which is entirely legitimate, but in many countries they tend to defend job security, as well as good and uniform working conditions for all teachers, irrespective of performance levels (Moe, 2011; Moe and Wiborg, 2017). While this may benefit teachers, it clashes with the interests of students. Other education providers and stakeholders may also have vested interests which are not necessarily well-aligned with the policies required to improve student performance. These profound conflicts of interest and the ways in which they have been resolved (or not) have had a major influence on education systems worldwide (Grindle, 2004; Moe and Wiborg, 2017).

At the same time, ideology started to play a significant role. The ideological divide is profound in many countries since it addresses core issues such as what the ultimate goal of the education system is: quality (political parties on the right of the spectrum) or equity (political parties on the left of the spectrum). Although no one questions the role of the state in funding education, there are major ideological divides regarding the role of the state versus private providers in school management. Ideology deeply permeates all major dimensions of the education system such as its architecture, curricular content, the degree of parental choice and competition that is allowed, and the rules of admission. Ideology also determines how political parties position themselves in relation to the vested interests of teacher unions, with those on the left generally supporting greater levels of investment, smaller class sizes and higher teacher salaries, i.e. the main union demands. In contrast, political parties on the right tend to support competition, accountability and student and teacher evaluations, which they believe improve quality and efficiency, against the interests of teacher unions. Obviously, ideological differences also include values and beliefs which are divisive in many societies (e.g. religion, abortion) and the question of whether and how they should be addressed in the curriculum.

Despite these general similarities, education systems became very country-specific, to the extent that there was a widespread assumption that they could not be directly compared. Thus, ideology and vested interests were the only powerful tools in educational debates which, as a consequence, became very polarised. Only in the last decades has there been increasing recognition about the need for evidence-based guidelines based on data from international comparisons. The hope was that solid evidence about the policies which lead to better student outcomes in some countries would be undisputed and would facilitate the reforms necessary to improve poor-performing education systems. Although international large-scale assessments (ILSAs) have provided a wealth of evidence by comparing the performance of many countries and trying to identify which policies lead to improved levels of student performance, they have not had a major impact on improving education systems. As we will examine in detail in this book, this has to do with a complex combination of factors: evidence from international surveys do lead to a few robust conclusions which clash heads-on with the powerful vested interests and are therefore ignored; other evidence is so context-dependent that it makes it difficult for policymakers to decide what applies to their specific context and, finally, some evidence is weak and the policy recommendations based on it have been heavily influenced by ideology.

1.2 The Social Function of Modern Education

To be able to improve education systems, societies need to agree first on their main purposes. As Terry Moe and Susanne Wiborg explain, education can boost human capital and economic growth, but it can also fuel patronage and corruption. Education can be a means of advancing social equity and upward mobility, but also of entrenching the existing class structure. Education may pursue the integration of migrants into a nation's culture or impose a common culture on unwilling groups. Education can be understood as a means of socialising citizens to democratic norms, or alternatively to authoritarian ideology and control. Education can promote religious tolerance and secularism, or privilege one religion at the expense (or even exclusion) of others (Moe and Wiborg, 2017, p. 1).

By identifying which of these many goals the education system should achieve, education policies have a very large impact on the political and social shape of nations in a vast array of dimensions. In fact, the prevailing visions about what education means and is intended to achieve are part of the fabric of the *material constitution* (Boldoni and Wilkinson, 2018) of the different countries.

Therefore, education, considered from the political science viewpoint, is an institutional arena of enormous potential, a shaper of the fundamentals of human society. Precisely because of this, governments have strong incentives to put this potential to use by actively involving themselves in the design, control and operation of education systems. Certainly, education's relevance from this perspective has been—until very recently—overlooked by mainstream political science. As Anja Jakoby and colleagues put it ten years ago: "In the discipline, education has remained a 'homeless' and widely underestimated topic during the last decades" (Jakoby *et al.*, 2010). More recently, Duke University political scientists Thomas Gift and Erik Wibbels have also regretted the paucity of comparative political science on education, highlighting the relative focus on education in disciplines such as sociology and, mostly, economics (Gift and Wibbels, 2014).

When we look at the interplay between nation building and the development of *mass schooling* systems, we find different trajectories. In a number of countries, like France and Spain, the first attempts to build a universal (primary) schooling system appeared when the countries established constitutions inspired by either liberal[1] (like the Spanish Constitution of 1812) or democratic (like the French *Convention* in 1793) principles and ideals (Puelles, 2010; Roche and Léon, 2018) that seek to establish mass schooling systems.

In some other countries the process of nation building and the development of mass schooling are less closely connected. But everywhere, at a certain point in time, mass schooling becomes a necessity because of the need to provide nascent industries with a labour force skilled enough (in terms of basic literacy and numeracy) to deal with the machinery and processes of those industries.

There were considerable time-lags in the development of those mass schooling systems in different countries, due to the different historic circumstances and timing of their respective processes of industrialisation. Amongst the pioneers of mass schooling, first Prussia (Reimers, 2020), then France (Roche and Léon, 2018) and the United Kingdom (Gillard, 2018) began building their mass education systems over 200 years ago, and other European nations have followed the same path at different points thereafter.

Conversely, in America, the education system as such, i.e. the education system that is today widely accepted and shared across the country, did not take shape until the early 1900s, fueled by progressive-era reforms that created a system based on bureaucratic administration, expertise, and non-partisan local democracy. Before this, in certain states (such as Massachusetts) during the early eighteenth century, there were attempts to follow the Prussian model (Reimers, 2020). Thus, at the federal level the United States was not a leader in shaping

---

1   'Liberal' here is used in the traditional political science concept of *liberalism*, an ideology advocating for individual freedom, consent and rule of law, as defined by philosophers and other thinkers in the Age of Enlightenment, not to the American concept of 'liberal' as a synonym of progressive or leftist ideals.

a public education system. However, through the combined actions of different levels of government, it eventually succeeded in taking over most European countries in terms of the scale of its coverage of basic and secondary education.

In the developed world, the full consolidation of mass or universal schooling including primary and lower secondary education took place during the twentieth century and more specifically in the immediate aftermath of the Second World War. The development of 'comprehensive' education, meaning a uniform track for all students up to the end of compulsory education, was one of the features of the welfare state that blossomed in Europe in the post-war years (Moe and Wiborg, 2017; Wiborg, 2009). Nonetheless, there were some remarkable exceptions to the uniformity of this pattern of comprehensiveness. The most conspicuous was Germany, which early on developed a well-functioning tracking system according to the requirements of its national industry (Busemeyer, 2015).

Extending education to the masses early on had enormous consequences for national economies, not least the growth of valuable human capital. In terms of how this process of mass schooling relates to economic growth and thriving societies, the example of the US is quite compelling. There, mass education served as the engine of economic growth that propelled the US to economic dominance during the twentieth century. The 'American century' in economy, military power, political influence and cultural impact has been fueled by an educational advantage over potential competitors for global leadership.

Over time, other countries followed the same path, expanding their public school systems. This process of extending education to all also entailed huge consequences for social equity. Universal education became the most relevant opportunity policy. It opened the door to increased social mobility, that not only lifted many in the lowest levels of the social pyramid from poverty, but also allowed access to middle class status to a substantial share of the working class (Frey, 2019; Moe and Wiborg, 2017).

In a nutshell, this era of educational expansion around the world covers a very long period, since it started at different moments in time and progressed at different speeds according to each country's political, economic and social circumstances. Building an education system entails major effort, since nations have to build the infrastructures, define governance arrangements, invest large amounts of funding, train and hire teachers, and design the architecture of the system. This long period, stretching from the nineteenth century to the years immediately after the Second World War in the mid-twentieth century, has been labeled as the "era of institutional formation" (Moe and Wiborg, 2017).

Once this process was completed in most, if not all, developed economies, we witnessed the dawn of a new era in education public policy, which started roughly during the 1980s and 1990s. The triggers for this transformation were globalisation, technological innovation, and intense economic competition. Human capital development was seen as crucial in order to compete in the new knowledge economy, and therefore higher levels of educational achievement were necessary.

To some extent, the crisis of the welfare state also prompted changes. The onset of fiscal austerity, demands for government efficiency, and rising disaffection with centralised, bureaucratic models of governance led to pressure for so-called neoliberal reforms to improve efficiency, such as the implementation of decentralisation processes, accountability mechanisms and the evaluation of student outcomes.

The emphasis shifted to performance and academic excellence: a new "era of performance-based reform" (Jakoby et al., 2010; Moe and Wiborg, 2017). Reformers sought major changes in institutions inherited from the past, so they faced all sorts of resistance from defenders of the institutional status quo, especially stakeholders with vested interests in the preservation of the existing system.

Indeed, this change in focus has had and continues to have huge consequences for the political economy of education reforms. More than fifteen years ago, Merilee Grindle, a Harvard specialist in comparative analysis, insightfully framed the rationale for the change in political response to reforms in both eras. Most reforms in the era of institutional formation ('access reforms') offered clear benefits at virtually no cost to a variety of direct stakeholders (from those building the infrastructures to teachers, administrators and school service personnel) and expanded opportunities and convenience for families. In these senses, they were 'easy' reforms, the kind that politicians were keen to undertake if they had the opportunity and the means to do so.

Almost the opposite is the case with regard to the era of 'performance–based reforms' ("quality-enhancing reforms" in

Grindle's wording) intended to improve efficiency and students' outcomes. Here, an array of stakeholders may have reason to fear that reforms will have a negative impact on their working conditions, their careers, the resources they receive or the institutional powers they have acquired. Tighter controls on efficiency and effectiveness, increased accountability and greater transparency of the governance system may be perceived as threatening by teachers, principals, unions, bureaucrats and many providers (for instance of textbooks, school meals, transport, etc.). Thus, opposition to new policies from stakeholders fearing the loss of valuable resources makes it much more difficult for governments to embark on reforms which are very costly in political terms. Such defiance will also involve major obstacles during the implementation process, which of course requires the collaboration of many of those who are likely to object to the reforms. As Grindle, following the seminal ideas of Mancur Olson on the logic of collective action (Olson, 1965), states, "losers have incentives to organize to protect the status quo; winners lack clear incentives to organize for change and therefore face difficult problems of collective action" (Grindle, 2004, p. 11).

In the case of education reforms, the crux of the matter is that unions and other stakeholders are well organised and have the political power required to defend the status quo, while those who would benefit from better outcomes (i.e., students and their families) do not.

1.3 To What Extent Do People Care about Education?

Although education is probably one of the policy agenda issues that has more practical implications for the majority of people, in most European countries it does not rank high in the list of public concerns as revealed by public opinion surveys. This does not mean that citizens do not have strong *opinions*, *attitudes* and even *values*[2] regarding education. They do. It does not mean either that public opinion does not have a role in determining the shape and fate of education reforms. It does (Busemeyer

---

2 'Opinions, attitudes and values' — following the metaphor coined by Sir Robert Worcester, are different expressions of depth and intensity for views that people may have on any given matter: "opinions: the ripples on the surface of the public's consciousness, shallow, and easily changed; attitudes: the currents below the surface, deeper and stronger; and values: the deep tides of public mood, slow to change, but powerful" (Worcester, 1983).

et al., 2020; Wert, 2019). Knowing or anticipating the reverberations on public opinion of education reforms is a key factor both in designing and implementing reforms, as well as in generating support or opposition to them.

However, education is not perceived as a top priority by most voters except at very specific times and places. The Eurobarometer, a robust serial survey conducted by the European Commission on representative national samples of EU countries' citizens (Eurobarometer, 2019) shows that only 12% of Europeans feel that education is a major concern at the national level, ranking it much lower than issues such as health, the environment, unemployment and pensions. Only in two European countries was the education system seen as one of the two major problems at the national level by over 20% of respondents: Sweden (26%) and Germany (23%).

It seems no coincidence that in both of these countries, at different moments, education became a top priority political and social issue, owing to unexpectedly mediocre PISA survey results. This happened in Germany when the results of the first PISA cycle (2000) were released at the end of 2001. The so-called "PISA shock" (Ertl, 2006; Gruber, 2006; Tillmann *et al.*, 2008) refers to the collective horror—not only in the educational establishment but also in the political elite, media and society as a whole —at the mediocre results of German students compared with other developed countries and the huge differences between high and low performers and between federal states. This "Tsunami-like impact" (Gruber, 2006) triggered a vast and long-lasting reform impulse that substantially changed the education landscape in one of the largest and richest countries of the European Union.

Similarly, in Sweden a clear decline in student performance became apparent after the 2012 PISA cycle (which was released in 2013), with Sweden ranking well below the OECD average, only above Hungary, Greece, Turkey, Chile and Mexico out of the then thirty-four members of the organisation. The links between this decline and governance reforms are discussed later, in Chapter 3.

In the US, conversely, education ranks among the top three political priorities, although it seems to be an important issue for a larger share of Democrats (76%) than Republicans (58%) (Pew Research Center, 2019). While few elections are won on the basis of educational promises, governments can be certain that they will face huge political costs if they attempt education reforms, due to major conflicts of interest with an array of powerful stakeholders and very visible ideological confrontations between political parties.

On the other hand, the beneficiaries of potential reforms are children who may acquire higher and more relevant knowledge levels and skills through education. As a consequence, they may obtain better jobs and enjoy a better quality of life when they become adults. However, this will always seem a long way off at the moment when political decisions are being made. It has been shown that, on aggregate, economies and societies gain greatly from having a highly skilled population: they become more productive and competitive in the "knowledge society" (Hanushek and Woessmann, 2015).

But this outcome inevitably seems too distant a future when governments are deciding whether or not to move forward with an education reform. This perhaps explains why few governments even dare to attempt to reform their education systems, because the balance in the short term tends to be negative. Electoral cycles—four or five years at most—are too short in all democracies, leading governments to reap politically relevant, low-hanging fruit achievable within a single electoral cycle. This is the conventional wisdom prevailing in most cases—although its rationale may be debatable[3]—and explains many governments' reluctance to embark on badly needed education reforms (Ball, 2013; Gomendio, 2017; Grindle, 2004; Wert, 2019).

1.4 The Goals of Education in the Knowledge Society

Although the goals of education as a public good have been — and continue to be—the target of never-ending debates from historical, sociological, political and even philosophical viewpoints, here we

---

[3] In particular, the idea that there is not sufficient low-hanging fruit in education reforms can be questioned in light of the swift improvement in student outcomes observed immediately after the enactment of education reforms in countries like Poland and Portugal. Although we acknowledge that our opinion may be biased, we are also persuaded that the unequivocal improvements in education outcomes in Spain, which became apparent in 2015 and 2016 (attainment, reduction of early school leavers, increase in VET enrolment, PISA, TIMSS and PIRLS and many others) were a direct result of the 2013 reforms we undertook.

will focus on how these goals have been redefined in present times by the megatrends shaping the knowledge economy and the knowledge society. This does not mean that those debates are over, or that they are unimportant: as we will see in detail in the next chapter, most of them are still very much alive and have a significant impact on education policy. But our focus here will be on how the megatrends currently at play are fundamentally changing the functional purposes of education, and how these changes affect the very meaning of education and the means by or moments at which it is delivered.

From this limited—in both time and scope—viewpoint, the main goal of education systems is to equip students with the knowledge and skills required to succeed in current and (if possible) future labour markets and societies. Traditionally, education systems prepared people for different types of jobs, depending on the level of education achieved and the field of knowledge in which the student specialised, as part of a 'once-in-a-lifetime', front-loaded educational experience. These educational qualifications would allow most people to get a job for life, or at least to secure successive jobs in the same sector for life, including job progression through on-the-job training and a seniority premium.

Thus, the relationship between the level of knowledge and skills that people acquired from the education system at an early age and the labour market outcomes was quite straightforward. Years of schooling and educational attainment worked as an efficient and undisputed proxy by which to assess human capital. Front-loaded education was the rule: the highest educational qualification obtained by students in their youth, when they left the education system, was the one and only measure. As such, it retained a powerful signaling value throughout an individual's lifetime.

A brief look at the relationship between economic history and the history of education reveals that education systems have responded to the increased demand for higher levels of skills generated by successive technological revolutions over time by expanding access to ever higher levels of educational attainment. This has led to the so-called "race between education and technology," a term coined by Harvard economists Claudia Goldin and Larry Katz (Goldin and Katz, 2009). Thus, during the nineteenth and twentieth centuries, education systems responded to the rise of skilled-biased technologies by expanding access to (what we now call) primary education and, once this was achieved, to secondary education, until these two levels became universal requirements.

The United States pioneered this early expansion of education from the mid-nineteenth century onwards, and it has been convincingly argued that this is the main reason behind the economic success of the United States during this golden era (Goldin and Katz, 2009). Most of Europe started to expand access to primary education towards the end of the nineteenth century, with major differences—as explained in the previous section—between countries in the timing and the type of education provided. Eventually the trend to expand access to higher levels of education reached tertiary education and, once again, the United States led this expansion after the Second World War, when the GI Bill enabled almost eight million veterans to attend high school, vocational school, or college (Altschuler and Blumin, 2009).

Countries in other regions such as Asia and Latin America started to make significant efforts to provide education to most of their populations much later. Despite this delay, some countries in Asia, such as South Korea or Singapore, identified education as the main enabler for the transformation and modernisation of their economies and societies. Although there are huge differences between the two countries—not least in size and population—both decided during the second half of the twentieth century to make education their top priority, and for decades invested relentlessly in improving their education systems in such a way that they have emerged as some of the best educated societies of the twenty-first century (Ansell, 2010; Sorensen, 1994; Yew, 2000). Once again, the effort to provide a good education to their citizens also led to economic and social prosperity. It seems fair to say that in certain Asian countries, education policies have been the fundamental engine propelling their economic and social leaps forward and elevating them to the ranks of developed nations.

1.5 Digitalisation: A Game Changer

Now, in the first quarter of the twenty-first century, the world has become a messier place. What labour markets demand in terms of knowledge and skills is changing fast due to the impact of megatrends, such as digitalisation, globalisation, demographic trends and migrations. In particular, digitalisation is leading to major changes in the workplace due to the automation of routine jobs and tasks that require low- to medium-level skills (Frey, 2019; OECD, 2019a-b). Thus, some jobs will disappear while others will undergo profound transformations, since workers will be required to perform high-skilled, non-routine tasks than cannot be automated.

It has been estimated that these trends will in one way or another affect around 50% of the workforce (OECD, 2019a). Digitalisation will also lead to the creation of new types of jobs (the so-called digital economy), but these are likely to be more demanding in terms of the skills required than those that are lost. Beyond the workplace, digitalisation has also dramatically modified the way people communicate, use services, obtain information and spend their leisure time, and adapting to the extensive use of digital technology for these purposes also requires new skillsets.

These changes represent a gigantic step in terms of the levels of knowledge and skills that people will require in order to adapt to and navigate this rapidly changing landscape (OECD, 2019b). In demanding and uncertain environments such as these, education systems are under huge pressure to become more efficient, more responsive to changing needs, and able to identify which bundles of skills people need and how to provide them.

In this case, increasing access to ever higher levels of educational attainment (university degrees and even upper levels of university education, such as master's and Ph.D. degrees) alone will not suffice. More profound changes are required. First, education systems that have already achieved universal access to compulsory education will need to put more emphasis on improving quality. As we will see, qualitative differences between education systems are so large that, in poor-quality systems, efforts to expand access to higher levels of educational attainment do not translate into the expected returns in skill levels. To put it bluntly, in some countries students learn very little at school.

As a result, proxies commonly used to measure human capital, such as years of education or proportion of university graduates, are becoming poor indicators of the actual level of knowledge and skills amongst the population. Moreover, students also need to acquire new skills such as adaptability to navigate an ever-changing environment, creativity to find innovative solutions to increasingly complex problems, and teamwork to bring together the expertise and perspectives of people from different cultural backgrounds. Finally, education systems need to be re-engineered as lifelong learning systems.

Lifelong learning is a widely used concept that is poorly understood and thus deserves explanation. Workplaces and societies are changing so fast that people will need to reskill and upskill many times during their lifetime. Workers who are currently in jobs that are at risk of becoming fully automated (the OECD estimates that this could be 14% of all current jobs) will need to make the transition to safer jobs; this will require a significant effort in terms of training (OECD, 2019b). Those who are in jobs for which a large proportion of current tasks could ultimately become automated (OECD estimates: 34%) will have to acquire higher-level skills in order to avoid being displaced as their jobs become more demanding. Finally, high-skilled workers tend to be more proactive in looking for opportunities to upskill, to get a promotion, or to move to new (potentially more creative and fulfilling) jobs as they emerge in the digital economy.

Thus, education systems will need to prepare students to become lifelong learners, who will engage in new learning and training experiences throughout their careers. Education will no longer be a one-off event that happens only in the early stages of the life-course. These opportunities to acquire new skills will allow people to move more frequently from one job to another, to look for jobs in different sectors, or to have different part-time jobs simultaneously. The flexibility of such non-linear trajectories will empower people to adapt to the decline and emergence of different economic sectors in the digital era. In this context, there is a profound debate to be had about whether or not a university degree obtained at the end of a person's first educational experience will matter as much as it did before. Given the difficulties that most universities seem to have in understanding and adapting to this new environment, some have suggested a new approach in which degrees and post-graduate education will become less meaningful, while short courses and other non-diploma formats will allow universities to play a pivotal role in the lifelong learning landscape (Pistone and Horn, 2016). Others, however, are keener on maintaining the traditional role of world-class universities centred on research and academic excellence, and wish to leave the provision of more market-oriented lifelong learning services to other providers (Willetts, 2017).

1.6 COVID-19: An Unexpected Disruption and an Accelerator of Change

As we write, in the spring of 2022, we are still coming to terms with the multidimensional consequences for education (as for many other areas) of the COVID-19 pandemic, which exploded in the winter of 2020. Although effective vaccines have been developed, the virus mutates and those variants which can overcome the immunity granted by natural infection or vaccination gain selective advantages and spread faster, displacing previous ones. Epidemiological models suggest that we will have to learn to live with COVID-19 for a long time, and maybe forever. Over the past two years, the pandemic has represented one of the greatest disruptions in history, with many countries shutting down their economies and confining people to their homes to slow down the expansion.

We do not intend to elaborate here on what COVID-19 will mean for the future of education and the future of work, since that exceeds the scope of this book. But it is clear that this unexpected situation has created the most important disruption to education in modern history. At a particular moment during the spring of 2020, over 90% of students worldwide were not attending school. According to UNESCO estimates, over 1.5 billion K-12 students have experienced school closures since the pandemic started. Previously, wars, earthquakes and epidemic outbursts had disrupted the delivery of education, but the impact of such disruption was always localised. This is a major global pandemic, which has erupted all over the world at great speed. Since technology now for the first time in history allows a good level of communication, work and learning, many countries have resorted to lockdowns and/or severe limitations on mobility and social interaction. After the past two years it seems clear that the pace at which digitalisation was previously unfolding has suddenly accelerated, creating a surge in the demand for new skills.

The impact on education as a consequence of school closures is huge. In many countries, students and teachers had to pivot quickly to online education. There has been a swift adoption of 'Emergency Remote Teaching' (ERT), "a temporary shift of instructional delivery to an alternate delivery mode due to crisis circumstances," something that is plainly different from "experiences that are planned from the beginning and designed to be online" (Hodges *et al.*, 2020).

As the first wave of infection receded, a number of countries reopened schools, either fully or partially, while others—mostly low- and middle-income countries—kept them closed for over a year (some for almost two years). Thus, learning losses have been huge, gaps have been magnified, and education systems need to find ways to overcome such delays. Over two years into the process, the extent to which technology has become integrated as a part of the learning process is still unclear, but a blended model seems likely to remain. The more general point that we wish to make is that this crisis has highlighted the need for education systems to adapt continuously to fast-changing environments and, sometimes, to drastic and unforeseen changes. The widespread educational losses as a result of the pandemic have generated an educational emergency.

Since one of the main roles of education systems is to equip students with the knowledge and skills required to integrate fully into the labour market and become active participants in their societies, education systems need to continuously reform themselves in order to successfully adapt to this rapidly changing environment and to flexibly deal with shocks of this kind.

Societies demand better outcomes from their education systems, because the benefits of acquiring higher levels of knowledge and skills have been exacerbated. To achieve better outcomes, poor-quality education systems require radical change, either because major elements must be improved or (more often) because many parts of their complex structure must change simultaneously in order for significant improvements to occur. Among better quality education systems, while the basic architecture and rules may be preserved over time, incremental improvements are required to keep up with the evolving landscape.

In order for education systems to improve over time, education reforms need to be enacted (and frequently) in order to adapt to changing circumstances. However, as we shall see, education reforms seem to be particularly difficult to set in motion, and to get approved and implemented. It is important to understand why.

The widely accepted view is that education reforms are politically costly in the short term, and that their benefits only become apparent in the long term, and even then are rather diffuse (Ball, 2013; Gomendio, 2017; Wert, 2019). The large costs arise mainly for two reasons.

First, most education reforms affect the way resources are distributed and/or increase the demands on teachers and stakeholders for quality, accountability and transparency; thus, they tend to face rejection from defenders of the status quo (Grindle, 2004; Moe, 2011; Moe and Wiborg, 2017). Second, education is an ideological battlefield in most countries (Adonis, 2012; Wert, 2019). This explains why all political parties introduce educational issues with a strong ideological component that will attract (or at least please) voters into their electoral manifestoes. Such issues may create deep divides between political parties and between voters, which may later be difficult to overcome.

While this argument may explain why few governments identify education as a priority in reformist agendas, it does not explain fully why when governments do have the will to embark on education reforms, they so often fail.

1.7 Why Are Reforms So Difficult?

The main question that we will address in the following chapters is: what makes education reforms so difficult to implement? We are persuaded that this is a central question, since many urgently needed education reforms often encounter obstacles so great that they cannot ultimately be implemented, and even those that do succeed are often reversed in the next political cycle.

To answer this broad question, we need to investigate the available evidence indicating which policies lead to better student outcomes, and consider how robust that evidence is; we must ascertain the economic and political costs associated with implementing these polices, and who is responsible for designing, implementing and funding these reforms. Before doing so, we will analyse the ideological underpinnings of education, and examine how they trickle down to a number of dimensions of educational policymaking.

2. Education and Ideology (Or Is It the Other Way Around?)

2.1. Ideology and Education: What Do We Mean?

We will start our journey by analysing the role that *ideology*, considered in a very broad sense, plays when it comes to defining education systems, their aims, shape, and drivers for reform. Hence, by *ideology* here, we mean any form of politically oriented conception of education based on strongly-held beliefs and values rather than evidence.

To start with, we address a paradox which is revealed by public opinion surveys and is present in the public discourse of political actors. The paradox goes like this: Only very naïve people think that ideology does not play a significant role in education. Most people know that it does. But an overwhelming majority of people subscribe to the idea that education should be kept far away from political battlefields and based on evidence.

Put in terms of the classic distinction coined by political scientists David Butler and Donald Stokes over fifty years ago (Butler and Stokes, 1969), most people think that education should be a *valence issue*, i.e., a question on which the whole body politic must come to a consensus that will last, while at the same time they recognise that in many instances it functions as a *position issue*, i.e., a key arena for political conflict.

There are several reasons that could explain both why education is very often the subject of bitter political confrontation, and why conventional wisdom stands against its politicisation. From a comparative education policy perspective, this is an issue of paramount importance when it comes to the analysis of education reforms, the roadblocks they realistically face, and the role that ideological battles play in creating those roadblocks.

In terms of the reasons as to why ideological confrontation is central in debates about education, these may be summarised as follows:

Political operators of every ideological affiliation believe that education is a process in which basic beliefs and values, *Weltanschauungen* or visions of the world, and consequently political or proto-political orientations are shaped (Davidson, 1996; Ehman, 1980; Faas, 2010). This common ground, in turn, leads to very different approaches on a number of issues that are perceived as the ideological backbone of education policy.

The most salient among these divisive issues are (i) the role of the state as [exclusive or dominant] education provider vs private and/or *social* providers; (ii) equity: education as an *equaliser* vs education as an *enabler*; (iii) the shape of the education system: its architecture, teachers, curriculum, and evaluations; and (iv) the funding of education.

But at the same time, there is also a widespread social consensus that education policy should be the subject of some sort of *national agreement* and should therefore be shielded from political confrontation. In different countries and at various moments in time, calls for such an agreement have prompted political and social initiatives to achieve this goal. Occasionally, these initiatives have led to the adoption of policies underpinned by very broad political agreements,[1] but more often than not they have been unsuccessful and frustrating.[2]

---

1   An example of one of these agreements was the No Child Left Behind Act in the United States, enforced in 2002 during the first term of George W. Bush's presidency. The initiative, which aimed to ensure rigorous external assessments at different stages of primary and secondary education as a condition for receiving federal funding, enjoyed almost full bi-partisan support.

2   A very close (in time and in geography for the authors) example of these failures was the pompously named Grand Political and Social National Pact for Education, which a committee in the Spanish Congress worked on for over one year in 2017–2018. Political parties on the left withdrew from the committee after the centre-right government refused to include in the recommendations an increase in national funding of 0.7% of GDP to achieve the expenditure benchmark that those on the left considered non-negotiable: public education expenditure of 5% of GDP. This case is interesting for what it tells us about the political manipulation of education expenditure. The flag of expenditure (i.e., overall expenditure, which is unrelated to more meaningful metrics, such as expenditure per student) serves very conveniently to get education agents to rally around.

If political operators feel—as they do—the need to pay lip service at the very least to the idea of a transversal agreement on education, this is basically because they know that a majority of voters adhere to that principle. Hence, political parties would never openly oppose the idea of a de-politicised approach to education, although in practice they do as much as they can to direct it along the ideological lines to which they adhere.

Here, we start by examining the most divisive issues surrounding education that follow basic ideological cleavages. We will deal separately with each issue, so as to consider how they combine to create more or less coherent *education ideologies*. After this, we will examine how—in our opinion—it is possible to overcome the ideological stalemate in which too many education systems seem to be trapped.

2.2 The Role of the State as an Education Provider

We begin with the role of the state as education provider. This has been a matter of philosophical and political debate since Ancient Greece (Burnet, 1903). For instance, no less than twenty-four centuries ago, Aristotle plainly stated that universal education was a function of the state, and was necessary to fulfil its duty of self-preservation: "Education is a function of the State, and is conducted, primarily at least, for the ends of the State [...] Since the whole State has but one end, it is plainly necessary that there should be one education for all the citizens" (Davidson, 1892).

Obviously, the meaning of the Ancient Greek word for 'education' to which Aristotle refers is substantially different from what we today understand by the term, just as the Aristotelian meaning for *'all citizens'* (i.e., natural born free men; not women, foreigners and slaves) has little to do with the modern, all-encompassing concept of citizenship.

Modern thought on education can be traced back to much later, at the end of the seventeenth century and during the Enlightenment, when philosophers and *maîtres à penser* like John Locke and Jean-Jacques Rousseau published the two most influential works on education in their time.

Locke's *Some Thoughts Concerning Education* (1693) was published almost seventy years before Rousseau's *Émile ou de l'Éducation* (1762), but both works are the fundamental pillars of educational thinking of the Enlightenment (in Locke's case, the debate is restricted to gentlemen's education, whilst Rousseau's work takes a far more democratic approach to the concept). Rousseau thinks that Locke's approach falls short of providing enough philosophical ground to the most important social function that can be conceived:

> In spite of all these books whose only aim, so they say, is public utility, the most useful of all arts, the art of training men, is still neglected. Even after Locke's book was written the subject remained almost untouched, and I fear that my book will leave it pretty much as it found it. (Rousseau, 1762)

However, for both thinkers it is more important to focus on *whom*, on which *values* and which *subjects* the education system ought to prioritise, rather than on *who* should be responsible for delivering them.

We can find some intellectual reflections more centred on the public provision of education by the beginning of the nineteenth century. For instance, as Fernando Reimers points out, in an 1801 letter of the diplomat and politician John Quincy Adams, who much later became the sixth president of the United States:

> [...] describes admiringly the success of Frederick the II who ruled Prussia from 1740 until 1785, in instituting a system of publicly funded schools to educate all children, for the purpose of teaching them to read and introducing them to science [...] Adams described how providing school masters' with a public wage enabled the creation of schools for elementary instruction of all classes of people. (Reimers, 2020, p. 2)

However, the main intellectual debate on this issue has its two fundamental milestones slightly later. In fact, the *grand narratives* on the role of the state in the provision of education for citizens can be dated to the period extending from the mid-nineteenth century to the early twentieth century. The most influential exponents of antagonistic views on private or public delivery of education are, respectively, John Stuart Mill and John Dewey.

John Stuart Mill is the undisputed standard-bearer of the argument in favour of private provision of education, although he also develops this thesis alongside his assertion that the state is responsible for making sure that every child, irrespective of the means of her[3] or his parents, has access to education. It is worthwhile to consider at some length Mill's phrasing of his argument in his most famous work, *On Liberty* (1859):

> Were the duty of enforcing universal education once admitted there would be an end to the difficulties about what the State should teach, and how it should teach, which now convert the subject into a mere battlefield for sects and parties, causing the time and labour which should have been spent in educating to be wasted in quarrelling about education. If the government would make up its mind to require for every child a good education, it might save itself the trouble of providing one. It might leave to parents to obtain the education where and how they pleased, and content itself with helping to pay the school fees of the poorer classes of children, and defraying the entire school expenses of those who have no one else to pay for them. (Mill, 1859)

Mill's thoughts should be read and understood with attention to the political, social and economic context of the time and place in which they were written. In those days, universal basic education was at best still in its infancy in the most advanced countries, such as the United Kingdom. In the period between the end of the First Industrial Revolution and the beginning of the Second, illiteracy rates in the UK, despite a steep decline over the first half of the nineteenth century, were still 30% among men and almost 40% among women (Clark, 2003). It is also noteworthy that, as Susanne Wiborg points out, in the UK the state's involvement in the provision of education was instituted rather late in comparison with other European countries, since basic education was in the hands of voluntary bodies, such as religious associations (Wiborg, 2009).

It is worth noting that Mill's central argument is about *choice* and, more precisely, the need to ensure that the state is at most a marginal education provider. In his previous work, published ten years before *On Liberty*, he addressed the possibility of public provision of education as one exception to his non-interference doctrine:

> Education, therefore, is one of those things which it is admissible in principle that a government should provide for the people. The case

---

[3] We refer to 'her' here because although Mill talks about 'the child' or 'children', it seems obvious from the context, the collaborative contribution of his wife Harriet and, mostly, his later work (Mill, 1861) that he strongly supported the education of girls on an equal footing, which was not a mainstream opinion in his era.

is one to which the reasons of the non-interference principle do not necessarily or universally extend. (Mill, 1848)

The apparent change in his view has been understood as the result of a natural evolution in his liberal doctrine, or simply as a question of wording: when Mill refers to the acceptability of the idea of 'government' providing education for the people, perhaps what he means is the provision of resources for education, rather than the direct involvement of the government in that provision. Even so, this view would ultimately change: what Mill advocates for in *On Liberty* limits government involvement to provision for poorer children, as opposed to for all children.

To summarise, Mill's educational philosophy combines a strong argument in favour of mass schooling with an equally strong argument against state provision thereof. Despite this, he is in favour of state funding—not necessarily delivery—of education for the poorer in society, and also permits—as an exception—state involvement in education provision to establish a standard of excellence.

The opposite viewpoint is espoused by American philosopher John Dewey in one of his most influential books, *Democracy and Education*, which was first published over a century ago (1916). For Dewey, public school is the melting pot by virtue of which it becomes possible to bring people from very diverse ethnic, social, religious and cultural backgrounds together, allowing them to be educated in mutual respect, recognition, tolerance and diversity.

> [T]he development of commerce, transportation, intercommunication, and emigration, countries like the United States are composed of a combination of different groups with different traditional customs. [...] The intermingling in the school of youth of different races, differing religions, and unlike customs creates for all a new and broader environment. [...] The assimilative force of the American public school is eloquent testimony to the efficacy of the common and balanced appeal. (Dewey, 1916)

Dewey's approach is still hugely influential with those advocating for public schools as the most important social equaliser. Nonetheless, this approach conforms quite poorly, from a factual viewpoint, to the reality in the United States. Two features of the schooling system—funding (mostly local) and admission criteria (where proximity to a school has a large weight)—make the American public school system a mechanism that reproduces and in fact magnifies social stratification rather than acting as an equaliser: students in most public schools simply reflect the social composition of the surrounding neighbourhood, and neighbourhoods tend to be quite homogeneous in terms of their social composition. In other words, while wealthy parents can (and do) invest in houses in affluent neighbourhoods so that their children may attend public schools with plenty of resources, underprivileged families cannot.

Interestingly enough, over sixty years after Dewey wrote his influential essay and despite a evidence showing that American public schools did not serve the melting pot ideal he had argued, Bruce Ackerman, a Yale professor of liberal leaning, also advocated for a fundamental role by the state via a state monopoly of public schools, precisely to avert the risk of parents *closing* their children into school environments that merely reproduce the attitudes, values and beliefs they hold dear and thus to avoid creating educational ghettos that favour segregation. He argues that it is the state's duty to expose children to experiences and ways of living diverse from those they see at home, and that only public schooling can achieve this anti-segregation objective (Ackerman, 1980).

From the perspective in which we are interested here, i.e., the question of how this issue of the state's role as education provider plays out in the build-up of a political narrative, and how this narrative relates to reality, the first thing to say is that none of the two *ideal types* (in the Weberian sense of the term) sketched by Mill and Dewey are to be found as such in reality. However, both ideal types remain very influential as ammunition for the ideological battle, at odds as both may be with the prevailing reality of national education systems.

When we move from the realm of theory to that of reality, what we find is a situation where both public and private provision of education have some role to play, although differences in the public and private sectors' respective shares of the school system are huge. Those differences follow trajectories for which culture and history explain more than strictly political cleavages.

In practice, only in a very limited number of countries and during specific political moments has the choice between a public and a private provision of education emerged as a dichotomy. In none of the seventy-two countries and economies participating in PISA 2015 did either publicly or privately managed schools account for 100% of the system (OECD, 2016a).[4]

But in a clear majority of countries the public school is predominant, accounting for the enrolment of 82% of all fifteen-year-old students in OECD countries (PISA, 2015; OECD, 2016a). Of the (then) thirty-four OECD member countries surveyed, public schools accounted for less than 50% of lower secondary education students only in four (Chile, Ireland, the Netherlands and the United Kingdom[5]). In the remaining countries and economies covered by PISA 2015, only Hong Kong and Macao have a large majority of private schools. The share of public schooling in (mostly) developing countries tends to be around or over 90%, with some exceptions where private schools have a more significant share of students (such as Colombia, Costa Rica, Indonesia, Lebanon, Peru, Taipei and the United Arab Emirates).

Since the 1990s there has been a trend in many countries for establishing a new type of publicly funded but privately managed school (known in the US and other countries as *charter schools*). This has reshaped the controversy about private vs public education, which has increasingly focused on whether charter schools should exist at all. Supporters claim that they offer a variety of choices in terms of values, subject specialisation and even religious faith that allows parents to exercise real choice. Detractors claim that, for the very same reasons, they contribute to the segregation of students, making societies less cohesive. But the main complaint is that such schools divert much-needed resources away from the public system. This represents the main (and potentially the only) issue that can mobilise parents against education reforms that seek to reduce or abolish charter schools, because in practice this would mean that parents lost the right to choose. The debate is therefore reframed as supporting parental choice or favouring

---

4 However, the prevalence of public schools (i.e., schools managed by a public entity, whatever its level) is closer to exclusivity in many countries. In 2015, in fourteen of the developed countries in the OECD, over 95% of students that sat the PISA test were enrolled in public schools (OECD, 2016a).

5 Management is the criterion used by PISA to define a school as public or private, irrespective of the funding body. In the case of the UK (not including Scotland) only schools managed by local education authorities (LEAs) are considered as public, while 'academies' entirely funded by national government, but managed mostly by not-for-profit entities, are considered private schools.

the idea that only public schools can ensure equity. This has become one of the most polarising issues in the educational debate.

Against this backdrop, it seems appropriate to ask why the state's role as education provider remains so politically polarising. The room for manoeuvre in moving from one system to the other is quite limited: except in revolutionary situations, or after very exceptional governance reforms,[6] the balance between public and private schools cannot change swiftly.

Nonetheless, even in the absence of more substantial practical implications, it looks as if parties remain confident in the mobilising power of the flag. Let us take an example: both the UK and Spain had elections in 2019. By comparing the statements on education in the respective electoral manifestos of the main left- and right-wing parties in both countries—in the UK, Labour and Conservative and in Spain, the PSOE (Spanish Socialist Workers' Party) and the PP (People's Party)— we can get a sense of how strongly this issue plays out in contemporary politics.

In the UK,

> The academies system is over-centralised, inefficient and undemocratic [...] And there is no evidence that academies deliver better results [...] We will end the fragmentation and marketisation [*sic*] of our school system by bringing free schools and academies back under control [...] of parents, teachers and local communities [...] Responsibility for delivery in education and support for young people will seat with local authorities, they will manage and have responsibility for school places, including the power to open new schools [...] We will ask the Social Justice Commission to advise on integrating private schools and creating a comprehensive education system. (Labour, 2019)

> We will continue to ensure that parents can choose the schools that best suit their children and best prepare them for the future. And we will continue to build more free schools. (Conservative, 2019)

---

6   In the UK the conversion of a majority of public secondary schools managed by the corresponding Local Education Authorities into academies managed by a trust and funded directly by the government is one such exception. This transformation of secondary education started in 2000 (under Tony Blair's leadership and inspired by Andrew Adonis) and was continued by both the Tory-Liberal Democrat coalition and the Conservative governments of Theresa May and Boris Johnson. Consequently, while in 2000 privately managed schools accounted for around 6% of all schools, today they account for nearly 60%, a shift largely owing to academies.

While in Spain,

> First and foremost, public school must be [...] a fair school, committed to the compensating for social and economic inequalities [...] We will reinforce the public service of education through inclusive public schools, turning back the privatising tide fostered by other parties and eliminating social demand as a criterion for education programming. (PSOE, 2019)

> We shall guarantee choice for families [...] Families will be able to choose the education model they wish for their children and the government should be responsive to that choice and respect the uniqueness of every centre [...] We shall extend the chartering of post-compulsory secondary education to every region. (PP, 2019)

These fragments from party manifestoes perfectly synthesise how the deeply entrenched mantras on the state's role as education provider play out in electoral competitions, even if quick implementation of major changes in the structure of education systems is unlikely. But parties stick to it and, notably, in many cases do not even bother to adjust it to reality. With remarkable stubbornness, "public school" on the left and "choice" on the right are the respective *cris de guerre* when it comes to education provision.

It should not necessarily be that way. One of the smartest education reformers of recent years, Andrew Adonis, who was Parliamentary Under-Secretary of State for Education in the UK during the Labour governments of both Tony Blair and Gordon Brown, referring to the two main challenges faced by English education, stresses that one is:

> [T]o forge a new settlement between state and private education [...] It is my view, after twenty years of engagement with schools of all types, that England will never have a world-class education system or a 'one nation' society, until state and private schools are part of a common national endeavour to develop the talents of all young people to the full. (Adonis, 2012)

This is in fact the challenge faced by many countries where public and private provision of education both have a significant presence. A mix of competition and cooperation resulting in positive emulation dynamics could and should raise the overall level of performance of any given education system. The precondition is of course that the application of rules to both allows for a level playing field and similar responses to equity concerns in both sub-systems.

The above discussion applies mostly to developed economies and mature democracies. When we focus on middle- and low-income countries, many of which are still struggling to achieve universal access to basic education, the state's engagement with education provision differs greatly from developed economies.

If a national education system's development level is "poor", according to the criteria of an influential McKinsey report (Mourshed et al., 2010) and the aim is to improve it to the next level ("fair"), most of the interventions (at the level of capacity-building in physical infrastructure, teacher training, and student support) require strong state leverage as well as substantial external development aid. The data on those middle-income countries participating in the most recent cycles of PISA show that in virtually all of them the share of publicly managed schools exceeds 95% for fifteen-year-old students.

However, in the past fifteen years or so, there has been a blossoming of so-called 'low-cost private schools' in middle-income and developing countries (Hanushek and Woessmann, 2015), most likely due to some endemic inability of governments in many of those countries to tackle issues such as teacher absenteeism, poor teacher quality, poor curricula and others, which all too often hinder progress in public education in less developed countries. There is evidence pointing to better student outcomes in these private schools compared with the public system. However, others argue that the evidence is inconclusive and that outcomes relate more to social differences between students than to the quality of teaching and learning in either type of centre (Akman et al., 2019; Ashley et al., 2014).

The overall question of the state's role as an education provider trickles down to other specific areas of education policy. Virtually every aspect of the system-level parameters (equity, functions, architecture, teachers, curriculum and evaluations) is dealt with differently according to both the state's actual involvement in the delivery of education and the ideological assumptions surrounding it.

Ideology, in fact, plays an important role in defining approaches to the main subjects that frame education systems. Kevin Smith's attempt to explain the deep ideological foundations of certain educational debates, published almost twenty years ago, defined two antagonistic creeds on education, 'public education' and 'the market':

> Public education and the market have both been described as secular religions [...] Though both represent broadly-held value systems, public education and the market are not particularly compatible creeds. Judging by the record of the past two decades, attempts to integrate the two tend to result in some sort of controversies associated with the most bitter sectarian debates. (Smith, 2003)

It is possible that antagonism continues to be central in the explanation of a number of those "sectarian debates" to which Smith refers. A good example can be found in a reader on global education reforms published a few years ago (Adamson and Darling-Hammond, 2016b). In it, some examples of the narrative against the market as a driving force in the education sector are presented in a rather radical way. For instance, Pasi Sahlberg, a renowned Finnish advocate of public education, links competition, standardisation, focus on literacy and numeracy, test-based accountability and choice as the main features of a supposedly damaging process that he has termed "GERM", which stands for 'Global Education Reform Movement' (Sahlberg, 2016). In our opinion this narrative is mainly driven by ideological assumptions rather than evidence-based policies drawn from robust data.

From a less ideological viewpoint, today any reference to the market should be qualified by considerations of the globalisation process as another driver of education reform beyond national boundaries. The influence of globalisation on education policies has somewhat blurred the boundaries between the left and the right on this issue, especially in those places where—at least, for some time—the mainstream left embraced the necessity for education systems to respond to the requirements of globalisation.

For instance, according to Stephen Ball's analysis of discourses on education reform in the UK during the Labour governments in the first decade of the twenty-first century and the coalition government that followed immediately thereafter, there was a certain thread of continuity on the issue of globalisation, while at the same time there was dissent on the question of how the education system should respond to it:

> However, here again, as well as the evident continuities between Labour and the Coalition, it is also important to point out the differences [...]

> Clearly, neither Labour nor Coalition education policies can be simply read off in their entirety from a global educational agenda. (Ball, 2013)

In the case of the UK, we may observe a certain 'incremental continuity' over relatively long periods in addressing some features of system-level education reform. For instance, the reforms of school governance were built up from 1986 until well into the twenty-first century, spanning across a number of both Tory and Labour governments (Adonis, 2012). There are clearly differences in the respective approaches, and some ebbs and flows in the reform stamina of these various governments. But in general, in the context of these two parties' different education ideologies, there was at least some willingness to accept that a number of specific measures worked well for the system and that there was no point in suppressing or changing them when a different party came to power.

Other countries also provide good examples of broad consensus across the political spectrum on some or most educational issues. Such agreements are more typical in countries where there is a political culture that underpins "consociational democracy" (Lijphart, 1969), i.e. politically fragmented societies that have developed a stable culture of cooperation between different parties, both in general strategies of government (through coalitions) and in debates over divisive issues, such as educational ideologies. A particularly compelling example would be Finland, where education and economic policies have been integrated and somehow shielded from political discontinuities:

> [B]oth education and economic development have been guided by integrated policies. Education policy has been articulated through five-year development plans that cover all the education and research sectors. These plans formed a bridge between the political mandates of outgoing and newly elected governments; hence, they became key instruments in creating sustainable political leadership in education. (Sahlberg, 2016)

2.3 Equity and the Function of Education: Equaliser or Enabler?

The debate about the social role that education has to play or the function that education serves both at an individual and micro-social level, as well as at macro-social or aggregate level, is deeply entangled with ideology.

From this viewpoint, we can identify certain fault lines of the debate which have to do with opposite visions of the social order not too dissimilar to those we have already observed on the state's role as education provider. These visions trickle down to more particular aspects of the education systems, as we will consider later.

On the one side, we have those favouring a public investment approach (Adamson and Åstrand, 2016: 2–12). The basic assumption is that only a strategy which keeps not just the provision of education but also the governance of the basic dimensions of the system in the hands of governments (and/or other public entities, such as regional, provincial or local authorities) will adequately:

- Achieve universal access to quality education, without leaving behind the underprivileged or vulnerable,
- Prepare students (and then citizens) for economy and democracy,
- Deliver equity, compensating for disadvantages and aiming at a level playing field for all.

The opposite view, labelled as 'privatisation' (Adamson and Åstrand, 2016), 'marketisation' (Bates et al., 2019) or 'choice' is grounded on a two-fold economic rationale:

> From the supply side, supporters of private education claim that efficiency is better served since private firms tend to be more efficient in delivering goods and services.
>
> While, from the demand side, the argument is that choice feeds competition and competition leads to higher quality. (Adamson and Åstrand, 2016)

This approach also claims that private provision delivers more equity. Choice not only benefits the affluent who can pay for private schools, but also low-income and minority students. Choice, publicly funded through vouchers or publicly funded charter schools, broadens the latter's educational opportunities, and prevents them from being confined to low-quality public schools.

At the end of the day, the claim for equity on each side relies on a different concept of equity. This is yet another never-ending debate on education. Discussion on equity and its requirements trickles down into the political arena in a more simplified form and on many occasions takes centre-stage in public conversations about education reform.

Although equity is a revolving issue in the education debate and we will find almost as many declinations of it as other, more specific topics with which we will be dealing, some sort of general framing of it seems necessary at this point.

Conceptually, equity covers a very broad definitional spectrum, from a libertarian idea of equity as simply equal treatment defined by law (Nozick, 1974) to an egalitarian concept for which equity involves compensation for differences in individuals' starting points in life. Such differences are not only connected with socio-economic status, but also with the unequal distribution of natural talent, as John Rawls pointed out in his discussion of meritocracy:

> [T]he principle that undeserved inequalities call for redress; and since inequalities of birth and social endowment are undeserved, these inequalities have to be compensated for. (Rawls, 1971)

However, if we want to get to grips with the more practical dimensions of equity in education, the first distinction to be made is probably between equity and equality, as expressed by Ben Levin in a seminal paper on the practical implications of equity for policymaking in education:

> There is general agreement that the aim of public policy cannot and should not be equality in the sense that everyone is the same or achieves the same outcomes [...] Rather, a commitment to equity suggests that differences in outcomes should not be attributable to differences in areas such as wealth, income, power or possessions. The question is always a practical one, then, of what state or degree of inequality is acceptable. (Levin, 2003)

It is in the gravitational balance between these two poles—equal opportunities for all and equal outcomes for all—that the battle between different conceptions of equity held by opposing ideological camps is fought. The problem here is that very often this difference in the meaning of equity becomes obscured in the debate. Consequently, this lack of consensus on what is meant by equity darkens rather than enlightens the debate itself.

There are many examples of these muddled and useless debates. There are many countries where equity (or lack thereof) has taken centre-stage in public discussion of education. We will show how, in absence of a shared operational definition of equity, the concept can be manipulated to the advantage of those opposing any given educational reform.

To better explore this question, we need to provide as neutral a definition of equity in education as possible, acknowledging that it is not the only possible—nor the only plausible—definition, but that it can at least accommodate most of the dimensions that are usually considered in debates about equity.

In our opinion, a good, adaptive definition of equity in education is that provided some years ago by OECD researchers Simon Field, Malgorzata Kuczera and Beatriz Pont:

> Equity in education has two dimensions. The first is fairness, which implies ensuring that personal and social circumstances—for example gender, socio-economic status or ethnic origin—should not be an obstacle to achieving educational potential. The second is inclusion, which implies ensuring a basic minimum standard of education for all—for example that everyone should be able to read, write and do simple arithmetic. (Field, Kuczera and Pont, 2007)

Focusing on these two practical dimensions, fairness and inclusion, allows us to sideline more philosophical debates that are hard to integrate or even to translate into the political narrative on equity that gets in the way of education reforms (OECD, 2012; Wert, 2019).

However, even if we narrow the focus to capture these two basic dimensions, we find huge disagreement on their implications. Ultimately, most of these disagreements pertain to the sphere of a fundamental cleavage in educational ideology. For some education policymakers, the main aim of education is social compensation. There is probably no clearer expression of this idea than the metaphor that the Chilean socialist former Minister of Education, Nicolás Eyzaguirre, used in a television interview to paraphrase the aims of his educational reform:

> [W]hat we have here are two runners on a paved track. One is running on high-speed skates, the other runs barefoot. The barefoot runner is public

education. Then, they tell me: Why don't you feed and train the barefoot runner? First, I have to get the other runner off his skates. (Fontaine and Urzúa, 2018)

Those opposing any form of educational privilege that could stem from private and selective provision of education face the issue of how to ban it without directly going against the foundations of liberal democracy. It is hard to find a rationale to deter—let alone to forbid up front—parents from investing their own resources in the best education they can offer their offspring.

The modulation of arguments can be quite diverse. In many cases, rather than voicing straightforward opposition to private education, the arguments point to its (supposed) deleterious effects on equity, along with denials of its (supposed) advantages. Those speaking out in favour of banning private education are rare, although every now and then a political campaign against private schools erupts.

One of the most recent of these happened in the UK on the eve of the 2019 election, when, at their pre-election conference in Brighton, Labour discussed and approved a motion promoted by the grassroots activist group Labour Against Private Schools (LAPS). The party voted in favour of abolishing fee-paying schools and redistributing their assets "democratically and fairly" for the benefit of all children (Verkaik, 2019). When translated into the party manifesto the wording of this pledge was slightly more nuanced, but the motion enjoyed the support of a majority of delegates. Waving the flag against private education still works on the left, particularly when a mainstream party in the centre-left becomes more radical and moves towards the left, as happened in the build-up to this particular election.

One particular expression of the conflicts arising in and around private provision of education and how these relate to equity concerns is the ongoing debate about 'shadow education'. This concept, meaning supplementary private tutoring to reinforce and/or enhance the learning outcomes of students mostly enrolled in public schools (Bray, 2013), is now a favourite target of those opposing private provision of education on grounds of equity.

Critics say that since private tutoring comes at a significant cost for families (European Commission, 2011) and represents a sizeable chunk of education investment, more regulatory attention should be paid to it to prevent it from magnifying already existing gaps in equity, as well as to guarantee standards in its provision.

More important is the fact that relevant international organisations are buying at least part—if not all—of this narrative. For instance, the European Commission published a position paper commissioned for the Network of Experts in Social Sciences on Education and Training (NESSE). The paper's main author was Mark Bray, a renowned specialist from Hong Kong University who has written extensively against shadow education. In the paper, equity-related concerns about shadow education are highlighted in unequivocal terms:

> All governments claim that they wish to reduce social inequalities and assist the disadvantaged sectors of society. If left to market forces, however, the shadow education system maintains and exacerbates inequalities. (European Commission, 2011)

Similarly, the OECD is also critical about shadow education because it assumes that it magnifies inequalities. Take this example from an assessment of the Greek education system conducted a few years ago:

> [I]t adds to existing inequalities, by allowing the affluent to give their children opportunities not available to others, and/or that it may be a financial burden on poorer households. Supplementary tutoring can exert undesirable pressure on young people by making the schooling day very long. (OECD, 2017a)

It is noteworthy, in our opinion, that this vein of criticism of families' efforts to improve their children's education is primarily concerned with a potential effect on equity rather than the likely impact on the learning outcomes of those benefiting from private tutoring. This vein of criticism assumes—quite apodictically—that only well-off families will be able to pay for it, when evidence from a number of countries shows that middle-class and even poorer families also make substantial efforts to invest as much as possible in their offspring's education. More importantly, none of these points address the main issue: parents are willing to invest resources in the education of their children because public schools are not meeting their expectations. So why not deal with the root of the problem rather than preventing parents from finding alternative ways to ensure a good quality education?

In other words, it seems reasonable to question the logical and moral grounds for preventing anyone from investing private money in their children's education simply so as to avoid the disparities that this may generate for those who—for economic and other reasons—are not making such investments. Again, as Eyzaguirre's above metaphor inadvertently suggests, a rather straightforward conclusion is missing here: rather than forbid private tutoring, it makes more sense to improve the quality of publicly funded education, making further investments unnecessary and benefitting all.

At the end of the day, this brings us to the big question: to what extent can the underlying ideal of education as an equaliser justify limiting—or even banning—the options for enhanced, improved or merely different types of education for those whose parents wish to invest their resources in improving the quality of their children's education? To what extent should the legitimate aspiration for a level playing field necessitate curtailment of those wishing to expand the boundaries of their educational achievement?

The wish to provide those students most in need with as many tools as possible to compensate for initial disadvantages and allow them to do better at school is a natural consequence of the ideal of equity and, as such, there is no reasonable objection to it. But it remains unclear why that ambition should be incompatible with the progress of those who simply want to use every resource available to them to do better as well.

A different vision of equity—equity as an enabler—is in our view needed to overcome the shortcomings and contradictions of the somewhat prevailing vision of equity as an equaliser. By this, we mean that the pursuit of a fairer and more inclusive education system basically has to do with the provision of the means, the resources, and the policies that are needed to allow every student—irrespective of personal or social circumstances—to reach the highest peak possible.

This vision of equity requires a focus on diversity. In the words of historian and former Labour politician Tristram Hunt, who was Shadow Secretary of State for Education and is now the Director of the Victoria and Albert Museum:

> Without necessarily jettisoning in its entirety the progressive advances of the welfare state, it is perhaps time to think more imaginatively about

precisely which equities are sacrosanct and which diversities worthy of encouragement. (Hunt, 2005)

Diversity, indeed, can be a better path than uniformity for achieving equity. In order to enable students to achieve their own potential, we must take into account their diverse needs and devise a system that helps them in many different ways. This does not exclude traditional compensation policies to help the underprivileged and the vulnerable, which are an essential component of both the fairness and the inclusion dimensions of equity. But there may be other pathways to develop diverse potential, and some leeway should therefore be allowed to students and families so that they can weigh their options, build their own itineraries, and choose from a range of educational trajectories the one that best suits their abilities, dispositions and ambitions.

However, the road to diversity is bumpy and an increasing emphasis on equity as the main goal of education systems is built on the premise that uniformity constitutes the only truly egalitarian policy, and equal outcomes constitute the only equitable goal. Comprehensiveness, the educational philosophy of the post-WW2 era that achieved widespread social-democratic support (Simon and Rubenstein, 1969), and its more modern adaptations continue to enjoy almost full consensus as the only strategy that leads to equality.

Where comprehensiveness denotes delaying tracking into academic and vocational paths until upper-secondary level, it is fair to say that this has been implemented in most (but not all) education systems, but we should also point out that some top-performing systems do have early tracking, and this does not seem to hinder their quality or their equity. Moreover, when comprehensive education policies have been implemented in their more radical forms (e.g., no ability grouping in any form, no choice of subjects) in non-egalitarian societies, this has led to the worst possible equality outcomes, such as high rates of early school leaving. The evidence thus far suggests that this is because radical comprehensive policies cannot deal appropriately with the huge levels of student heterogeneity in non-egalitarian societies.

The seemingly indestructible link between equity and uniformity created by an extreme version of the comprehensiveness ideology has been kept alive, even after the failures of that doctrine have in many places become apparent. Since the notion of comprehensiveness as the only fair education policy seems to have become an indestructible belief for a substantial part of the educational establishment, any attempts to diversify educational pathways to accommodate differences and channel them positively tend to clash with the equity advocates, who will almost invariably try to discredit them on counts of elitism or segregation.

The alternative explanation is rarely considered: that comprehensiveness does work in societies—such as the Nordic states—that were egalitarian before the implementation of these educational policies. In these societies, students and their parents enjoy rather high and uniform levels of skills, and thus do not require policies to deal with major differences between students when they start school.

In summary, equity is a very important component of any well-functioning education system. But since equity is a "complex" (Martínez, 2017) or even "elusive" concept (Wert, 2019), its translation into educational policies is shaped in diverse ways. While the very idea of equity is supported by scholars and policymakers of every ideological affiliation, the range of meanings ascribed to it covers a very broad spectrum.

For those on the left, educational equity is the main mechanism for equalising societies, compensating for differences in wealth (material and/or symbolic) and thus diminishing or even suppressing the "reproductive function" (Bourdieu and Passeron, 1970) of education. Equity is a means to equality: first in educational outcomes and ultimately in social outcomes. Education is an equaliser or even 'the equaliser'. In the most extreme iteration of this ideological framework, maximising equity is the yardstick against which the success of an education system must be assessed.

Conversely, for those on the right, equity should be understood—and acted upon in policy terms—as providing equal opportunities for every student to minimise the impact of their socio-economic status or other personal factors by providing compensatory measures, and to reach their fullest potential in educational outcomes according to talent, character and effort. Education in this framework is an enabler.

Ultimately, none of the two extreme frameworks can reasonably be expected to function as more than an aspiration in the real world. Equality is impossible to achieve due to insurmountable differences among students and the different levels of effort that students with similar abilities are willing to display. Similarly, perfect equal opportunities do not exist in the real world, because underprivileged students face challenges at many levels beyond the school environment. However, education systems should aim to achieve both quality and equity by providing additional support to disadvantaged students while also allowing those with potential to excel. As we will see, some countries have achieved an adequate balance between the two.

2.4 The Shape of Education: Architecture, Teachers, Curricula and Assessments

The ideological divide trickles down to a great number of issues on the education agenda. Here we will consider how the different ideological visions of education exert their influence on the narratives about the main features shaping education systems. We have included four, which are most subject to ideological dispute: architecture, teachers, curriculum and assessments. We have deliberately avoided a consideration of pedagogical issues, not because they lack ideological dissent, but because pedagogy is beyond the scope of this book.

2.4.1 Architecture of the Education System

At first glance, the basic architecture of the education system seems to be an aspect that is less exposed to political quarrels. At this level, global convergence has gradually taken place such that structural features (stages, progression and graduation) tend to be very similar, almost identical, in the developed world. This process of convergence, driven by many factors, such as peer learning between countries and increased mobility of students and teachers, which requires mutual recognition of degrees, has gone through a considerable acceleration process over the past fifty years (Parkyn, 1969; Spring, 2015)

Therefore, the degree of ideological dissent over the structure of the education system is very limited in the majority of countries, if it exists at all. When there is some divergence, it tends to be relatively mild and peripheral.

The main exception—and in some countries a very important one—has to do with the scope of comprehensiveness of the system.

The diversification of pathways in secondary education into general academic programmes and vocational programmes has been a matter of political conflict in some countries. In particular, the educational stage at which this diversification takes place is a highly controversial issue with many ideological implications.

So-called 'early tracking' (a loaded title with a negative subtext), which refers to the diversification of tracks before the end of compulsory education, is a typical instance. Supporters of comprehensiveness, which include a majority of parties on the left, including most mainstream social democrats, will oppose early tracking on the grounds that it "segregates" students, setting low performers on a less attractive educational trajectory and limiting their chances to thrive in labour and in life. On top of this, they argue that disadvantaged students will bear the burden of that segregation as they have more chances of being low performers, or of being perceived as low performers.

In contrast, among those policymakers who favour the diversification of educational trajectories—mostly, but not exclusively, liberals and conservatives—the rationale is that creating the possibility of following a more job-oriented curriculum at the end (or very near to it) of compulsory secondary education (around ninth or eleventh grade, depending on the country's system) diminishes early school leaving because it offers a range of choices to students who would quit school altogether if vocational education and training (hereafter VET) programmes were not offered early enough.

Comprehensive education theory is largely built on the idea that keeping all students on exactly the same track until the end of compulsory education is a fundamental element of equity. This assumption warrants some fact-checking.

To begin with, since the formal length of compulsory education has changed over time, the precise meaning of flexibility at the end of it has also changed. For instance,

- In the UK, prior to 1944, school was compulsory up to the age of fourteen, from 1944–1972 it was compulsory up to the age of fifteen, and from 1972 onwards it has been compulsory up to the age of sixteen.
- In France, before 1959, school was compulsory up to the age of fourteen; from 1959–2020 it was compulsory up to the age

of sixteen and in 2020, a new act made education compulsory following different paths up to the age of eighteen.

- In Spain, compulsory education up to the age of fourteen was established in 1970; twenty years later it was extended to the age of sixteen, and there is currently an ongoing debate about extending it to the age of eighteen.
- In the US, there is no federal legislation on compulsory schooling. Individual state legislation and Supreme Court rulings have led to a variety of situations across the country regarding not only the length of mandatory schooling but also whether conventional schooling can be made mandatory, or homeschooling is allowed. A number of libertarians (Caplan, 2018) and others fiercely oppose any attempts to extend further compulsory schooling.

Generally speaking, there is an ongoing movement in most developed countries to extend compulsory education up to the age of eighteen. Previous experiences in different countries show that extending mandatory education is not *per se* a guarantee of higher educational performance.

One of the unintended consequences of extending compulsory education is that it may well result in an increase of early school leavers. Thus, as homogeneous compulsory education spans more and more years, the education system needs to deal with the different performance levels present in the student population in different ways. If the education system has failed to support those students lagging behind they are likely to opt out. In addition, those students who are more interested in applied subjects may decide not to continue in on the academic path for longer. This was the case in Spain after the implementation of a new education law in 1990 (*Ley Orgánica General del Sistema Educativo*, known as LOGSE), which was passed by the PSOE (the socialist party). The law extended the upper age bracket for compulsory secondary education from fourteen to sixteen years and implemented a uniform curriculum up to the end of that stage. As a result, the choice of a vocational track was not possible until two years later, which led to high rates of early school leaving, particularly among males (Felgueroso *et al.*, 2013).

Since then, early school leaving has reached very high levels (around 30%) and became an endemic problem for the Spanish education system, leading to high rates of youth unemployment and low levels of skills among a substantial proportion of the adult population. All future attempts to tackle this problem—for instance by giving students in the last years of lower-secondary education the option to choose between academic and applied versions of the same subjects such as mathematics (not tracks)[7]—were furiously criticised by parties on the left and unions, on the grounds that they promoted segregation and threatened equity, despite ample evidence showing that these policies led to increased enrolment in VET and a parallel decrease in early school leaving (Wert, 2019).

It seems shocking that some would argue that not having any options to choose between academic vs applied versions of the same subjects until the end of compulsory education is more relevant in equity terms than decreasing rates of early school leaving. This case illustrates the convoluted nature of debates muddled by ideology and oblivious to empirical evidence. Beyond that, this and similar cases illustrate the long-standing prejudice against VET.

2.4.2 Teachers

Since teachers are at the core of education policy it seems inevitable that they are the target of ideologically charged education debates. In general, parties on the left (supporting the interests of teachers' unions) are in favour of hiring as many teachers as possible and in most instances are against them being evaluated, given incentives linked to performance, or dismissed for poor performance. On the other hand, parties on the right tend to be more frugal in hiring, and to support teacher evaluations and performance-related incentives.

Of course, behind this broad left-right opposition, there is more nuance on institutional arrangements about recruitment, training, career

---

7   This was achieved through the *Ley Orgánica para la Mejora de la Calidad Educativa*, or LOMCE (Law for the Improvement of Quality in Education), which was approved in Parliament on 9 December 2013. It consisted of amendments to around one third of the provisions of the *Ley Orgánica de Educación*, LOE, passed in 2006. These amendments were basically aimed at addressing the main weaknesses of the system (high early school leaving and low VET enrolment) and were supported by strong international evidence.

progression and compensation of teachers, which makes ideological debates on specific issues concerning teachers quite heterogeneous.

Public teachers are recruited and employed in quite different ways depending on the country. The main difference is whether they are tenured civil servants or ordinary employees, even if their employer is a public institution. Civil servants enjoy a strong shield against redundancy or dismissal and are protected by collective bargaining agreements. On the other hand, teachers employed on general labour terms, with open-ended or fixed-term contracts, are—in theory—less protected, as they can be made redundant or fired for a variety of reasons.

In most of continental Europe, as in Latin America, teachers are, with some nuances depending on their formal status, predominantly civil servants. Historical conceptions of the state as the main education provider, along with the prevalent institutional arrangements in the process of building the welfare state, have led to teachers being granted the status of civil servants, a privileged position in terms of job stability, workload and, often, also salary.

On the contrary, in Anglo-Saxon countries, most notably in the UK and the US, but also Australia and others, there is a much more flexible, adaptive, and diversified process for recruiting teachers. There are differences between and within these countries (because of the federal system in the US or devolution in the UK) but, all in all, these systems are flexible in their approach to different kinds of employment, so that they are able to develop and retain teaching talent, while fostering links between permanence and performance in order to avoid the burden of keeping ineffective teachers on school payrolls. However, some argue that in practice, given the real asymmetries in the distribution of power between the micro level (school boards and individual schools) and teachers' unions, it is highly unlikely that a teacher with poor performance would be fired (Moe, 2006).

These differences have an impact on the importance and shape of ideological debates about the teaching profession and the role of teachers in education. At face value, parties on both sides of the political spectrum would likely hold similar views on the importance of teachers, the need to enhance their status and working conditions and their crucial role in educational policymaking. But the precise nature of the conflicts and cleavages that sometimes emerge in the education debate reveal different conceptions of the teaching profession.

At this point, a very important factor that drives huge differences among those countries with more mature and developed education systems and others is the degree and type of professional development and institutionalisation of teachers. Where teachers—whether they are civil servants or employees—are recruited through selective processes and entry to the profession demands rigorous and high standards, they tend to be institutionally recognised as professionals commanding social respect and recognition. In these cases, although there may be political conflicts about certain aspects of their training, career paths or compensation, such conflicts will be channelled by political parties and teachers' unions on the basis of a well-established framework that will prevent escalation.

When the recruitment of teachers is neither selective nor based on merit, their training is of low quality, and unions gain much power due to their large membership and their capacity to penetrate ministerial and governmental structures, education outcomes are weaker, and it is in the interests of teacher unions to protect their large membership by rejecting any attempts to raise standards or link performance to incentives. In this context, conflicts between teachers and reformist policymakers can and do spiral, often resulting in very long strikes or even more serious public disorders.

This was the case in Mexico in 2013, after the newly-elected President Enrique Peña Nieto had launched an urgent education reform in 2012. The reform included a provision that secondary education teachers be periodically assessed, with those failing open to being fired. Although the reform had a strong parliamentary support (it was part of the *Pacto por México*, signed by the main political parties), it met strong opposition from the teachers' union *Coordinadora Nacional de Trabajadores de la Enseñanza* (CNTE), which fought against it in very radical terms, including a very long strike in some states and an encampment in Mexico City's most iconic square (Plaza del Zócalo) which was occupied for over five months. Despite this fierce resistance, the Secretary of Public Education, Aurelio Nuño, successfully persevered with the reform until the populist government of Andrés Manuel López Obrador repealed it altogether, and also suppressed teacher assessments.

Anything having to do with teachers is extremely sensitive from a political point of view. Students and their parents tend to have strong emotional attachments to teachers, and often a rather diffuse understanding of school performance. In many countries there is a high level of unionisation among teachers, but even in those countries where affiliation with teachers' unions is not particularly high, unions are nonetheless quite powerful as they serve as the voice of teachers, and the only channel of communication between teachers and policymakers, as well as all other stakeholders. In those countries where there is a variety of unions representing a diversified teaching profession this multiplicity facilitates dialogue, mainly because different unions do not act in unison either supporting or rejecting particular policies and, therefore, hold less political power. But such diversity requires that governments listen to all of the different voices and try to accommodate different interests. Conversely, there are places where a particular union is very predominant or even monopolistic. In these cases, a false sense of professional unanimity can be created around issues on which there is no such agreement.

There is growing concern among the institutionalised representation of teacher unions about their risk of being portrayed as a self-serving group more focused on their own interests than those of students. A research review on the role of teachers' unions on education reforms, commissioned by the powerful National Education Association, the main American union, clearly articulates this concern:

> In contrast to the portrayal of self-serving unions advocating for teacher benefits at the expense of student learning [...] many unions have adopted the 'new unionism,' a more collaborative approach to collective bargaining emphasizing the importance of increasing the scope of unions' role in decision making to include professional and reform agendas. (Bascia and Osmond, 2012)

It is perfectly understandable that teachers' unions speak out about improving the working conditions of their affiliates, negotiating better salaries, or enhancing teachers' status in society. Ultimately, this is what unions were created for. But these perfectly respectable objectives sometimes collide with the purposes of educational reform. This is the case whenever education reformers feel the need to address initial and/or pre-service training, professional development, assessment, or teacher career tracks in their reforms, and their proposals are opposed by teachers, who fear that their privileges could be threatened by the changes. In these cases, the narrative is often distorted by ignoring the legitimate corporative aims and presenting the opposition to reforms in the name of the interest of students, equity, or any other sacrosanct educational dogma, so as to elicit support or sympathy from families and the public at large.

In fact, teachers' unions are well aware of the leverage they can provide when it comes to the implementation of education reforms. Let us consider, for instance, how Fred van Leeuwen, then Secretary General of Education International, the global umbrella federation of teachers' unions, put it:

> All the evidence shows that successful education systems rely on strong self-confident teaching unions working in partnerships with governments on education policies [...] This fact seems surprising to many—particularly those who believe that it is quite possible to terrify teachers into accepting the latest imposed reform. (Bascia and Osmond, 2013)

In summary, teachers are a fundamental gear in the education engine and as such they play a key role in the definition and implementation of education policy, insofar as their stance determines to a great extent whether a given reform will succeed or fail. Both professional and ideological considerations matter, and sometimes it is difficult to ascertain to which of those categories a given teachers' response to a policy measure belongs. Moreover, teachers in a vast majority of countries enjoy a very positive public image (as is the case with other professions delivering public goods, like health workers) and, especially on issues which directly affect them (salaries, class size), public opinion tends to support their demands. Therefore, every effort to provide education reforms with a clear-cut narrative that makes teachers understand it, buy into it or, at least, that keeps them neutral towards it will be worthwhile.

2.4.3 Curriculum and Ideology

As for the ideological debates focused on curricula, an important distinction must be made for the sake of clarity. There is an influential current of literature on the topic, stemming from the seminal work of critical pedagogue Michael W. Apple (Apple, 1979 and 1982) focused on the way curricula are a reflection of the clashes and imbalances of power existing in a society both in political and cultural terms. This line of analysis, following in the footsteps of the work of sociologists Pierre Bourdieu and Jean-Claude Passeron on social reproduction (Bourdieu and Passeron, 1970) and Marxist philosopher Louis Althusser on the ideological state apparatuses (Althusser, 1970), explores from a structural Marxist perspective the relationship between curricula and social and political hegemony. The well-known work of Peter Berger and Thomas Luckmann (Berger and Luckmann, 1966) on the social construction of reality has had a big influence on educationalists questioning the possibility of basing curricula on "objective" knowledge (Christodoulou, 2014).

This is not the kind of intellectual construction in which we are primarily interested here, though we will briefly return to it later, at the end of this section. From the analytical perspective that we follow in this book, the question we want to explore instead is much more down to earth: how debates on curricular approaches and content reflect on, and are driven by, educational ideologies. We try to identify and analyse how the curriculum is approached by education policymakers and experts according to overall ideological conceptions.

Having defined our focus, it is also necessary to note upfront that, unlike other educational topics (like those we have dealt with above), political ideology sometimes trickles down to curricula less openly, and can work as an undercover component of an education debate (Wahlstrom, 2018).

Reading between the lines in these debates, we find a set of issues with varying degrees of salience in place and time around: (*i*) the usefulness of a national curriculum and how it relates to student outcomes; (*ii*) the content of curricula, or who decides what; and (*iii*) how curricula should deal with 'position issues' which are divisive and how they keep pace with the changing requirements of the megatrends shaping our world and its evolving values and beliefs.

The ideological ground of the debate about the need for and function of a national curriculum varies according to the particular country. In the US, it was mainly to do with the dynamics of federal vs state competency. As a matter of fact, the success of the Common

Core Standards Initiative owed much to the cooperative approach of its advocates.[8] It was through a voluntary network of governors sharing best practices by peer learning and the Council of Chief State School Officers that the initiative was shaped and then taken up by an overwhelming majority of states. It enjoyed widespread bipartisan support, as its broad adoption makes evident. It probably would never have happened if the impulse had come from the federal level of government. Instead, the horizontal approach, along with the voluntary condition of the decision to adopt the standards, made it easier for states to accept it.

In other federal or quasi-federal countries where education systems are co-governed by the national government and the regional governments (such as Germany or Spain), there are different approaches to curriculum content. In the case of Germany, where the Constitution (Grundgesetz, 1949: articles 7 and 30) enshrines the federal government with the function of "general supervision" of the school system, in practice public education is basically under the purview of individual regions (*Länder*). Under this regulatory framework, the question of a national curriculum has been dealt with consensually, not too dissimilarly to the pattern we have seen in the United States, through agreements reached in the Conference of Education Ministers of the sixteen *Länder* (Kultusministerkonferenz, KMK).

In Spain, there is a defined constitutional role assigned to the national government in education, which is to promote basic legislation which defines the architecture of the system and general rules, while implementation is the responsibility of regional governments. This division of responsibilities has allowed different approaches to the role of central and regional governments in defining curricular content. Until 2013, the curriculum of each and every subject was split between central government and regions, with a percentage assigned to each: central government was responsible for between 55–65% and regions were responsible for between 45–35%, depending on whether they had an official vernacular tongue. This led to educational problems

---

8   The Common Core Standards Initiative was launched in 2009 by state leaders, including governors and state commissioners of education from forty-eight states, two territories and the District of Columbia (Common Core Standards Initiative, 2020). Today the standards have been adopted by forty-one states, the District of Columbia, four territories and the Department of Defense Education Activities.

such as a lack of alignment between the curriculum content defined by central government and regions, and a growing divergence between the curricular content actually studied in different regions by students who would obtain the same national degree. It also led to political problems, since regions with strong nationalistic movements introduced changes to subjects such as history or geography which proved instrumental in creating national identity and animosity against central government. The next major legislative change (LOMCE, 2013) implemented a different approach in order to avoid these problems: central government became responsible for the content of certain subjects and regional governments became responsible for the content of others, but the percentages remained the same. This system was reversed in 2020 when the current socialist-populist government used this issue as a concession to secessionist parties in exchange for support to approve the budget (Gomendio, 2020a). As a consequence, regional governments are now responsible for a greater share of the curricular contents of every subject than ever before. Control of education has proven to be the most powerful tool for nationalistic movements.

Meanwhile, in the UK a national curriculum was introduced by Kenneth Baker (who served as Secretary of State for Education from 1986 to 1989, under Margaret Thatcher's premiership) in 1988 as a fundamental element of the Education Reform Act. At the outset, it applied to K-12 education in England and Wales, although because of devolution it no longer applies to Wales. The act was not supported by the main opposition party (Labour), although the first clarion call in favour of a national curriculum had been made by Labour Prime Minister James Callagham in his famous Ruskin College speech on the challenges faced by the UK (Woodward, 2001), some twelve years before the new act was approved in Parliament.

When a national curriculum was finally passed, Labour opposed it on the grounds that it was removing educational power from local authorities and schools to national government. But their main objection was the claim that a national curriculum was against equity, since it established the same standards for the well-off and the underprivileged. In the words of Hillary Armstrong, then Labour spokesperson on schools,

> [I] see the Act as returning to an elitist system and an admission of an elitist system in education [...] You cannot have a mass education system without bringing everyone up to at least a minimum standard [...] The problem with the Act is that in establishing a national curriculum, the government takes away the local autonomy. (Armstrong, 1990)

But in this case, the main opposition force was not political. The most vocal opposition came from teachers. There was a widespread outcry across the teaching profession that remains alive more than twenty years on:

> In 1988, when I had been teaching for about 20 years, something dreadful happened: the national curriculum was introduced. (Hanson, 2018)

Why was it dreadful? The underlying argument in most cases had to do with something teachers and teachers' unions called the invasion of the "secret garden" (Gillard, 1988; McCulloch, 2000), the space teachers assumed was their own in deciding what to teach and how to teach it. Twenty years after its implementation, the national curriculum had been accepted (Swift, 2009) or at least grudgingly tolerated by teachers (Shepherd, 2009), but the campaign in favour of its simplification and improvements to its flexibility and focus remains a persistent fixture of England's teaching landscape.

Beyond this mostly corporative approach to the debate on curricula, on many occasions the burning ideological issues on curricula have to do with the curricular consideration of topics or subjects that are, at given moments in time, a matter of debate in society. Thus, debates about whether issues like religion, citizenship education or LGBTQIA+ identities are to be taught in schools, and how they should be dealt with become the focus of public debate on the curriculum. In addition, in countries where there are strong pro-independence tensions, history also becomes a contentious curricular issue.

There is an old, but still ongoing, debate on these issues. From a philosophical viewpoint, the seminal work of political scientist Amy Gutmann linked it with a more general question about what she calls "principled" education, meaning a discussion on what education is for, regarding individuals, society and the state, and consequently, the roles that different stakeholders should play.

From this angle, she elaborates on the different theories of authority in education: the "family state", the "state of families" and the "state of individuals". In the family state the authority of education lies with the state, in the state of families parents will hold that authority, and in the state of individuals authority will be placed with students themselves, in the sense of allowing them to define as freely as possible the "good life" that they want to pursue. In the end, Gutmann assumes that none of the three theories can provide a general answer to all divisive issues, because all three are incomplete, as conceptions of good life are contested (Gutmann, 1999).

These differing views are a powerful factor to explain the 'cultural wars' that often thwart education reforms. To quote only some examples and how they have affected education reforms in different times and places, in the UK, at the same time as the Education Reform Act was being discussed in Parliament (1988), Section 28 of the Local Government Act prohibited Local Authorities from "intentionally promot[ing] homosexuality or publish[ing] material with the intention to promote homosexuality" and from "promot[ing] the teaching in any maintained school of the acceptability of homosexuality as a pretended family relationship".

The origin of the public debate that led to the approval of this contentious clause in the context of a Local Government Act had taken place two years before, when it was discovered that some schools under the oversight of the Inner London Education Authority were using a picture book (*Jenny Lives with Eric and Martin*) in which a young gay couple were raising a five-year-old daughter, who is the biological child of one of them. The tabloids created a considerable furore over it and Kenneth Baker, then Education Secretary, involved himself and the government in the quarrel, ordering the withdrawal of the book and summoning Local Education Authorities to avoid "condoning" homosexuality as an acceptable relationship or lifestyle (Chitty, 1999). Although it was unrelated to the Education Reform Act, the issue somewhat tainted the public image of the reform, which was perceived as more influenced by old-fashioned conservatism than it really was.

Twenty years later, we faced a very similar situation in Spain during the process of debating and passing the LOMCE in 2013. This piece of legislation was intended to address chronic weaknesses in Spain's education system: very high rates of early school leaving, as well as high rates of grade repetition, very limited VET enrolment, poor student outcomes and little autonomy for schools. The law follows an evidence-based approach and does not pursue ideological aims. But due to bitter political circumstances and the budget cuts on education expenditure that took place during the financial crisis (2009–2013), the structural content of the law was completely overlooked in the public debate. Instead, public attention focused on the budget cuts (as if they were a part of the law, which they were not) as well as relatively minor aspects of the curricular content, especially those which could serve as harbingers of ideological confrontation: religious curriculum, single-sex education, citizenship education and the mandatory use of Spanish (the common official language) alongside vernacular regional languages throughout the country (Wert, 2019).[9]

These two particular cases illustrate how curricular issues that are not central to the curriculum itself, and which in some cases are not even part of the curriculum, can have a decisive impact on the fate of education reforms. As with other dimensions of the education process, when ideology seems to be rejected at the door, it makes its way through the window. The pervasive shadow of ideology is cast over material and procedural issues of the education system, and the curriculum is no exception.

---

9   This issue is perhaps hard to understand for non-Spanish readers and some clarification is in order. The devolution process in Spain has developed over the past forty years after the passing of a new constitution in 1978. In seven regions, vernacular languages are co-official with the common Spanish language. These vernacular languages were given importance as learning languages in those regions, but only in Catalonia had Spanish in practice been eliminated as a language for teaching and learning, while in all other regions using another vernacular official language, a strategy of dual language or language choice was in place. Even when some families in Catalonia asked for bilingual teaching and learning in Spanish and Catalan, the Catalonia education authority systematically applied the principle of "linguistic immersion", meaning all teaching (except teaching of Spanish language) takes place in the vernacular Catalan. In LOMCE we introduced some provisions to enforce the choice of having a mix of both Spanish and Catalan as teaching and learning languages, but the Constitutional Court dismissed it on the grounds—debatable in our opinion—that this was beyond the national government's power on education. A ruling of the *Tribunal Superior de Justicia de Cataluña*—the highest court at the regional level—in 2020 finally established that at least 25% of the teaching in primary and secondary education has to take place in Spanish. This ruling is systematically ignored by Catalan education authorities, who stubbornly stick to "linguistic immersion".

And finally, a word must be said about the more openly ideologically framed curriculum sustained by the school of critical pedagogy (Darder *et al.*, 2017), to which we referred earlier. The main assumptions of critical pedagogy on the curriculum and ideology in the school are summarised as follows:

> Anyone who has paid attention to the debates on curriculum and school reform knows that schooling is a decidedly political enterprise. The question in teaching (as well as teacher education and school reform) is not whether to allow political discourse in schools or whether to advocate or not, but the nature and extent of political discourse and advocacy. (Ross and Vinson, 2014)

For critical pedagogy, teaching and the curriculum are fundamentally about creating a critical conscience in students that will allow them to free themselves from the dominant frame and achieve conscience of their social situation as a first step in challenging and ultimately changing that situation. From the perspective of this educational philosophy (which is clearly not mainstream, but very active and influential in education colleges), education in general and the curriculum in particular have to be considered as the tools needed to:

> [E]ducate [students] to contest workplace inequalities, imagine democratically organized forms of work, and identify and challenge those injustices that contradict and undercut the most fundamental principles of freedom, equality and respect for all people who make up the global public sphere. Public education is about more than a job preparation or even critical consciousness raising; it is also about imagining different futures and politics as a form of intervention in public life. (Giroux and Giroux, 2006)

In summary, when it comes to the relationship between curriculum and ideology, we find a number of levels at which ideology has a strong influence on the inclusion in or exclusion from the curriculum of issues that are contentious in society and/or how should they be included. Sometimes, those issues—having to do with political orientations, moral values and societal trends—take centre-stage in the public debate on education and may, purposefully or by chance, distract attention from the core issues at stake.

Another aspect on which ideology exerts some influence on the curriculum paths followed by a country is the degree of centralisation or decentralisation in determining curriculum content, particularly in federal or quasi-federal systems, where significant educational decision-making has been devolved to regions. In some cases, the very idea of a national curriculum is at stake. Strategies of cooperation between regions to try and achieve consensus on curricular content seem to be a more fruitful approach than vertical imposition of decisions made by the national government on to regions. But trade-offs are particularly challenging, especially when there are loyalty issues between regional governments and the national government. Education, and specifically curriculum ownership, can provide a convenient arena for confrontation for those challenging the authority of a national government to define basic rules on education. Catalonia in Spain, a region with a powerful secessionist movement, provides a telling example of this with multiple dimensions, from the use of official and co-official languages (in this case Spanish and Catalan) in schools, to the curricular content of subjects such as history or geography.

Also, the curriculum is a battlefront in terms of a more general ideological approach to education, as held by the critical pedagogy movement, for which education is not only (or not mainly) a process focused on acquiring the competencies to thrive in life and in work, but also (or mainly) a process through which students learn to challenge the prevailing social order and engage in its transformation. For this school of thought, the curriculum is just another tool to change the world.

2.4.4 Assessments and Ideology.

At first glance, it may seem counterintuitive to think about assessments as an issue which plays a significant role in the ideological debate. However, assessments are not only a burning issue in the educational debate but also one in which—openly or covertly—ideology drives many of the ongoing debates.

Assessments have an important place in the history of education and have been the focus of much controversy. From centuries ago, what we could call a 'theory on assessment' has been developing alongside the historical development of education policies. As David McArthur put it, "educational assessment in the West has a long but very irregular history" (McArthur, 1987).

Assessments were first developed in Imperial China (around 581 CE), and were designed as a tool to detect talent in the vast Chinese Empire and to integrate the selected scholars by making them officials (mandarins) (Wooldridge, 2021). The aim of assessments was to find talent in remote areas irrespective of social background, thus breaking the tight-knit circles of powerful families and dynasties and enriching the civil service with talented people who otherwise would not have had a chance. In this way, China became the first meritocracy based on talent. Authority shifted from inheritance and wealth to performance in competitive examinations. Irrespective of their background, mandarins ruled the system. The examination system lasted for a very long period (over 1000 years) because it served vital social purposes and was improved over time by adjustments that made it more objective and the introduction of blind grading to avoid biases. In 1601 Matteo Ricci became the first European to enter the Forbidden City and described in detail a system where the elite owed its position to brain power, rather than inherited wealth and political favour, as was the case in the rest of the world. Eventually, the West started paying attention to the Chinese model and integrating some of its features, but the ancestors of what we today call assessments are not recorded in the West until the fifteenth century. Although assessments were originally designed as a tool to measure talent objectively in an attempt to break down the barriers of wealth, inheritance and political influence, they have been the target of endless debates which have recently become criticisms arguing that they achieve precisely the opposite, i.e. assessments are increasingly regarded as discriminatory tools (McArthur, 1987).

The more education became integrated in the state's operational perimeter, the more assessments were developed and formalised to serve a number of purposes. Originally, those purposes had more to do with adjusting the capacities of the system to a demand of education that in many occasions exceeded those capacities, and assessments ensured that objective and efficient criteria were used to identify candidates with talent. This approach clearly suffered from limitations since not every student had access to the same level of quality education.

Together with this primary objective, assessments developed a culture of evaluation at other levels including the quality of teaching, the performance of specific centres, issues about equity and others. An ever-growing complexity and formalisation of assessments takes shape as education becomes one of the pillars of public policy. Assessment becomes a science and a standard practice at every level of the education system. It also becomes a field of specialisation for researchers, experts and practitioners (psychometricians, subject matter experts and others).

The "past century was also the century of mental tests, when educational assessment came into widespread practice" (Pellegrino, 2004). A number of factors explain its blossoming (OECD, 2013). Some have to do with the evolution of education policies, others with constraints of systems capability, and a third group relates to the development of scientific and technical tools to reliably measure knowledge and skills acquired in the education process.

From the specific viewpoint that we wish to address here, i.e., the link between assessments and ideology, the issue of whether students and/or teachers should be assessed, when, how and with which consequences, has become more political over time. The ways in which politics plays out in this field are diverse, but political questions have become more influential over time. For instance, some years ago Tony Scott summarised the radical critique of assessments in these openly political terms:

> We need to ask new questions. Sophisticated, informed, critical examination of the politics of assessment can enable students to step outside of these binaries, critique the present use of testing, and imagine and pursue alternatives. Examining the political aspects of large-scale assessment highlights its historical contingency and its ideological function. (Scott, 2004)

What Scott and others argue—following an argument similar to the radical critique of curricula—is that assessments are basically tools to sustain and reinforce the reproductive function of education. And even if they acknowledge that arguments favouring assessments may deserve some consideration, they conclude that the political harm to education systems caused by external assessments clearly outweighs its presumed benefits.

Besides this critique, which is anchored in hard political beliefs, there is a much more pragmatic critical approach to assessments rooted in professional grievances of teachers, school principals and educational experts, which basically argues that assessments have the following negative consequences (which are exacerbated in external and standardised assessments):

i. Curtail the pedagogical creativity of teachers and autonomy of schools (Priestley *et al.*, 2015).

ii. Create a negative competition dynamic (Steiner-Khamsi, 2003).

iii. Hinder productive teaching and learning experiences by replacing them with "teaching to the test" instruction (Popham, 2001).

iv. Generate inequality since students from disadvantaged backgrounds tend to perform worse in assessments (Baker and O'Neil, 1994).

v. Serve the purposes of uniformisation and globalisation of education (Sahlberg, 2006).

Both the depth and the breadth of these critiques are very diverse. Some of them deserve to be taken seriously, while others lack ground and merely disguise corporatist demands. Generally speaking, most of the critiques seem to attribute to assessments a number of negative features that are not necessarily associated with the tool itself, but rather with the specific ways in which they are designed and implemented. From a more political viewpoint, these criticisms are generally supported by parties on the left and teachers' unions, as they advocate for a system in which competitive dimensions are reduced to a minimum and there is no direct or indirect evaluation of teachers.

The most widely accepted criticism of assessments is that they diminish the agency or the autonomy of teachers, principals and schools. However, this is something that can only happen when teachers enjoy a considerable degree of freedom to determine knowledge content and pedagogy in the first place, which depends to a large extent on the regulatory framework for curricula and standards. From this viewpoint, the broader the degree of autonomy at the curricular and standards level that a system allows, the more important the accountability mechanisms in place for evaluating how autonomy is being used. In this respect, the most efficient accountability tool is a robust system of external and standardised assessments. The evidence shows that a large degree of autonomy needs to be coupled with accountability, in order to ensure that the decisions taken do improve student performance.

This argument is often developed further to suggest that external standardised evaluations should be replaced with continuous evaluations by teachers, who know their students better. While the last part of the argument is obvious, it also misses the point entirely. Precisely because teachers only know the students who attend their classrooms, it may be difficult for them to assess them in relation to the rest of the student population. Thus, an effective teacher who is able to achieve large learning gains among his/her students will have little knowledge of the performance of students in other schools, which tends to show a large degree of variation. Furthermore, the evidence shows that most teachers assume that their students' grades should follow a bell-shaped curve, so that a few will have either high or low grades, and the rest will lie somewhere in between. Thus, a teacher whose students perform at high levels does not give them all high grades, in the same way that teachers whose students underperform do not give them all low grades. The only way for these hidden differences to emerge is through the assessment of all students according to the same standards. For this reason, external evaluations are the only objective and fair way to assess all students. This does not mean that continuous evaluation by teachers is not useful, and as a result many education systems calculate the final grades according to a formula which takes both kinds of assessment into account.

The other argument which is gaining ground is that external and standardised assessments are unfair because underprivileged children tend to perform worse. This argument is used to label such assessments as discriminatory and to reject them. In the context of the ideological debate, what really matters is whether it is true that assessments are designed in such a way that make them unfair. The typical example would be an assessment which requires knowledge or skills that have not been taught in schools in deprived areas. The fact that, in all countries, student socio-economic background has a significant impact on student performance suggests that the trend for students from poor backgrounds to underperform is real and not an artifact of the assessment design, but that the causes are complex and linked to differences between schools and social environments. Thus, rather than regarding assessments as a biased tool, they should be regarded as a useful tool which detects which students are in need of additional support and, at a higher level, when the education system fails to support disadvantaged students. Getting rid of assessments will not improve the system, it will just hide its deficiencies and turn a blind eye.

At the end of the day, a substantial proportion of these critiques are a reflection of a broader ideological framework that rejects external assessment because it interprets it as part of the process leading to so-called 'marketization' and 'choice' in education. In reality, it probably reflects fears of a clear way of making teachers accountable for their students' performance.

This is the basic ideological fabric of the movements—like, for instance, the 'anti-GERM movement' developed by Pasi Sahlberg and others—which oppose external standardised assessments, in particular those labelled as 'high-stakes assessments' (i.e., those with academic consequences). As this is an issue to which we will return in more detail when examining the evidence provided by ILSA and ILSA-like surveys, we will simply point out here that ideology plays a meaningful role even on the many occasions in which the argument against assessments appears at first sight to be based only on technical, pedagogical or instrumental reasons. As Sahlberg himself puts it:

> Education reforms focused on increasing external control of schools, teachers and students through inspections, evaluations and assessments that led to an increase of regulations in schools and decreased autonomy of teachers. At the same time, however, the neo-liberal movement increased the freedom of choice in education. (Sahlberg, 2006)

Let's take the 'teaching to the test' argument. At face value, the objection states that when significant instructional time is devoted to high-stakes test preparation, 'item teaching', i.e. teaching of those items that recurrently appear in the tests, it is at the expense of 'curriculum teaching', i.e. the teaching of high-order skills that has a more fundamental impact on the student learning experience. This is certainly a widely accepted criticism. But the evidence supporting the damages attributed to this teaching strategy is rather scarce, if not non-existent. Ultimately, as William J. Popham, one of the pioneers of the battle against 'teaching to the test' admits, often the frontier between these two kinds of teaching is blurred and sometimes some teaching to the test—if the tests are appropriately designed and clear to teachers—could be acceptable. Even so, the reservations he has towards 'item teaching' are so paramount that his conclusion is strikingly strong:

> I'm not sure whether item-teaching is, technically, a high crime or a misdemeanor. But because it can harm children, I lean toward the high crimes label—and such instructionally criminal conduct is increasing. (Popham, 2001)

On the opposite side of the spectrum, there is a narrative that illustrates the benefits of external standardised tests for providing the systems with a powerful tool for improvement. Eric Hanushek, the most articulate and influential advocate of testing, in a recent paper co-authored with Annika Bergbauer and Ludwig Woessmann, has summarised it eloquently:

> Our results indicate that assessment systems that use standardized tests to compare outcomes across schools and students lead to greater student outcomes [...] Most interestingly from an international perspective is the finding that assessment systems are more important for school systems that are performing poorly. [...] Overall, the results from international comparisons of performance suggest that school systems gain from measuring how their students and schools are doing and where they stand in a comparative way. (Bergbauer, Hanushek and Woessmann, 2019)

The authors condense into these sentences the key takeaways of a robust body of evidence accumulated across many years, particularly over the past two decades when the OECD, IEA and others have been collecting and analysing ILSAs or ILSA-like assessments. Obviously, as suggested by David Kamens and Connie McNeely, there is a strong link between the demand for national and international assessments and the reforms of national education systems to make them more effective, more accountable and better-aligned with the requirements of the globalisation process:

> [N]ational assessments are linked to efforts to reform educational systems and are often themselves stimuli for further cycles of reform [...] [T]he international acceptance of testing comes from key international forces in the world polity that are associated with the accelerated globalization of national and international, cultural, economic and political structures. (Kamens and McNeely, 2010)

In absence of a strong external evaluation culture, reforms which introduce national external standardised assessments risk becoming highly politicised in a negative way and dealt with in strictly political terms. This was something we experienced quite painfully when introducing these national external and standardised assessments in the LOMCE.

At least from a public opinion perspective, it may well be said that this was precisely the key element to create a hostile environment towards the reform on the whole, aligning against it not just the political opposition but also teachers' and students' unions. In this particular case, they were able to create a powerful straw man, assimilating the new assessments to old national exams that were in place during the Franco regime—and quite long before it—the so-called *reválidas*.[10] Such assessments were feared because they represented bottlenecks in access to university. The assessments we had designed were not even close to the *reválidas* in purpose or in content, but that association was extremely damaging. The conversation was fundamentally misled by that framing, a telling example of the processes that George Lakoff described some years ago (Lakoff, 2004). And once the concept of *reválidas* won the framing battle, the reform was seriously harmed (Wert, 2019).

In summary, the relationship between ideology and assessments is probably less clear-cut than that existing between ideology and teachers or the curriculum. The main reason for this is that assessments' divides appear at first glance to pertain to the domain of professional debate rather than political orientations. Sometimes this is true. But often there are also political and ideological underpinnings to the stances taken on assessments. In recent times, criticism based upon the idea that assessments and evaluations are "systemically" unfair, as disadvantaged students do perform worse no matter how much effort and energy they put into it (Sandel, 2020), is becoming dominant in liberal circles. The evidence provided by ILSAs on the advantages of assessments is

---

10 *Reválidas* (literally: validation exams) were national examinations at the end of the eighth and tenth grades, introduced as early as the mid-nineteenth century as a 'pass or fail' exam required to progress from the first to the second stage of secondary education and, from there, to university. They are wrongly linked to the Franco regime and, most of all, they are associated in the social imaginary with the purpose of restricting access to the upper levels of the education pyramid and therefore they bear an implicit mark of segregation and elitism.

conclusive. At the same time, this evidence is rejected or at least ignored. This paradox is central for an explanation of the paucity of consensus as well as of how vested interests and ideological prejudices play out in the educational field.

2.5 Funding of Education and Ideology

Funding is the most difficult conundrum in the educational debate. It is the crossroads where ideology, vested interests and evidence meet and, to put it very mildly, not necessarily on amicable terms (Wert, 2019).

Obviously, funding means different things in a developed economy and in developing economies. The issues around which the public conversation on educational funding revolves are quite diverse. The degree and focus of politicisation of the debate about funding is also different.

Every education system initially goes through an "era of institutional formation" followed, in the case of developed economies, by a subsequent "era of performance-based reforms" (Moe and Wiborg, 2017). When a system is at the institutional formation stage—as most developing countries are—the main purpose is access, i.e., the provision of basic literacy and numeracy skills for the whole youth population. To achieve that goal, public funding has to provide for the physical infrastructures of schools and the workforce of trained teachers, as well as some additional resources, like free meals or textbooks, so that students from disadvantaged backgrounds are supported and incentivised not to quit school prematurely. For countries still at this stage, there is no question that further increases in funding are required as the education system expands.

Such consensual arrangements about funding of education are in some cases elevated to the constitution. This is the case in Costa Rica. Article 78 of its constitution, introduced by an amendment in 2011, mandates that public expenditure for public education must reach at least 8% of GDP (Rodríguez Ramírez, 2015). Certainly—and the case of Costa Rica is a good example—these kinds of commitments *per se* do not get the job done, because they do not directly improve students' outcomes. But they at least provide the resources required to grant access to a growing number of students (Wert, 2019).

The situation is entirely different when it comes to mature education systems. When the main issue is no longer access, but improvement of performance, things change dramatically.

Public expenditure on education amounts to a substantial chunk of all public expenditure. In OECD countries, public spending on education represents on average 4% of GDP and 10% of total public expenditure. This equates to the second largest public expenditure in social services, lower only than public expenditure for healthcare (Busemeyer, Garritzmann and Neimanns, 2020; OECD, 2019). Intrinsically, this does not explain why funding has become so politicised: in most countries, with some exceptions, like the US, healthcare expenditure is less contentious than education expenditure, although it is significantly larger than the latter.[11] But a combination of elements contribute to making education funding a controversial issue. These include different conceptions of the role of the state, deeply entrenched vested interests and opposing views about the desirable outcomes of education.

Teachers' unions, political parties, families and other stakeholders of the education community could engage in sensible debates about these elements. But, often, they get trapped in never-ending discussions that have little to do with evidence and are much more closely related to corporate interests, ideological preconceptions, and a combination of both. The effort to disentangle these diverse elements is essential to understand the complexities of the political economy of education reforms.

Indeed, almost every aspect of funding is affected by unclear rules, disputed assumptions and undercover interests. To drive the discussion on objective evidence seems an almost impossible task. The basic premise is that higher levels of investment will lead to improvements in quality. However, the evidence does not support this claim. Higher levels of investment basically mean two things: smaller class sizes, which necessitates the hiring of more teachers, and higher teacher salaries. Obviously, these are the factors that teachers' unions care most about,

---

11 During the COVID-19 crisis, healthcare expenditure became a hot political issue, especially in those countries hit hardest by the pandemic like the US, the UK, Spain or Italy. But this was a 'one-off' debate rather than a permanent fixture in the political landscape, as the debate on education funding tends to be in many countries.

so they will argue that increases in investment benefit children, when in fact they are protecting their own interests. The strongly-held belief that more investment equals better quality makes finding evidence unnecessary in the public debate.

Ideological stance plays an important role: parties on the left and the right hold different views on *where* and *how* to spend in education and, to a lesser extent, on *how much* public money has to be spent. Only libertarians—and not all of them—think that too much tax money is spent on education, against an overwhelming majority on both sides of the political spectrum that supports increases in educational expenditure. But it is likely that this unanimity has more to do with the perception that high educational expenditure is very popular among all sectors of the electorate, than with a genuine belief in its worth. As one of the most incisive (and radical) exponents of the minority view, libertarian economist Bryan Caplan, put it:

> American opinion is typical. In the General Social Survey, 74% favor *more* education funding, 21% favor the status quo and only 5% favor cuts. Education enjoys bipartisan allegiance [...] What inspires this panideological affection? Proeducation industrial policy is so popular advocates have little need to share their reasons. (Caplan, 2018)

But if virtually everybody across the political spectrum agrees—or, at least, does not openly disagree—with the idea that education expenditure should increase, differences are huge when it comes to defining the targets of the expenditure, its relationship (or lack thereof) with performance and outcomes, or the accountability mechanisms in place to ensure that funds are properly and efficiently spent. Here, the views of each camp point in very different directions. Parties on the right support a careful allocation of resources to incentivise better outcomes, expediency in dealing with low performance (including closing down seriously underperforming schools), robust high stakes assessments to enable objective measurement of the successes and failures and, first and foremost, wide *devolution* of education resources to private providers to foster choice and quality.

On the other side of the political spectrum, the focus is instead on equitable allocation of resources. Normally this means more funding to support vulnerable students, to provide alternative strategies for those lagging behind, smaller class sizes and more funding for teacher training and development. Individuals on the left of the debate also fiercely oppose the allocation of public funding to entities other than public schools, like chartered schools and even more fiercely oppose 'vouchers' systems, through which not only chartered schools but private, for-profit education providers can access public funding.

Stanford political scientist Terry Moe has studied thoroughly how vested interests, especially those of teachers' unions, have been a powerful impediment to various attempts to reform American schools. Since his seminal work on this topic ten years ago (Moe, 2011), he has not only convincingly explained the American school stagnation, but has further articulated a general theory on how vested interests have enjoyed great power and influence in defining the fate of reforms at a global scale (Moe, 2019; Moe and Wiborg, 2017). In his most recent work on the issue, he has summarised his vision as follows:

> The teachers' unions promote the job interests of their members [...] [T]hey are the key to understanding how the unions behave in politics [...] These job interests are not the same as the interests of children or the requirements of effective education, and indeed often come into conflict with them. The conflict is not what the teachers' unions intend or want. But it is unavoidable because of the misalignment of interests. (Moe, 2019)

Although there are some elements of this theory that may vary depending on cultural, historical, and institutional factors at the national level, the bulk of it can be applied to virtually every developed education system.

As Moe clearly points out, this is neither an argument against teachers, nor even an argument against teachers' unions. They—particularly unions—do precisely what they are supposed to do and what they have been created for. They also exploit a situational advantage, namely "the positive image that teachers hold with parents and the larger public" (Moe, 2019). The point is that those vested interests would lead to policies squarely at odds with some of the more robust evidence gathered by research—ILSAs and other sources—on dimensions crucial to education funding.

Unions rarely express the real reasons behind their rejections of reforms. Instead, they disguise their vested interests and develop a narrative designed to make them look like they are trying to protect the interests of students. A clear example is provided by Susanne Wiborg in a quote from Danish teachers' union representatives explaining how they frame their rejection of pro-choice policies:

> We are not telling the school boards that the way of organising the free choice policies cost eight teacher positions. We rather talk about the pedagogical aspects and limitations of having too many children in classrooms that are too [physically] small. (Wiborg and Larsen, 2017)

When reforms are undertaken in the context of reductions in investment, this factor will be enough to kill the reform no matter how well-designed or well-intended. This is because powerful vested interests will reject such reforms fiercely, and the public will tend to agree with a narrative which automatically links budget cuts to serious harm to the education system. We experienced a situation of this sort in the process of negotiating education reforms in Spain in 2012 and 2013. Due to economic circumstances—a very stringent fiscal consolidation in the aftermath of the 2008 financial crisis, we were seeking "a very difficult reform, under impossible conditions" (Wert, 2019). Some fiscal consolidation measures reduced educational expenditure. Hiring of teachers to replace those taking retirement was reduced to a minimum (10% replacement rate). Instead, teachers on short temporary contracts were hired to replace those going into retirement. Certain other measures were also enacted by the education authorities (regional governments) by means of a blanket authorisation from the national government to allow them to reduce expenditure. These included longer teaching hours, no replacement of teachers on sick leave for less than ten days, and some others that had an impact on the working conditions of teachers.

This was a one-off piece of legislation unrelated, except for the timing, to wider education reforms. But the proximity in timing was a fatal blow to the reform: "budget cuts" in education became the overwhelming narrative, and as a result both reforms and cuts were confounded with one another in the public opinion.

On top of this, fiscal consolidation meant that monetary resources for the implementation of the reform were very scarce. In fact, the only additional resource we were able to bring to the table was a grant of the European Social Fund, earmarked for the development of VET, of one billion euros over a five-year period. This represented merely less than 0.5% of annual education public expenditure. The two previous system-level reforms of education—LOGSE in 1990 and LOE in 2006—received much more substantial economic backing. In 1990, the resources for implementation amounted to the equivalent of four billion euros (in 2013 figures), while in 2006, the package was even more generous, at six billion euros (Wert, 2019). It goes without saying that the bulk of those resources went to decreasing class sizes and increasing teacher salaries.

Under these constraints, we faced totally hostile opposition from teachers' unions. Teachers' unionism in Spain is ideologically multifaceted. Although some of the stronger unions have a distinctive leftist leaning, there are also other unions with a centre-right leaning. Every single one agreed to oppose the reform because there was nothing in it that would improve their salaries or working conditions, nor any measures that would increase union membership. Unions developed a public narrative that they rejected the reform because the aim was to privatise education and increase equity gaps. However, at private meetings they explained that they were prepared to change their stance if we included some sweeteners for them, such as an increase in the rate of teacher replacement and a reduction in teaching hours. We knew, as they did, that both demands would not possibly pass through the very exacting filter of the Finance Ministry. But, even if the debate ultimately proved to be rhetorical, it made it crystal clear to us where the problems lay.

2.6 Conclusions

In this chapter we have tried to disentangle the complex relations between education policy and ideology with a focus on how those ideological beliefs affect evidence-based education reforms. There is without any doubt a very deeply entrenched relationship between ideology, taken in a broad sense, and education policy.

Could it be otherwise? The answer, in our opinion, is clearly negative, insofar as education is one of the backbones of social life and it would be inconceivable that ideology could be kept apart from it. As we have examined, there are deep and legitimate ideological differences on many aspects of education including its very meaning and its philosophical, moral and political dimensions. But perhaps the major ideological divide is about its primary aim, and whether that is to promote equity or to advance quality.

However, at the same time, this does not necessarily mean that ideology should always or in most cases become a roadblock on the journey towards performance-oriented reforms. No democratic country can avoid some ideological debate about education policy and there are probably no good reasons why such a debate should not take place. However, some democracies have managed to reach a much-needed consensus to protect those aspects of education policy that are most relevant in achieving good student outcomes alongside ideological quarrels, while others have not. The ability to reach a consensus on core issues related to student performance to a large extent determines the feasibility, durability and sustainability of education reforms.

We talk about 'democracies' rather than 'countries': in non-democratic countries there is no need to overcome ideological disputes on education because there is only one ideology that counts. And, particularly when we talk about education, let us not forget that, contrary to Juan Linz and Alfred Stepan's famous assertion twenty-five years ago that democracy was "the only game in town" (Linz and Stepan, 1996) or Francis Fukuyama's notion of "the end of History" (Fukuyama, 1992), democracy is now no longer the only universally accepted system of government (Mounk, 2018). Actually, when we look at some of the education systems recognised as best in class by the most influential sources (like the OECD or IEA) we find remarkable success stories in East Asian countries, which are either full democracies who agree to manage education systems in a practical and non-ideological way, semi-democracies—in the sense of having limited political competitiveness—or authoritarian regimes (like the People's Republic of China).[12]

But when it comes to democracies and, more specifically, liberal democracies—the political system which prevails in a great majority of developed countries—there is a burning need to find a way to prevent ideological battles from hindering education reforms.

In this chapter we have referred to some examples of broad agreements across the political spectrum regarding certain central education policies. The 'No Child Left Behind' Act on elementary and

---

12 To be precise, we should refer to those areas of the People's Republic of China that the Chinese authorities select as they please to be included in international comparisons. These are urban and economically privileged cities and regions, most likely far above average in student outcomes than regions elsewhere in the country.

secondary education in the US was passed in 2001 by an overwhelming majority (90% in both the Senate and the House of Representatives) after being sponsored by Democrats and Republicans alike.

A most divisive educational issue, namely the role of the state in education provision and the role of families in choosing the school they want their children to attend, has been dealt with in the UK over the past twenty years through some sort of 'silent agreement'. The policy of replacing low-performing 'modern comprehensives', managed by local authorities, with 'academies', managed by private or social sponsors, was first designed and implemented under a Labour government. It was then further developed by the Conservative-Liberal Democrat coalition government and was then given priority by a Tory government (Adonis, 2012; Gibb, 2017).

In the Republic of Ireland some form of consensualism on education has been taking place since the second half of the twentieth century (Lynch, 1987). As former Minister for Education and Skills, Ruairy Quinn, a seasoned Labour politician, explained to us when we met during the LOMCE debate in Spain, the solution consisted in developing the ability to agree on keeping the basics and to disagree on the accidental, understanding that non-essential elements of the system are open to change according to the political and social atmosphere of the moment, and of course according to which party has won the election (Quinn, 2012).

However, all in all, these examples represent the exception as opposed to the rule. In many countries—and Spain is a very telling case—it seems impossible to build a consensus on the basics of the education system, so that political changes do not disrupt it and energies can be directed towards improving the outcomes of the system, instead of revisiting circular and mostly unproductive debates on polarising issues which need to be set aside to allow performance-oriented reforms.

Which elements should ideally be hedged from ideological disputes to avoid hindering such performance-oriented reforms? We believe that policies on the architecture of the education system, basic curriculum, teacher training, development and careers, assessment and funding allocation would all benefit most from a broad, transversal agreement between the different political actors.

At the same time, it is important to reject the idea—broadly accepted as 'conventional wisdom' in many countries—that education laws should be immutable in order to avoid dangerous disruptions to the teaching and learning experiences of students and the instructional practice of teachers. Of course, education laws and education policies have to change as often as necessary. They must for instance adapt to changes in the environment that open new avenues to education and provide new opportunities to students and teachers. But it is important to protect cardinal elements of education policy from mere ideological battles through a broad agreement which, at the very least, should identify the areas open to change as a result of party politics, and those shielded from such change. Ideology will probably never disappear from the education policy landscape. But, if attention is focused on those cardinal elements and the more polarising issues are kept at bay (Roldán and Cabrales, 2020), we could avoid reforms being made and unmade from one electoral swing to the next. Agreements of this kind—including agreements on disagreements—would represent significant progress and remove roadblocks on the highway of evidence-based education reforms.

3. The Governance of Education Systems

How They Constrain or Facilitate the Implementation of Reforms

3.1 Why Governance Matters

In Chapter 1 we sketched a very brief historical summary of how states became systematically involved in building education systems in modern times. From the onset of that process countries have had to take key decisions regarding the governance models of their education systems. Those decisions have been affected by constitutional arrangements, history and culture. Their main dimensions are linked to authority (who decides what at the different levels of government, particularly in federal or quasi-federal states), stakeholder involvement (the role that different stakeholders play at different stages of policy design and implementation) and funding (who pays for what in the different stages of the education process). The models designed during these early stages to a large extent constrained how and to what extent education systems could evolve.

In this chapter we will examine how governance arrangements can facilitate or hinder reforms. By 'governance arrangements', we mean the distribution of power and responsibilities between different levels of government, the financial incentives, the generation and control of resources, the interests of stakeholders outside government, and the existence of vetoes used to block reforms either by different levels of government or by stakeholders.

3.2 The Power of Governments

As explained in Chapter 1, the role of governments in relation to education has changed over time. Until the nineteenth century, most governments played little, if any, role in education. However, at different points in time, governments became involved in building mass schooling systems. We have already described the beginning of this process for Germany (or then Prussia) and France over 200 years ago. The German system ultimately became very decentralised while the French system was and still is very centralised. The process began even later for other countries in Europe, while in the United States mass schooling developed gradually from the mid-1800s at a state level, but a decentralised nationwide system did not emerge until the 1900s. The US became a pioneer in universal access to education, while European countries took longer to expand access to education, both from the elites to all, and from primary schools to secondary schools. The fact that the US achieved universal access to education earlier has been considered the main reason for its economic leadership during a long period of sustained growth and prosperity (Goldin and Katz, 2009).

As we have already described in more detail, during the early phase of educational expansion, as the number of students enrolled increased so too did the resources allocated to public education, whose share of public budgets grew. Schools were built, classrooms were equipped and more and more teachers were hired. As the education system expanded, an institutional structure was created to manage its increasing complexity. In this way, education became a crucial function of government and a complex network of actors benefited from the growing resources.

The most relevant of these actors are teachers, since the sheer size of the teaching force made governments in many countries the largest employers. In most countries this development coincided with the emergence of the welfare state, and education became a right rather than a privilege. The so-called "access reforms" (Grindle, 2004) in the "era of institutional formation" (Moe and Wiborg, 2017b) were reforms in which virtually every stakeholder had a clear win and obviously this contributed to smooth introduction, painless implementation and sustainability over time.

Then, once universal access to education was achieved, education systems moved into a second phase, which Merilee Grindle terms "quality-enhancing reforms" (Grindle, 2004), while Terry Moe and Susan Wiborg labeled it "the era of performance-based reform" (Moe and Wiborg, 2017b). Starting in the late 1970s and 1980s, when globalisation and technological change became powerful forces in labour markets, governments started to struggle to deliver on the increasing demands of welfare states. Ageing societies required increases in spending on health and pensions, and investment in education continued to grow even in countries in which demographic trends led to smaller cohorts of children.

Thus, governments were forced to seek efficiency and flexibility from their systems. Most countries responded by implementing reforms which decentralised their education and health systems, on the understanding that localised management would lead to greater efficiency, since the decision-making process could be more readily adapted to individual circumstances. In the case of education, decentralisation was often accompanied by accountability and choice. Efficiency requires the implementation of strategies to maximise returns (defined as improved student outcomes) for each unit of investment. This meant a shift from the traditional focus on inputs (amount of resources invested) to outputs (student performance) and then to outcomes (human capital growth). Thus, accountability was often (but not always) linked with the development of new mechanisms to evaluate student performance. In this way, governments were no longer held responsible just for the delivery of the education service, but for the quality of education they delivered. Whether improvements in student performance did indeed happen or not will be the focus of later chapters.

During the expansion phase, the interests of government and stakeholders were largely aligned, because everyone benefited from a growing system, larger budgets and the hiring of more teachers. However, once universal access was achieved and governments began to seek efficiency, major conflicts of interest emerged. First, decentralisation led to tensions between central government and regions or local authorities regarding the level of decision-making power and the amount of resources that would be transferred. Second, accountability and choice were strongly resisted by teachers' unions, which perceived them as threats to the teaching force and to their power.

In this difficult environment, reforms can only happen when the following set of conditions is met: governments have real power, there is commitment across parties over time (and across levels of government) to a path of reform, and stakeholders with vested interests have no veto points. The power of governments largely depends on the shape of party systems and the parliamentary arithmetic. Here, two distinct features are at play. In bi-partisan or quasi bi-partisan systems the party in government generally enjoys a majority in parliament and is thus more likely to attempt education reforms. However, in multi-party systems, governments are normally supported by a coalition of different parties and there may be important differences in cohesiveness, and substantial ideological or tactical distances between the coalition parties. In these cases, disagreements over the content of reforms can hinder or prevent reforms altogether (Adonis, 2013).

However, achieving approval by parliament is just the first step. Many reforms actually fail during the implementation phase, either because education administrations at the regional or local level refuse to collaborate, or because a different political party wins the next general election and brings the reform process to a halt. Thus, continuity over time can only be ensured when a given political party remains in power for long enough, or when major political parties agree on the basic and most relevant issues, putting their most divisive ideological differences aside. Some East Asian countries, such as Singapore, are good examples of the first pattern. In fact, they show that profound, long-term reform is more likely when governments do not have to deal with the complexities of different parties holding power at different times and are relatively free from union constraints. While this may be an important part of the recipe for the astonishing success of education reforms in these countries, whether the lack of full democratic competition is a fair price to pay is another matter.

Agreement between all major political parties has been the case in the UK, where Conservative, Labour and Conservative-Liberal Democrat coalition governments have built upon the reforms of preceding governments over time. New Labour (1997–2010) established the rules for the development of a new model of schools labelled "academies", which allowed failing public schools to be removed from local authority control and placed under the watch of central government, governed by a board appointed by a sponsor and accountable to the Department for Education (Adonis, 2012). The academy model was supported and expanded by the subsequent Conservative-Lib Dem coalition government (2010–2015) and has become such a success that in recent years more than 70% of all secondary schools have become self-governed, as well as funded by and accountable to central government (Wiborg, 2017).

Academies are run by non-state providers and have more autonomy on a range of issues such as curriculum, conditions for staff, hiring and dismissals of teachers. In addition, 'free schools' are new schools that follow a similar model and have been opened at the request of parents. Thus, agreement on the need to grant more autonomy to schools and to shift from local to central oversight has revolutionised the education system in the UK. This is also a good example of how reforms tend to face less resistance when they start as a small-scale pilot experiment, which is then allowed to expand based on its success, rather than as a wholesale change abruptly imposed on the whole system (Adonis, 2012).

Coalition governments, which are quite common across Europe,[1] face a different kind of challenge. Coalition governments can only agree on an agenda of reforms either by focusing exclusively on those already agreed beforehand, by setting aside major ideological divides, or if the weakest party relents. As we have seen, education tends to elicit strong ideological views, so compromises may be more difficult to achieve than in other sectors. The other alternative, a U-turn by the weaker party, has serious ramifications, as the example of the Liberal Democrats going against their pledge when the coalition government approved an increase to university tuition fees demonstrates (Willets, 2017).

Since the financial crash of 2008, in many countries a strong polarisation of political views has set in, fed by mounting insecurities and fears about the future. In Europe, this process has given rise to "insurgent parties" (Dennison and Pardjis, 2016) on both the extreme left and right, which have gradually attracted more voters. These are

---

1 As of 2023, there are coalition governments in twenty of the twenty-seven member states of the European Union.

often populists from outside of mainstream politics, who claim that they can free the government from corruption and outdated rules, and who offer simplistic solutions to complex problems. This process has been referred to as "the rise of outsiders" (Richards, 2017). The emergence of such outsiders into the political arena has been facilitated by the deep insecurities that globalisation and digitalisation have generated. These include the fear of being displaced from jobs, either by outsourcing (globalisation), immigration (demographic trends), or automation and robots (technological change).

These are indeed complex problems that make governments look weaker, because they cannot easily be solved, particularly at the national level. Outsiders at the extreme fringes, who are politically inexperienced and naïve, are bold enough to claim to have simple solutions and to act on behalf of those "left behind". The power of this narrative should not be underestimated, since it has allowed many such fringe parties to gain enough power to join government. Since their messages are strongly ideological (whether on the right or the left) the discourse on education focuses on the most divisive issues. This makes reforms even more difficult.

Reforms are more likely to survive in the long term if governments engage stakeholders. Some countries have a tradition of consensus building, which has led to institutional arrangements that facilitate stakeholder participation. Agreement between different political parties and stakeholders has been the norm among Nordic countries, which are classic examples of "corporativism". It can be defined as an "institutional arrangement so that important political-economic decisions are reached via negotiations between or in consultation with peak-level representation of employees and employers or other interest groups and the state" (Kenworthy, 2003). In some central European countries, like the Netherlands or Belgium, so-called "consociationalism" pushes different and even antagonistic parties to work together in government and implement agreed-upon policies (Lijphart, 1977). This culture of consensus building may slow down the reform process but makes sustainability in the long term more likely.

Some countries have tried to implement similar institutional arrangements, organising bodies or committees in which stakeholders may participate. These can have merely consultative functions or be a part of the policymaking process, normally through their influence on legislative or executive bodies that can be veto points for reforms (Moe, 2017b). The most powerful stakeholders in education are by far teachers' unions, but others include parents' associations, employers' associations, non-state providers, research institutes and non-profit organisations.

The involvement of stakeholders in the reform process is a complex endeavour. On the one hand, there are clear benefits derived from involving stakeholders in the reform process (OECD, 2019b and 2020). First, stakeholders may contribute valuable information about the multiple effects of certain policies and regulations, which policymakers may lack. Second, a reform agreed with stakeholders has political legitimacy, which may strongly influence public opinion, maximise the support of those participating in the implementation phase and increase the chances of continuity in the long term.

The downside of engaging many actors in the reform process is that some may use the opportunity to resort to particularistic bargaining, rather than joint problem solving (Busemeyer, 2015; OECD, 2020). If one actor is seen as participating for the sake of obtaining benefits, others will follow suit. In the best-case scenario, the decisions taken will not surpass the threshold of "least common denominator policies", diluting the initial reform to the extent that it becomes ineffective. In the worst cases, government may find itself in gridlock due to major underlying conflicts of interest which are disguised in the public discourse as good intentions.

Since most education reforms have significant distributional implications, this is more often than not the case. In countries where there is no tradition of consensus building, the mere establishment of similar structures to those in Nordic countries and constant appeals for consensus-based reforms alone will not do the trick. Thus, idyllic as it may sound, broad consensus between actors with vested interests and reformers is not always possible (Allègre, 2000). We might even say that any prior commitment by government to make a reform contingent on achieving consensus between many actors may backfire, because it entitles actors who may wish to extract more resources not only to oppose the reform but also to threaten to block reforms unless their demands are satisfied.

Thus, governments face many obstacles when trying to approve and implement education reforms, which often have nothing to do with the intended outcomes of the reform in terms of improved student performance. Weak governments are unlikely to try, strong governments need to ensure that political parties mutually agree on a long-term reform path by setting aside ideological issues which are important to their voters, and vested interests from powerful stakeholders may block any attempt. As a result, many reforms are not successfully implemented, and changes of government from one political cycle to the next lead to new reforms which *de facto* cancel previous ones.

3.3 The Dilemmas of Multi-Level States: When Power Is Shared between Different Levels of Government

Education and training systems remain basically a national responsibility. The belief that education should remain a national policy is so ingrained, that even when countries organise themselves under the umbrella of supranational entities, such as the European Union, these have no direct responsibilities over education systems and can only support their member states by defining overall targets and offering incentives and support (funding, tools and advice). Many have argued that a powerful process of globalisation of education is taking place nowadays. Some adopt a neutral stance towards it (Ball, 2013) while others are openly critical, associating it with a "marketization" and "privatization" of education (Sahlberg, 2006). However, this trend does not substantially change the fact that education continues to be placed under the authority of national governments.

Strong government involvement makes education a very powerful tool for governments to socialise citizens to the beliefs and values that each nation wishes to preserve, to create a sense of national identity by influencing the narrative about each nation´s history, to modulate the degree of ambition in terms of boosting human capital and economic growth, and to strike the right balance between equity and excellence. Thus, curricular contents, teacher training and professional development programmes, the degree of ambition in terms of student outcomes required to obtain degrees and how to measure them, are to some extent defined by each national government. For this reason, education has been regarded for a long time as a policy sector that shows greater heterogeneity between countries.

While any attempts to allow core elements of education policy to be defined and managed above the country level have been universally rejected, there has been a widespread trend to delegate many decision-making powers to sub-national governments. In a few countries, such as France or Japan, education is centralised and central government remains by far the main decision-making power. But over the last decades, education systems in most countries have become decentralised to different extents and in different ways.

There are basically two concurrent rationales for this decentralisation. One has to do with the constitutional framework of the state, and particularly with the diverse varieties of multi-level, multi-confederate, federal or quasi-federal states (Ornelas, 2003; Wung *et al.*, 2017). Among those multi-level states, it may be worth distinguishing between those with a formally federal constitution (e.g. Australia, Belgium, Canada, Germany and the United States) and those without (e.g. the Netherlands, Spain, Scandinavian countries and the UK). Among formally federal countries, most decision-making powers have been conferred or delegated to sub-national governments (such as German *Länder* or Canadian provinces) which are primarily responsible for their education systems. In contrast, other countries remain formally unitary, but have *de facto* become decentralised, and these tend to delegate mostly the management of schools and some decision-making powers, to sub-national entities (regions, states and/or local authorities) (Busemeyer, 2015; OECD, 2019b; OECD, 2020). In most of these cases, national governments retain core competences, such as the responsibility of designing the architecture of the educational system and defining the standards required for students to obtain educational degrees. Depending on the model of decentralisation, regions or local authorities may be responsible for fundraising, may receive transfers from national governments, or both.

The other factor underpinning this trend of decentralisation is the understanding that many decisions should be taken at the regional or local level according to the specific needs of that geographical area, thus making the system more efficient and adaptable. In principle this makes sense since, in many countries, regions differ greatly in terms of their labour markets, business fabrics, the medium- and long-term objectives for their economies, and even their cultural backgrounds.

However, as we shall see, decentralisation has led to such a huge divergence in the skill levels of different regions that these have in many cases become larger than the differences between countries. The growing disparities between the skill levels of regional populations have become a major concern, since these are the main source of inequality within countries, leading to huge differences in unemployment rates, job quality, and citizen wellbeing (Cheshire *et al.*, 2014).

In a way, the opposite extremes (i.e. totally centralised vs formally confederate and federal countries), operate within clear frameworks in which either central or sub-national governments hold most of the power in terms of decision-making, as well as responsibilities for raising and investing funds allocated to education. But they face challenges of a very different nature. While centralised systems in large and diverse countries must implement models and rules to deal with such heterogeneity, formally federal countries must put in place more complex governance arrangements, since they involve more actors who may have divergent interests. Thus, the implementation of reforms (at least at the systemic level) requires vertical coordination between different levels of government, as well as horizontal coordination among sub-national governing bodies.

There is no clear-cut evidence suggesting that centralised or decentralised educational systems are of better or worse quality; in fact, there are multiple examples of good and bad performing systems in both models. Singapore is an outstanding example of a centralised system which was in a very difficult starting point just fifty years ago, as a low-skilled economy, but has improved rapidly over time to the extent that, in recent decades, it has become a top performer according to international surveys.

This success is the result of a complex set of factors, but teacher quality is widely recognised as a key element. The fact that the Singaporean education system is centralised has allowed it to develop very demanding and homogeneous standards for teachers both in pre-service and in-service training, as well as uniform performance evaluations. The strong emphasis on teacher professional development goes much further than in most other countries: during their careers, teachers spend a considerable proportion of their time training at the teachers' academy, ensuring very high standards all round. This is an example of a good policy which can only be implemented homogeneously in a centralised system, thus ensuring teaching excellence in all schools. However, it is also true that this model, which ensures quality of teaching across the whole system, has also proven successful in a small city-state where opposition from political actors and teachers' unions is very limited. To what extent it is scalable remains an open question.

Among centralised systems it may be easier, from a governance point of view, to elaborate, approve and implement uniform policies across the whole territory, because central government does not need to negotiate the reform with sub-national levels of government, nor does it depend on them for its implementation. However, when central government is the sole actor trying to make reform happen, it becomes an easier target for stakeholders outside government who may develop fierce resistance and will focus their efforts on a very visible target ensuring a highly politicised confrontation. This is the case in France, a country which has not excelled in international surveys and where education reforms tend to trigger massive protests due to strong opposition from powerful unions (Allègre, 2000; Dobbins, 2017).

Formally federal countries also define clear frameworks in which regional or local governments have the most decision-making power and are generally responsible for raising most of the funds invested in education. In this case the level of complexity in terms of governance is higher, as it requires both horizontal and vertical alignment. Common standards need to be negotiated between sub-national entities, and some decisions must be agreed with central government. The required alignment between different actors suggests that systemic reforms are bound to fail when agreements cannot be reached. While this governance model has allowed Canada[2] to develop a good education system, according to international surveys, a similar model has led to average results in the United States.

---

2   Canada is probably the most extreme case of decentralisation among the developed countries, to the extent that there is not a specific Ministry for Education, and coordination takes place without vertical intervention through the *Council of Ministers of Education Canada* (CMEC) of the different provinces and territories.

One example that can help us to understand the complexities involved in the governance of education in federal countries is Germany's process for deciding the curricula for dual vocational education and training. The *Länder* (states) are primarily responsible for education policy. Thus, the school-based component is regulated by the individual states, while the workplace component is regulated by the federal government. The sharing of responsibilities on different aspects of one specific policy area (Dual VET) requires coordination between the *Länder*, as well as complex negotiations with federal government, to ensure that the school-based and work-based components complement each other. Since on-the-job training is an important component of dual vocational education, social partners (employers and unions) also play a significant role in this decision-making process (Busemeyer, 2015; OECD, 2020).

Countries whose education systems are not decentralised to the same extent apply models that fall somewhere in between the two extremes. This makes governance arrangements more complex, and often less clear. In these cases, central government and provinces/regions/states share more responsibilities or have complementary responsibilities, making the decision-making process more complex and making conflicts of interest more probable. In most of these decentralised models, central government retains major responsibilities in defining the architecture of the education system, the basic rules of its functioning, the standards required to obtain degrees, and standards for teachers. Sub-national entities may share some of these responsibilities, but they are mainly in charge of the management and delivery of the education systems in their territory.

To be efficient, these models require a very clear division of responsibilities for each level of government, as well as the institution of effective accountability mechanisms. If the boundaries are blurred, it seems inevitable that tensions will arise in relation to how much power each level of government holds and who is to blame when things go wrong. These conflicts will become exacerbated when a single political party holds power in central government, but the individual regions are mostly governed by other political parties. If this is the case, education reforms are often doomed when central government is responsible for elaborating basic education laws, which are approved by national parliaments, but sub-national governments are in charge of their implementation.

To give an idea of the diversity of arrangements within this decentralised model, we will focus on the curriculum, a core element of every education system. In the Netherlands, there is no national curriculum but central government defines the standards required to obtain degrees through national exams at the end of each stage. Thus, schools have a big say in defining many aspects of the curricula. In the words of one Dutch Minister of Education when explaining to us the logic behind this arrangement, "we set the goals and schools can decide how they manage to get their students to those standards; in other words, it is up to schools to decide the how". In other countries, central government is responsible for the national curriculum, but over time the degree of involvement has diminished with national curricula becoming less detailed and more schematic. For example, in Finland central government does define a national curriculum, which contains the main objectives and core contents (Lähdemakï, 2019). Within this overall framework, local curricula are designed by municipalities and schools decide on the details. Similar governance arrangements are in place in most Scandinavian countries.

Finally, in countries such as Spain, central government and the regions share the responsibility of defining the curriculum, and the balance is defined in terms of percentages (around half each). On this basis, two models have been implemented. After education was decentralised, central government and regions were assigned the same percentage of the curriculum for each and every subject. This gave rise to two problems. First, regions tended to make their share of the curriculum very local in flavour, particularly in subjects such as geography and history. Thus, while the share of the curriculum defined by central government was very broad, the other half was narrow. Depending on the subject and the grade, this may or may not result in a reasonable balance. Second, it became clear that a definition of responsibilities in terms of percentages was difficult to assess, raising questions as to whether these percentages actually referred to the number of teaching hours, the number of pages in textbooks, or other, equally meaningless metrics. More worryingly, some regions with strong nationalistic movements introduced biases into their narratives of Spanish history or even geography that were factually wrong (such as the existence of a Catalan State in the Middle Ages) but proved very effective in educating many generations in the belief that these historical events and geographical disparities justified the quest for a return to an independent state that had never truly existed (Wert, 2019).

To overcome these issues, the education reform approved in 2013 (LOMCE) adopted a substantially different approach which divided subjects into three blocks. Core subjects (which included Spanish history) were compulsory and became the full responsibility of the national government; for a second group of subjects, there was a certain degree of choice with the national government defining the evaluation standards, but regions reserving the right to expand on certain content; finally, regions were given full responsibility for a third set of subjects, which were optional. These three blocks of subjects were designed in such a way that every level of government had a fair share in the project of defining the curriculum. However, most regions (and particularly those with strong nationalistic movements) raised concerns over this new model, which they regarded as an attempt by central government to "re-centralise" education. When there are tensions between the roles of central government and regions, the fear of re-centralisation, whether this is a genuine prospect or not, is a recurrent issue. In most cases, regions use this (mis)perception to justify demands for more power and resources. In other words, the fear of re-centralisation is often used as a red herring to achieve greater decentralisation in practice.

3.4 The Process of Decentralisation: A Bumpy Road

In some countries, education systems were created from the very beginning as centralised or federal systems, but in others the education systems began as centralised systems that then underwent a process of decentralisation later on. The transfer of responsibilities to sub-national levels is a complex process in which many things can go wrong. When this happens, there is a real risk that the quality of the education system will suffer. To begin with, the decision as to which responsibilities are delegated or transferred and which are not should not be the result of political conflicts of interest about which level of government will end up having more decision-making power and greater control over funds. Instead, the first step should be to elaborate a detailed map of how the different responsibilities should be distributed, designed with the aim of improving the quality and equity of the system. Sub-national entities should not fully assume new responsibilities unless there is first a process of capacity building, which allows them to develop the expertise required to fulfil their new roles effectively. Once sub-national governments start to perform their new responsibilities, accountability mechanisms should be implemented to ensure that the right decisions are made and students are benefiting from the new governance arrangements.

There are many countries in which the process of decentralisation itself has been too rushed, messy or has led to a blurred division of responsibilities and has therefore damaged the efficiency and the quality of the education system. Depending on whether the problems were eventually corrected, the damage may or may not have been reversed later on. Sweden is a good example of a country that transitioned from a centralised system to a decentralised system without paying enough attention to capacity building and accountability before transferring the responsibilities. This resulted in a dysfunctional system and a sharp decline in student performance, according to PISA (Blanchenay *et al.*, 2014; OECD, 2015a).

Until 1990, Sweden was known to have one of the most centralised education systems in Europe, which was seen as a major component of the country's welfare state. During the 1990s, a series of reforms led to the transfer of responsibilities for the provision of primary, secondary and adult education to municipalities. The aim of these decentralisation reforms was to improve efficiency on the assumption that all resources would be allocated where they were most needed (NAE, 2009). As a result, municipalities became responsible for the allocation of funds to schools, as well as for many other decisions regarding schooling, curriculum choice, the hiring of principals, teacher wages, and working conditions. At the same time, the role of central government was greatly reduced, although it retained the responsibility for setting national educational goals and evaluating the results of the education system. In relation to funding, central government transferred the responsibility for allocating resources to schools, but retained the responsibility for raising them through taxes. Transfers of funds from central government came in the form of grants to municipalities earmarked for education, but were then integrated into a larger lump sum which enabled municipalities to decide how much to invest in education as opposed to other responsibilities such as public health and social services.

It soon became clear that the speed of these reforms did not give municipalities enough time to prepare and adjust to their new responsibilities. The sudden shift of responsibilities from central government to municipalities took place without the necessary support for capacity building, which led to student underperformance because municipalities were unprepared in terms of organisation, leadership and know-how. In addition, few accountability mechanisms had been put in place to assess the outcomes of such a massive shift. Increased awareness of the problems that many municipalities were facing, as well as their negative impacts on student outcomes and completion rates, led central government to implement greater accountability through the National Agency for Education, mainly by reintroducing school inspections. The inspecting bodies were subsequently granted powers to use sanctions if schools failed to achieve the national learning goals.

These shortcomings, together with the complexity of the new system (with almost 300 municipalities and many more private providers sharing responsibility for education), led to a major decline in student performance, according to PISA, until 2012 when it reached the lowest levels. The results of PISA 2012 were presented by Sweden's National Agency for Education, whose Director General Anna Ekström said: "We are astonished by the depth and breadth of the downturn. There is a sharp deterioration and it is serious" (Radio Sweden, 3 Dec 2013). But the reasons for this decline became very contentious in the political arena. The Education Minister at the time, Jan Björklund (Liberal Party), blamed the Social Democrats by stating that "[in 2012] pupils had gone through all nine years of compulsory schooling with the old curricula and old scores [...] PISA 2012 is thus not an evaluation of the new school policy, but the nail in the coffin for the old". He also referred to the reforms of the 1990s, when school policy was transferred from the state level to the local municipal level, as "a failure" (Radio Sweden, 3 December 2013). On the other hand, the Social Democrat leader Stefan Löfven said the results were a "national crisis". As a consequence, education became the top priority issue in the next general election of 2014. A government inquiry into the matter concluded that the decentralisation reforms had meant that, in the words of political scientist Leif Lewin, "the government had largely abdicated from its responsibility in relation to the country´s school system" (SOU, 2014).

Over the next years a series of reforms gave central government more powers in relation to school funding, emphasised the impact of national exams on student grades, and gave the school inspection body the powers to close down schools that were underperforming. Since 2012 student performance has improved in Sweden, returning to the levels achieved in the first PISA cycle (2000). While the impact of a poorly implemented decentralisation process on student performance is not disputed, it is true that its effects are difficult to disentangle from those of other reforms that were implemented at the same time, such as the creation of independent schools and the encouragement of school choice by families. However, another government inquiry concluded that there is no evidence that school choice reforms are to blame for the decline in student performance. Furthermore, while school choice did lead to an increased segregation of pupils according to their socio-economic backgrounds, it did not magnify the impact of family background on student performance (IFAU, 2014). Because the Swedish case has been so thoroughly examined, and there have been clear trends in declining performance first, followed by improvements thereafter, we view it as one of the most revealing case studies of what can go wrong in a decentralisation process, and how to resolve it.

3.5 Funding. Who Raises the Money and Who Spends it?

Governance arrangements not only define the areas of responsibility in terms of decision-making by different levels of government, they also set the rules about who raises the funding through taxes, who has the capacity to set tax rates, and who spends the funds and how. As we have seen in the previous section, centralised and formally federalist countries tend to have a clear division of responsibilities in terms of decision-making, which is normally well-aligned with funding responsibilities, because either central government or individual regions perform both.

In federal systems such as Germany and Switzerland, the *Länder* raise most of the taxes and decide how to allocate the funds to education.

However, this is not always the case. Although Austria is also a formally federal country, the federal level retains greater legislative competences for education policy than Germany or Canada. It also follows a so-called 'distributional federalism' model. This means that most of the tax revenue is generated at the federal level and, through the Fiscal Adjustment Act, these funds are then partially transferred to provinces and municipalities based on quotas, which are negotiated between different levels of government (Nusche *et al.*, 2016). This system creates some tension between the responsibility to raise funds and the capacity to spend (Bruneforth *et al.*, 2015). If accountability mechanisms and monitoring systems are not properly developed, it may lead to overspending or misallocation of funds by lower levels of government, as has been pointed out by the Austrian Court of Audit (*Rechnungshof* reports, 2011 and 2012).

This kind of misalignment between the level of government in charge of raising taxes and the level of government deciding how the funds will be spent is common among decentralised systems. Giving authorities at the regional, provincial, or local levels the power to distribute resources among schools may lead to a more efficient use of resources given their knowledge of local needs. However, lack of transparency on how the resources are used and what the outcomes are may lead to mistrust from central government, which holds responsibility for raising the funding. Existing research on fiscal federalism shows that giving lower levels of government the power to spend without any corresponding responsibility for raising those funds sets strong incentives for overspending (Busemeyer, 2008). Within the Austrian education system, vocational schools are a clear example that provincial government spending becomes more efficient when the responsibility for raising the funds is shared by the provincial and federal governments (Nusche *et al.*, 2015).

Completely decentralising not only the decision-making power, but also all responsibilities in terms of raising the required funds is not an adequate solution. This is because it leads to a different sort of problem, namely that of equity. When the resources required by education systems come mostly from taxes raised at the regional or local level, basic socio-economic differences between areas may lead to major disparities in available funds. This can reinforce existing inequalities at the regional or local level, by generating major gaps in the quality of the education that students receive, which in turn lead to substantial differences in the skill levels of the population. The United States is a clear example of this inequality trap, since public schools are funded mostly by local property taxes. Thus, rich neighbourhoods raise plenty of funds for their schools, while poor areas struggle. The cycle is perpetuated as only wealthy families can afford to buy houses in rich neighbourhoods and continue to send their kids to free and well-funded public schools.

The solution to this conundrum seems to be for higher levels of government to compensate, at least partly, for socio-economic differences between regions or local authorities. In the state of Massachusetts, the Education Reform Act (MERA) (Baker, 2019; Rowe, 2016) resulted in a major increase in state funding for public schools, especially in poorer areas (Dee and Levine, 2004). In exchange for receiving funding, schools were required to align their curricula with standards set by the state and to participate in a state-wide student assessment system. Accountability measures were also introduced so that low-performing schools were subject to state intervention and, if their performance did not improve, they could be closed down by the state administration. To evaluate the performance of schools and school districts, Massachusetts built an information management system that included not only student assessment results, but also other indicators such as graduation rates and absenteeism.

At the federal level, the 2001 No Child Left Behind Act (NCLB) expanded the role of federal government in public education by providing additional funding in exchange for an assessment and accountability system. To receive federal funds, states had to implement assessment tests and evaluate school quality according to a set of common standards. Although the 2015 Every Student Succeeds Act (ESSA) relaxed the level of federal control, states are still required to implement student assessments.

Even in a formally federal country like Germany, the federal government provides funds to the *Länder* to compensate for socio-economic differences. Thus, in decentralised systems it is important that central and sub-national governments share responsibility for raising the funds that are required for their education systems. Co-responsibility between national government and individual regions will generate the incentives required for ensuring that resources are allocated efficiently. On the other hand, co-responsibility from central governments will play an important role in ensuring the re-distribution of resources raised through taxes, to promote equity across the whole country, i.e. to ensure that all students have access to equal educational opportunities. Thus, central government becomes the guarantor of equity at the national level and regional governments are responsible for the efficient use of allocated resources.

For the complex governance arrangements in decentralised systems to work, central government must also implement accountability mechanisms in exchange for the funds transferred to regions, so as to ensure that they are allocated efficiently (OECD, 2017a). These accountability mechanisms normally include common curricular standards and national assessments, and push for the creation of information systems that measure the quality of the education system through indicators such as rates of early school leaving and upper-secondary graduation rates. When these accountability mechanisms are not implemented by central government and regions have little or no role in fundraising, the wrong incentives take over. Regions may enter into an endless political battle to obtain more and more resources from central government, but they have no incentives to ensure that they are allocated in such a way as to ensure the quality and equity of their sub-systems.

Unfortunately, this is the case in many decentralised countries, so we will use the case of Spain as an example to illustrate what can go wrong in the absence of co-responsibility and accountability. In Spain the national government is responsible for raising most of the public funds through taxes, although some taxes have been transferred to regions. Thus, education, health and social affairs are funded by taxes raised by central government, which are then transferred to regions as a lump-sum, following a formula which takes into account population size, demographic factors and degree of dispersion, as well as some degree of re-distribution from rich to poor regions. As expected, this formula is the source of constant disputes between those regions that feel that it does not benefit them as much as others.

It is the responsibility of individual regions to decide how to distribute these funds between education, health and social affairs, and as a result the level of investment in education varies greatly from one to another. The magnitude of the transfers from central government to regions is such that regional governments manage around 83% of the funds invested in education. However, accountability mechanisms are lacking: there are no common standards, no national assessments, no national targets, and most regions have not implemented external evaluations of student performance (Gomendio, 2021; Wert, 2019). Levels of funding are therefore unrelated to levels of performance of regions or schools, their improvement or decline. Furthermore, central government has no say when schools consistently underperform (which in fact is difficult to identify, given the lack of a common metric by which to measure student performance). In such a system, central government cannot act as a guarantor of equity and there are no incentives for regions to improve the quality of their sub-systems. Consequently, there are huge regional disparities in student performance (as revealed by international surveys), which translate into major regional differences in rates of early school leaving, NEETs and youth unemployment.

The lack of national assessment and common standards is particularly surprising given that the degrees for lower- and upper-secondary education are national, meaning that they are awarded by the Ministry of Education, and therefore the responsibility of central government. This implies that students receive the same national degrees, despite of the fact that overall student performance levels differ by more than one year of schooling between regions according to international surveys. Attempts to introduce national standardised evaluations and common curricula for core subjects via the reform approved in 2013 (LOMCE) were fiercely rejected by regions as a form of "re-centralisation". This illustrates the difficulty of introducing accountability mechanisms after the transfer of funds and responsibilities has taken place. Ideally, the right combination of transfers of funds from and accountability mechanisms to central government should be mutually agreed upon during the decentralisation process. Otherwise, regions gain decision-making power and national funds, without any obligation to enforce accountability mechanisms in exchange.

The lack of co-responsibility for fundraising also generates an imbalance between central government and regions in terms of the political costs of providing adequate resources. When central government raises most of the funding through taxes and then transfers the resources for education, health and social services, this sets the scene for a never-ending battle for more funds between regions. The narratives that regional policymakers develop to justify their claims to more resources from central government, often lead to the popular perception that central government is to blame on the one hand for not providing enough resources for public services, and on the other hand for setting taxes which are generally perceived as too high or unfair. The extent to which people disassociate these two critiques is surprising. We unfortunately learnt this the hard way when working in central government.

In 2012 Spain was going through the worst of the financial crisis and had to make difficult choices to control the deficit and to avoid the immediate risk of needing to be 'rescued', i.e. of receiving critical financial aid from the European Union, the European Central Bank and the International Monetary Fund on the condition of severe cuts to pensions and other welfare tools, as well as public salaries (Wert, 2020). As we have seen above, it is the regions who make decisions about how to invest the funds transferred by central government in education, health and social affairs. So there was little that central government could do except to introduce flexibility on issues regulated by basic law in order to allow regions to control their own spending. In education, basic law determines a wide range of variables such as student-teacher ratios, number of teaching hours, replacement rates of teachers on leave, and so on. Greater flexibility was granted to regions on mostly unpopular measures such as increases to student-teacher ratios.

To cut a long story short, on the whole, regions decided to implement larger budget cuts in education than in health. In educational metrics there was ample room for improving efficiency since for example decades of steady decreases in student-teacher ratios meant that Spain's was one of the lowest in Europe; in fact, even after the increases, student-teacher ratios remained below the OECD average. However, a very strong narrative was constructed around the "budget cuts" and the supposed damage they inflicted on public education; this causal link that was taken for granted, despite the lack of evidence. Central government was blamed for this and strong opposition was mounted to the measures, with regions watching on in relief. The political costs were so great that the education reform we designed at the Ministry of Education met with fierce resistance. This was because, amidst all the confusion caused by the blame games, people believed that the reform (which did not address these issues and was not approved until late 2013 nor implemented until the start of the 2014–2015 school year) was responsible for the budget cuts (which were actually implemented in 2012 by the regions). This tainted the public view of the education reform before it was even born.

The case of Portugal illustrates very well the extent to which political costs are dependent on the possibility of transferring the blame. In contrast to Spain, from 2011–2014 Portugal was subject to international bailout, which included major austerity measures mandatorily imposed by the so-called *troika* (the European Commission, the European Central Bank and the International Monetary Fund). Budget cuts in education were comparatively larger and many teachers lost their jobs, as a number of very small rural schools were consolidated into bigger ones allowing for greater cost efficiency. However, as the then Minister of Education Nuno Crato explained to us, people perceived that these decisions were imposed by Brussels and therefore the Portuguese national government did not suffer politically as much from the budget cuts.

While centralised and formally decentralised systems tend to have clear boundaries, other decentralised systems tend to have blurry lines of responsibility in terms of both decision making and funding, which may be difficult for citizens to understand. This conveys the risk that specific levels of government will not be held politically accountable for the decisions that they make, thus creating incentives for destructive blame games. These toxic dynamics may also lead the public to fear that the use of resources by different levels of government is inefficient and creates unnecessary duplicities. In terms of implementing education reforms, ill-defined areas of responsibility may lead to power struggles which generate endless disputes between different levels of government about who is entitled to make certain decisions, or simply may cause sub-national governments to refuse to implement decisions made by central government.

3.6 The Role of Stakeholders

The main role of education systems is to equip students with the knowledge and skills that will allow them to obtain good jobs, to push the frontiers of innovation, to become active participants in their societies and to improve their wellbeing. Thus, education systems have been developed to serve students.

Following this logic, the main stakeholders should be parents, who have a direct interest in the benefits that their children will obtain from a good quality education system. However, in most countries they have not become influential stakeholders, probably because they are rarely well-organised and also because the benefits for them as a group are rather diffuse. It could be that parents care about whether the system gives them the opportunity to choose the kind of education that they think is best for their children, rather than about the quality of the system as a whole. In fact, when choosing a school parents seem to prioritise aspects such as discipline, safety, school environment, and reputation over academic achievement (OECD, 2013a). In some countries parents have limited information on the performance levels of specific schools, let alone the whole system. When reforms do directly limit their capacity to choose what they feel is best for their children, they will react. For example, when charter schools are at risk of being closed down, those parents who hold strong beliefs about the adequacy of charter schools for their children will mobilise (Moe, 2017a).

It could also be argued that businesses which benefit from hiring highly skilled workers, and could therefore contribute valuable information about labour market needs, should also be expected to be major stakeholders. It seems fair to say that in many countries they have an influence over vocational education and training systems, which are designed facilitate access to labour markets, and which require the collaboration of firms for on-the-job training schemes (Busemeyer, 2015). Their influence over other parts of the education system seems much weaker.

Those who receive direct and quantifiable resources from the education system constitute an entirely different group of stakeholders. Since education systems have become large institutional structures with high shares of public investment, they generate vested interests among the people and groups on the receiving end of this massive pipeline of resources (Moe and Wiborg, 2017).

The extent to which most educational reforms do imply the (re)distribution of resources is not always obvious. Investment in education is mostly assigned to teacher salaries. In fact, 80% of current education expenditure goes to staff (OECD, 2014). As education systems have expanded, the number of teachers hired has grown to such an extent that in many countries governments are now the single largest employers. Therefore, policies that modify either the number of teachers or their salaries have a huge impact on the total amount of resources invested and how they are allocated. Any changes to class size will have a direct impact on the number of teachers that the system requires, as will changes to the number of hours that teachers are expected to work.

Our experience in government taught us that many issues that are seemingly unrelated to resources quickly reveal unforeseen links to major distributional conflicts. A clear case was the reaction to our decision to delegate greater autonomy to schools in terms of setting curricula, so that they could decide how many hours to devote to each subject, as a major pillar of the LOMCE education reform. Since the number of teaching hours for each subject equates to the number of specialised teachers required in any given field, we ended up spending many hours meeting with teachers' association representatives from different fields of knowledge and unions who (to our surprise) seemed to agree on one general principle. They agreed that central government should retain the decision-making power to determine the number of hours per subject for each grade, but seemed to have very different points of view as to which subjects required more hours.

Any providers of resources required by schools or students may also become influential stakeholders during reforms, particularly if they provide resources that are purchased annually, such as textbooks. Reforms that change the content of the curriculum may imply significant benefits or losses for publishers. Similarly, policies that facilitate the establishment of school libraries so that students can share books, and schools do not have to choose one textbook for all students, are met with strong resistance, although they clearly benefit families.

It is teachers as a group that, due to the sheer size of the teaching force and the fact that they are the direct beneficiaries of most of the funding, have incentives to get organised in order to protect their rights and fight for better working conditions and higher salaries. Thus, teachers all over the world have organised themselves through unions, which have become powerful and visible political players. The main objective of teacher unions is to defend the interests of their members and to enlarge the teaching force so as to gain more power. In principle, there is nothing wrong with this mission, since it is the very reason for their existence. But major conflicts of interest can arise when unions oppose reforms designed to improve student outcomes, because they perceive them as a threat to teachers' existing privileges.

The education system provides teachers with jobs, salaries, careers and security. As employees, they have vested interests. Most unions defend teachers' contract provisions which seek security and uniformity, at the expense of incentives for good teachers. They also tend to limit school principals' autonomy to build their teams (i.e. to hire and dismiss their teachers). Thus, most unions favour salary rules based on seniority above performance-linked incentives and mechanisms for joining the teaching force that prioritise seniority over merit, as well as transfer rules that give senior teachers the first pick of available jobs and rules that make it virtually impossible to dismiss underperforming teachers (Moe and Wiborg, 2017).

This set of rules is meant to protect the interests of teachers, particularly low-performing teachers, who refuse any form of accountability (except so-called 'self-evaluation'). As a result, unions outright reject the idea of a distinction between high- and low-performing teachers. Clearly these rules go against the interests of students who would benefit from having a more flexible system and more accountable teachers, which would increase their chances of a good or excellent education. In fact, it has been shown that dismissing a small percentage of the lowest-performing teachers in the US would have a huge positive impact on student outcomes (Hanushek *et al.*, 2013). Furthermore, there is a clear link between the skill levels of teachers and the performance levels of their students (Hanushek *et al.*, 2019).

Unions may argue that they support these rules, because their role is to protect teachers at large. This cannot be contested. Huge vested interests have made unions powerful, precisely because they have effectively protected teachers´ working conditions. But this also should not be twisted. Unions often try to hide this fact and to disguise it as attempts to make the system fairer or better for students. This leads to powerful union narratives which may obscure the real conflicts of interest that lie behind their support or rejection of reforms.

There are many examples of this narrative, but they all share similar features, so we have chosen those that are closer to our direct professional experience. This does not imply that they are the best ones, or the most extreme ones, just the ones that we are most familiar with. They do have a wider implication, closely related with the purpose of this book, as these examples tell us about a narrative supported by an international organization, such as the OECD, which has a major impact on the global narrative about education and has a unique role in identifying good practices that lead to better student outcomes by generating comparative international evidence.

The International Summit of the Teaching Profession (ISTP) is the highest-level meeting that the OECD organises on education. In fact, the meeting is co-organised with Education International (EI), which is a global federation of teachers' unions from over 170 countries representing over 30 million teachers. Attendance is by invitation only. The rules agreed by both stipulate that only the top twenty performing countries in PISA, plus the ten that have improved the most, can attend as long as the Education Minister and the leader of the most powerful national union agree to sit hand-in-hand. Education ministers and union leaders have the same speaking rights. The agenda and format of the meeting is agreed in great detail by the OECD and EI.

At the ISTP meeting held in Finland in 2019, David Edwards, Secretary-General of EI stated:

> [G]lobally, when one thinks about Finland one thinks about Finnish teachers. But not everyone always gets the whole picture. Apparently, make every school a good public school, trust teachers, value their labour rights and representatives and give them the time, respect and resources to collaborate and innovate and teach, didn't fit into the bumper sticker that certain so-called reformers wanted to sell.

He went on to argue that the reason why Finland was a top performer in education was that no attempts were made "to disrupt or squeeze in additional instruction hours or lower teachers' qualifications or bust unions or pay teachers by student test scores". Finally, he claimed that members of the teachers' union in Finland had told him that "the conservatives wanted more resources for gifted education and the liberals wanted all students to be treated as gifted" (Edwards, 2019).

In summary, EI interprets that the success of Finnish students in PISA is entirely attributable to the fact that teachers are "trusted", an oxymoron which actually implies that teachers should not be evaluated, nor be made accountable for student outcomes, nor have performance-related pay. Furthermore, a narrative is built around the argument that Finnish teachers are successful mainly because of their labour rights and the resources and freedom that they are granted. It is true that, when Finland unexpectedly emerged as the top performer in the first cycle of PISA, the most widespread conclusion was that it was due to the high quality of the national teaching force. However, unions quickly elaborated an interpretation better-aligned with their interests, claiming that "trust in teachers" was the key; this narrative has been adopted by many unions in other countries to reject attempts to evaluate teachers and to make them accountable for student outcomes (Wiborg, 2017b). What seems surprising is that EI would make this argument in 2019, after Finland had experienced a marked decline in PISA scores since 2000, particularly in mathematics and science. In other words, the strong narrative of trust in teachers and the freedom required to be innovative was supported by both EI and the OECD long after the evidence from PISA suggested that this was the wrong (or at least not the whole) explanation.

Interestingly, a couple of years earlier, EI rejected the argument that teacher quality was a key element among top-performing systems, using reports from the OECD as evidence. At the ISTP meeting held in 2017 in Scotland, the then General Secretary of EI, Fred van Leeuwen, claimed that the 2011 summit report was clear that "the frequently cited claim that the best performing education systems [...] recruit their teachers from the top-third of graduates [...] is not supported by the evidence". And he urged for the establishment of "safeguards against an overreliance on standardised assessments" and the establishment of a "holistic approach to school evaluation with a raised profile for school self-evaluation", a recommendation based on the OECD's Review of Evaluation and Assessment in Education (OECD, 2013b; van Leeuwen, 2017).

These quotes from successive EI General Secretaries actually neatly summarise the narrative built by many unions all over the world. The basic elements are that the education system, and by implication students, will benefit from strong unions which ensure good working conditions for all teachers (irrespective of their performance), and societies that do not demand accountability measures because they trust their teachers, but are willing to provide a large share of resources for the system. While this set of rules clearly favours teachers, as we will see later, there is no clear evidence that it improves student outcomes. As revolutionary as it may sound, what benefits teachers does not necessarily benefit students.

In their quest to further improve the conditions of the teaching force, EI led an initiative to seek evidence linking teacher stress, wellbeing, and excessive work-load to a concept labelled "self-efficacy", which refers to teachers' subjective perceptions of their own performance. The concept of "self-efficacy" is employed loosely as an equivalent to the actual impact that teachers have on student performance. The OECD agreed to include a new module on the next cycle of its major international large-scale survey of teachers' perceptions (TALIS 2018) to analyse these issues.

As happens with most subjective reports, there are serious limitations in how teachers perceive their "self-efficacy", which must be taken into account when interpreting these data. A comparison of the countries included in TALIS 2013 clearly shows that, overall, most teachers feel "well or very well prepared" in terms of the content of the subject being taught, with the average being 93% (OECD, 2014b). This seems to be an over-optimistic perception, given that the sample includes countries that differ to a large extent in student outcomes (according to PISA). In fact, teachers in countries where fifteen-year-olds have low levels of performance (according to PISA), seem to show the highest levels of self-confidence. In low-performing countries such as Brazil, Chile, Malaysia, Italy and Spain, the proportion of teachers that feel well- or very well-prepared is over 95%, while in high-performing countries like Finland and Japan the percentage of perceived self-efficacy drops to 72% and 76% respectively. Similarly, according to TALIS 2018, the proportion of teachers who think they can "get students to believe they can do well in school work" is very high among some low-performing countries in

PISA—such as Colombia (98%), Brazil (97%), United Arab Emirates (94%), Argentina (93%)—and lower among some top-performing countries such as Singapore (85%) and Korea (87%) (OECD 2020b).

When taken together, TALIS (teachers' perceptions) and PISA (student outcomes) data clearly show that teachers in countries where students have low performance levels show high confidence in their level of preparedness and in the impact of their teaching on student outcomes, while the level of teachers´ confidence decreases in countries where students are top performers. Therefore, the biases in the perceptions of teachers in low-performing countries seem to have more to do with the fact that they work in environments which are not demanding than with their real impact on student performance. On the contrary, teachers in countries where students have high levels of performance seem to feel that they should prepare more and improve their efficiency further. Given that these biases are clear, it seems odd that so few efforts have been made to link teachers´ perceptions and working practices to the actual performance of students, when TALIS and PISA provide a wealth of information on both.

The TALIS 2018 survey included forty-eight countries and economies, 15,000 schools and 260,000 teachers (OECD, 2020b). The results showed that 90% of teachers claimed that they chose to enter the profession in order to have a positive impact on the development of children, but that issues to do with job security and working conditions were also paramount (secure job: 70%; reliable income: 65%; steady career: 65%). Of course, teachers are no different from people working in many other sectors where job security and salaries are important. But teachers´ views on their work seem to run counter to the persistent claims made by unions about poor working conditions.

In some ways, teachers do stand out from other professions: 90% of teachers report being satisfied with their job. This proportion is even higher in some low-performing countries such as Argentina (CABA),[3] Colombia, Mexico, and Italy, and the percentage is lowest for countries in which students perform better (UK: 77%; Japan: 82%). In addition, only 18% of teachers suffer a lot of stress, mainly because of their administrative workloads. Furthermore, most teachers work

---

3   CABA (Ciudad Autónoma of Buenos Aires) was the only Argentine region participating in TALIS 2018.

on permanent contracts, with only 18% hired on temporary contracts (mostly young people who have recently joined the teaching force). Finally, appraisal is linked to some form of career promotion or salary increase for only 41% of teachers.

The results of this large international survey (TALIS) do show the extent to which unions have been successful in improving the working conditions of teachers, while shielding them from the potentially negative consequences of teacher evaluations. However, they highlight the fact that teachers in countries with poor-performing education systems seem to be more confident and more satisfied than their counterparts in top-performing countries. Thus, the concluding claim of the OECD's TALIS 2018 report that "good working conditions can improve teachers' overall wellbeing, job commitment and efficiency" (OECD, 2020b) does not seem to be supported by the data that TALIS and PISA generate. Since teachers' reports of 'self-efficacy' bear little relationship to the performance of their students, it seems important to treat the two separately.

This type of narrative has provided unions with the 'fuel' to demand direct participation in education policy and the legitimacy to act as powerful stakeholders in supporting or rejecting education reforms. In fact, the OECD (which is a member-led organisation funded by governments) often makes claims such as "[t]eacher engagement in the development and implementation of educational reform is crucial and school reform will not work unless it is supported from the bottom up" or "[i]t requires teachers to contribute as the architects of change, not just its implementers. Some of the most successful reforms are those supported by strong unions rather than those that keep the union role weak" (OECD, 2015b; Schleicher, 2011 and 2015).

It is clear that education reforms are unlikely to have an impact if they do not count on the support and understanding of teachers who, ultimately, will have to implement changes in the classroom. However, this is different from arguing that teachers and unions should participate in the design of reforms. The claim that the most successful reforms are those supported by strong unions fails to acknowledge the fact that in many countries strong unions have blocked reforms when their interests were in conflict with those of students (Moe and Wiborg, 2017).

Countries differ to a large extent in the level of political power that unions have achieved, whether or not they have veto powers, and the role that they have played in relation to education reforms. In Latin American countries, unions have established strong links with Ministries of Education and political parties, and their leaders frequently hold relevant positions in both (Bruns and Luque, 2014; Grindle, 2004). They are highly organised, enjoy great visibility and have the capacity to bring education systems to a halt. Sadly, Latin American countries are known for the long strikes that unions have organised against reforms, which inflict clear damage on the learning trajectories of students.

Mexico represents an extreme case because the close relationship between its largest teachers' union (SNTE) and the PRI, the hegemonic political party of Mexico for nearly a century, has allowed the former to gain immense power and acquire plenty of resources (Chambers-Ju and Finger, 2017). The close relationship even allowed the union to place members in key positions within the country's huge education bureaucracy. The union regulated entry into the profession, ensuring that merit played no role, and acting as a broker since teacher positions could be sold or bequeathed to next of kin. The union received a proportion of the salaries of all teachers and eventually accumulated massive resources, to the extent that its leader was eventually arrested on charges of corruption. The control by the teachers' union of jobs, salaries and promotions led to high rates of teacher absenteeism. According to *The Economist*, 13% of the teacher payroll (or 298,000 teachers) did not show up for work; the practice became so widespread that these 'teachers' became known as *"aviadores"* or "ghost" teachers (*The Economist*, 2014). It is clear that these practices did not benefit students in any way, and this is a primary reason for the very poor levels of student performance in Mexico.

Unions are known to be very powerful in the US and France, and in both countries that have been very effective in blocking reforms. In the US, unions opposed all major reforms (Moe, 2017a) including "No Child Left Behind", which required states to test students and made schools accountable, but in the end was diluted to the extent that there were no consequences for teachers and "Race to the Top", which included a charter reform perceived by unions as a threat, since jobs and resources could be transferred to them if parents chose to send their children to such schools. Evidence from the United States shows that, while unions tend to be successful at increasing the amount of funding that goes to schools, this does not necessarily improve student outcomes (Hoxby, 1996).

In France the unions have supported low institutional autonomy, centralisation and high expenditure (Dobbins, 2014 and 2017). Unions emerged at the same time as the construction of the very centralised education system during the Third Republic (1870–1940)[4] and have become so powerful that they are regarded as co-managers of education with successive governments, who wish to be seen to be seeking consensus. However, unions have been said to follow "teacher rent seeking behaviour" (Vedder and Gallaway, 1991). They have opposed all efforts to decentralise education, in order to retain the power that they already exercise within central government, to prevent teacher salaries from becoming fragmented, and to avoid the potential loss of their public service status. Centralisation provides unions with one single target on which to focus their efforts, increasing their visibility, and it has the additional effect of politicising all issues and enhancing media attention while attracting the support of the public. French unions also oppose evaluations and accountability of teachers and schools, so there are no means to reward or sanction teachers for their performance.

Nordic countries represent classic cases of '"corporatism", with unions integrated into decision-making structures designed to promote moderation and balance (Wiborg, 2017b). Although these systems have a long tradition of making policy decisions based on broad consensus, this does not imply that teacher unions have supported all education reforms. As education systems became decentralised in the 1990s, unions resisted becoming employees of the municipalities because this would diminish their collective bargaining power and could generate heterogeneity in teacher salaries and working conditions.

In summary, in their efforts to improve teachers´ working conditions, most unions have resisted attempts to decentralise education systems,

---

4   The traditional level of centralisation of French education was so extreme not only at the macro policy level but also at the micro level that Jules Ferry, an influential Minister of Education at the end of the nineteenth century, used to say, checking his pocket watch at nine in the morning: "Right now, every student in France is having dictation under the supervision of the teacher" (Blanquer, 2016).

to make the training of teachers more demanding, to design hiring processes which are more selective and based on merit, to dismiss underperforming teachers, to link teachers' pay to student performance and to give principals more power to build their teams of teachers. In fact, in some countries unions have gone to the extreme of opposing reforms to implement standardised, external student assessments, which they regard (rightly) as an indirect way of assessing the teachers themselves, arguing that teachers should be "trusted", that they know better, and that they should perform "self-evaluations".

As Moe and Wiborg (2017) argue, in those countries where teachers' unions have the power to veto reforms, they have successfully opposed many of those aiming to improve student performance. However, in other countries, unions do not have veto powers. In this case, the alliance that unions have traditionally established with political parties on the left of the political spectrum has enabled the former to have a major impact on the education policy implemented when the latter were in government. As we will see, this has led to the widespread implementation of policies which favour teachers but do not have a clear impact on student outcomes (such as lower ratios and higher salaries for all teachers), while policies that clearly impact the performance of students (such as student assessments and demanding criteria for hiring teachers) face major obstacles.

3.7 A Special Case: Governance of VET Systems

As we have noted in the previous chapters, it can be said that VET is probably the most country-specific of all components of an education system. Specificity derives from different elements. In the chapter on ideology, we mentioned how the question of tracking students' academic or vocational trajectories from an early stage of K-12 plays out in the ideological debate on comprehensiveness. Also in this chapter, when analysing governance in multi-level states and the involvement of stakeholders, we have anticipated that VET requires more complex governance models than other elements of K-12, insofar as the relationship between the economic and social agents translates into multi-stakeholder governance arrangements. As a result, differences between countries in VET governance are greater than in other educational areas.

The most convincing theoretical framework to root these differences in political, economic and institutional factors is, in our opinion, that proposed twenty years ago by the American political scientist Peter Hall and British political economist David Soskice on "varieties of capitalism" (Hall and Soskice, 2001). According to this framework, in a nutshell, historic, cultural and mostly institutional factors have led to two varieties of capitalism (VoC) in different countries. The ways in which firms coordinate a number of relational spheres (including VET) differ between "liberal market economies" (LMEs) and "coordinated market economies" (CMEs). In LMEs those spheres are coordinated fundamentally through hierarchy and competitive market arrangements. Instead, in CMEs there is a strong recourse to non-market relationships and collaborative arrangements. Although some have argued that the VoC framework does not seamlessly apply to the domain of education (Ansell, 2010), it certainly provides a good theoretical foundation for satisfactory explanations on the differences between VET governance models, as developed extensively by German political scientist Marius Busemeyer (Busemeyer, 2009 and 2015).

Another significant theoretical framework along this line—to some extent filling in some of the gaps of the VoC theory—is that developed by MIT political scientist Kathleen Thelen on institutional evolution and path dependency (Thelen, 2004). She states that institutions are from the outset shaped by historical events that explain not only their national variations, but also the substantial differences in a number of their policies, such as VET systems. Institutions evolve over time, adapting to changes in the environment, but their original shape creates a path dependency and feedback effects that explain many of the different trajectories followed by developed countries in their VET strategies (or lack thereof).

According to these frameworks, the different pathways followed by countries in shaping both upper-secondary and tertiary education are not only determined by partisan cleavages, but also by differences in formal and informal institutional arrangements pertaining not only to the political sphere but also to economic and social actors. And in the context of VET, the key requirement seems to be that in "coordinated market economies [...] coordination among economic actors via strong associations and corporatist institutions facilitates the formation of cross-class coalitions that support the maintenance of VET" (Busemeyer, 2015).

Those countries where these forms of collaborative coordination between different economic actors prevail can institute VET systems in which employers and unions agree to cooperate in the design, funding and deployment of an alternative to university education which provides high-quality training and well-paid jobs to young people who have practical or applied (rather than academic) dispositions, inclinations or skill sets. This alternative seems to work better when employers are deeply committed to training through systems of 'Dual VET' (like that prevailing in Germany) than in the so-called 'statist skill-formation regime', of which Sweden would be the best example. Both models can be found in CMEs, and their respective prevalence is to a great extent explained by partisan politics: where centre-right (mostly, Christian democrats) governments are predominant, we find a strong Dual VET model, while in countries tending towards centre-left (social-democrats), we tend to find the statist model.

Instead, in LMEs, in the absence of such cross-class compromises (both between employers and unions, as well as political parties on the left and the right), VET has lost importance as a 'respectable' alternative to university education, and enrolment has declined or even fallen off entirely.

Here we find a very interesting paradox. From both an economic and social viewpoint, the evidence suggests that a robust and well-functioning VET system provides enhanced productivity (through better matches of skills and jobs) as well as less inequality (through stable and well-paid jobs for skilled workers that have gone through a VET pathway). The telling examples of Germany, Austria and Switzerland in Europe or Singapore in Southeast Asia should normally suffice to dispel fierce criticism to VET on grounds of inequality, segregation and unfairness.

This is not the case. The reasons have to do with the substance, shape and governance of VET systems. They have to do with substance, because the idea of different pathways during secondary education clashes with the comprehensiveness doctrine, which has been and still is the backbone of educational philosophy for a majority of leftist (mainly social-democrat) parties in Europe.[5] They have to do with shape and governance because in LME systems, where cross-class coalitions are hard if not impossible to achieve, unions are extremely reluctant to engage with employers in training schemes and to work with them on governance. Something similar happens with employers, who will not be keen on building up the mutual trust with unions to commit themselves to this shared responsibility.

Here is the fundamental issue: a well-functioning VET system requires a good connection with the employment system, in order to match the skill formation plans with the evolving demands of the labour market. This connection is harder to achieve if employers are not a part of the governance of the system. Also, since labour markets hold significant sub-national (regional and local) specificity, the connections between the VET system and the employment system do require a very demanding level of granularity. A close-knit relationship between employers, unions and the different layers of government to put in place a well-functioning governance scheme for VET is required in order to make that scheme effective and responsive to changes in the labour market. The most typical examples of such systems are Dual VET systems.

The Dual VET systems that have been developed mostly in Germany, Austria and Switzerland rest on a number of pre-conditions that can be more easily achieved in CMEs than in LMEs. The first and foremost of these is mutual trust, since there is an array of conflicting interests to arbitrate in the governance of these systems. Employers will be interested in a model of training as practical and specific as possible, so that it meets their needs in the shortest possible time. Unions will instead advocate for a broader and more transferable skill-set to be covered by the training model, so that apprentices do not get stuck in too narrow a bundle of skills that hinders their opportunities to open up their job chances. And governments, meanwhile, will pursue different aims from an educational and employment vantage point, including eventual conflicts of interest between their different departments.

There are a number of trade-offs to be negotiated between the different poles of the Dual VET system. Ultimately, most of them have

---

5 Conspicuous exceptions, naturally, are social democrats in CME countries like Germany or Austria.

to do with the structure of incentives to engage firms, unions and apprentices themselves (Cedefop, 2009; European Training Foundation, 2018; Kuczera, 2017; OECD, 2018). When it comes to firms, incentives, in the form of direct subsidies, in-kind contributions or tax credits, must avoid the risk of producing deadweight losses, i.e., subsidising firms for training expenses which they would have incurred even if such subsidies were not available. In the early developmental stages of a Dual VET strategy, identifying the most effective levers to engage all the relevant actors of the complicated stakeholder structure becomes the make-or-break factor of the initiative.

Another complex issue has to do with the whole-of-government approach that is required to make it work smoothly. Typically, two different departments of the particular level of government responsible for the delivery of VET—whether the national, regional or, less frequently, local level—namely education and employment departments, must agree on how to combine their respective (and often conflicting) interests in the design and governance of Dual VET. Education departments will try to bring to the process a fair share of foundation skills (literacy, mathematics and science, fundamentally) as key ingredients of a clear pathway towards effective lifelong learning. Employment departments will be more interested in reskilling strategies allowing for 'quick fixes' in employment crises and strategies to facilitate smooth transitions to new jobs, including those in different sectors.

From a more general viewpoint, beyond the specificities of Dual VET, the problems faced by VET governance are clearly a lot more country-specific than those related to other areas or stages of K-12 education. The reason for this is self-evident: while academic or general programmes are intended to provide generic knowledge and competencies, VET programmes put more focus on those specific skills that are in demand with employers. Many of those skills are subject to a much higher rate of change than academic subjects and they must be calibrated and adapted according to the evolving needs of the labour market. On top of that, labour markets demand different skills according to sectoral specialisation, firm size, labour regulations and many other factors. Additionally, the specific model of "human capital formation" (Iversen and Stephens, 2008) that prevails in each country moulds the shape, orientation and governance of VET differently.

Hence, coordination mechanisms must be put in place to make the VET engine work. First, coordination between the different levels of government (national, regional and local) is required, as well as coordination between different departments within each level (education and employment). As explained above, this is probably the most 'universal' issue of governance of VET systems. There is a 'natural' conflict of interest between educational VET authorities and employment authorities, as explained above, in terms of the relative shares of school-based components and on-the-job training components, and also in terms of the broadness and transferability of skills in the curriculum.

Second, coordination between employers and the education and employment authorities responsible for VET in governments is also required. If formal or informal coordination mechanisms do not exist or are ineffective, there will be a growing divergence between the supply of skills that the VET system provides and the fast-changing demands from employers, thereby damaging the employment outlook of VET graduates.

Third, some level of coordination between unions and employers is also mandatory. A well-functioning VET system cannot be developed if there is systematic hostility from the unions against it. And unions are generally reluctant to engage in VET systems governance unless their 'fairness' conditions are taken into consideration. When a country only develops a school-based system, unions are less concerned about its governance. Instead, when the system has a strong component of on-the-job training or firm-based learning, unions feel they have 'skin in the game' and are keen to set conditions: broad and highly transferable skill-sets, decent wages and social security arrangements for apprentices, limitations on firm-specific skills in order to avoid undesired ties between the apprentice and the firm providing the training.

In summary, a whole-of-government approach, strong coordination with economic and social actors, and mutual trust between the parties seem to be essential pre-requisites for a well-governed VET system.

In an ideal situation, such engagement and coordination should be achieved by the establishment of formal governance partnerships. But this is not always achievable. By default, informal coordination mechanisms can do part of the job. Foundations or other types of voluntary associations that bring together the different stakeholders (especially the economic and social ones) have proven to be instrumental in fostering greater and faster development of VET initiatives. This seems to be particularly the case in those countries where a cultural tradition of apprenticeships has never developed, or has been lost over time.

Ultimately, that coordination and shared sense of purpose is more necessary in those nations where the social value of VET has been very scarce, or has deteriorated over time.

In the case of the United States, as the most prototypical example of an LME, VET was not historically a major concern in federal public policy until the 1970s (Kreising, 2001). In the past fifty years it has received more political attention, with a number of pieces of legislation trying to address the issue of shortages of skilled workers that the education system seemed unable to solve. But in fact, vocational training is almost non-existent in high school and, on the other hand, tertiary VET education (two-year community colleges) represents quite a meagre fraction of overall enrolment in higher education: according to the latest data, enrolment in two-year programmes among Americans aged eighteen to twenty-four represents only 10% of this age cohort, while 30% of those youngsters are taking four-year university programmes (Hussar *et al.*, 2020). Actually, community colleges have a larger intake of working adults taking courses than of younger full-time students.[6] Apparently, even when there is some consensus that appropriate VET education would improve both employability and skills among young Americans, it seems impossible to overcome the absence of a 'VET culture' in an education environment with virtually no VET alternative in secondary education, and a tertiary VET supply that cannot compete with university education.

Spain is a good case study for why the perception of VET as a useful pathway deteriorated in many education systems, and the track ultimately faded away. In 1990 new legislation which extended compulsory education for two years (from age fourteen to age sixteen) was implemented. A totally comprehensive system was put in place which offered no choices between subjects or tracks until the end of compulsory education. All students had to follow the same curriculum.

---

6   While total enrolment in tertiary VET is around 5 million, a large majority of those enrolled—over 3 million—are in paid work over thirty hours a week, taking courses as part of their lifelong learning strategies.

A major consequence was that students who wished to follow the VET pathway had to spend two additional years following the same academic track. As a result, many dropped out of school. Thus, early school leaving increased to around 30% and remained at such high levels for decades (Felgueroso *et al.*, 2013). In more than 50% of cases, students who dropped out were lagging so far behind that they did not even obtain the compulsory lower-secondary degree. Thus, almost one in every three students was expelled from the education system without the most basic levels of knowledge and skills, a heavy burden that would limit their chances for the rest of their lives.

Beyond this major flaw, there was an additional detrimental impact. The new legislation did not modernise VET, which remained focused on low-skilled manual jobs. Historically, this had allowed many students to make a quick transition to the labour market, but the economy was changing and many jobs were demanding higher levels of skills. The disconnect between what VET offered and the changing needs of the labour market implied that VET did not lead to the middle- and high-skilled jobs that the economy was offering. VET became outdated, targeting a decreasing share of the labour market consisting of low-skilled jobs, and became attractive only to low-performing students. As a consequence, there was a growing perception that only university degrees led to high-quality jobs, and most families became convinced that this was the only path that would ensure their children's success in life. Over the years, enrolment in VET decreased and access to university expanded rapidly. But the hopes that these trends reflected equal opportunities for high-quality jobs among students proved itself to be a mirage: rates of early school leaving remained stubbornly high (30%) and rates of unemployment among university graduates were high compared to other countries. The latter was partly the consequence of students choosing fields of study which were not in demand in the labour market, partly due to the low quality of most universities. The opportunities provided by modernised VET systems with strong links to firms were lost.

These deficiencies were addressed by the new reforms we undertook first in 2012 (Dual VET) and then in the education reform of 2013 (LOMCE). A major aim of the reform was to decrease early school leaving by modernising VET and to make it more attractive to students with a broad range of levels of performance who aspired to obtain middle-skilled jobs. Both reforms gave firms a relevant role in relation to on-the-job training, which had disappeared from educational VET. The impact was substantial and rapid: enrolment in VET grew at an unprecedented pace in the following years while early school leaving decreased.

3.8. Conclusions

Governance arrangements are a fundamental component of any education reform, insofar as matters such as who decides what (authority), if and how different stakeholders must be involved in the reform process (stakeholder involvement), and who must pay for what (funding) do decisively shape an education system. Most reforms at the system level have an impact on how responsibilities in terms of decision-making and/or funding are shared, and how resources are distributed. Thus, the governance arrangements may facilitate or hinder reforms. In this chapter, we have dealt with these governance dimensions and their relationship with reform experiences.

Education reforms are difficult. The political economy of these reforms shows that they face difficulties due to a variety of factors. One is time: almost everywhere, the political cycle is much shorter than the reform cycle. Governments can be discouraged from embarking on complex reforms if they are not sure they will have enough time to implement them or to reap their fruits politically. From this viewpoint, reforms seem to be more easily implemented in countries where electoral competition is limited or nonexistent, or where most political parties agree on a pragmatic (non-ideological) long-term approach to education policies.

Another factor has to do with the kind and intensity of involvement in policymaking of stakeholders apart from government, especially teachers, and the extent to which their interests are conflicting. Governance reforms seeking to improve student performance may be perceived as a threat by teacher unions, particularly if accountability mechanisms linking student outcomes with the possibility of firing the least effective teachers, or establishing salary incentives to compensate merit and effectiveness over seniority are introduced. In these cases, if teachers' unions have veto points in the policy process, they will probably use them to stop or hinder the reform. Getting stakeholders, and especially teachers, aligned with a reform aids its successful implementation, but this does not mean that alignment must be a condition of reforms.

Clearly, the most important governance dimension in education reforms is the (re)distribution of power/authority among the different levels of government. Different countries' education systems have different degrees of centralisation according to constitutional arrangements (federal vs centralised), and also historical traditions like, for instance, the role municipalities played at the onset of mass schooling. While federal systems and centralised systems have a clear division of responsibilities assigned either to central government or the regions, many *de facto* decentralised systems are somewhere in between and suffer from a lack of clear definition of responsibilities and accountability mechanisms. Evidence shows that the degree of centralisation or decentralisation *per se* does not have a decisive impact on the outcomes of the system, as many confounding factors intervene. But reforms are more difficult in decentralised systems because many more actors with different interests have a say, and a role to play. Coordination mechanisms between the different administrations involved are required, and clear rules on responsibility and accountability seem to be the crucial elements for making such systems work smoothly and effectively. The level of difficulty increases in systems which are *de facto* decentralised but in which the definition of responsibilities is blurred; this leads to never-ending tensions about the degree of power and resources that each level of government has or should have. In the worst-case scenario, central government may approve reforms that are hijacked by regional governments, who oversee implementation.

The main evidence in terms of policy suggests that changes in governance arrangements must be carefully orchestrated and preparation for them is essential. In particular, decentralisation processes (when authority is transferred from central to regional or local levels of government) without capacity-building may fail, making the system ineffective. Similarly, decentralisation processes in which regions do not have a role in fundraising run the risk of overspending, and those without proper accountability mechanisms in place lack the incentives and control mechanisms needed to ensure that the eventual decisions will improve student performance and equity.

Funding rules—basically which role the different levels of government have in raising and allocating funds for education—are key in the process of devising and enacting reforms. Again, clear delineation of funding responsibilities between the different levels of government is necessary to ensure appropriate levels of accountability. In many countries, funding comes from more than one level of government (national and regional, or national and local, or all three combined). Regional contributions are key in order to ensure co-responsibility and an effective use of resources, while central funding helps to minimise the impact of regional disparities on levels of investment. Since funding is one of the most contentious dimensions in any given education reform, there are ample possibilities that reforms may fail or get curtailed if re-distributional issues prompt one or several of the stakeholders to use it as a means to hinder or veto the reforms. Political manipulation and blame-gaming often arise when it comes to funding. Different levels of government can argue about how reforms affect their funding contributions, teachers' unions may argue that a lack or inadequacy of funding affects teachers' earnings or career prospects, and any of them can find room for manoeuvre to protect their vested interest, which they disguise as general interest or students' interest.

This takes us to the overall question of vested interests and how they play out in education reforms. Education is clearly a multi-stakeholder aspect of political and social life. Governments, teachers and principals, other education providers (like teaching material providers), families and students themselves are relevant stakeholders. But their respective levels of involvement, cohesiveness or bargaining power are very different.

In the process of reforms, the stakeholders with more 'skin in the game' (teachers unions mainly) will be keen to weaponise arguments (including noble ideals such as equity) to block reforms, when in reality they are protecting their own vested interests. In the current stage of education reforms (reforms oriented to improve performance and quality), more often than not, teachers may perceive those aspects of the reform aimed at making them accountable for student outcomes, or linking pay to those outcomes, as threatening. Consequently, they will try to redirect the narrative towards supposed or imagined damages to students' wellbeing, inclusion, equity or any other educational values. There is nothing wrong with teachers acting collectively in defence of their conditions. There is something wrong with them hiding their real motives and disguising them as altruistic efforts to protect students' interests.

VET governance is a particular case within the governance aspect of education reforms. Given the stronger links between VET and the needs of the labour market, its governance arrangements require the participation of employers, firms and workers' unions as stakeholders. In those systems where there is a well-functioning VET system, this translates to a relevant place for these economic and social stakeholders at the governance table, including in decisions on funding. Reforms of VET governance seeking to better align it with labour market demands can only succeed where there is a shared commitment among economic, social and government stakeholders to find common ground.

4. ILSAs: Do They Count?

4.1 What Do International Metrics Measure?

International large-scale assessments (ILSAs) were started by the International Association for the Evaluation of Educational Achievement (IEA). In 1995 the first TIMSS (Trends in International Mathematics and Science Study) survey was conducted in over forty countries at five grade levels (third, fourth, seventh and eighth grades, as well as the final year of secondary school). Students were assessed in mathematics and science and a parallel analysis of the school curricula was conducted with the aim of finding links between the two. TIMSS was subsequently designed as a "quasi-longitudinal study" assessing a cohort of students in fourth grade and four years later again in eighth grade. The survey has been conducted every four years and in 2015 the sample included fifty-seven countries and seven regional jurisdictions. A different survey, "TIMSS Advanced", targets the final year of secondary school (twelfth grade in many countries) and assesses student achievement in advanced mathematics and physics. The IEA has also developed an international survey to assess reading literacy among fourth grade students every five years (PIRLS: Progress in International Reading Literacy Study). It started in 2001 with thirty-five participating countries and in 2016 it covered fifty countries and eleven regions.

In 2000, the Organisation for Economic Cooperation and Development (OECD) started its own survey, PISA (Programme for International Student Assessment). It assesses three domains: scientific literacy, mathematics and reading literacy, and in each cycle one of these is the main domain. It runs every three years, which means that each subject is treated as the main domain every nine years, and evaluates fifteen-year-olds irrespective of their grade. Thus, it compares students who have been at school for different lengths of time depending on the age at which compulsory schooling starts in different countries. In addition, the proportion of fifteen-year-olds in different grades included in the sample varies depending on the rate of grade repetition in each country. The geographical coverage of PISA has grown from forty-three countries/economies in 2000 to seventy-nine in 2018.

Thus, the three major international large-scale assessments (PIRLS, TIMSS and PISA) measure the same domains (reading, mathematics and science), but the methodology, length of the cycle and the target population (as defined by student age or grade) are different. The IEA surveys (PIRLS and TIMSS) sample all students in each classroom focusing on specific grades and have been designed to analyse the extent to which students have acquired curriculum-based content (Martin *et al.*, 2016; Mullis *et al.*, 2016 and 2017). On the other hand, PISA samples fifteen-year-olds in different grades (eighth, ninth, tenth and eleventh grades) and has defined its goal as an assessment of how the knowledge and skills acquired are applied to meet real-life challenges and to solve problems in unfamiliar settings (OECD, 2001 and 2019c). Unlike IEA surveys, PISA does not attempt to relate differences in curricular content between countries to student outcomes. Instead, the knowledge and skills considered relevant for "knowledge-based societies" are decided by groups of experts. This approach recognises explicitly that PISA scores are the result of the combined impact of school, home and the social environment, making the links between PISA results and school policies more tenuous. Despite this, PISA claims to be more policy-oriented than IEA's assessments and in fact PISA publications include many analyses to try to identify which good practices distinguish well-performing countries (OECD 2016b, 2019c, and 2019d). Participating countries first included mostly OECD members, i.e. largely high-income countries, but then expanded beyond the OECD perimeter to include low- and middle-income countries, which (as we shall see) required adjustments to the methodology.

The value of ILSAs lies in providing international benchmarks, which allow comparisons between countries in student performance using the same metrics. The fact that the main ILSAs measure student performance periodically also makes it possible to analyse trends over time. Initially these international surveys faced skepticism because of the deeply ingrained belief that education systems are too different to allow any meaningful comparison.

Critics also argued that their methodologies were flawed and that differences between countries focused too much on a narrow set of subjects and failed to capture important outcomes of the education systems. As an increasing number of countries has joined these international surveys, trust in them has grown, as has their influence on the narrative around good practices in education policy. This is mainly because they have promoted much-needed analyses on the good practices that lead to improvements in certain countries and the policies that top-performing countries have implemented (Cordero *et al.*, 2013 and 2018; Gustafsson and Rosen, 2014; Hanushek and Woessmann, 2011 and 2014; Hopfenbeck *et al.*, 2018; Johansson, 2016; Klieme, 2013; Lockheed and Wagemaker, 2013; Strietholt *et al.*, 2014). It is important to remember that drawing causal inferences remains controversial mainly due to the cross-sectional nature of the samples.

Over the years the public profile of international surveys, and PISA in particular, has grown. Media and policymakers eagerly await the results of each cycle to find out how their countries perform in relation to others and whether student outcomes have improved or declined since the last cycle. This has increased awareness among policymakers and citizens of the quality of their education systems. It has also contributed to a shift in the debate about education, from an emphasis on inputs (amount of resources invested) to an emphasis on outputs (student performance).

But the heightened media and political impact also has its drawbacks. It inevitably leads to a very narrow focus on the ranking between countries, and to oversimplistic hypotheses concerning the impact of policies implemented by different governments. In the worst-case scenario, it also leads to destructive blame games when countries perform poorly; this is a major concern among low- and middle-income countries which expect to perform badly but wish to be able to measure the progress of their education systems. Thus, international surveys, particularly PISA, have become powerful tools in the political debate. This is a reality that must be acknowledged and raises the bar for ILSAs to be reliable and accountable.

4.2. ILSAs: What Do They Tell Us?

Differences between and within Countries
Differences between Countries

International surveys have revealed large differences in student performance between countries which are equivalent to several years of schooling, showing that differences in the quality of education systems are much larger than expected. The difference between the top-performing country and the lowest-performing country is equivalent to more than seven years of schooling according to PISA (OECD, 2016a); in other words, what an eight-year-old has learned in a country with a good-quality education system is roughly equivalent to what a fifteen-year-old knows in a low-performing system. Thus, differences in the quality of education systems mean that students in different countries end compulsory education with a shocking difference in knowledge and skills. These findings show that years of schooling is not a reliable proxy measure for students' levels of knowledge and skills, because how much students learn in a school year differs greatly from country to country. In other words, education systems differ to a large degree in their effectiveness, or productivity, which are measured as learning progress made by students per time unit.

One might also question the usefulness of viewing the educational attainment of adults as the main measure of a country's human capital and talent, since students at the end of any educational stage (including compulsory education, i.e. lower-secondary) will have very different levels of performance in different countries. The worrying conclusion is that, while the expansion of educational opportunities has led to high returns in terms of skills and knowledge in countries with good-quality education systems, universal access to school and improved enrolment rates at higher levels of education have delivered very poor results in terms of human capital growth among low-performers.

As the number of countries participating in ILSAs has increased over time, the top performers have changed with different cycles, but some trends remain very solid. Perhaps the most telling and consistent of them has been the excellent performance among students from East Asia. The first country from the region to participate in international surveys was

Japan, which achieved the very top positions from the beginning: second in mathematics in 1964 (First International Mathematics Study among thirteen-year-olds) and first in the second mathematics study (1980–1982). It also outperformed most participating countries in science from very early on, achieving first in the First Science Study in 1970 for both ten-year-old and fourteen-year-old students (1970 First Science Study) and maintaining the very top position in the next science survey in 1984. As other countries from East Asia joined, they were recognised as top performers: Hong Kong in 1982 in mathematics and science, Singapore and South Korea in science in 1984.

The outstanding levels of performance among East Asian countries became even more apparent in TIMSS 1995, when the four top performers were all from the region: Singapore, Korea, Japan and Hong Kong, both in eighth-grade (out of thirty-nine participating countries) and fourth-grade mathematics (out of twenty-five countries) (Harmon *et al.* 1997). In TIMSS 1999 the best-performing countries in mathematics were Singapore, Korea, Taiwan, Hong Kong, and Japan (out of thirty-eight participants) (Martin *et al.*, 2000; Mullis *et al.*, 2000). These countries remained top performers in mathematics and science in the next cycles of TIMSS and, as other countries from the region joined, most emerged as top performers. In the last cycles (2015 and 2019) the top-performing countries in mathematics (fourth grade and eighth grade) were Singapore, Korea, Hong Kong, Chinese Taipei and Japan (Mullis *et al.*, 2016; Mullis *et al.*, 2020). The gap in performance between this block and other participating countries was substantial. These countries were also among the top performers in science but did not occupy all of the top positions as a block in this subject (Martin *et al.*, 2016; Mullis *et al.*, 2020).

The results in PISA confirm the same trends, but with a slightly different composition of participating countries from East Asia. In the first PISA cycle (2000) Japan and Korea (both OECD members) achieved the top positions in the ranking and remained top performers in successive cycles (OECD, 2001; OECD, 2019c; OECD, 2019d). Hong Kong-China became the top performer when it joined in the next cycle (2003), and also remained among the top performers in the following year (OECD, 2004). Shanghai and Singapore broke the mould from 2009 onwards (OECD, 2010), with Shanghai outperforming all other countries in all three domains in 2009 and 2012 (OECD, 2014c), and Singapore becoming the top performer in all three domains in 2015 (OECD, 2016a). In 2018, China chose to be represented by four provinces (Beijing, Shanghai, Jiansu and Zheijiang, or B-S-J-Z), which outperformed all other countries in all domains (OECD, 2019c). Just to give an idea of the extent to which countries in Asia excel, the top performers in mathematics in PISA 2012 were (in descending order): Shanghai-China, Singapore, Hong Kong-China, Chinese Taipei, Korea, Macao-China and Japan. The difference between Shanghai-China and Peru (the highest and lowest performers) was equivalent to over six years of schooling.

The exceptions from East Asia are countries with considerably lower GDP and levels of investment per student, such as the Philippines and Indonesia, which have tended to performer very poorly, and Thailand and Malaysia, which have performed somewhat better both in TIMSS and PISA.

Perhaps the most meaningful change over time is that most of the countries that have joined these surveys in the last cycles are low- and middle-income countries, so the number of low-performing countries has increased substantially over time and the gap between the top- and lowest-performing countries has enlarged. This is particularly pronounced in PISA, which started as a survey designed mainly for OECD countries and then made a proactive effort to expand to include a much broader range of countries. To exemplify the magnitude of this transformation, suffice it to say that in the first PISA cycle, Mexico (an OECD member) and Brazil were the lowest performers and the only two countries from Latin America. By 2018, ten Latin American countries had joined, and they all performed well below OECD levels, but Mexico outperformed twenty-four other participating countries, such as Philippines, Kosovo, Lebanon and Morocco, despite its own performance not actually having improved.

In many ways, Latin America is the opposite of East Asia, because countries in this region show consistently low levels of performance and little improvement over time. In fact, in all international comparisons Latin American students are among the lowest performing of all participating countries. In PISA 2015, all Latin American countries were ranked significantly below the OECD average (OECD, 2016a). Within this group the highest performer was Chile and the lowest was the

Dominican Republic. The difference in performance between Chile and the OECD average was over one year of schooling, while the difference between the lowest performer (Dominican Republic) and the top performer (Singapore) was over five years of schooling. Furthermore, there is no relationship between years of schooling and student performance across Latin American countries, given that students seem to make little progress in learning in each individual year that they spend at school (Hanushek and Woessmann, 2015). Thus, policies which try to compensate for the low quality of education by adding more years of compulsory schooling will not lead to any significant improvements in student performance.

Do Different ILSAs Tell the same story?

Studies comparing how countries perform in both PISA and TIMSS have shown that country averages are strongly correlated in the two years in which both surveys were conducted simultaneously: 2003 (Wu, 2010) and 2015 (Klieme, 2016). Thus, both surveys seem to provide similar information on how students from different countries perform in mathematics and science. Relatively minor differences can partly be attributed to the design of the surveys, and partly to the fact that all students in TIMSS are in the same grade and have experienced the same years of schooling, while PISA targets fifteen-year-olds irrespective of grade (countries show major differences in the rate of grade repetition and in the age at which compulsory schooling starts) (Wu, 2010).

The general picture that arises from both surveys shows three clusters of countries: East Asian countries are top-performers, European and North American countries together with New Zealand and Australia are mid-performers, and countries in Africa, Latin America and the Near Middle East are poor performers.

Looking in more detail at countries' performances, it seems that East Asian countries perform comparatively better in TIMSS than PISA, while some Nordic and English-speaking countries seem to perform better in PISA than TIMSS (Klieme, 2016; Wu, 2010). Many hypotheses have been put forward to explain these differences, but the most widely accepted suggests that students in East Asian countries may focus more on learning the curricular content, which is more accurately captured by

TIMSS, while in Nordic and English-speaking countries more emphasis is placed on problem solving, which may be better assessed by PISA. A relationship has also been reported between fourth graders' performance in PIRLS 2011 and reading performance in PISA 2018, which are assumed to correspond roughly to the same birth cohort of students (OECD, 2019c). It is worth highlighting that East Asian countries as a group do not outperform countries in Europe and English-speaking countries in reading to the extent they do in mathematics and science.

Differences within Countries

As we have seen, differences between countries in student performance are large, but differences between students within the same country are even larger. In many decentralised countries, major differences between the quality of different regions' education systems are a chief source of inequality. Differences in levels of student performance lead to large differences in the skill levels of the adult population which, in turn, are related to employment levels, economic growth and prosperity (Cheshire *et al.*, 2014; OECD, 2016d; OECD, 2019b).

Many low-performing regions fall into the so-called 'low skills trap' since their labour markets are based on low-skilled jobs and there are few incentives for education systems to become more demanding and efficient; in these contexts students feel that the returns of education are low and tend to leave school as soon as they reach the age at which attendance is no longer compulsory, in many cases before having attained the compulsory education diploma (OECD, 2015c; OECD, 2017b).

These differences have been analysed in more detail in Spain and Italy, since both countries show large regional differences, and most regions have an extended sample in PISA that allows meaningful comparisons. To simplify what is a very complex scenario, in both countries, poorer regions in the south tend to perform badly, while richer regions in the north achieve better student outcomes. However, in Spain some relatively poor regions in the north (Galicia) and the centre (Castilla y León) are the best performers in PISA. Also, as we shall see, there is no relationship at the regional level between the level of investment in education and student outcomes.

Data at the regional level show that the PISA average for Spain hides major differences between regions (Gomendio, 2021; OECD, 2015c; Wert, 2019). Thus, in PISA 2015 the difference between the top-performing region in science (Castilla y León) and the lowest performing region (Andalucía) is the equivalent of more than one year of schooling. Eleven out of the seventeen Spanish regions perform above the OECD average, and six perform below it. In Italy, regional differences are even larger and are equivalent to more than two years of schooling. Thus, mediocre average results at the national level conceal diversity within countries where some regions are actually top performers, while others are low performers according to PISA rankings.

In Spain, rates of grade repetition are very high (2015: 36.1% in Spain vs 13% OECD average) and show large regional differences, with the number of students repeating at least one grade ranging from 25% to 45% (Gomendio, 2021; Wert, 2019). It is important to remember that PISA samples fifteen-year-olds in different grades and that students who repeat a grade perform much worse. To understand the extent to which grade repetition influences PISA scores in Spain, it should be noted that in PISA 2015 the sample included 67.9% of fifteen-year-olds in tenth grade, while 23.4% were one year behind and 8.6% were two years behind (OECD, 2016a). Regional differences in the rate of grade repetition explain to a large extent the variation in student outcomes in PISA. Grade repetition, in turn, is a good proxy for rates of early school leaving. Students who repeat grades are much likelier to drop out of school later on, become NEETs and suffer high rates of unemployment. Thus, there is a clear relationship between regional levels of student performance, differences in rates of grade repetition and early school leaving which, in turn, have a major impact on rates of youth unemployment.

In contrast, in Italy grade repetition rates are lower but truancy rates are higher, and both explain to a large extent differences between regions in PISA scores (Hippe *et al.*, 2018). These large regional differences are by no means unique to Southern Europe. In Canada the difference between the top-performing region (Alberta) and the lowest-performing region (Saskatchewan) is also larger than one year of schooling, while in the United States the level of performance of Massachusetts is so much higher than Puerto Rico that it is equivalent to more than three years of schooling (OECD, 2016a).

In order to understand the level of variation in student performance within countries, it is important to look at the proportion of students that reach different levels of proficiency. International surveys establish thresholds below which students are assumed to have failed to achieve the most basic skills, and above which students can be considered excellent. A comparative analysis with data from seventy-seven countries which participated in different international surveys shows that among top-performing countries the share of students who do not acquire basic skills in mathematics and science is less than 5%, while among low-performing countries the share of functionally illiterate students ranges from 40% to 80% (Hanushek and Woessmann, 2015). On the other hand, the share of excellent student ranges from 10% to 20% among top-performing countries to almost non-existent among low-performing countries. These findings highlight the fact that low-performing countries are not only unable to allow excellent students to reach their full potential, but they also fail to equip a large share of students with the most basic skills.

4.3. ILSAs: Trends Over Time

For most countries, comparing how students perform over time is crucial, since this is the main source of information through which to infer whether the implementation of certain policies has had the expected positive outcomes. Changes over time are also the main focus of political battles, as different political parties engage in debates about which government was responsible for improvements or declines. However, in this crucial aspect ILSAs differ to a large extent, leaving policymakers to decide which survey is more reliable or better-suited to measure the impact of specific policies.

In a nutshell, while PISA finds no significant change over time (2000–2018), both TIMMS and PIRLS detect improvements in most participating countries. To understand the extent to which these surveys diverge in the changes that they detect or fail to detect, we will just provide an overall summary avoiding excessive technicalities.

When the last two cycles of PISA are compared, mean performance for the sixty-three countries that participated in both 2015 and 2018 remained stable in reading, mathematics and science (OECD, 2019c). When changes are analysed separately for participating countries, we find that only four countries improved in reading between 2015 and 2018, while thirteen declined and forty-six remained stable. Furthermore, in twenty-four countries out of the sixty-three, no changes were observed in any of the three domains. When longer periods are considered, there are sixty-five countries that participated both in PISA 2018 and at least one other PISA cycle before PISA 2015. Out of these sixty-five countries, seven countries/economies improved in all three domains, seven declined in all domains, and thirteen showed no changes in any of the three domains. When only OECD countries are considered, PISA detects no changes between 2000 and 2018.

In contrast, data from PIRLS and TIMSS show clear improvements overall. From 2015 until 2019, out of the forty-five countries participating in both cycles in TIMSS (fourth grade mathematics) fourteen improved, only eight declined and twenty-three did not change substantially; among eighth grade students (mathematics), out of thirty-three countries, thirteen improved and only four declined (Mullis *et al.*, 2020). When a longer timeframe is considered (2007–2019), out of twenty-one countries participating in fourth grade mathematics, fourteen improved and none declined, and out of twenty-three countries participating in eighth grade mathematics, sixteen improved and only two declined. Similar patterns of change over time emerged for student performance in science.

In summary, when the last two cycles are considered only 6% of participating countries improve according to PISA, while 40% of participating countries improve in TIMSS. When changes since the first cycle are considered, only 10% of PISA participating countries improve, while 50% of TIMSS participating countries improve (since 1995). Obviously, the participating countries in both surveys are not identical, although there is a substantial degree of overlap. Despite this, the contrast between the flatness in PISA trends and the positive TIMSS and PIRLS trends points to differences between surveys, rather than between participating countries.

This conclusion is supported by evidence from specific countries which shows that the trends over time identified by TIMSS and PISA are strikingly different. Australia and South Korea show a substantial decline over successive cycles in mathematics according to PISA (2003–2018), while they show clear improvements over the same period according to TIMSS (2003–2019). In the case of Chile, Japan, Lithuania and the US, PISA findings show no improvement between 2003 and 2018, while TIMSS reveals major improvements over a similar timeframe (2003–2019). Thus, a pattern emerges in which TIMSS uncovers improvements where PISA fails to detect changes, or TIMSS shows no changes where PISA finds declines. In both cases, TIMSS reveals a more positive evolution over time for many countries than PISA.

Further analyses reveal that until 2011/2012 the number of countries which improved or declined was more or less the same when comparing TIMSS and PISA. However, since 2015 more countries showed declines in PISA and, in some cases, the same countries showed improvements in TIMSS (Klieme, 2016). The conclusion from this study is that the lack of sensitivity to changes shown by PISA is the consequence of a new mode of assessment adopted in PISA 2015. Detailed studies conducted within countries have shown that, in countries such as Germany, the methodological changes implemented in PISA 2015, which include moving from paper to computer-based assessments, as well as changes in the way students' scores were calculated, had a negative impact (Robitzsch et al., 2020). Further changes introduced in 2018 seem to have been even more disruptive, leading to the withdrawal of PISA results for countries such as Spain and Vietnam.

In 2018 PISA introduced substantial changes aimed at improving the sensitivity of the survey at low levels of student performance, in order to deal with the problems generated by the fact that many low- and middle-income countries had joined PISA. Since these countries tended to have poor levels of performance, PISA was of little use beyond stating the obvious. Furthermore, governments faced strong criticism from political opponents when the poor results were made public, so the political costs of engaging with PISA were high, and the benefits limited. This became a constraint to the ambitious targets that PISA had set in terms of increasing the number of participating countries. In an effort to maximise the amount of information that could be provided to the increasing share of low-performing countries, PISA introduced a number of changes to improve its sensitivity at low levels of student performance. However, these changes may have been made at the expense of the consistency required to detect changes over time and, in at least a few countries, at the expense of the reliability of the PISA 2018 results.

In 2018, PISA merged some items from the PISA for Development framework (OECD, 2017c), which was developed to measure low levels of performance among fifteen-year-olds (in and out of school) in low- and middle-income countries. These included a new section on "reading-fluency", which in theory was designed to assess in more detail the reading skills of students in the lower proficiency levels (OECD, 2019c, p. 270).

In practice, this section seemed designed to assess whether students had the cognitive skills to distinguish if short sentences make sense or not, rather than reading fluency. Examples include short sentences such as "airplanes are made of dogs", to which students had to reply 'yes' or 'no'. A significant proportion of students in some countries, such as Spain, gave patterned responses (all 'yes' or all 'no'), but then continued onto more difficult items and responded according to their true level of proficiency (OECD 2019c, Annex A9). Although the section on Spain claims that this problem is unique to this country (OECD, 2019c, p. 208), in a different section the OECD reports that this pattern of behaviour ("straightlining") was also present in over 2% of the high-performing students in at least seven other countries (including top performers such as South Korea) and even higher in countries such as Kazakhstan (6%) and the Dominican Republic (5%) (OECD, 2019c, p. 202). No data are provided on the prevalence of straightlining behaviour among all students. The OECD recognises that it is possible that some students "did not read the instructions carefully" or that "the unusual response format of the reading fluency tasks triggered disengaged response behavior".

Any problems with this initial section may have had major implications for the whole assessment because in 2018 PISA introduced another major change: it was designed for the first time as an "adaptive test". This means that students were assigned to comparatively easy or comparatively difficult stages later on, depending on how they performed at initial stages. This contrasts with PISA 2015 and previous cycles, when the test format did not change over the course of the assessment based on how students had performed at previous stages. It is also worth mentioning that this adaptive testing cannot be used in the paper-based assessments. Thus, any anomalies in the first section improperly labelled as "reading fluency" may have led not only to low scores, but more importantly to mistakes in how students were assigned to easy or difficult tests for the rest of the assessment.

In the case of Spain, the OECD withdrew the results for the main domain (reading) from the official launch of its report in December 2019, after complaints from several regional governments about major problems with the data. This led to unprecedented concerns about the unreliability and unaccountability of PISA (*El Mundo*: "La Comunidad de Madrid pide a la OCDE que retire todo el informe PISA por errores de un calibre considerable: Toda la prueba está contaminada", 29 Nov 2019; *El Mundo*: "Las sombras de PISA: ¿hay que creerse el informe tras los errores detectados?", 2 December 2019; *El País*: "Madrid pide que no se publique ningún dato de PISA porque todo está contaminado", 30 November 2019; *La Razón*: "Madrid llama chapucera a la OCDE por el informe PISA", 2 December 2019). Surprisingly, the OECD then published the same results in July 2020, although it made it clear that the results were not comparable to previous cycles (OECD, 2019c, Annex A9). The OECD claimed that Spanish students were "negatively disposed towards the PISA test and did not try their best to demonstrate their proficiency", thus failing to assume any responsibility. Furthermore, according to the OECD the same results that were initially withdrawn were published months later at the request of the Ministry of Education, generating widespread concern about the OECD giving in to political pressures from a government that wished to use unreliable data to justify the need for an education reform that had been announced well before PISA 2018 data were even available (*El País*: "Falta de interés y cansancio en mitad de los exámenes finales: así explica la OCDE las "anomalías" del informe PISA en España", 23 July 2020; *El Mundo*: "La OCDE atribuye los errores del PISA a la "disposición negativa" de los alumnos españoles por coincidir varios exámenes", 23 July, 2020).

In 2018, the PISA results for a different group of countries were also deemed unreliable or did not meet 'PISA technical standards'.

These included Vietnam, which was praised as a top performer in PISA 2012, and a number of relevant countries such as Hong Kong (China), Netherlands, Portugal, the United Kingdom and the United States. While the results for Vietnam have not been published by the OECD, the government has informed national media of the PISA scores that were provided by the OECD (*Viet Nam News*: "VN gets high scores but not named in PISA 2018 rankings", 6 Dec 2019). The results for the other countries were published by the OECD because they were accepted as "largely comparable" (OECD, 2019c), but raised major concerns (for a detailed analysis of the UK see Jerrim, 2021).

The OECD concludes that the lack of progress detected by PISA is the result of countries not implementing the right policies, by which it means the policies that the OECD recommends (OECD, 2019c). In the words of OECD Education Director, Andreas Schleicher, PISA has:

> become the world's premier yardstick for evaluating the quality, equity and efficiency of school systems, and an influential force in education reform. It has helped policy makers lower the cost of political action by backing difficult decisions with evidence—but it has also raised the political cost of inaction by exposing areas where policy and practice are unsatisfactory. (OECD, 2019c)

In our opinion, it is unfair to make governments responsible for the apparent lack of progress made by countries, given that the OECD has not provided satisfactory explanations about the impact of methodological changes and the reliability of the scores. For many governments, PISA is a high-stakes exam of the kind that PISA itself no longer supports when making recommendations to countries about student assessments. By participating in PISA, governments expose themselves to huge media impact and to the blame games that are so often part of the political debate. This means that the results will have major implications about how particular education policies or reforms are perceived by societies. In exchange, PISA must remain accountable when the results generate reasonable doubts. As an evidence-based organization, the OECD should also examine the possibility that PISA has lost the sensitivity required to detect the changes unveiled by other ILSAs.

Let us assume, just for the sake of the argument, that the OECD is right in that countries have not improved the quality of their education systems because they have failed to implement those policies which, according to PISA, lead to better student outcomes. This would imply that the OECD has not achieved the self-proclaimed status of a global player in education, since countries have not listened to or acted upon the lessons that PISA has to offer (indeed, this is PISA's own conclusion). But there is an even more worrying hypothesis not contemplated by PISA, that those countries which have followed the OECD's recommendations have not noticed improvements in student performance.

In the following section, we will examine in more detail the argument that PISA has substantially changed the balance of costs and benefits derived from implementing education reforms by "backing difficult decisions with evidence". Given the doubts about the reliability of PISA 2018, we will focus mostly on earlier cycles.

4.4. Evidence from ILSAs on Effective Policies

In this section, we will review the evidence available on education policies which has led to improvements in student outcomes, focusing mostly on the data generated by ILSAs. While the OECD has made great efforts to make PISA an "influential force in education reform", the IEA does not focus on drawing conclusions about which policies lead to better outcomes, beyond more specific analyses of the curriculum. Thus, over successive cycles, the number of analyses aimed at identifying which policies are linked to better student outcomes has grown in PISA publications. These include links between student outcomes, which are measured directly, and factors about the school and home environment which are addressed in questionnaires answered by students and principals. Since the OECD advises governments directly and PISA has a substantial media impact, these conclusions have reached many policymakers and have influenced public opinion.

However, PISA statistical analyses are almost exclusively correlations which cannot establish causal effects. To overcome this limitation, a number of researchers have used more sophisticated statistical techniques to more reliably identify causal factors, and many of them have included in their analyses not just PISA data, but also data from other ILSAs. In this section we will review the policy recommendations elaborated by the OECD based on PISA data and analyse how robust the evidence on which they are based is. We will also look at the conclusions of non-OECD researchers who have independently analysed data from ILSAs. We do not intend to review all of the available literature, so we will only refer to studies which are not based on ILSA data when they are required to support or refute specific conclusions. Our main purpose is to assess the robustness of those policy recommendations as evidence-based pieces of advice.

It is important to note that as the number of PISA participating countries has increased over time, some conclusions have changed. It is also worth pointing out that as the diversity of participating countries has increased, the pertinence of extrapolating good practices directly between countries has been questioned.

Investment in Education

Since 2006 PISA has considered the relationship between student outcomes and countries' GDP or investment in education (measured as investment per student from the ages of six to fifteen). Although the percentage of GDP allocated to education is a widely used measure, it is heavily influenced by demographic factors. Thus, a similar percentage of GDP invested in education will result in high investments per student in countries with ageing populations, and low investments per student in countries with larger cohorts of young people. To avoid this confounding factor, we focus on levels of investment per student.

Investment per student can be analysed in purely monetary terms (absolute investment), in monetary terms corrected by purchasing power parity (investment relative to prices in any given country), or in relation to either per capita GDP or per capita public expenditure (investment relative to income or public expenditure). A combination of all three metrics provides quite a complex outlook, not just on how much a country invests in education, but also on how education is prioritised (or not) in public policy.

In 2006 and 2009, no relationship was found between investment in education and student performance (OECD, 2007 and 2010), but as more countries joined, from 2012 to 2015 a clear pattern began to emerge. PISA data show that below a certain threshold (which is established as 50,000 USD, after accounting for purchasing power parities [PPP]), there is a strong positive relationship between investment per student and performance in PISA, which all but disappears above this threshold (OECD, 2014a and 2016a).

Most of the countries below this threshold are low- and middle-income countries that have not reached universal access to education and/or countries where students only spend a few years in school. Therefore, these countries are still at the stage where further investment is needed to build schools, provide them with the necessary resources and hire more teachers. In PISA 2012 and 2015, this included all participating Latin American countries and others such as Thailand, where only between 50% and 70% of fifteen-year-olds are enrolled at school. Still, the fact that all countries below this threshold have low levels of student performance means that, for the share of fifteen-year-olds that remain in school, the quality is very low. This implies that there is a minimum level of investment below which the limited resources are not enough to develop a quality education system. But there seems to be one exception.

The only outlier is Vietnam, a country which, despite having one of the lowest levels of investment per student, achieved PISA scores similar to those of countries above the threshold, such as Germany and Canada, and higher than the United States, Portugal or Sweden. However, while among top-performing countries most, if not all, students are in school at the age of fifteen, in Vietnam less than 50% of fifteen-year-olds are enrolled at school. It is in fact the only top-performing country that has such a small proportion of fifteen-year-olds in school, followed by China (B-S-J-G) where 64% of fifteen-year-olds are in school. It seems reasonable to assume that fifteen-year-olds who have already left school (or never attended in the first place) have a low level of performance, so including these out-of-school students in the sample would dramatically lower the performance of these two countries which PISA regards as top-performers. Furthermore, it raises the question of whether these countries achieve such high performance levels precisely because disadvantaged students or students from rural areas are not integrated into the schooling system (OECD, 2016a).

The most revealing finding is the fact that, above a relatively low level of investment, there is no relationship whatsoever between investment per student and student performance. These countries represent a wide range of levels of investment, from just over 50,000 to almost 200,000

USD (PPP) invested per student between the ages of six and fifteen. Thus, countries that invest up to four times more than others do not achieve better student outcomes. The group of countries which is above this threshold is large and diverse: all of Europe (including the UK), the United States, Canada, Australia, New Zealand and most countries in East Asia. Some countries which are just above the threshold in terms of investment are top performers (such as Estonia), while others invest much more and obtain poor results (such as Luxembourg). And while certain intermediate factors may explain such differences (Estonia is a very homogeneous and egalitarian society; Luxembourg is very unequal and the share of immigrant students, at 55%, is by far the largest among OECD countries) they clearly demonstrate that investment *per se* is no guarantee of success.

Further support for this conclusion comes from studies carried out at a more granular level, which have compared the level of investment per student for different regions within the same country. One of the advantages of these studies is that regions in any one country are more similar to each other in terms of their education system, its institutional structure and the mechanisms that define how it is funded, than different countries participating in large international surveys. Thus, studies which compare regions avoid many of the confounding factors that studies which compare countries encounter. In Spain, where regions decide how much to invest in education from a lump sum transferred by the central government (which covers education, health and social affairs), there are remarkable differences in the level of investment per student between regions: some regions invest twice as much as others. Despite these large differences, there is no relationship between levels of investment in education and student performance (Gomendio, 2021; Wert, 2019).

Another way to analyse the impact of investment on student outcomes is to look at increases or decreases over time in levels of investment, and whether or not they are aligned with student outcomes. In the 2012 cycle, PISA found no relationship between changes in investment between 2003 and 2012 and changes in PISA scores. Although the vast majority of countries significantly increased education investment over this period, many of them experienced a decline in student performance. An independent analysis of changes in expenditure per student from 2000 until 2010 and changes in PISA reading scores from 2000 until 2012 also suggests no relationship between the two (Hanushek and Woessmann, 2015).

Most reviews of the vast amount of work which has analysed in different ways the impact of educational expenditure on student outcomes concludes that this lack of relationship is a very robust finding (Hanushek, 2003; Hanushek and Woessmann, 2011; Woessmann, 2007a). Detailed studies of changes in investment in specific countries over longer periods of time using more sources of data have also failed to show that those changes lead to changes in student outcomes. In the US, there have been dramatic increases in spending per student from 1960 to 2016 (expenditure has more than quadrupled over that period), but student performance has remained rather stable and similar to the OECD average (Hanushek, 2021). In Spain, the education budget doubled between 2000 and 2009, but mediocre student outcomes did not significantly change during this period (Gomendio, 2021; Wert, 2019). Conversely, after the global financial crisis, regions in Spain started to reduce the budgets assigned to education and did not increase them again until 2016; contrary to all expectations, student performance had improved in mathematics and science in TIMSS 2015, further improvements in reading were detected in PIRLS 2016, and PISA 2015 also detected improvements of a lesser magnitude (Gomendio, 2021).

The evidence showing that investment *per se* is unrelated to student outcomes is the most solid evidence available about what does not work in education. These findings contradict the most widely accepted premise in any debate on education: the higher the input (investment) the better the outcome (student performance). They also contradict the reverse premise: that budget cuts in education will inevitably lead to a decline in student outcomes. To explain why the total amount of resources is not a determinant of student outcomes, it has been argued that what is most important is how resources are invested. But what does this mean?

To analyse this claim in more detail, it is important to understand how investment in education is allocated. More than 90% of total expenditure on education is devoted to current expenditure (average across OECD countries) given that education is labour-intensive. In primary and secondary education, around 61% of current expenditure is allocated to funding teachers, about 16% is allocated to compensating other staff and 23% to other expenditure, such as meals and transportation for students (OECD, 2016b). Thus, the majority of resources assigned to education depend on two factors: the number of teachers (which is, in turn, the product of the number of students and the ratio of students per teacher) and teacher salaries. In the next sections, we will analyse evidence of the impact of teacher salaries and class size on student performance.

Teacher Quality and Salaries

It is widely accepted that the success of any education system relies to a large extent on the quality of its teachers. However, the concept has proven to be elusive (Gomendio, 2017). The best evidence comes from longitudinal studies, which have tracked student performance over time. These "value-added analyses" have shown that there are large differences between teachers in terms of classroom outcomes: differences in the progress made by students with weak teachers when compared to those with great teachers may represent as much as one grade (Hanushek, 1992; Hanushek and Rivkin, 2010 and 2012; Rivkin *et al.*, 2005; Rockoff, 2004). In turn, these differences in learning progress thanks to exposure to effective teachers have a large impact on access to higher levels of education (university) and higher income (Chetty *et al.*, 2014). Thus, we know that teachers make a difference, but what makes teachers different?

There are so far no concrete conclusions in the quest to identify which traits make teachers effective. Both PISA´s own analyses and others have found no relationship between traits which are easy to quantify, such as teacher education, certification or professional development, and student outcomes (Chingos and Peterson, 2011; Glewwe *et al.*, 2014; Hanushek and Rivkin, 2006; Hanushek and Woessmann, 2015; Harris and Sass, 2011). This is probably due to the fact that in most countries, teachers hold university degrees and have some form of professional development, but these similarities mask large differences in the training requirements, as well as the quality and content of degrees and in-service training.

According to school principals who participated in PISA 2015, the average student in OECD countries attends a school where 84% of teachers have been fully certified, with some countries reaching over 90% (such as Ireland, Japan and Australia), and a few falling below 60% (such as Mexico and Chile) (Gomendio, 2017). However, the fact that teachers hold university degrees in most countries should not lead to the conclusion that they all have similar levels of knowledge and skills. There are major national differences in terms of how demanding education systems' entry requirements are, and the levels of knowledge and skills that trainee teachers acquire by the end of their degree. While in Latin America, students applying to education degrees generally have lower grades in university entrance exams than students applying to other degrees (Bruns and Luque, 2015), in other countries education degrees are much more selective. It is also important to consider that there are large differences in quality: the skills acquired by university graduates in low-quality systems are lower than those of secondary students in high-quality systems (OECD, 2016d).

Similarly, while some countries have very effective models of professional development, others do not. Most countries follow a rather traditional model offering courses and workshops which do not have any impact on their teaching practices or knowledge levels (Gomendio, 2017; Opfer, 2016). But some top performers have developed very effective models of teacher training and professional development: in Singapore, teachers are entitled to 100 paid hours of professional development each year, and the National Institute of Education, as well as the Academy of Teachers, provides high-quality training for the upskilling of teachers (Gomendio, 2017).

Given the importance of having effective teachers to achieve high levels of student performance, it is surprising how little direct information there is comparing teachers' knowledge and skills in different countries. The one international survey that assessed teachers' knowledge focused on mathematics (TEDS-M, 2008) and showed large differences between countries both in primary and secondary education, with teachers in Singapore and Switzerland reaching the highest scores, and teachers in Chile and Philippines receiving very low scores (Tatto, 2014; Tatto *et al.*, 2012).

It is remarkable that, despite the efforts made by ILSAs to understand effective teaching practices, none has been able to find direct links to student outcomes. The OECD Teaching and Learning International

Survey (TALIS) asks teachers about their working conditions and subjective perceptions of their "effectiveness", but there is no major programme in place to link these findings with student outcomes (as measured by PISA). The so-called TALIS-PISA link has a very limited number of participating countries and does not provide clear-cut results (OECD, 2021a).

The only relevant international comparative analysis in this context has used data from the survey of adult skills (PIAAC), which does not include teachers as a target subpopulation, but does include a small proportion in the general sample. This study has found a strong correlation between the skill levels of teachers (PIAAC data) and student performance (PISA data) across countries (Hanushek et al., 2019). These findings clearly show that teachers' skill levels differ to a large extent, and that these differences do matter, since only highly skilled teachers are able to achieve good student outcomes. They also show that degrees and certificates are not good indicators of the real skill levels of teachers, because of large differences in the quality of those degrees between countries. There are different ways in which teachers in different countries may achieve different skill levels. Since the survey of adult skills (PIAAC) shows that there are large differences between countries in terms of skill levels of adult populations, teachers´ skills could be merely a reflection of these population differences. In other words, teachers may be more skilled in some countries just because they are part of an adult population with higher skill levels.

Alternatively, teachers in different countries may represent different levels of skills within their country's range: in some countries the education system may allow university graduates with relatively low skill levels to become teachers, while more demanding education systems may ensure that (among those with a university degree) only those who have achieved high skill levels can become teachers. This study shows that differences between countries in terms of teachers' skill levels are mainly the result of policy choices on where teachers fall on the spectrum of a country´s university graduates. Out of thirty-one countries included in this analysis, teachers in Finland have the highest skill levels because they score highly amongst Finnish graduates, who already perform higher than many other countries. In contrast, Denmark has a similar skills distribution, but teachers have lower skill levels than other university graduates. If we consider countries where the skill levels of the population are lower, such as Chile, teachers have relatively high skill levels compared to other university graduates, while in Italy, teachers come from the lower range of the skills distribution spectrum.

These findings highlight the importance of establishing mechanisms and incentives to ensure that good candidates are attracted into the teaching profession and that their education and training is demanding. In the policy debate, the conclusion of an influential McKinsey report has now become a *cliché*: "the quality of an educational system cannot exceed the quality of its teachers" (Barber and Mourshed, 2007). This report also concludes that "the top-performing systems recruit their teachers from the top third of each cohort graduate from their school system" (Barber and Mourshed, 2007). However, the findings of a wide-ranging comparative study show that some countries, such as Singapore and South Korea, perform better than expected from the skills of the teaching force, while others such as Sweden or Greece perform worse than expected (Hanushek *et al.*, 2019).

Thus, while teachers have a major impact on student outcomes, other aspects of the education system also play an important role, such as high curricular standards and effective student assessments. The findings also show that in no country do teachers fall at the very top of the national distribution of graduates. However, this finding should be treated with caution, since the PIAAC survey assesses the adult population from the age of sixteen to sixty-four. Countries which have started to implement policies to attract highly skilled graduates into the profession during the last decades may only see the impact of this selective approach among young teachers. If these countries have a large proportion of old teachers included in the overall sample, the effects of new policies may be diluted. Thus, these results do not dispute the fact that in countries like Singapore and Finland, in the last decades only 20% of secondary school students who apply to teacher education programmes are accepted, and all applicants fall within the top range of student performance (Barber and Mourshed, 2007).

Given that only highly skilled teachers can achieve good student outcomes, it is often assumed that high salaries are required to attract good candidates into the teaching profession and to retain the most effective teachers. This has led to a substantial increase in teachers' salaries among OECD countries between 2000 and 2010. For countries for which data are available, teacher salaries continued to increase from 2010 until 2014, despite the financial crisis (OECD, 2016b). Although PISA´s correlations have found no significant relationship between teachers´ salaries and student outcomes, in some cycles it has claimed that they are linked (e.g. OECD, 2013a, Fig. IV.1.10, p. 43), while in others it has recognised that they are not (OECD, 2016b and 2019c), which makes policy recommendations rather confusing. According to PISA 2015, countries such as Finland, Japan or Canada achieve good student outcomes with average teachers´ salaries (relative to per capita GDP), while countries such as the United Arab Emirates, Qatar or Mexico have poor student performance despite higher relative teacher salaries (PISA 2016d, Vol. II, Fig II.6.7). Other studies looking at the relationship between student outcomes and teachers´ salaries have found no clear link (Hanushek and Woessmann, 2015).

It has been suggested that incentives such as performance-related teacher pay may be more important than absolute values. Cross-country studies have indeed found this to be the case, since students have better outcomes in countries where teachers receive performance-related pay, and introducing performance-related pay has improved outcomes in a number of countries (Atkinson *et al.*, 2009; Hanushek and Woessmann, 2015; Podgursky and Springer, 2007; Woessmann, 2011). Performance-related pay could represent an incentive for existing teachers to work harder (referred to as 'effort' margin), or it could make the teaching profession more attractive to candidates who are likely to benefit from such working conditions while making the system more effective at retaining effective teachers (the so-called 'selection' margin).

The evidence seems to suggest that the latter is more important in leading to an improvement in student outcomes. Several studies have shown that, when teachers have high initial salaries but flat trajectories (i.e. small increases thereafter), teaching turns into a low-risk/low-returns profession that is unattractive for highly skilled and ambitious individuals (Bruns and Luque; 2015; Corcoran, Evans and Schwab, 2004; Eide, Goldhaber, and Brewer, 2004; Fredriksson and Ockert, 2007; Hernani-Limarino, 2005; Hoxby and Leigh, 2004). Thus, incentive-based policies that enhance teacher accountability can improve student outcomes at a fraction of the cost of reforms that uniformly increase teacher salaries across the board (Bruns *et al.*, 2011, Bruns and Luque, 2015).

Class Size

Class size explains to a large extent why, beyond a certain threshold, the amount of resources invested in education is unrelated to student outcomes. The measure of reducing class size involves the highest cost, because it requires hiring more teachers, and more often than not the benefits (if any) are small.

It is a widespread assumption that large classes may constrain the degree of attention that teachers may devote to each of their students, that this may lead to less support for struggling students, and overall to poor concentration among students, or even a lack of discipline. As a result, large class sizes are assumed to lead to poor student outcomes. This is such a strong belief that governments have made huge financial investments to decrease class size over time. Between 2005 and 2014, the average class size among OECD countries decreased and, despite the 2008 financial crisis, class size continued to decrease between 2010 and 2014 (OECD, 2016b). As a consequence, the average class size in public schools among OECD countries was twenty-one in primary schools and twenty-three in lower-secondary schools in 2014 (OECD, 2016b).

There have been massive investments to decrease class size over time despite the lack of evidence linking it to student outcomes. No single PISA cycle has shown a significant correlation between the two variables when countries are compared, but the policy recommendations have changed over time. Comparisons within countries in PISA 2015 showed that, in most countries, students in schools with larger classes tend to perform better (OECD, 2016b and 2016c). However, these analyses should be treated with caution because it is unclear how or whether they accounted for the fact that larger class sizes are found in schools in rich neighbourhoods, in urban areas and in public schools.

In the same PISA cycle, a comparison between countries showed no relationship between class size and student performance, since some top performers in East Asia have classes of over thirty-five students (B-S-J-G China, Japan, Chinese Taipei, Macao-China), but some low performers also have similar class sizes (Dominican Republic, Brazil, Mexico or

Turkey). Conversely, countries with class sizes of less than twenty-five students include both top performers such as Estonia or Finland and poor performers such as Greece and Moldova (PISA, 2016d).

Thus, in its 2015 cycle PISA points out that large class sizes may result in positive trade-offs, such as freeing up time for teachers to prepare their lessons, or to engage in peer learning and professional development. They may have other benefits such as exposing many students to high-quality teachers. The OECD concludes that, since large classes lead to excellent performance in schools in East Asia, and across OECD countries students in large classes perform better, "governments should seriously consider the opportunity costs of reducing class size" (OECD, 2016d).

In contrast, the conclusions from PISA 2018 clearly recommend fewer students per class in order to improve outcomes, despite the data showing only weak and statistically insignificant correlations between both variables and the consistent finding that the top-performing systems in PISA have very large class sizes (OECD, 2019e). The mixed messages in the last PISA cycle are probably the result of the addition of many low-performing countries with large class sizes, such as the Philippines, Panama and Saudi Arabia (with around forty to forty-five students per class). This is a clear example of the limitations of correlational approaches, and of the contradictory policy recommendations that follow as the sample of countries changes over time due to the increased participation of low- or middle-income countries which tend to perform poorly.

More robust analyses using data from a variety of ILSAs to compare different countries have found that class size does not impact student performance (Cordero *et al.*, 2018; Hanushek and Woessmann, 2015; Woessmann, 2007; Woessmann and West, 2006), as have inter-regional studies within certain countries (Gomendio, 2021; Wert, 2019). As Nobel Prize winner Michael Kremer bluntly put it, adding "more-of-the-same inputs" (whether teachers, textbooks or other resources) has no impact on student performance (Kremer *et al.*, 2013). This conclusion comes from an experimental (RCT: randomised control trial) study in Kenya in which new teachers were hired on temporary contracts to reduce class size; despite a reduction in class size from eighty-two to forty-four students, those students who were randomly assigned to remain with the same teacher did not show any improvements, while learning did improve among those students placed with new teachers, probably due to the latter's incentive to perform well and prove themselves because of their short-term contracts (Duflo et al., 2015).

This experimental study clearly shows that in education systems where teachers have low skill levels, smaller classrooms will not solve the core problem. Conversely, in high-quality education systems, highly skilled teachers still achieve good student outcomes in large classrooms. This seems to be the case in East Asian countries, but whether this is only related to the fact that teachers are very effective, or to a more complex set of issues such as the high degree of discipline in the classroom, remains to be seen. These findings have led to intense academic disputes, but have had no impact on policy, since most countries have continued to reduce class size by hiring more teachers, despite the low benefits and high costs involved. We will discuss why in the next chapter.

Student Assessments

In most OECD education systems, there are national external standardised assessments for students at the end of lower- or upper-secondary level, or both. Central government is responsible for standardising both lower- and upper-secondary evaluations in most countries, although in decentralised systems this responsibility has been transferred to states/regions (e.g. Belgium, Germany and the US). The results of national assessments are used to obtain degrees and to determine students' entry to a higher grade or education level. In many education systems, the results of upper-secondary examinations are also used to grant access to tertiary institutions or degrees.

Over time PISA has changed its own conclusions on the impact of assessments. In 2006 and 2009, PISA correlations showed that external standardised evaluations had a large and positive impact on student performance, but in subsequent cycles PISA warned against the dangers of "high stakes" exams, i.e. student assessments with academic consequences (OECD, 2007, 2010b and 2013b). Apparently, the reason for this change in policy recommendations is that analyses carried out in later cycles focused on the uses of standardised tests and concluded that they had a negative impact on student performance if they were used to adapt teaching to students' needs, to identify aspects of instruction or the curriculum that could be improved, to make decisions about retaining or promoting students, or to make judgements about teachers' effectiveness (OECD, 2016d, Fig. II.4.24). This leaves the question of what assessments should be used for.

In contrast, other analyses have consistently found that countries which have curriculum-based external exit exams tend to outperform countries without them (Bishop, 1997 and 2006; Hanushek and Woessmann, 2011 and 2015; Woessmann, 2018). In decentralised countries such as Canada and Germany, students perform better in regions with external exit exams, and strong accountability systems in states in the US improve student performance (Bishop, 1999; Graham and Husted, 1993; Hanushek and Woessmann, 2015; Jacob, 2005; Lüdemann, 2011; Piopiunik *et al.*, 2012). These improvements occur because standardised external evaluations are powerful signals for both students and teachers of the level of knowledge and skills expected at the end of each educational stage, allowing them to align their level of effort with these goals, and promoting practices which support students who are struggling to reach these targets. When these evaluations have direct consequences for students they also serve as powerful incentives for them to make the necessary effort to learn, hold teachers and principals accountable for the results, provide the evidence required to evaluate school and classroom practices, and allow policymakers to identify which schools or areas of the education system are performing well and which are falling behind and require improvements (Bishop, 2006; Fuchs and Woessmann, 2007). Student assessments also provide the necessary evidence about learning gains to evaluate whether policy decisions are having the expected positive outcomes across the system.

Critics argue that standardised tests may reinforce the advantages of schools with students from high socio-economic backgrounds, that they may demotivate low-performing students, or that teachers may narrow their teaching to the goals set by them (so-called 'teaching to the test'); these potential negative effects are presumed to be magnified when 'high stakes' (i.e. academic consequences) are linked to exit examinations (Clarke *et al.*, 2000 and 2003; Dee and Jacob, 2006; Dufaux, 2012; Hooge, Burns and Wilkoszewski, 2012; Jacob, 2005; Koretz, 2005; Koretz *et al.*, 1991; Ladd and Walsh, 2002; OECD, 2013b; Papay *et al.*, 2008). While these criticisms highlight the need to design the tests adequately and to apply their results constructively to improve the quality of the education system, they do not provide any evidence that student performance is better when there are no evaluations. Furthermore, 'high stakes' make students and teachers care about exit exams and incentivise the whole education system to achieve the set standards. Diluting the consequences of exams by implementing evaluations with low standards or no academic impact would defeat the purpose of improving student performance. The important question here is: where is the evidence that a lack of evaluation leads to better outcomes or reduces the risk of students from low socio-economic backgrounds dropping out because they fear that they may not reach such ambitious targets?

There are few countries with no evaluations, but they provide a very firm answer. Spain and Greece are exceptions within the EU in that they have not implemented standardised evaluations. In these two cases, the reasons for not doing so are similar: fear of negative consequences outweighs the possibility of positive consequences. Furthermore, in these countries there have been dictatorships in the not-too-distant history which still cast a long shadow over the perceptions of many educational issues. In Spain, as explained in the chapter on ideology, the concept of external student evaluations is immediately associated with those in place during the Franco regime, which were specifically designed as bottlenecks to limit the number of students going to university. Thus, any form of evaluation is assumed to have the goal of segregating students and is perceived as a barrier designed to prevent students from low socio-economic backgrounds from going to university (Gomendio, 2021; Wert, 2019). In Greece, the fact that poor results in evaluations were in the distant past used to dismiss teachers taints any debate on the positive impact of evaluations with the fear of punitive outcomes for teachers (OECD, 2017d).

So, what are the real consequences of not having evaluations? They go far beyond the mediocre performance of students in these countries, because in fact they magnify the effects that they are intended to avoid. Traditionally, Spain and (to a lesser extent) Greece have suffered high rates of early school leaving in relation to other European countries, thus generating the worst form of inequity in any education system. These exceptions to the general rule show that, in the absence of clear and uniform standards for all students, anyone struggling may go unnoticed, and the system lacks incentives to support them because the goals are non-existent. As a consequence, the gap between those students with difficult starting points and others widens as they grow older, until they lose all hope that the education system has anything to offer them and ultimately drop out.

Thus, a lack of standardised evaluations leads to the worst form of segregation for disadvantaged students, and to poor results overall. Some countries in Latin America also lack evaluations, and the arguments for not implementing them are very similar: i.e., as a measure that supposedly protects students from discrimination and teachers from unfair consequences. In South America, this also leads to poor performance among students, large inequities due to the strong impact of family socio-economic background and low quality of teaching (Bruns and Luque, 2015).

Since national evaluations define the same standards for all students, they also minimise the risk of geographical inequalities. Spain is an interesting counterexample, as an unfortunate exception within the EU in that it lacks national and regional standardised external evaluations. As a result, Spain has huge regional disparities in student outcomes (Gomendio, 2021; Wert, 2019). Thus, national standardised evaluations are also the main tool that central governments have to ensure equity, i.e. that students in different regions achieve similar standards (Gomendio, 2017).

The debate surrounding the correct uses of student assessments seems to have had a clear impact since, according to PISA 2018 (OECD, 2019d), there has been a decline in the frequency with which student assessments are used to compare school performance and to make decisions about promoting or retaining students. There has also been a very marked decline in their use in judging teachers' effectiveness.

School Autonomy

Countries with good-quality education systems train highly skilled teachers and professional principals (who tend to enjoy high levels of school autonomy) to ensure that they have the flexibility to make the most appropriate decisions for their student population in terms of curricula, pedagogical methods and allocation of resources.

Based on the fact that high-quality education systems tend to grant schools a high degree of autonomy, PISA makes a general recommendation that countries give more autonomy to schools in order to improve student performance (OECD, 2013a, 2016d and 2019d). Over the cycles, conclusions have focused on those aspects on which decision-making responsibilities should be transferred to schools, such as budgetary resources, curricular content or assessments. More importantly, since 2009 PISA has established a relationship between autonomy and accountability, making it clear that both should go hand-in-hand. This has been the trend in most OECD countries which have increased school autonomy, while at the same time implementing greater accountability in terms of outcomes (student performance). In this way, principals and teachers have increasingly been able to make decisions in their schools that they feel are best-suited to the specific needs of their students. At the same time, regional or central governments have developed more elaborate ways in which to evaluate whether their policy decisions do lead to better student performance and to implement corrective mechanisms if they do not. Other studies also support the conclusion that greater school autonomy will only lead to improved student performance when strong accountability measures are implemented, because this prevents opportunistic decision-making behaviour by agents who may pursue their own interests rather than seeking to improve student performance (Hanushek and Woessmann, 2015; Woessmann, 2007).

This is one of the policy recommendations that has been widely applauded and has become part of the policy package that is recommended to many low-performing countries (OECD, 2018a). This is unfortunate, since there is a large amount of evidence showing that school autonomy will only bring benefits when principals and teachers are prepared to use those responsibilities in an effective way (Hanushek, Link and Woessmann, 2013; Hanushek and Woessmann, 2015). This requires highly skilled teachers and principals who have been trained to take on leadership responsibilities.

In other words, the fact that schools have a large degree of autonomy in countries such as Finland, the Netherlands or Hong Kong does not mean that granting more autonomy to schools in Greece, Turkey or Mexico would improve their results. In fact, it would mean the opposite. Other studies have shown that school autonomy improves student performance in countries with high-quality education systems but has a negative impact upon student performance in developing countries (Hanushek, Link and Woessmann, 2013). This is a classic example of the mistake of extrapolating those practices which work in mature, high-quality education systems and importing them to low-performing systems before they are ready to take the required steps. Improving education systems requires a carefully orchestrated sequence of steps. School autonomy is one of the last steps in that sequence, because it is first necessary to deal with the quality of teachers and to build up principals' capacity to be true leaders.

This kind of policy advice on school autonomy highlights the errors that are often made when features that are common among top-performing systems are transformed into recommendations to low-performing systems without careful attention to the context. School autonomy in itself does not improve student outcomes; necessary preconditions are that teachers have already achieved a high level of skills and principals have been trained as leaders. A closely linked example is the frequent recommendation that teachers should be allowed to innovate. There is evidence for this argument in Finland, where teacher innovation is regarded as one of the key features of the system's success (Gomendio, 2017). But in countries where teachers have not achieved a similar level of skills, they need guidance much more than the freedom to innovate (Barber and Mourshed, 2007). This is why the choice of quality textbooks in low- and middle-income countries is key. Textbooks conversely play a much less significant role in countries where teachers are ready to be creative, innovate and use a wide array of educational resources.

It is surprising that policy recommendations regarding the autonomy of schools and principals tend to avoid advising that principals should be able to choose the teachers that join their schools, and dismiss those that are underperforming. In fact, many education systems have developed mechanisms that allow more senior teachers to choose the school where they work, but do not grant principals the power to select teachers or dismiss low-performing teachers. A few pilot experiments have shown the positive impact of empowering principals to make decisions on the teachers in their schools. In Chicago, principals were allowed to dismiss teachers who they regarded as unsatisfactory while they were on probation; research showed that dismissed teachers did have higher rates of absenteeism, low performance rates and a negative impact on students, thus corroborating principals' capacity to correctly identify low-performing teachers (Jacob, 2012; Jacob and Lefgren, 2008; Jacob and Levitt, 2003). But the findings went further, since absenteeism also decreased among tenured teachers in these schools. It has also been shown that dismissing the lowest 10% of teachers has a substantial impact on student performance (Hanushek, 2009). In any other sector, the importance that leaders attach to their autonomy to build their teams is well-established and is not up for debate. We will discuss possible reasons for the generalised refusal to grant this power to principals in the next chapter.

School Choice: Public vs Private Schools

Most education systems allow the co-existence of different types of schools, which fall into three categories: (*i*) public schools are funded and managed by government; (*ii*) the so-called government-dependent private schools by PISA (also known as charter schools in some countries) are funded by government and managed by NGOs or religious organisations; and (*iii*) private schools are for-profit and are privately owned and run.

When only two broad categories are considered, government-dependent private schools can be considered either public or private. Since the mere existence of these schools is a controversial issue in many countries, it is revealing that supporters tend to label them as 'public' and detractors as 'private'. As a matter of fact, in many analyses PISA considers both charter (government-funded) and private (for-profit) schools as a single category, and compares this too broad and basically heterogeneous category against public schools. The consequences of this are two-fold. First, the analyses are not granular enough to consider in full the three categories and to draw clear conclusions about charter schools, which are the focus of much controversy in some countries. But, second, PISA takes a side about the nature of these schools, supporting the critical stance that some radical advocates of public education express when arguing that public funds should only be allocated to schools run by governments.

In our view, charter schools are funded by governments, who are responsible for ensuring that all citizens can exercise their right to education by providing adequate school places. Thus, they are part of the network of public schools that must ensure that all children have access to quality education and are bound to follow most of the basic rules defined by governments, just like schools managed by governments. Our position in relation to the definition does not in any way convey a bias or prejudice about government-dependent private schools, but we wish to flag it, because it affects how analyses are carried out and conclusions are drawn.

There is great variation among countries in the proportion of students that attend different types of schools and in the extent to which parents can choose the school that they think is most appropriate for their children. Among OECD countries, about 82% of fifteen-year-old students attend public schools, around 14% attend government-dependent private schools, and just over 4% attend private schools (OECD, 2016b, Table II.4.7.). However, these averages hide a large degree of variation between OECD countries. In around half of the countries more than 90% of students attend public schools, and in most countries the proportion of students attending private schools is rather low (ranging between 0% and 10% at most), although there are a few exceptions, such as Japan (28%).

The proportion of students attending government-dependent private schools is over 50% in countries such as Belgium, Chile, Ireland, the Netherlands or the UK. In a few education systems, the vast majority of students attend government-dependent private schools, as is the case in Hong Kong (93.3%) and Macao (China) (83.2%). Among government-dependent private schools, there is also variation in the types of organisations that run schools: across OECD countries 39% of students enrolled in these schools attend schools run by a religious organisation, 53% are in schools run by another non-profit organisation, and 8% attend schools run by a for-profit organisation (OECD, 2016b, Table II.4.7).

In countries such as Belgium and the Netherlands, government-dependent private schools have a long history because they have traditionally been regarded as an effective way for the public education system to offer parents a broad range of choices including, but not limited to, different religious faiths (Fontaine and Urzúa, 2018; Nusche et al., 2015; OECD, 2017e). In this way, historical confrontations about which religion, if any, should be taught at school were solved by allowing different types of schools to co-exist and enabling parents to exert meaningful choices. It has been argued that the principles of freedom of religion paved the way for school choice to become one of the pillars of these education systems (Patrinos, 2011). In other countries, the Church had a historical role in creating the first schools, which were eventually integrated into the public system as government-dependent private schools. This is the case in Ireland and Hong Kong, which have a large proportion of government-dependent private schools, most of which are run by the Catholic Church (Renehan and Williams, 2015; Tan, 1997).

More recently (from the 1990s onwards), a group of countries has introduced reforms aimed at enhancing school choice in order to make the education system more sensitive to the increasingly varied needs of societies which have become more diverse and plural, as well as to enhance quality and stimulate innovation. These countries include New Zealand, Spain, the United Kingdom and the United States. In the United Kingdom, the changes have gone beyond developing a model of government-funded private schools, since Tony Blair's Labour government's introduction of so-called 'academies', which entailed a major change in governance: the responsibility and the funding shifted from local authorities to central government, and new accountability mechanisms were put in place (Adonis, 2012; Wiborg, 2017a). These major changes were originally introduced to tackle the large number of low-performing public schools in the UK. The model was further expanded by consecutive governments and it has grown so rapidly that at present nearly 70% of publicly funded secondary schools are academies.

We will not address in this section the ongoing debate about whether parents should have the right to ensure that they can send their children to schools which are aligned with their views on pedagogical approaches, discipline, values or religious faith, or whether this choice should be limited because it may increase social and cultural segregation (Elacqua, 2012; Levin, Cornelisz and Hanisch-Cerda, 2013; OECD, 2017e; Renzulli and Evans, 2005; Saporito, 2003). Instead, we will focus on whether school choice does improve student performance by stimulating competition and, in doing so, enhancing efficiency and innovation (Chapman and Salokangas, 2012; Jiménez and Paqueo, 1996). Since reforms which have expanded school choice have also implemented new accountability mechanisms which focus on student performance, rather than the traditional focus on inputs and processes, it is important to consider both simultaneously. We will also look at the evidence for the claim that school choice increases inequality because middle-class families tend to exert their choice and send their children to government-funded, privately managed schools, which detract resources from public schools where students from disadvantaged backgrounds tend to remain.

When addressing this issue, PISA tends to group government-funded private schools with private schools and compare this broad group against public schools. Thus, the analyses are not granular enough to compare the three categories and to draw clear conclusions about government-dependent private schools, which are the focus of much controversy. Data from PISA have consistently shown that student performance is better in private schools (OECD, 2010b, 2013a and 2016b). However, after accounting for socio-economic status, in twenty-two education systems students in public schools score higher than students in private schools, while in nine systems they score lower than students in private schools (OECD, 2016d). This reflects differences in the extent to which students are selected by socio-economic status from country to country.

It is worth noting that the percentage of students enrolled in government-dependent private schools is positively correlated with average scores of student performance at the national level, but there is no association with equity (OECD, 2016d). The positive impact of government-dependent private schools on student achievement is correlated with the greater levels of autonomy granted to these schools (OECD, 2016d), combined with better accountability mechanisms based on outputs, i.e. student performance (Nusche *et al.*, 2015). Further analyses have also established that a major causal factor linking school choice and the existence of government-dependent private schools to improved student outcomes is enhanced competition between schools to improve student performance so as to become more attractive to parents (Hanushek and Woessmann, 2015, West and Woessmann 2010; Woessmann, 2007b; Woessmann et al., 2009).

A recurrent theme in the policy debate concerning government-dependent private schools is whether they only achieve better student outcomes because they select students according to socio-economic background or level of performance. Several studies show that this is not necessarily the case. In the case of academies in the UK, recent studies have shown that the conversion of underperforming schools to this new model has led to improvements in the performance of students who were already attending the same school before its transition to the new model, and that the degree of improvement is greater among schools that gained larger degrees of autonomy from the conversion (Eyles and Machin, 2019). This work clearly shows that a dramatic change in the governance and accountability mechanisms of these schools improved the performance of those students who attended them prior to their conversion to academies, thus eliminating the possibility that improved student performance was the result of academies selecting high-performing students. Other studies carried out in charter schools on school admission policies based on 'lotteries' have shown that the performance of pupils who were 'lotteried' into charter schools improved, while the performance of those who were not accepted did not (Abdulkadiroglu et al., 2011; Angrist et al., 2010, 2013 and 2016; Dobbie and Fryer, 2011, 2013 and 2014; Hoxby, Murarka and Kang, 2009).

The data also show that government-dependent private schools tend to be much more cost-effective than public schools, since the former tend to provide education at a lower cost per student than the latter (Hanushek and Woessmann, 2015; Howell and Peterson, 2002). Although the reasons for this are to some extent country-specific, in most cases it is the result of a combination of factors including teachers in government-dependent private schools investing more time in teaching, these schools having larger class sizes, and their principals having more control over the hiring of teachers.

However, when government-dependent private schools receive too little funding from government, they may not be able to afford to provide free education and may instead charge tuition fees or add-on fees for extra-curricular activities. Since this undermines the principle of free school choice, it is important that enough funding is provided by governments and that these schools do not charge additional fees or follow selective admissions policies. Regulatory mechanisms should be implemented to prevent government-dependent private schools from targeting families who can afford to pay for their children's education and/or the best-performing students, since both would lead to a wider inequality gap (OECD, 2017e).

A rather recent phenomenon which seems to be growing fast in some developing countries is the emergence of low-cost private schools, which tend to produce better student outcomes at a much lower cost than public schools (Amjad and MacLeod, 2014; Barber, 2013; Van de Berg *et al.*, 2017).

Student Socio-economic Background

International comparisons have consistently revealed that no education system has been able to prevent the impact of socio-economic background on student performance. The reasons for the strong influence that family background exerts are complex and include many factors, such as the degree of stimulation that children receive from their parents and home environment before they enter school, how much children can learn from their parents own skill levels, the expectations that parents from different backgrounds may have for how their children should perform at school, the quality of the support that parents can provide for their children's learning needs, and the value that they place on education.

According to PISA, the impact of socio-economic background is universal since students from privileged backgrounds perform better than underprivileged students in all countries. However, it is also true that good-quality education systems raise the performance of all students, while even privileged students fail to achieve high levels of performance among low-quality education systems. As a result, PISA comparative data consistently show that students from low socio-economic backgrounds in good-quality education systems outperform privileged students in low-quality education systems (OECD, 2013a and 2016d). These data suggest that high-quality education systems have more power to improve the performance of poor students than low-quality systems' ability to improve rich students' performance. But there is more to the story than this.

The fact that education quality improves the outcomes of all students challenges the widespread assumption that quality is achieved mostly by improving the performance of privileged students, at the expense of students from low socio-economic backgrounds. On the other hand, privileged students in poor-quality education systems cannot completely escape the overall poor levels of performance. To put it bluntly, money cannot overcome the limitations of underperforming education systems, probably because there are features of the system (such as low-quality teachers and curricula, a lack of accountability mechanisms or assessments with low standards) which are pervasive. It also calls into question the argument that equity can only be achieved by lowering standards to ensure that underprivileged students do not fall behind, fail evaluations, drop out, or fail to obtain degrees. In fact, these findings show that the opposite is true, since students from low socio-economic backgrounds perform very well in good-quality education systems, probably because there are compensatory measures that ensure that they get the support that they need in order to achieve high standards.

But the fact remains that, within each country, socio-economic background always has a major impact on student performance. According to PISA 2015, it is the single greatest influencing factor in student performance, when compared to many others (OECD, 2016d). This has been interpreted by some as a depressing sign that none of the education policies that have been implemented so far have allowed disadvantaged students to overcome their 'fate' as low performers. But there is a brighter side to this rather gloomy interpretation. The extent of the impact of family background varies greatly from country to country. There is an intense debate about whether this is because some societies are more equitable than others (and this is also reflected in the outcomes of education systems), or whether some education systems are more effective at diminishing the influence of social and economic inequities. Since we know that some countries, such as Nordic countries, are more equitable than others, such as Latin American countries, it seems reasonable to ask to what extent can education systems be expected to compensate for large social and economic disparities.

Other studies have adopted a more sophisticated approach which has shed light on this difficult issue. What is missing in PISA's comparative data is that, when comparing the performance of students from different percentiles of the socio-economic range, the relative wealth of the country is not considered. It seems obvious that the poorest students in Finland are not as poor as those in Colombia. Furthermore, PISA also fails to take into account the fact that some countries still have not reached universal access to education, and in others a substantial proportion of students drop out of school before they reach fifteen years of age. One clear example of this oversight is Vietnam, a country which was hailed as an outstanding example of equity in PISA 2015, when the fact is that over 50% of the fifteen-year-old population does not attend school and is therefore not even assessed by this survey (OECD 2016 b, Fig. I.6.2). In fact, PISA claims that "the world is no longer divided between rich and well-educated nations and poor and badly educated ones: the 10% most disadvantaged students in Vietnam compare favourably to the average student in the OECD area" (OECD, 2016b, p. 4). It is misleading to make these statements when Vietnam has the lowest proportion of fifteen-year-olds enrolled in school of all PISA participating countries, and it seems reasonable to assume that the other 50% not enrolled in schools come from very poor family backgrounds. This is not an isolated example. In most Latin American countries, a substantial proportion of students are no longer in school by the age of fifteen, so any analyses concerning the impact of socio-economic background seriously underestimate its real impact (OECD, 2016b).

Using a different approach that takes into account both national income and household income, it becomes clear that both matter. The performance of primary students (using data from TIMSS, PIRLS, and two other regional multi-country assessments, Latin American LLECE and African PASEC) is strongly correlated with household income in real, purchasing-power-parity dollars across countries, but students with the same level of household resources have different educational outcomes depending on the wealth of their country of residence (Patel and Sandefur, 2020). The reason for this is that student outcomes are also strongly linked to GDP per capita, except in oil-rich countries where the wealth of the country does not translate into improved student performance (an educational version of the 'curse of the commodities'). As a result, poor students in rich countries perform better than rich students in poor countries. So countries do indeed seem to be divided between rich and well-educated countries and poor and badly educated countries, contrary to the OECD's claim.

This study also provides new insights on the impact of economic inequality within countries. Among countries with high levels of inequity (as measured by the Gini coefficient), the impact of household income on student performance is much greater than among more egalitarian societies. Thus, household income has a greater impact on student performance in countries like Colombia, Brazil or Guatemala than it does in economically equitable societies such as Finland or Norway. It is worth pointing out that economic inequality often goes hand-in-hand with the range of differences in skills of the adult population (OECD, 2016e). While most parents in Finland have high skill levels, only a small proportion of parents in Latin American countries achieve similar skill levels. Thus, the relationship between the degree of inequality and the extent of the impact of parental income is most likely not just about how much parents can invest in education, but also about how much children can learn from their parents and their home environment. This finding has important implications. It suggests that education systems cannot overcome the impact of social and economic inequalities when these are profound.

It also cautions against the risk of establishing causal links between specific education policies and equitable outcomes in egalitarian societies, as well as the risk of assuming that transferring those policies to countries with high levels of inequity will successfully reduce inequality in student outcomes. It seems more likely that social and economic equity permeates education systems which, therefore, do not require major interventions against inequity. The prime example is the widespread assumption that because Finland has equitable education outcomes its policies should be extrapolated to countries where inequality is rampant. It seems more likely that Finland can afford those policies because social and economic inequality is not a major issue. Countries with high levels of economic inequality may require different policies from those with low levels of economic inequality, because they are each addressing completely different challenges. In a context of strong economic and social disparities, students from low socio-economic backgrounds may need additional support, more personalised attention and more flexible pathways, which are not required in more egalitarian societies.

The fact remains that most education systems aim to achieve quality and equity without trade-offs between the two. Equity has two main dimensions: *fairness* implies that personal circumstances (such as gender, socio-economic or migrant status) should not have any major impact on student outcomes; *inclusion* implies ensuring a basic minimum standard of education for all (Field *et al.*, 2007). This two-dimensional definition is important because it asserts the need to prevent students from falling below a certain threshold, and it also avoids claiming that equity requires similar outcomes. Instead, it emphasises the need to minimise the impact on student outcomes of factors which are known to hinder learning.

We will now review the evidence concerning which factors influence equity in outcomes, and which policies seem more effective at enhancing equity.

Dealing with Student Diversity: Is Diversification a Form of Segregation?

A major challenge for education systems is how to deal effectively with the degree of student heterogeneity found within a single grade or classroom, or how to ensure that struggling students are not left behind while allowing those top performers to advance more rapidly. A number of policies have been developed with this aim.

First, many countries have implemented some form of 'ability grouping', which sorts students according to their level of academic performance in different groups or classes at primary and/or lower-secondary level. The term 'ability grouping' includes a wide array of practices. In its most extreme form, students may be sorted into different classes for all subjects (a practice referred to as 'tracking' in English-speaking countries). Softer versions of ability grouping involve students being divided into different groups within the same class for certain subjects.

Second, all countries have differentiated trajectories which students can choose in upper-secondary education, but some countries start much earlier. Traditionally, the major divide has been between academic programmes and vocational education and training (or apprenticeships), but students are also allowed to choose different paths within the academic track. A few countries have also developed several trajectories which represent different combinations of academic and VET-oriented content. The separation of students into academic and VET trajectories is labelled in PISA publications as 'tracking', generating some confusion with extreme forms of ability grouping.

Third, when these practices are not implemented or do not prove efficient enough in reducing student heterogeneity in performance, some students may lag so far behind that they make little progress in one grade; in these extreme cases most education systems resort to grade repetition, which means that these students remain in the same grade for another year in order to allow them to catch up and increase their chances of continuing to make progress in the education system.

There is an intense controversy both among policymakers and academics about the pros and cons of practices which aim to reduce student heterogeneity in academic performance. The clear advantage is that teachers will find it easier to make progress if they teach a group of students with a similar level of performance who can thus follow a similar pace and have similar needs. When teachers are faced with a heterogeneous group of students their efficiency may be compromised, since they must make choices about whether to focus on the low-performers, the top-performers or a bit of both, thus failing to meet the very diverse needs of their students. But opponents claim that any practices which separate students according to performance will harm low-performing students who will not be allowed to learn from their high-achieving peers, thus exacerbating inequality, and in most cases will lead to discrimination based on socio-economic background or immigrant status. From this viewpoint, these practices are seen as non-inclusive and referred to in a derogatory way as 'segregation'. The recommendations from PISA are consistent with this discourse and therefore discourage countries from any practice which aims to reduce student heterogeneity in performance, because it is assumed that it will lead to segregation and will increase inequity. Thus, PISA does not recommend ability grouping, early tracking or grade repetition. Let us look at the evidence.

Is Student Heterogeneity within Classrooms Really a Major Problem in Most Education Systems?

A detailed analysis of the education system in Chile may provide a clue (Fontaine and Urzúa, 2018). According to the reports by principals to the PISA questionnaire, in Chile 70% of students are in classrooms where the main barrier to learning is the heterogeneity in student performance. Further in-depth interviews with teachers in Chile reveal that they feel that this degree of diversity in levels of skills and knowledge within schools and classrooms is the main challenge that they face in their struggle to make progress in learning. It is well-known that social inequity is a major issue in Chile, as well as in many Latin American countries. Therefore, the broader issue is whether the education system can compensate for the inequity that is so prevalent in some societies, and how. The authors conclude that, in the context of such a large degree of social and economic disparities, treating all students equally will generate unequal results which do not reflect merit (Fontaine and Urzúa, 2018). Thus, it is possible that education systems can only deal with such levels of heterogeneity by implementing mechanisms which organise students into groups that reduce performance disparities, so that teachers can be more effective in ensuring learning. In other words, a large degree of heterogeneity in student performance may require the implementation of measures to allow teachers to manage it. But is this challenge unique to countries with large social and economic inequality?

If we dig deeper in the principal reports for PISA 2012, which is a key element of the study in Chile, the results are truly shocking. In 86% of countries (fifty-five out of sixty-four countries) more principals identify "teachers having to teach students of heterogeneous ability levels within the same class" as a bigger obstacle to learning than any of the other ten potential barriers, which include "teachers not being well prepared for classes", "teachers having to teach students of diverse ethnic backgrounds (i.e. language, culture) within the same class" and "teachers' low expectations of students" (OECD, 2013a). Thus, student heterogeneity in terms of ability is regarded as the main barrier to learning in most countries.

Furthermore, in those few countries where principals do not believe that student heterogeneity is the main issue, it is still among the top three barriers. For example, in Australia and Italy, around 35% of principals believe that student heterogeneity is an obstacle to learning which is similar to or slightly higher than the proportion who believe that "staff resisting change" is an obstacle too. Similarly, in the United Kingdom, 14% of principals reported that student heterogeneity is an obstacle to learning, while only a slightly higher proportion believe that "teachers not meeting individual students' needs", "teacher absenteeism" and "staff resisting change" are barriers to learning. In countries where teacher absenteeism is prevalent (e.g. Uruguay and Tunisia), it is cited by a similar proportion of principals as a barrier to learning than student heterogeneity, which gives an idea of the extent to which principals regard the latter as a major problem. In contrast, in many countries where most principals identify student heterogeneity as an obstacle to learning, the distance from other potential barriers tends to be much larger. This is the case in Colombia, Chile, Portugal and Spain, where 70–80% of principals identify student heterogeneity as a barrier to learning, while other potential obstacles are only considered relevant by 25–40% of principals.

These data show that in most countries, most principals believe that student heterogeneity in terms of ability is a major obstacle to learning. This is even the case among top performers such as Finland, Singapore or Hong Kong. The issue of how to allow a heterogeneous classroom to make progress without leaving struggling students behind, or preventing those who excel from continuing to advance, is a universal and major challenge. While providing individualised teaching to each student seems the optimal strategy, this is rarely possible and requires a highly skilled teaching force, plus a combination of technology-enabled resources and technology-savvy teachers, to create a bespoke 'personal learning environment' for every learner. This task is easier said than done. Hence, in most cases teachers may be more effective when student heterogeneity is reduced by separating students into ability groups, different trajectories, or in extreme cases resorting to grade repetition.

Grade Repetition

The approach that PISA adopted when defining its target population is different from other ILSAs in that it assesses fifteen-year-olds irrespective of the actual grade in which they are studying. Thus, PISA evaluates the performance of fifteen-year-old students in the grade corresponding to their age (modal grade), as well as those in lower grades because at some point they have remained in the same grade level for an additional year (either once or several times) due to low academic performance. Only fifteen-year-old students who remain in primary education are excluded from PISA's consideration.

Among OECD countries an average of 11% of students participating in PISA reported that they had repeated a grade at least once, but the variation between countries is very large. In some countries, the rate of grade repetition is below 5% (mainly Nordic countries and countries in East Asia, such as Denmark, Sweden, Finland, Iceland, Estonia, Singapore, Japan and Korea), while in others over 20% of students report having repeated a grade at least once (Spain, Portugal and all Latin American countries participating in PISA 2018). In Colombia over 40% of students have repeated a grade at least once, and in Morocco this figure stands at over 50% (OECD, 2019c).

The OECD refers to grade repetition as "vertical stratification". Students in disadvantaged schools are four times more likely to repeat a grade at least once (20%) than students in advantaged schools (5%), and there is an ongoing debate about whether this is due to the impact of socio-economic background on student performance, or to discrimination against these students because of the low expectations that teachers may have (OECD, 2020c). Unsurprisingly, students who have repeated a grade at least once show substantially lower levels of performance in PISA, corroborating international metrics on the poor academic performance of students who resit a grade. Unsurprisingly too, countries where grade repetition is more prevalent score lower in PISA, since a larger proportion of the fifteen-year-olds in the PISA sample have fallen behind, are in lower grades and show lower levels of performance. Surprisingly, the recommendation that PISA makes based on these findings is that, because students who have repeated a grade perform at a lower level, countries should avoid grade repetition. This misses the point entirely.

First, the almost exclusive use of correlations in PISA is itself problematic because it leads to a well-known statistical problem: 'reverse causality'. When two variables are positively or negatively associated it is not possible to conclude which is the causal factor, or if both are caused by a third factor which has not been included in the analysis. If a correlation is wrongly used to draw conclusions about causality, a common mistake is to identify one of the two variables as the causal factor, when it is actually the other (i.e. reverse causality). This seems to be one of those cases. Grade repetition and low student performance are associated, not because grade repetition lowers student performance, but rather because low student performance leads to grade repetition.

Second, the goal of grade repetition is to allow students who are lagging so far behind that they cannot follow what is being taught to them to catch up and to have a second chance to learn what they could not manage the first time. But they are expected to catch up with their peers during this second go at the same grade, and not with the former peers who have moved on to the next grade. Thus, the expectation that students who remain in lower grades should perform similarly to those who move on to the modal grade is misplaced, since fifteen-year-old students who have repeated a grade have not been exposed to the same curricular content and teachers as students in the modal grade. Thus, while PISA has much to say about the extent to which education systems equip fifteen-year-olds in each country with the required knowledge and skills (irrespective of their grades), and this seems to us a valuable contribution, it cannot draw the conclusion that grade repetition harms performance by comparing students in different grades with the same metrics. The result is obvious, and the expectation is unfounded.

At the individual level, the relevant question is whether grade repetition does allow students who have fallen behind to catch up, and thus whether it improves their chances of progressing in their education. The counterfactual, i.e. whether students lagging behind would have made greater progress if they had been allowed to move onto the next grade, cannot be tested. At the systemic level it is important to understand why grade repetition is more prevalent in some education systems, what the alternatives are, and what the costs and benefits are. Since grade repetition is the consequence of differences in the performance levels of students in the same grade which the education system considers insurmountable, it is important to understand whether such large differences are the consequence of very different starting points in compulsory education, due to differences in socio-economic background, immigrant status, or other factors. Alternatively, large differences between students could be due to the education system's failure to compensate early on for different starting points and to provide the support that struggling students need before it is too late.

According to the information provided by the reports from principals and students to PISA 2012 questionnaires, in many of the countries in which grade repetition is rare, a relatively low proportion of principals think that the main impediment to learning is "teachers having to teach students of heterogeneous ability levels within the same class" (OECD, 2013a and 2014c). This is the case among European countries with low rates of grade repetition such as Denmark, Sweden, Iceland or Estonia, where between 39% and 56% of principals identify student heterogeneity as the main obstacle to learning. However, this is not the case in Japan, where grade repetition is forbidden, despite 72% of principals believing that student heterogeneity is the main barrier to learning. In contrast, among countries with high rates of grade repetition, a larger proportion of principals tend to identify student heterogeneity within the classroom as an obstacle to learning (Spain: 66%, Portugal 68%, Chile 71%, Uruguay 75%, Colombia 80%).

These findings suggest that, while grade repetition is a last-resort mechanism, some countries make more frequent use of it, either because the student population is more heterogeneous than in other countries when they start compulsory education, and/or because alternative mechanisms implemented to deal with student heterogeneity (if any) have not been effective by the time students reach the age of fifteen. Still, grade repetition seems to be an inefficient strategy because students who repeat grades are more likely to drop out of school and regions with higher rates of grade repetition also suffer higher rates of early school leaving and youth unemployment (Gomendio, 2021; Wert, 2019). It has also been suggested that students who repeat a grade develop more negative attitudes towards school (Ikeda and García, 2014; Rumberger and Lim, 2008; Thompson and Cunnigham, 2000; West, 2012), although other studies have found that student retention impacts positively on achievement (Allen *et al.*, 2009). The high costs of grade repetition for the education system compounds its limited efficacy. The total cost of grade repetition can represent 10% or more of some countries' annual national expenditure on primary and secondary education (OECD, 2016b; Wert, 2019).

Grade repetition therefore seems a radical and costly measure, which is not effective because it is quite a rough and crude practice which intends to address low performance after students have fallen dramatically behind by making students go through a whole year of the same curricular content and teaching practices that did not work the first time. However, merely recommending that grade repetition should not occur is not helpful, because it does not address the issue of how to avoid such large differences between students and how to support students who are lagging behind early enough. In other words, education systems need to know what the alternatives are, not just to be told what they should not do.

Spain is a good example of how designing an education system with the theoretical aim of achieving equity has led to one of the least equitable outcomes. It is also very revealing that PISA is blind to the clear signs of inequity in the Spanish system and has reinforced the myth that Spain has sacrificed excellence in the pursuit of equity.

In a nutshell, for decades the Spanish education system has banned all practices that were suspicious of segregating students, such as ability grouping or early tracking. It has also refused to implement external standardised national (or regional) assessments at the end of lower- and upper-secondary education because they are widely regarded as unfairly discriminating against students from poor socio-economic backgrounds. Thus, the education system is not only unable to deal with the diversity of students entering schools, but actually allows differences between students to increase as they age, precisely because it does not allow any differential treatment of students. The lack of assessments in primary education means that students from difficult starting points are not identified early enough and therefore do not get the additional support they need. The lack of standardised evaluations at the end of lower- and upper-secondary education means that there are no clear goals that students need to reach, leaving both students and teachers without any incentives. As a result, students who are struggling do not have ways to catch up, and those who could become top performers are not given the opportunity to excel.

According to PISA, the system is flat, with a small proportion of top-performing students and the same proportion of low performers as the OECD average, which leads to overall mediocre results. This flatness may be wrongly interpreted as reflective of equitable outcomes, since no factor—including socio-economic background—can be identified as having a major impact when levels of performance are uniformly poor. But what PISA fails to detect is that struggling students gradually fall further and further behind until they eventually start repeating grades and ultimately drop out. As a result, the rate of grade repetition in Spain at age fifteen was around 40% from 2000 until 2011, and the rate of early school leaving was 26% in 2011. In conclusion, although it may seem counterintuitive, not implementing practices that allow differential treatment of students according to their academic performance for fear of generating inequality may lead to the worst type of inequality: students being excluded from the education system because they have been lagging behind for years and have lost any motivation or hope that it has something to offer them. These students leave with such low levels of knowledge and skills that they face high levels of unemployment during their lifetimes and are very reluctant to engage in any form of adult learning (Gomendio, 2021; Wert, 2019).

Ability Grouping

Separating students into groups according to their ability for some subjects is the least drastic strategy and, according to PISA, does lead to better student performance without having any negative impact on equity (OECD, 2020c). Among OECD countries, grouping students into different classes is quite common, since 46% of students attend schools whose principal reported this practice, with 38% of students being grouped for some subjects and only 8% for all subjects (OECD, 2016). Ability grouping within classes is even more common: 55% of students attend classes where there is ability grouping, in most cases only for some subjects (50% students) and in a few cases for all subjects (5%). Thus, the benefits of sorting students into more homogeneous groups with varying levels of difficulty seems to improve student performance, while avoiding the potential costs linked to low-performing students being unable to learn from their higher-achieving peers (Collins and Gan, 2013; Garelick, 2013; Zimmer, 2003).

An experimental study in Kenya sheds light on the controversy around the benefits and costs of separating students into different groups according to their academic performance (Duflo, Dupas and Kremer, 2011). The study was carried out in primary schools that hired an additional teacher and were therefore able to split classes into two (average class size was eighty-three before hiring a new teacher). In half of these schools, students were split according to their academic performance (so-called 'tracking' schools), while in the other half students were randomly assigned to each class ('non-tracking' schools).

The results showed that all students benefited from 'tracking' because teachers were able to make more progress when dealing with a more homogeneous class, while no improvements were observed when class size was reduced but students were randomly assigned to each class. The positive impact on reading and numeracy was clear both for top- and low-performing students. Thus, the benefits for low-performing students clearly offset any potential negative effects of being placed with similarly performing peers. Furthermore, these gains persisted after the programme ended, suggesting that students acquired core skills that facilitated learning later on. Interestingly, the students who benefited the most were low-performing students who were assigned to contract teachers, suggesting that more homogeneous ability groupings and teachers with the right incentives achieve larger gains for low-performing students.

This study was conducted in the context of high levels of student heterogeneity, since students in Kenya differ in age, school readiness and support at home. But the study is unique because its experimental approach allows the establishment of causal relationships that contradict established dogmas: class size reduction *per se* did not have a significant impact on student performance, but assigning students to different classes according to their level of academic performance did. It is possible that in countries were student heterogeneity is smaller, other less drastic strategies—such as online resources or ability grouping within classes—may be enough to help teachers deal with student diversity.

The important conclusion is that teachers can make greater progress in learning when diversity in student performance is reduced, and this can be accomplished in different ways. As long as these practices reduce heterogeneity by focusing on levels of performance (rather than socio-economic background or immigrant status), they will not increase inequality, because struggling students will benefit the most. The most effective strategy will depend on the level of student heterogeneity in schools which, in turn, depends on external factors such as the degree of social and economic inequality, differences in the levels of educational attainment and skills among parents, proportion of immigrants, and proportion of students enrolled in pre-school education. In conclusion, ability grouping cannot be universally recommended, because it is strongly context-dependent.

Vocational Education and Training (VET) and Apprenticeships

Most education systems have developed "academic or general" and "vocational education and training or apprenticeship" (VET) programmes at school, with the exception of most English-speaking countries which do not offer differentiated VET programmes in school. The main difference is that academic programmes focus on theoretical knowledge, while VET programmes focus on applied skills which are more closely linked to the needs of the labour market. Thus, while academic programmes have traditionally been the main pathway for those who wish to access university, VET programmes have been designed as a more direct route through which to enter the labour market or to continue into tertiary VET.

Education systems in most OECD countries are 'comprehensive', which means that all students follow the same programme until the end of lower-secondary education. Thus, students choose between the academic and VET programmes at the age of sixteen when they move into upper-secondary education. In a few countries, this choice is made much earlier: at ten years old (Austria and Germany), twelve years old (e.g. Belgium, Netherlands, Switzerland, Singapore) or thirteen years old (e.g. Luxembourg). Most of the countries where the choice is made earlier offer several programmes that cover a range of combinations of theoretical and applied knowledge, while most of the countries where VET is only available in upper-secondary education have two clearly distinguished paths (VET and academic).

Over many cycles PISA has consistently claimed that the performance of fifteen-year-olds in VET programmes is lower than that of students on academic tracks (OECD, 2013a, 2016d and 2020c). This has led to the conclusion that following a VET programme before the end of compulsory education has a negative impact on student performance and increases inequality, because students from low socio-economic backgrounds are more likely to choose or be assigned to VET. Based on these findings, one of PISA's strongest recommendations is that countries should delay the start of VET programmes as the lesser of two evils (OECD, 2013a, 2016d, 2020c). Since this recommendation and its wide acceptance has had a major impact on the education policy debate, it deserves detailed scrutiny here.

The first issue is that, as mentioned before, in most OECD countries the choice between academic and VET programmes does not take place until students enter upper-secondary education, in most cases at the age of sixteen. Since PISA evaluates fifteen-year-olds, in most countries it cannot assess students in VET programmes. To circumvent this problem, PISA includes as VET students those enrolled in what it calls "pre-vocational" programmes. This is grossly misleading since in most countries these programmes are specifically designed for very low-performing students who are deemed unlikely to obtain a lower-secondary degree. Thus, these programmes are normally designed for a tiny minority of students who need an alternative path to obtain a different educational degree. Despite this questionable tactic, the sample sizes for most countries remain very low: in almost half (46%) of the thirty-five OECD countries considered, the percentage of students in pre-vocational or VET programmes is less than 1%, with many countries having no students at all in this category (OECD, 2016d).

It seems questionable that PISA would draw any solid conclusions from such small sample sizes. But in fact, PISA argues that the negative impact of VET (or pre-vocational programmes) on student performance is greatest among some of those countries with the lowest proportion of fifteen-year-olds enrolled in such programmes. Ireland (0.8%), Spain (0.9%) and Georgia (1.7%) are among the five countries for which PISA claims that the negative impact on performance is largest (OECD, 2016d, Fig. II.5.10). To generalise from so-called 'pre-vocational' programmes which are designed for a minority of students with very low levels of performance seems first to be another case of reverse causality, and second to be very misleading, since VET programmes have different designs and objectives and target different students.

It is also a matter of concern that countries that are well-known for having developed VET systems at earlier ages and to a much larger extent than most others are treated in PISA 2015 (OECD, 2016b, Table II.5.14) as having very few students enrolled in such programmes. For example, Germany and Switzerland, which are prime examples of European countries with well-developed VET systems from early ages, only have 2.7% and 9.2% of fifteen-year-old students enrolled in VET according to PISA, a much lower proportion of students than has widely been reported for those countries, even by other OECD publications (OECD, 2020d: over 20% of fifteen to twenty-four-year-olds are enrolled in VET in both countries). Other non-OECD countries which have developed a combination of academic and VET programmes from early ages, such as Singapore, have no students enrolled in VET according to PISA. It is unclear whether these problems are to do with the quality of the data or with how programmes have been classified but, in any case, they do not reliably represent those education systems.

The second issue is that what PISA results actually show is that student performance is lower in VET programmes in half of the countries considered (50%), not significantly different from academic programmes in a third of the countries considered, and higher than that of students in academic programmes in 20% of the countries considered (OECD, 2016d). Thus, fifteen-year-olds enrolled in VET or pre-vocational programmes have lower levels of performance in some countries, but by no means in all countries. In Luxembourg, Switzerland, Japan and most Latin American countries, students in VET programmes perform better than students in academic programmes.

Finally, in some of the countries with the highest rates of enrolment of fifteen-year-old students in VET programmes, such as Austria (71%), Italy (50%) and the Czech Republic (33%), the performance of these students is similar to that of students in academic programmes. Furthemore, if we consider those countries where students can choose between academic and VET programmes at early ages, PISA finds lower performance among VET students in Belgium (twelve years) and the Netherlands (twelve years), no significant difference between academic and VET students in Austria (ten years) and Germany (ten years), and better performance among VET students in Switzerland (twelve years) and Luxembourg (thirteen years) (OECD 2016d).

In conclusion, since PISA assesses the performance of fifteen-year-olds, and in most countries the choice between academic and VET programmes does not take place until upper-secondary education when students are older, this survey cannot properly address the question of whether students enrolled in VET have different levels of performance from those following academic programmes. Even among education systems where differentiation between both types of programmes starts at an early age (i.e. between ten and thirteen years), there is no conclusive evidence that VET students perform worse in PISA. Thus, the widely accepted recommendation that VET should be delayed as much as possible to avoid generating inequalities at early ages seems unfounded.

The point is not whether VET should be delayed in order to postpone any assumed pernicious effects upon student performance as far as possible. The question is which VET models avoid such harmful effects. To understand this, it is necessary to undertake a brief historical overview (Busemeyer and Trampusch, 2011; OECD, 2018b and 2019b).

Traditionally, apprenticeships were designed to train people in a specific set of skills required to enter a trade. In some countries, these apprenticeship systems remain strong and are the responsibility of firms, who set the standards, provide the training, and offer contracts. This is the case for Germany and Switzerland. But in most countries the traditional apprenticeship model declined as education systems expanded and developed vocational education and training programmes which led to educational degrees. Initially, these VET systems were designed as an alternative pathway for students with low academic performance and equipped them with a rather narrow set of technical skills that allowed them to move rapidly into low-skilled manual jobs. In contrast, students with higher academic performance who aspired to get high-quality, well-paid jobs followed the academic track that allowed access to university. However, this model has become obsolete over time since societies have gradually become more educated and a greater proportion of people have higher levels of skills, and thus aspire to obtain high quality jobs. In parallel, most countries have evolved into knowledge economies where many traditional low-skilled jobs have disappeared due to automation and outsourcing, and a greater share of the labour market consists of middle- and high-skilled jobs (OECD, 2020e).

These changes have led to a major transformation of VET systems in many countries (Busemeyer and Trampusch, 2011; OECD, 2019b, 2020d and 2020e). Modern VET systems are designed for students of all levels of performance, since they prepare them to obtain good quality jobs in high demand. In order to become attractive to a broader range of students, these VET programmes equip participants with strong foundation skills so that they can engage in lifelong learning. This is badly needed in rapidly changing labour markets where people can no longer expect to have a 'job for life' and may even need to move from one sector to another. In fact, modern VET systems offer many advantages in dynamic labour markets, since their strong links with the labour market allow them to more easily track the changes taking place (due to the impact of megatrends) and to respond more efficiently by equipping people with the right skill bundles.

Ideally, education systems should create bridges between academic and VET programmes, so that the latter are not regarded as dead ends, and students in both programmes have the possibility of moving into tertiary education. In addition, VET programmes are more effective when they establish links with the labour market by increasing the amount of time that students spend training at work; this will ensure that they acquire the skills required by the labour market, and will avoid the need for VET schools to constantly update equipment in order to track changes taking place in working environments (OECD, 2018b).

The available data clearly show that VET systems represent smoother transitions to the labour market, since upper-secondary VET graduates enjoy higher employment rates than upper-secondary graduates in academic programmes (OECD, 2020d and 2020e). Furthermore, in more than 30% of OECD countries, upper-secondary VET students have similar or higher rates of employability than tertiary graduates (OECD, 2020d), highlighting the fact that a university degree is not the only (or necessarily the best) route to a job. The countries in which secondary VET graduates enjoy higher employment rates tend to have a strong component of work-based learning, as is the case in Austria, Germany, Sweden and Switzerland (OECD, 2020d). Some studies suggest that this advantage weakens over people's lifetimes, possibly because the skillset that VET students acquire becomes obsolete over time, due to technological and structural changes in the labour market (Brunello and Rocco, 2017; Forster *et al.*, 2016; Hanushek *et al.*, 2011 and 2017; Rozer and Bol, 2019). Most VET graduates are employed in middle-skill and low-skill occupations, but 20% of young VET graduates are employed in high-skill occupations (OECD, 2020e). However, this share increases in countries like Germany and Switzerland, where more than one third of VET graduates work in high-skill occupations.

In conclusion, VET systems facilitate school-to-work transitions, resulting in better labour market outcomes for VET graduates compared to general education graduates and, in some countries, even higher than those of tertiary graduates. Countries with strong VET systems which have adapted to the increased demand for high levels of skills from labour markets do ensure that VET graduates work in middle- and high-skills occupations. In parallel, VET systems are effective in reducing dropout rates, since they offer a more applied, work-based learning environment which may be better-suited to students who are not motivated by the academic programmes, or who need to enter the labour market earlier (Henriques *et al.*, 2018; Kulik, 1998). This was clearly the case in Spain, where an education reform which modernised VET and made it more attractive to a wider range of students resulted in a substantial reduction in early school leaving (Gomendio, 2021; Wert, 2019).

4.5. Conclusions

The evidence provided by ILSAs has proven to be very useful for comparing education systems directly and assessing how they evolve over time. These international benchmarks have revealed huge differences in student performance between education systems, raising important questions about which factors improve quality. The vast amount of data generated have allowed quantitative analyses to identify these factors, and have contributed to a much-needed shift in the educational debate from inputs (i.e. investment) to outputs (i.e. student outcomes).

The international surveys differ in the target population, periodicity and methodology, and focus on evaluating student performance in reading, mathematics and science. While PIRLS and TIMSS assess how much students in specific grades in primary and secondary education learn from the curriculum, PISA claims to measure the extent to which fifteen-year-olds (irrespective of grade) have acquired twenty-first century skills and are able to solve unfamiliar problems in knowledge-based societies. Thus, while PIRLS and TIMSS establish clear links with the curriculum taught in school, PISA openly defines a more ambitious target: to measure what fifteen-year-olds can do with the knowledge acquired, irrespective of whether it has been learned at school, at home, or in their social environment. Despite the more tenuous links between what PISA measures and the learning achieved at school, PISA is more policy-oriented and boasts about its impact on education policies.

When ILSAs are compared in terms of national performance, a very consistent picture with clear geographical differences emerges: top performers are countries in East Asia, low performers are mostly low- and middle-income countries in Latin America, Africa and the Near Middle East, and mid-performers are mostly European and North American countries alongside New Zealand and Australia. International surveys also reveal that differences between regions within countries are sometimes larger than differences between countries. Thus, despite their differences, ILSAs seem measure similar features of student performance.

In contrast, there seem to be significant differences between surveys when trends over time are analysed: while PISA claims that between 2000 (first cycle) and 2018 (last cycle) no significant changes in student performance occurred in most participating countries or in OECD countries, both PIRLS and TIMSS reveal a more positive trend of improved performance in many more countries. The divergence between PISA and the other surveys seems to have become more accentuated in 2015 and 2018 when PISA introduced substantial methodological changes to respond to the needs of an increasing number of low- and middle-income participating countries. Thus, in order to provide more granular information to low- and middle-income countries about student performance at the lower end of the range, the reliability and comparability of the information provided to high-income countries may have been sacrificed. This highlights the trade-offs when surveys grow rapidly in terms of participating countries and performance levels to the extent that newcomers, who tend to have low levels of performance, need different types of information in order for the survey to be relevant.

In any case, the fact that according to PISA no significant improvements have taken place after almost two decades represents a failure of its self-proclaimed mission: to identify good practices, to advise governments on which policies should be implemented and, in this way, to enhance student performance all over the world. PISA claims that policymakers are at fault because they have failed to implement such good practices, but before shifting the blame to governments, a detailed analysis of PISA recommendations is required to refute alternative hypotheses. What are the main PISA policy recommendations? Are they consistent and solid?

The most robust conclusion from international surveys is that, above a rather low threshold, levels of investment are unrelated to student performance. This holds true for most participating countries, with the exception of the poorer nations. The lack of association also becomes apparent when regions within countries are compared in terms of investment per student. Similarly, changes in levels of investment over time are unrelated to changes in student performance. In other words, increases in investment do not lead to better student outcomes, and decreases in investment do not lead to declines in student outcomes. It is remarkable that the most solid conclusion has had so little impact on the educational debate, which systematically assumes that there is a causal link between levels of investment and quality. It has been argued that what matters is how resources are invested, rather than the absolute amount.

After universal access to education has been achieved and schools and facilities have been built, which is the case in most countries that participate in ILSAs, investment in education mostly translates into investment in teachers (and other staff). As a result, total investment is the result of two main variables: the number of teachers (which is in turn the result of the number of students and class size) and their salaries. The evidence clearly shows that class size has no impact on student performance but, after making this conclusion clear in all previous cycles, in 2018 PISA does recommend reducing class size for reasons that remain unclear and are not supported by the data provided in this cycle (or any other). Countries in East Asia have very large class sizes because they have made a conscious trade-off: they invest most of their resources in selecting, training and paying a high-quality, albeit reduced, teaching force.

In other countries, this has not been possible because class size is what matters most to unions, since it determines the number of teachers and therefore the size of their membership and ultimately their power. In addition, parents intuitively associate small class sizes with individualised teaching and a higher quality of education. These conflicts of interest have meant a high political cost for increasing or even maintaining class sizes in most countries. This has led to decreases in class size over time, a trend which has major consequences in the medium to long term: resources are needed to pay salaries to a larger number of teachers and therefore selection processes are not as demanding, training is of a lower quality and professional development is poorly elaborated. The dire consequences of this choice are particularly apparent in Latin American countries.

There is also no evidence that teacher salaries are associated with student outcomes, although they need to be above a certain threshold in order to attract good candidates. However, incentives linked to performance do have a positive impact on student learning gains. The additional advantage of such policies is that performance-related pay requires a fraction of the resources that are needed to implement salary increases at the systemic level. However, such incentives are rare.

It is truly remarkable that despite consensus about the relevance of teacher quality to achieve good student outcomes, so little is known about what makes teachers effective. Studies have shown that the impact of a good or bad teacher on student performance is huge, but the precise features that make teachers effective remains unclear to the extent that the OECD refers to this gap in knowledge as "the black box". The main drawback seems to be that few attempts have been made to link student performance to teacher quality, beyond subjective assessments of 'self-efficacy' made by principals and teachers themselves. In addition, those variables which are easy to quantify such as educational degrees or years of experience do not reveal any clear links, since teachers in most countries have university degrees or certificates but the quality differs dramatically from country to country. One exception is a study which finds a strong relationship between the level of basic skills (numeracy and literacy, as measured by PIAAC) of teachers and student performance, and also shows that high levels of skills among teachers are the result of selection processes which target teaching candidates at the top end of their country's skills distribution.

Perhaps the next most robust finding is that external and standardised student assessments (also known as 'exit exams') are linked to higher levels of student performance. However, the consistency of this result sharply contrasts with how PISA recommendations have evolved over time: in the first cycles PISA reached clear conclusions based on comparative evidence about the positive impact of such student assessments, but eventually started to warn against the negative side-effects of high-stakes exams (such as undue pressure on students and teachers with a negative impact on their wellbeing or potential discrimination against disadvantaged students who may lose motivation when faced with ambitious targets) until it shifted to a narrative that supported so-called 'formative assessments' by teachers.

Clearly such assessments are also useful, but there is no reason why they should not be combined with external assessments, which define the same standards for all schools and teachers, are useful tools for detecting struggling students early enough to provide them with effective support, represent clear incentives for all students and teachers to achieve common targets, and provide information about how different schools or regions are performing using the same metrics in case interventions are required. Many analyses using data from PISA and other ILSAs have shown that exit exams have a clear impact on student performance, so it is unclear why PISA's policy recommendation has changed over time.

The evidence from international surveys also shows that giving more autonomy to schools has a positive impact, but only under certain conditions. The first is that greater autonomy leads to better student outcomes when implemented along with accountability measures. Greater school autonomy means many things: principals may have more decision-making power in relation to budget allocation, the degree of specialisation in certain knowledge areas, or the amount of time assigned to different subjects, while teachers may be able to decide which materials they will use, their pedagogical practices, internal assessments, and (to a certain extent) curricular content. But it is surprising that in most countries school autonomy is not what matters the most: principals are rarely able to select their teachers, nor do they have the power to dismiss underperforming teachers. When these responsibilities are transferred to principals and teachers, it is important to evaluate whether they make the right decisions to improve student performance. This is why accountability mechanisms, which in most cases are based on the results of standardised external assessments, should go hand-in-hand with more autonomy.

The second condition for school autonomy to work is that both principals and teachers must have high levels of skills and receive the necessary training before assuming new responsibilities. The evidence indicates that while greater school autonomy has a positive impact when teacher quality is at good levels, it has a negative impact in developing countries where low teacher quality implies that the education system is more efficient if there are stricter guidelines about the curriculum, assessments, and classroom materials. PISA often fails to acknowledge the conditionality attached to granting schools greater autonomy in order to ensure their effectiveness, and makes a universal recommendation in favour of high levels of school autonomy.

The extent to which parents should be able to choose the type of school which they think is best for their children is the subject of much controversy. The complexity of the debate is partly due to the fact that for parental choice to be meaningful, there needs to be a diverse array of schools. Such heterogeneity is achieved mainly through government-funded, privately managed (charter) schools. The mere existence of this type of school is a highly charged political issue in many countries, with supporters arguing that they represent the diversity of values prevalent in modern societies, and detractors claiming that they create even more profound divides in societies where cultural integration remains problematic, and that admission policies tend to favour students from privileged backgrounds, leaving disadvantaged students and migrants overrepresented in public schools.

PISA's analyses cannot contribute to this debate because all of their comparisons lump government-funded, privately managed schools and private schools into a single category. More detailed analyses using data from ILSAs clearly show that competition between different types of schools leads to improvements in student performance and provide very solid evidence that government-funded, privately managed schools are more efficient in the sense that they achieve better outcomes with fewer resources. This is partly because they have more autonomy and more accountability, and principals have much more power to choose their team of teachers, an option which is usually lacking in public schools.

In political, academic and media debates, the most contentious issues have to do with the other dimension of education systems: equity. This is due to the strong ideological component of such debates, as well as the difficulties associated with interpreting different ways of measuring it. While it is widely accepted that quality is measured by student performance, equity is multidimensional, and many different measures have been proposed that actually convey very different types of information. All analyses of data from ILSAs reveal that student socio-economic background is the factor that has the greatest impact on student performance. The impact of family socio-economic background is evident in all countries, but to different extents. The broader and most challenging question is to what extent such differences between countries reflect how egalitarian societies are, or whether they are mainly the result of the implementation of policies that minimise the impact of inequity.

What the data tells us is that good-quality education systems raise the performance of all students, but those in the top percentiles of a country's socio-economic distribution perform better than those in lower percentiles. PISA concludes that since differences between countries in student performance are huge, poor students in good-quality education systems perform better than privileged students in countries with low-quality education systems. But this conclusion fails to take into account the fact that students in the lowest percentiles in rich countries are not as poor as those in the equivalent percentiles in poor countries.

More sophisticated analyses using data from ILSAs have provided a more realistic and complex picture: poor students in rich countries (which tend to have higher-quality education systems) actually perform better than rich students in poor countries. This is probably the consequence of systemic deficiencies, such as low curricular standards, teachers with low levels of skills and poorly designed assessments, which parental resources cannot overcome. These studies also show that in countries with high levels of inequity (as measured by the Gini coefficient) the impact of household income upon student performance is much greater than in more egalitarian societies.

These findings have important implications. They suggest that education systems cannot overcome the impact of social and economic inequalities when these are profound. They also caution against establishing causal links between specific education policies which have been deployed in egalitarian societies with equitable outcomes (since the confounding variable is that high levels of equity are already present in such countries), as well as the risk of assuming that transferring those policies to countries with high levels of inequity will contribute to the reduction of inequality in student outcomes. It seems more likely that social and economic equity permeates education systems which, as a result, do not require major interventions against inequity, while less egalitarian societies face very different challenges that do require specific policies to minimise the impact of inequality.

A major challenge for education systems, which is exacerbated in countries with high levels of inequity, is the question of how to deal effectively with the degree of student heterogeneity found in the same grades and classrooms, and ensure that struggling students are not left behind while those that can become top performers advance at a more rapid pace. In most countries, principals and teachers identify differences between students' levels of performance as the main obstacle to learning, but this challenge is magnified in less egalitarian societies. Thus, a number of policies have been developed to reduce variation in student ability when it compromises learning gains. These include ability grouping, separation of students into academic and vocational tracks, and grade repetition. There is intense controversy both among policymakers and academics about the pros and cons of practices which aim to reduce student heterogeneity in academic performance. The clear advantage is that teachers will find it easier to make progress if they teach a group of students with a similar level of performance who can follow at a similar pace and have similar needs.

When teachers are faced with a heterogeneous group of students, their efficiency may be compromised, since they must make choices about whether to focus on the low-performers, the top-performers or the average students, thus failing to meet the very diverse needs of their students. But opponents claim that any practices which separate students according to performance will harm low-performing students who will not be allowed to learn from their high-achieving peers, thus exacerbating inequality, and in most cases leading to discrimination based on socio-economic background or immigrant status. From this viewpoint, these practices are seen as non-inclusive and are referred to pejoratively as "segregation".

The recommendations from PISA are consistent with this discourse and therefore discourage countries from any practice which aims to reduce heterogeneity in student performance, because it is assumed that this approach will lead to segregation and will increase inequity. Thus, PISA does not recommend ability grouping, early tracking or grade repetition.

These conclusions are not supported by PISA data, so they must be challenged, even if they align with mainstream ideas. In the case of VET, PISA data cannot compare the performance of fifteen-year-olds in academic vs VET programmes because in most countries the latter do not start until the age of sixteen. Thus, the data used to support this conclusion are flimsy at best. In the case of grade repetition, PISA seems to fall into the well-known reverse causality trap: since the performance of students who repeat a grade is lower, grade repetition lowers performance. Obviously, when students repeat a grade it is because their level of performance is much lower, and not the other way round. Finally, conclusions regarding ability grouping suffer from a similar problem: if ability grouping is used more often when student performance levels show huge variation in non-egalitarian societies, the association between the two cannot be used as proof that ability grouping increases inequality.

The available evidence suggests that practices which aim to reduce student heterogeneity and cater for different needs and interests, such as ability grouping and differentiated general and VET programmes, do not decrease student performance. Furthermore, ability grouping seems to benefit low-performing students the most, while VET programmes can decrease early school leaving and equip students with the skills required to obtain middle- and high-skill jobs without compromising their performance. Obviously, any differential treatment of students carries a hidden risk of discrimination. Poorly designed ability grouping could result in students from low socio-economic backgrounds being unfairly assigned to low-performing groups, therefore limiting their chances of making progress. Similarly, old-fashioned VET systems may target students from underprivileged backgrounds and equip them with such a narrow set of skills that they can only aspire to low-skill jobs. The fear that education systems may fall into these traps does not seem to be supported by the evidence. But it is this fear that leads to recommendations to treat all students equally, which is widely regarded as an inclusive strategy.

Contrary to conventional wisdom, the evidence suggests that not allowing any differentiation may lead to inequitable outcomes, at least in some contexts. It seems reasonable to argue that in countries where there are major differences in the skill levels of the population, differentiation is needed to a greater extent than in more uniform societies. This is the case because in societies where parents' abilities, not only in terms of resources but also in terms of skills, differ to a large extent, children born to parents with low skill levels will have a much more difficult starting point when entering compulsory education. In the worst-case scenario, a lack of ability grouping may leave struggling students behind and, if there are no other alternatives, these students will lag further and further behind until they start repeating grades. A lack of alternative learning paths such as VET programmes that could be more attractive to students seeking more practical training may result in high drop-out rates. The needs of disadvantaged students will not be addressed if they receive the same treatment as other students. This may be a safeguard against potential discrimination but it is by no means a solution to the very real problems. When student heterogeneity becomes an obstacle to learning, offering different pathways allows the education system to have the flexibility to adapt to the diverse needs of the student population.

In conclusion, PISA claims that the evidence it provides about good practices lowers the cost of reforms to policymakers and increases the costs of inaction. The detailed review of the evidence provided by

PISA and other ILSAs unfortunately shows that this is not the case for three main reasons: (a) since most good practices are strongly context-dependent, it is difficult for policymakers to understand precisely what applies to their own country; (b) PISA conclusions are based on its own analyses, which are limited to correlations that cannot establish causal links; and (c) some of the conclusions that PISA draws are not supported by strong and objective data.

Nonetheless, data from ILSAs have proven incredibly useful when more sophisticated statistical techniques have been used, but there are only a few robust conclusions about the factors that do or do not have an impact on student performance: investment in education does not equal quality and the corollary is that class size and teacher salaries do not have any impact; teacher quality matters a lot, but a clear understanding of what it entails is still lacking; student assessments and school choice do have a positive impact; school autonomy has a positive impact only in high-quality education systems and when implemented along with accountability mechanisms; policies that minimise student heterogeneity are required in unequal societies, but not in egalitarian societies, where there are higher levels of student uniformity.

5. Does the Evidence Count?

5.1. What Can We Learn from Top-Performing Countries?

When the results from ILSAs are made public, some countries seem surprised to find themselves as top performers, others shocked to realise that they perform worse than they expected, and others still seem oblivious. We will try to understand the different reactions and the lessons learned both from top and low performers. We will start by considering what top performers have taught the rest of the world (and themselves).

Finland

The very first PISA cycle took place in 2000 and included a relatively small number (thirty-one) of mostly OECD countries; thus, the magnitude of the differences found between countries was smaller than in later cycles when a larger number of more diverse countries participated. Finland emerged as the top performer in reading (the main domain), but not in mathematics and science, domains in which Asian countries, such as Japan and Korea, were already top performers (OECD, 2001).

Since then, Finland has become a legend in educational circles, with international organisations, academics, policymakers and unions trying to understand what aspects of its education system have led to such high performance among students. The interest in learning from Finland´s success has grown to such an extent that it has become a common destination for 'education-tourism', with policymakers flocking in to see for themselves how this miracle was achieved. But the truth is that Finland did not expect such high levels of student performance and had difficulty interpreting why it was so successful. A report co-sponsored by the OECD and the Institute for Educational Research at the University of Jyväskylä noted that the PISA results have been both a source of "great joy" and a "somewhat puzzling experience" (Grubb et al., 2005). Thus, all interpretations focused on analysing Finland *after* its success was revealed.

Even the OECD sent teams to Finland to understand what made the education system so successful. The main conclusions from these first visits identified several factors, the most salient of which were comprehensive schooling, teacher quality, school autonomy and commitment to equality (Grubb et al., 2005; Valijarvi et al., 2002). In this way, high levels of equity were seen from the very beginning as a key to success in terms of high student performance (i.e. quality), rather than as a different dimension of the education system. This is somewhat surprising since, according to PISA 2000 results, Finland performed worse in terms of equity than countries such as Japan, Spain, Mexico or Korea (OECD, 2001). We will come back to the links between these two dimensions of the education system, i.e. quality and equity, later.

Most analyses highlighted the fact that teachers in Finland go through a highly selective process to enter university and receive demanding, high-quality training; as a consequence, the teaching profession is highly regarded, teachers are given independence to innovate, and there is a well-functioning system of professional development, although salaries are not high in relation to other countries (Grubb et al., 2005; OECD, 2014a). The fact that teachers in Finland enjoy more independence than in other countries has rapidly led to the idea that "the secret to Finnish education is trust", a conclusion that the OECD maintains to this day, despite Finland's decline in performance after the first PISA cycle (Schleicher, 2018 and 2020).

The teachers' unions rapidly capitalised on this narrative, which became very popular. The Finnish unions argued that the success of the education system was due to the high skills of teachers thanks to the quality of their university education, their level of autonomy and a presumed student-centred approach. They also used the fact that levels of investment and teacher salaries were lower than in other European countries to demand more resources (Rautalin and Pertti, 2007). The emphasis on the quality of teachers obviously minimises the impact of education reforms, as well as the role of families in supporting their children. Thus, while unions were happy to acknowledge the high quality of teachers, they ignored other aspects and used the fact that levels of investment were comparatively low to reinforce their demands, rather than acknowledging that the good results most likely revealed an efficient use of resources.

Over time the narrative about the success of Finland crystallised in an ideal of education systems that most unions supported and that has had a major impact worldwide. This ideal claims first and foremost that teachers should be *trusted*, an attractive turn of phrase which actually means that teachers should not be evaluated for their work and should be given autonomy to decide how and what to teach in exchange for no accountability. In the most extreme cases, it is argued that students should not be evaluated either, except continuously by their own teachers, because there is a risk that student performance could be used to evaluate teachers indirectly. This ideal also encompasses the entire range of so-called 'comprehensive policies', which goes much further than rejecting tracking until the age of sixteen, by denouncing all forms of diversification as segregation. This overstretched interpretation of Finland's success brought the OECD and the unions closer together, since they found common ground in articulating a narrative which saw trust in teachers as paramount for education reforms to prosper. In a book which attempts to give a personal view of the main PISA findings, Andreas Schleicher states:

> policy makers need to build strong support about the aims of education reform and engage stakeholders, especially teachers, in formulating and implementing policy responses [...] many of the countries with the strongest student performance also have strong teachers' unions [...] [...] the higher a country ranks on the PISA league tables, the more likely it is that the country works constructively with its teachers' organizations and treats its teachers as trusted professional partners. (Schleicher, 2018)

The rationale that the most effective way to prevent unions from derailing reforms is to give them a relevant role in designing those reforms is simple and clear, but in our view misses the point entirely, because the vested interests of teacher unions are often not aligned with what is required to improve student performance. The claims of a link between student performance and the strength of unions are not supported by data. Quite the opposite (Moe and Wiborg, 2017). While it is true that myths tend to drift further and further away from hard evidence, because the strength of the narrative at some point becomes more powerful than the evidence itself, it is still surprising that the OECD has fed this narrative in the absence of robust data.

A whole school of thought (and industry) has been created around this notion, so the literature is vast. We will quote just one well-known supporter of this interpretation, who makes crystal-clear the political underpinnings of the trust doctrine:

> this book does not suggest that tougher competition, more data, abolishing teacher unions, opening more charter schools, or employing corporate-world management models in education systems will bring about a resolution to these [education] crises—quite the opposite. The main message of this book is that there is another way to improve education systems, one that is different from the market-based reform ideology [...] it includes improving the teaching force, limiting student testing to a necessary minimum, placing responsibility and trust before accountability, investing in equity in education, and handing over school- and district-level leadership to experienced education professionals (Sahlberg, 2021)

Soon after Finland was identified by PISA as an education "superpower", its performance started to decline, a process which has steadily continued up to the last PISA cycle. Two mutually non-exclusive hypotheses may help us explain the inconsistency in the construction of a powerful narrative around Finland as a role model for the rest of the world, as its actual performance was deteriorating. One possibility is that the explanations of Finland's success in 2000 are either wrong or have gaps because, although the country has continued to implement what were identified as 'good practices', its performance has worsened, mainly due to an increase in the proportion of students performing poorly in all domains, and an increased impact of socio-economic background on student outcomes (Ahonen, 2021; Rautalin, 2018).

Another possibility is that the policies which were effective in a very specific context, i.e. when Finland had a rather uniform population, a deeply egalitarian society and a network of small schools, did not work as the Finnish population became more diverse with the arrival of immigrants (Harju-Luukkainen and McElvany, 2018). If this is the case, then sticking to supposedly good practices while basking in its popularity as an education superpower may have prevented Finland from making the necessary reforms (Rautalin and Pertti, 2007).

One of the problems with the interpretations of causal relationships is that they often do not take into account "time lags" (Oates, 2010). Since PISA assesses fifteen-year-olds, the impact of changes which affect the whole education system (for example, improved teacher training) on student performance at this age may go back as far as ten years which is more or less the amount of time that students have spent in school, although other policies may have a visible impact within a shorter timeframe. Thus, in some cases student performance according to PISA has more to do with the education system that has been in place for the last ten years or longer, than with current models. In Finland the high standards for teaching qualifications were set in 1979, when all teachers (including primary teachers) were required to have a master´s degree, in addition to a undergraduate degree (Ahonen, 2021; Oates, 2015; Sahlgren, 2015). But the roots of the Finnish success in reading may extend further back. In Finland improvements in student performance were mostly the result of reforms that took place in the 1960s, which were centralised, at a time when strong control by the state was exerted over accountability, a detailed national curriculum and the inspection system (Frassinelli, 2006; Oates, 2010 and 2015; Sahlgren, 2015; Simola, 2005). Relaxation of these measures only took place once curriculum coherence and a highly skilled teaching force were in place. The impact of previous education models and of early reforms is strongly supported by evidence from international test scores available before PISA started, which clearly show that Finnish students were performing poorly and below other European countries in 1975, and improved rapidly until 2000, the year when the first PISA cycle took place (Hanushek and Woessmann, 2015).

Another common problem with the interpretation of causal relationships using PISA data is that, as we have seen, it cannot disentangle the impact of schooling from that of family and culture, because of how student performance is assessed. Finnish society has traditionally placed great emphasis on literacy and early family learning plays a very important role (Aunio *et al.*, 2006; Oates, 2010 and 2015; Sahlgren, 2015). In addition, historical and cultural factors have also contributed to the teaching profession's high social status, since teachers have played an important role in the national project to create a Finnish-speaking culture (Sahlgren, 2015).

The inconsistencies in the interpretations of the Finnish success may have to do with the fact that it was a top performer in the very first PISA cycle, when no conclusions had yet been elaborated about good practices. However, the growing disconnect between the country's declining student performance over time and the increasing impact of a narrative focused on comprehensive policies and equity, as well as autonomy and a lack of accountability for teachers, is worrying. To be more precise, although Finland remained a top performer among OECD countries for several cycles, its success was ultimately eclipsed by East Asian countries.

East Asian Countries

As its performance continued to decline, Finland eventually ranked below other OECD countries as well (in PISA 2015 and 2018 Finland ranked fourth and seventh respectively in reading, fifth and sixth respectively in science and thirteenth and sixteenth respectively in mathematics) (OECD, 2016b, 2019c). Given the extraordinary and consistent performance of some regions of China, and countries such as Hong Kong, Japan, Korea, Singapore and Taiwan in all ILSAs, what lessons have been drawn from them, and to what extent are these compatible with the narrative about Finland?

Surprisingly, no comparable narrative to that of Finland has been built around the outstanding and sustained success of this group of countries. Since most of these countries emerged as top performers in other ILSAs well before they joined PISA (see Chapter 4), it is obvious that (as was the case in Finland) they did not improve by adopting the good practices recommended by the OECD.

Some of them, such as Singapore and Korea, do share some historical background with Finland: these countries had few natural resources, so they decided early on to focus on developing their human capital in order to improve their economies and societies. In addition, they were at a turning point in their histories when building a national identity through education was crucial. Their ability to plan in the long term, to implement consistent policies over time, and to adapt them as their education systems gradually improved led to the most successful cases in the history of education reforms.

As the data from the survey of adult skills (PIAAC) shows, adult populations in both Singapore and Korea had very low levels of skills around sixty years ago compared to all OECD countries (OECD, 2016d). However, rapid improvements in their education systems led to the acquisition of increasingly higher levels of skills over time, until younger generations became top performers in those ILSAs in which they participated. Thus, in about fifty years Singapore and Korea had evolved from being the underdogs to becoming the best players in the world. From then on, this group of East Asian countries was seemingly in another galaxy, with student performance continuing to improve with no apparent ceiling while most OECD countries remained stagnant or declined. As expected by educational reformists, improved student outcomes led to such exceptional economic growth and social prosperity that the phenomenon is commonly referred to as the "East Asian Miracle".

The capacity to plan in the long term is due to several factors. Some of these countries are semi-democracies where the same political party has been in power for decades, such as Singapore, or authoritarian regimes without real political competition, such as China. Others are full democracies with different political parties alternating in power, but there seems to be a high degree of consensus ranking education as a top priority, and a shared understanding of which policies lead to better outcomes, with no major ideological divisions on education. In most of these countries, teachers' unions either do not exist or have no real power to veto reforms, shut down schools or mobilise masses against them. The reforms which led to rapid improvements of these education systems started recently and from a pragmatic perspective: an understanding of the power of education to transform societies, as well as to propel economic growth and enhance wellbeing.

The undeniable success of these countries makes it clear that governments can and do get it right, and that the lack of capacity of teachers' unions to veto reforms in order to defend their vested interests greatly facilitates the improvement of education systems. In this respect, the conclusions from countries in East Asia come into conflict with the narrative built around Finland.

Countries in Europe and North America were shocked at first, but then found solace in the idea that differences in success were mainly due to cultural differences, with families in Asia putting undue pressure on their children to achieve high levels of performance through endless hours of rote learning, leading to high levels of stress (Takayama, 2017). This explanation fails to take into account the fact that students in these countries outperform others not just in tasks that require memorising knowledge, but in complex problem-solving, critical thinking and collaborative tasks as well (OECD 2016b, 2019c).

Although it is widely recognised that families in Asia consider their children´s education a high priority, the levels of stress differ substantially between countries. In Korea, access to a few prestigious universities is regarded as crucial for professional success, so there is a huge bottleneck for this level of education, and families respond by sending their children to academies (*hagwon*) (OECD, 2014d) after school hours to enhance their learning opportunities. The government is aware of the pressure on students and has devised a number of policies to try to ameliorate it. However, these are unlikely to work as long as the bottleneck to enter the few top universities continues. In contrast, children in Singapore, Hong Kong or Taiwan are not subject to such high levels of stress and still achieve excellent results. This success seems to come in each instance from a very efficient school system, in addition to the high value that families place on good academic results, which they instil in their children, and the responsibility that students assume for their own performance.

This group of countries clearly shows that education systems can improve very fast when societies as a whole identify education as *the* priority for the future of their country, families become involved in inculcating the value of good educational outcomes in their children, and governments have the capacity to plan in the long term, because the chances that reforms will be blocked are minimised due to the lack of veto power from unions and the absence of profound ideological divides. But the question still remains: given that in this context governments have greater leeway in making decisions, what are the policies that they have put in place?

Education systems in these countries show a great degree of variation, so we will concentrate on the commonalities which are known to have a positive impact on student outcomes. We will also analyse whether the policies that were identified as having a relevant role in the case of Finland have been implemented by countries in East Asia.

We will start with a brief historical account of the education reforms in Singapore and South Korea. This choice is based on the fact that both education systems have improved very rapidly over the last fifty years and successive governments have made the roadmap for each stage explicit, providing a rare and unique opportunity for us to understand which policies were implemented and how they changed over time.

Singapore

In Singapore, the Ministry of Education was first established in 1955 by the colonial government before this city-state became independent (Doraisamy, 1969; Norrudin, 2018). The first step was to provide six years of free primary education to all children, which required a substantial investment in the construction of schools, their equipment, as well as the training and hiring of teachers. Before then, the education system consisted mostly of private schools teaching in Chinese, Tamil and Malay, besides the government-aided mission schools that taught in English. In the second half of the 1950s, the aim was to establish a national education system where all schools would follow the same curriculum, use the same textbooks, have national exams, and be taught via a bilingual model of instruction (English and the mother tongue). To achieve this goal, schools would only receive government funding if they complied with a set of regulations, a rule which was initially rejected by the Chinese schools.

After independence, in the 1970s, new solutions were sought to address the main weaknesses of the system: high drop-out rates in primary and secondary education, and low levels of literacy (Lee, 2008; Norrudin, 2018; Soon, 1988; Turnbull, 2009; Wilson, 1978). The New Education System (NES), introduced in 1979, implemented three tracks both in primary and secondary schools according to students' academic ability, so that they could learn at different paces according to their needs, and maximise their chances of reaching their full potential and obtaining jobs.

This streaming system generated much controversy and was debated in parliament for four days; some feared that children in the low-performing tracks would suffer from reduced access to university, but others supported the measure because they felt it would minimise drop-out rates, which are far worse outcomes. In order to balance the risks and advantages, the system was designed flexibly so that streaming started three to four years after the beginning of primary school, and students who performed better or worse than expected would be moved to other tracks. Two tracks were mostly academic, and the third was entirely vocational. This streaming system was implemented in secondary schools in 1980 and led to huge improvements: the proportion of students who passed the national exams increased from 60% to 90% and drop-out rates decreased both in secondary education (from 36% to 6%) and in primary education (from 29% to 8%). The streaming system has subsequently been modified to ensure that all students reach their full potential. In 2017 it was replaced in primary education with ability grouping. But tracks remain in place today in lower-secondary education, with students following different tracks from the age of twelve, depending on the grades they obtain in the Primary School Leaving Examination (PSLE). The success of this model in an international context is reflected in the fact that Singapore emerged as a top performer in TIMSS in 1995 (Harmon et al., 1997) and has remained a top performer in different ILSAs ever since.

From the very beginning, teacher quality was identified as a priority. The Teachers's Training College was established in 1950 to train primary teachers but later expanded to secondary teachers (Loh and Hu, 2019; Norrudin, 2018). In 1973, it was transformed into the Institute of Education and later became the National Institute of Education, which offers high-quality undergraduate and diploma programmes and professional development for teachers, and carries out research on efficient teaching practices. Professional development has been elaborated to the extent that teachers can opt for different trajectories depending on the career paths available to them: teachers, mentors, principals or policymakers. Such importance is placed on the lifelong learning of teachers that teachers are entitled to 100 paid hours of professional development each year (Bautista et al., 2015). The emphasis on teachers' professional development was taken one step further in 2010, when the Ministry of Education introduced the requirement that every school becomes a 'professional learning community' (PLC), with every teacher participating in learning activities with colleagues (Academy of Singapore Teachers, 2012; Dimmock and Tan, 2015). As a consequence, teachers spend less time in the classroom and more time engaged in collaborative activities with other teachers. In order to free up time for all these activities, class size is larger than in most OECD countries. In other words, there is a clear trade-off between time spent in professional development and class size.

Teachers enjoy high social prestige and receive competitive salaries. The main contribution of this highly skilled teaching force to the design of education policies takes place through direct collaboration with the government: teachers with experience in the classroom may take up positions at the Ministry of Education and, in this way, they participate in improving the education system. Despite the high skills of teachers and principals, they do not enjoy high levels of autonomy in schools and classrooms, in terms of resources, curriculum or assessments, which remain under central control (Dimmock, 2011; Dimmock and Tan, 2015; Gopinathan and Deng, 2006).

Assessments are national, high-stakes examinations at the end of key learning stages (primary fourth and sixth grades, GCE "O" levels in lower-secondary school, and GCE "A" levels in upper-secondary school), and the results are used to place students in different tracks from the age of twelve (Tan, Chow and Goh, 2008). The fact that students follow different pathways from an early age does not prevent them from attaining high levels of performance.

South Korea

The recent history of South Korea is the other main example of an education system which has managed to evolve in a few decades from what was basically an illiterate population to a consistent top performer in all international surveys. In 1945 only 22% of adults were literate, by 1970 adult literacy had increased to 87% and by the late 1980s it was estimated at 93%. South Korea has emerged as a top performer in all international surveys since 1975 (Hanushek and Woessmann, 2015).

In the 1950s, after the Korean War, South Korea was one of the poorest countries in the world, with an economy based largely on agriculture. Today it is the twelfth largest economy and is an advanced, high-tech nation. This amazing rate of economic development was clearly associated with the incredible success of its education system, as is the case in Singapore. The main difference is that while Singapore is a small city-state, South Korea is a large country. Thus, the latter shows that fast improvements in education can also be accomplished at a large scale. Furthermore, rapid improvements in student performance can occur alongside fast expansion of access to education for large numbers of students (Tucker, 2019).

In the 1950s, the decision-making power was taken away from local boards and education became centralised. The Ministry of Education became responsible for the management of schools, allocation of resources, curriculum development, textbook guidelines and teachers, thus concentrating most resources and decision-making power centrally (KEDI, 2015; KICE, 2012; Ministry of Education, 2017and 2020). Under the influence of the US occupation, South Korea adopted a similar structural design: six years of elementary education, six years of secondary education and three years of high school with different tracks from the age of fifteen. In the 1950s, elementary education was made compulsory for all children. Later, in 1985, compulsory education was extended by a further three years, and was eventually extended until the end of lower-secondary education (fifteen years). The expansion of access to schools took place so rapidly that the number of high schools increased from 640 in 1960 to 2,218 in 2007, while the number of students enrolled increased from 273,434 in 1960 to 2.3 million in 1990 (data provided by Ministry of Education Korea, 2017 and 2020).

Teaching is tightly regulated by the government, which sets high standards (Kang and Hong, 2008). Entrance into the teaching profession is highly competitive. As in other East Asian top-performing countries, teachers are recruited from the top third of each cohort of graduates (top 5% in Korea, top 30% in Singapore and Japan) (Barber and Mourshed, 2007). They receive high-quality training at university and must take a very selective Teacher Employment Examination to obtain a tenured position in a public school. Teachers enjoy high salaries and the social prestige that they deserve. Professional development for teachers is well-developed and of a high quality, and good performance at in-service training is linked to promotion and pay rates. After three years on the job, teachers must complete an additional training programme to earn a higher-level Grade I Teacher Certificate. Teachers' unions were illegal until 1999, when a new law allowed their existence as part of the membership negotiations held between South Korea and the OECD.

The national curriculum is updated every ten years by government and there are strong accountability measures in place. All schools' performances in Korean national assessments are publicly available since 2008 (OECD, 2012a, 2014d and 2016b).

Competition over admission into a few top universities is fierce, so families put pressure on their children to achieve high levels of performance and are eager to invest in their children attending the *hagwons* (private academies) (Kim and Lee, 2001 and 2010). When we visited Korea, we learned that the government had implemented curfews at ten p.m. to prevent students from spending long hours studying at night, although students in *hagwons* became quite effective at hiding when a patrol turned up. Another measure introduced by the government in a further attempt to lower levels of stress and promote 'happy education' is the 'free semester', when students do not have to take exams. In order to relieve the pressure on students, in the 1980s the Ministry of Education implemented reforms aimed at increasing university enrolment. As a result, although secondary schools do offer vocational tracks, the high return of attendance top universities led to a dramatic expansion of admissions and a high rate of university enrolment (Park and Jang, 2014). Between the early 1980s and the mid-2000s the tertiary gross enrolment ratio increased fivefold, with the number of students increasing from 539,000 in 1980 to 3.3 million in 2015.

However, this strategy backfired, when the financial crisis of 2008 led to large numbers of young graduates losing their jobs. According to a survey from the Korea Research Institute for Vocational Education and Training, in 2013 nearly four in every ten young workers were overeducated. As the returns of a university degree declined, so did the number of students attending university, while the government started to promote vocational education and training as well as apprenticeships.

Finland and East Asian Countries: Similarities and Differences

The examples of Singapore and South Korea reveal how education systems can improve, rapidly transforming illiterate populations into the world's top-performing students. It is beyond the scope of this book to provide a detailed description of the education systems in other top-performing East Asian countries, which have a longer and more complex history. From what we have seen so far, these countries share one clear feature with Finland: an outstanding teaching force, which is the result of highly selective processes to ensure that the best-performing students enter university to study education, that they receive high-quality training (on subject content as well as pedagogy), that they are evaluated for their performance, and that they continue to upskill and reskill through professional development. This conclusion can be safely expanded to other East Asian countries. As is the case in Finland, in this group of countries teachers enjoy high social prestige. But this is where the similarities seemingly end.

Contrary to the myth of Finnish success, trust in teachers in East Asia does not mean that the system is blind to what teachers do, or that most responsibilities are transferred. In fact, in all East Asian countries teachers are evaluated based on the results of their students in assessments, to a much larger extent than in most OECD countries (OECD, 2019d). Thus, teachers are trusted because they are highly skilled and their teaching practices are very effective. In addition, high curricular standards are set by government, as well as demanding assessments for students, both of which tend to be under strong central control.

While individual teachers can play a significant role in collaborating with government to continuously improve education systems, unions play either little or no role. This is also the case in Japan, perhaps the East Asian country where unions have been present for longest, although they face stricter constraints than in Western democracies. As local public officials, they are denied the right to strike and the right to collective bargaining (Araki, 2002; Aspinall, 2017). It is therefore a fact that in East Asian countries education systems have rapidly improved their performance in the absence of major opposition from unions, but with the collaboration of teachers.

If we analyse in detail other aspects of the Finnish myth, we find further discrepancies. According to this narrative, one of the main elements in the Finnish success is school autonomy. However, teachers and principals in Singapore and China have low levels of autonomy in the use of resources, curricula, assessment and appointment of teachers, and Korea and Japan also have low levels of autonomy in terms of use of resources; in contrast, Hong Kong and Taiwan have high levels of autonomy in all of the above aspects, which is probably because, for historical reasons, many of the schools are privately managed (OECD, 2016c; Tan, 1997). Thus, high levels of school and teacher autonomy do not seem to be a necessary prerequisite for becoming a top performer, even in a country with an exceedingly high-skilled teaching force, like Singapore.

The other major element of the Finnish success narrative is comprehensive education and equity. The case of Singapore shows that ability grouping in primary education and early tracking into different academic/vocational trajectories from the start of lower-secondary education has not in any way prevented rapid educational progress, to the extent that the country has become a top performer in just a few decades. In fact, the case of Singapore shows that on this journey, streaming has been very efficient in preventing drop-out rates and allowing all students to progress at their own pace, while avoiding grade repetition, which is non-existent or very rare in all East Asian top performers.

This case clearly shows that the potential risks associated with early tracking can be prevented by achieving a good balance between the different tracks and student performance, allowing the flexibility to move to other tracks when a student's level of performance changes, and ensuring that all tracks equip students with solid foundations. In fact, when early tracking is designed in this way, the data from Singapore obtained by PISA show that it does allow all students to reach their full potential, leading to a high proportion of top performers and very few low performers.

Finally, the Finnish narrative claims that comprehensive schooling has led not only to excellent student performance, but more importantly to equity: uniformly high student performance. If these factors are linked, then we should expect much lower equity among East Asian countries and, in particular, Singapore, which follows a radically different model of early tracking. Once again, the data from East Asian countries clash with the Finnish narrative. As we have already discussed, equity has two dimensions: inclusion, which refers to the proportion of students that fail to reach basic levels of attainment, and fairness, which refers to the impact of socio-economic background (or other personal factors) on student performance. In terms of inclusion, according to data from PISA 2015, the proportion of students who fail to achieve Level 2 (defined as the minimum level of achievement required) is equally low in Singapore (10%) and Finland (11%), and is almost half what it is in OECD countries (OECD average: 21%) in most East Asian top performers (OECD, 2016b and 2016c).

Thus, neither the early tracking in Singapore, nor the lower levels of school and teacher autonomy in other East Asian countries, result in a larger proportion of students failing to achieve basic proficiency levels. Quite the opposite, in fact. In terms of fairness, the impact of family background on student performance is slightly higher in Singapore and China than in Finland, but the remaining East Asian countries show similar or lower values than the OECD average (OECD, 2016b and 2016c). Thus, rapid improvements have been achieved without sacrificing equity, but comprehensive policies and teacher autonomy are not significant ingredients in the recipe of success in East Asia.

In the face of clear contradictions between the policies implemented by top-performing countries in East Asia and the narrative built around the comparatively short-lived success of Finland, the OECD has continued to support the narrative on the virtues of comprehensive education, school autonomy and trust in teachers. This seems surprising, given that, according to PISA, Singapore outperforms Finland in some domains by the equivalent of more than one year of schooling, which is no small difference (OECD, 2016b). This stubbornness has led to a lack of transparency on the data from China and other countries, for the sake of preserving a particular narrative.

China and Vietnam: How to Read the PISA Data

Before we move on to the next section, we feel that a note of caution concerning PISA data from China and Vietnam is needed. China participated for the first time in 2009, and was only represented by Shanghai, one of the wealthiest cities in the country. The fact that Shanghai-China emerged as the top performer shocked many Western countries, and raised concerns about China outperforming other countries in terms of human capital development similar to the fears that Sputnik had sparked years before about Russia's unexpected success in space technology. The OECD's Secretary General placed a huge emphasis on this result:

> the stunning success of Shanghai-China, which tops every league table in this assessment by a clear margin, shows what can be achieved with moderate economic resources and in a diverse social context. In mathematics, more than a quarter of Shanghai-China's 15-year-olds can conceptualise, generalise, and creatively use information based on their own investigations and modelling of complex problem situations. They can apply insight and understanding and develop new approaches and strategies when addressing novel situations. In the OECD area, just 3% of students reach that level of performance (OECD, 2010a)

According to PISA, Shanghai was also a top performer in terms of equity, since their analyses seemed to show that the impact of socio-economic background was small. In fact, nothing seemed to have a negative impact on the performance of Chinese students; the sample had a very large proportion of top-performing students and almost no low-performing students when compared to other countries. The success of Shanghai, which was attributed to China as a whole, continued in PISA 2012, but critics argued that a sample from one of the wealthiest cities was not representative and could not be compared to samples from other countries which included rich and poor regions, as well as rural and urban areas (Loveless, 2013a, 2013b, and 2014).

It was also argued that the PISA sample did not include students whose families had emigrated from rural areas to Shanghai because they were not allowed in secondary schools following the *hukou* system which restricts rural migrants´ access to urban social services including education and health (Roberts, 2013; Tao *et al.*, 2013). According to *The Economist* ("China's left-behind", 17 October 2015; "The plight of China's 'left-behind' children", 10 April 2021), around 270 million Chinese workers have moved from their villages to rural areas looking for work; most do not take their children with them. The Chinese call these children the "left-behind children" and it is estimated that in 2010 there were 61 million children under the age of seventeen left behind in rural areas, with most of them being cared for by grandparents or more distant relatives. In addition, 36 million children had moved with their families to cities, but the *hukou* system denies them access to state schools or health care, so they are also neglected.

As a response to these criticisms, in 2015 the sample was expanded to include Beijing, Shanghai, Jiangsu and Guangdong (B-S-J-G), but the results dropped and China was outperformed by other countries (ranking tenth in science) (OECD, 2016b). For reasons that the OECD has not explained, the sample for China was modified again in the next cycle, since Guangdong was substituted with Zhejiang, a change which propelled China (this time with a different combination of samples from B-S-J-Z) to the top position in the ranking (OECD, 2019c). Once again, the OECD made an effort to highlight the success of "China":

> Among its many findings, our PISA 2018 assessment shows that 15-year-old students in the four provinces/municipalities of China that participated in the study—Beijing, Shanghai, Jiangsu and Zhejiang—outperformed by a large margin their peers from all of the other 78 participating education systems, in mathematics and science. Moreover, the 10% most disadvantaged students in these four jurisdictions also showed better reading skills than those of the average student in OECD countries, as well as skills similar to the 10% most advantaged students in some of these countries (OECD, 2019c)

Of course, the main problem with these results is that, in contrast to what happens in other countries, the PISA sample does not seem representative in any way of the whole country. Furthermore, the lack of transparency has led to serious concerns about whether the samples are even representative of these regions, or whether they leave out immigrant students and students from lower socio-economic backgrounds (Loveless, 2019). To understand the scale of the problem it is worth taking into account that in PISA 2018 the sample size in China included just 12,058 students and 362 schools, which represents less than 1% of the potential sample (a total of 1,221,747 fifteen-year-olds in those regions according to PISA); the sample size was much larger in many countries with comparably tiny population sizes, for instance in Spain the sample size was 35,943 students (7.9% of all fifteen-year-olds).

Furthermore, in PISA 2015 the proportion of fifteen-year-old students in B-S-J-G China enrolled in school was 64%; thus, 36% of students were not enrolled either because they had left school at an earlier age or because they never attended school. It seems reasonable to assume that these students were either from rural areas or disadvantaged backgrounds.

A sample of students with such limitations is not representative of the performance of a country, as we know from the large degree of regional variation that exists in all countries that have measured it. In this case, the sample in China has changed over time in what can only be interpreted as an effort to reach the top position through a focus on cities or regions which enjoy higher levels of wealth than the rest of the country. It seems no coincidence that the provinces included in PISA 2018 are those with the highest levels of GDP per capita; for instance Guangdong was replaced by Zhejiang which has a higher GDP per capita. Thus, PISA is choosing to assess only wealthy coastal regions in China, disregarding the fact that rural areas are much poorer, to the extent that children suffer from severe health issues (Loveless, 2019; *The Economist*, 2015 and 2021). But even in this biased and privileged sample, more than a third of fifteen-year-olds were not enrolled in school. Thus, to draw any conclusions about China being a top-performing country and to try to embellish the story by adding that it also enjoys high levels of equity seems totally unfounded. The insistence on stating that the supposedly "most disadvantaged children in China" outperform advantaged students in OECD countries shows a craving for headlines which is incompatible with robust evidence. Similarly, the OECD's Secretary General, speaking on Vietnam in the 2015 cycle, stated:

> the data also show that the world is no longer divided between rich and well-educated nations and poor and badly educated ones: the 10% most disadvantaged students in Vietnam compare favourably to the average student in the OECD area (PISA, 2016a).

Here again the problem is that more than 50% of fifteen-year-olds were not enrolled in school, strongly suggesting that the most disadvantaged students were not included in the PISA sample (OECD, 2016b). To add to the lack of transparency, data from Vietnam were not made public by the OECD in the next cycle (2018), although the authorities did receive the data from the OECD and published them in national media.

The OECD has gone to great lengths in its effort to try to build a positive narrative around the Chinese educational system: in a Country Note summarising the results for China in PISA 2015, it praises the fact that "Admission to upper secondary school is not based on a single entrance exam. More emphasis has been placed on comprehensive evaluations, including students' *'ideological and moral qualities'* (OECD, 2016f). While many countries have decided to balance the results of high-stakes exams with the work that students have carried out during the previous year(s), it is in our view inadmissible that the OECD would regard as good practice the Chinese authorities' emphasis on ideological obedience to an authoritarian regime as a prerequisite for education.

5.2. What Can We Learn from Low Performers? The Latin American Story

Latin America has followed the opposite path to that of East Asia. In 1960 the region had higher schooling levels and the average income exceeded that in East Asia (Hanushek and Woessmann, 2015). It seems shocking that, despite this clear advantage, Latin America today lags so far behind East Asia in terms of human capital, economic growth rates and per capita income (Hanushek and Woessmann, 2015).

The answer to this puzzle is that while Latin America has made a huge effort in terms of increasing enrolment rates, years of schooling and even access to tertiary education, the quality of education systems in the region remains very poor. Economic growth (measured as regional annual growth rates) is closely linked to knowledge capital but only when measured as student performance in ILSAs, which is a reliable indicator of the level of knowledge and skills in the population. However, economic growth is unrelated to years of schooling, because it is not a good index of human capital in countries where education systems are of poor quality. Since students in Latin America perform badly in ILSAs, the failure to develop its human capital explains why Latin America went from being a relatively rich region fifty years ago to a relatively poor one today (Hanushek and Woessmann, 2015).

When the average performance in different ILSAs is calculated for seventy-seven countries for the period stretching from 1964 to 2003, the sixteen Latin American countries included in the sample consistently underperform, not only compared to top-performing East Asian countries, but also to European and Commonwealth OECD countries (Hanushek and Woessmann, 2015). According to this analysis, the top-performing country in Latin America is Uruguay, which performs well below the lowest-performing countries in Europe (Greece and Portugal). From 2000 onwards, an increasing number of Latin American countries has joined PISA. Eight countries from the region participated in PISA 2015, all of them performing well below the OECD average (OECD, 2016b). The gap between the top-performing country in the region (Chile) and the OECD average is equivalent to more than one year of schooling; the difference between the top regional performer (Chile) and the lowest performer in the region (Dominican Republic) is equivalent to three years of schooling, and the abysmal difference between the lowest-performing country (Dominican Republic) and the top performer (Singapore) in this PISA cycle is equivalent to seven years of schooling, which is close to the average number of years of compulsory schooling in many countries in Latin America (OECD 2016b).

In short, students in Latin America learn very little, because the education systems are very inefficient. While the share of low-performing students is very high, there are almost no high-performing students. Despite this poor level of performance, most countries in Latin America have not improved over the last decades. The exceptions are Peru, where student performance has improved substantially, and Chile and Colombia, which have also shown learning gains (OECD, 2019c)

As a consequence of the low quality of education systems in Latin America, despite the huge effort made in terms of expanding access to education, most of the adult population has very low levels of literacy and numeracy (OECD, 2016e). The extent to which higher levels of educational attainment in Latin America have not had the expected returns of improved knowledge and skills is illustrated by the fact that the level of basic skills acquired by tertiary graduates in Peru, Mexico and Ecuador is lower than that of people who have not attained an upper-secondary education in most OECD participating countries in the survey of adult skills (PIAAC) (OECD, 2016e).

There seems to be widespread recognition that the low quality of teachers in Latin America is the major constraint on the region´s education progress and that the major obstacle to raising teacher quality is neither economic nor technical, but rather political, i.e. the opposition of teachers' unions which are very powerful and active stakeholders (Bruns and Luque, 2015; Bruns *et al.*, 2019; Chambers-Ju and Finger, 2017; Grindle, 2004). Although the proportion of teachers with university degrees has increased over the years (in Brazil from 19% in 1995 to 62% in 2010), the students who enter education degrees are academically weaker than the overall pool of tertiary students in those countries according to their grades in university entrance exams (Bruns and Luque, 2015). In addition, teacher education degrees do not seem to equip future teachers with the knowledge required, since there seems to be a large mismatch between teachers' formal credentials and their real cognitive skills (Tatto, 2014; TEDS-M, 2008). Thus, in Latin America the lack of appropriate selection and training mechanisms means that future teachers tend to be low performers, which is precisely the opposite of East Asian countries.

At odds with the policies implemented by top performers, teacher salaries tend to be flat with no incentives linked to performance, and there are few accountability mechanisms, meaning that teacher absenteeism is common in many countries. Despite many attempts to implement them, no teacher evaluations are in place in most countries, and there is no clear career structure (Bruns and Luque, 2015). Thus, most teachers have a job for life, which trades potentially higher earnings for stability. These features of teachers' working conditions are mostly the result of huge pressures from the unions in Latin America, which are very powerful by global standards (Bruns and Luque, 2015; Bruns *et al.*, 2019; Chambers-Ju and Finger, 2017; Grindle, 2004). This is because unions in the region have large memberships which facilitate coordinated actions, such as long strikes and school closures, as well as large public demonstrations in the streets (Bruns and Luque, 2015; Bruns *et al.*, 2019; Chambers-Ju and Finger, 2017; Corrales, 2005; Grindle, 2004; Kaufman and Nelson, 2004; Palamidessi and Legarralde, 2006). While this is not unique to Latin America, since teachers' unions tend to be the largest in the public sector in most countries due to the sheer size of the teaching force, Latin American unions have gained more power by developing strong alliances with political parties (particularly on the left) and have penetrated governments by occupying key positions in the structure of Ministries of Education.

The most extreme example is Mexico, where the unions control key positions both at the federal and state levels and many education ministers were former state-level union heads (Chambers-Ju and Finger, 2017). Unions in Latin America have opposed changes necessary to improve the quality of teachers to a larger extent than other regions/ countries, such as measures seeking higher standards of entry into teaching programmes, better education training programmes, incentives linked to performance, evaluation of teachers and standardised student assessments.

The fierce rejection to these policies is the result of major conflicts of interest between what unions regard as threats to their power and to the favourable working conditions of their members, and the policies necessary to improve teacher quality and enhance student performance. In other words, in countries where teacher quality is low and unions defend the interests of the existing workforce, any measure that may threaten job stability, reduce the size of the teaching workforce, make jobs more demanding or risk the loss of benefits as a consequence of unfavorable evaluations on performance, are vigorously opposed. The deepest conflicts tend to arise in relation to policies concerning the evaluation of teachers. Although reforms addressing this aspect have established attractive incentives for good performers and offered support for teachers who need to improve, the risk that teachers who consistently underperform may be sanctioned or even dismissed seems to override any benefits for high-performing teachers or learning gains for students. Attempts to implement evaluation systems have elicited strong responses from unions in many countries, including violent strikes in Ecuador and Peru (Bruns and Luque, 2015).

In contrast, unions exert strong political pressure in favour of reforms which aim to reduce class size. The benefits for unions are huge, since this means hiring more teachers and therefore expanding the number of members, which is an attractive option for teachers because it facilitates their work and is popular with parents. However, when unions put pressure on governments to reduce class size, they strategically hide these benefits for their members and instead argue that smaller class sizes will facilitate individualised attention to students and therefore increase the quality of teaching.

This narrative is false because, as we have seen, all the available evidence shows that reducing class size *per se* does not have a positive impact on student performance (Bruns and Luque, 2015; Hanushek, 2002; Hanushek and Woessmann, 2015). However, parents are easily convinced that a small class size leads to higher quality of schooling. Thus, governments face huge pressures that have led to a decrease in class size in many Latin American countries, to the extent that nine countries in the region (Argentina, Brazil, Chile, Costa Rica, Cuba, Ecuador, Panama, Paraguay, and Uruguay) have lower class sizes than many better-performing OECD countries, despite this measure being very costly in economic terms (Bruns and Luque, 2015).

But the costs of investing resources in reducing class size are profound and long-term because there are trade-offs involved, which do not seem apparent to other stakeholders. As we have seen in the case of top-performing countries in East Asia, these countries have very large class sizes because they choose to invest the resources in teacher selection, training and professional development. Thus, investment goes to a smaller, more selective, better-trained and higher-paid teaching force, which achieves much better student outcomes. Governments must choose between investing resources in high-quality teachers or decreasing class size. To put it in simple terms: high quality teachers can achieve rapid learning gains in a class with many students but decreasing class size, while keeping the quality of the teaching force low, will not improve student performance. The appeal of small classes to parents and the huge incentives that unions have to reduce class size imply that governments are caught in a double bind between the high political costs of refusing a popular measure and the long-term costs to the quality of the education system. So far, where the political costs seem insurmountable, governments have had little choice but to reduce class size, a trend which is not only present in Latin America but in most OECD countries.

Education systems in Latin America are characterised by their large degrees of inequality. In terms of *inclusion*, the results from PISA reveal a terrible tragedy: between 40% and 60% of the fifteen-year-olds at school in Uruguay, Costa Rica, Mexico, Colombia, Brazil and Peru are low performers, in Chile the proportion is slightly lower (35%) but in the Dominican Republic it amounts to over 80% of students. Compared to the OECD average of 21% of students, this represents a huge failure of education systems (OECD, 2016b, 2016c and 2018a). But the picture is even bleaker if we take into account the fact that drop-out rates are high, so in most countries in the region between 25% and 40% of fifteen-year-olds are no longer in school; it seems reasonable to assume that those students who have dropped out of school have even lower levels of performance, leading to the conclusion that the overall level of performance among the whole population of fifteen-year-olds is even worse than PISA data suggest.

In terms of *fairness* the impact of family socio-economic background on student performance is higher than the average for the OECD in most Latin American countries, but not all. It should be taken into account that the impact of socio-economic background tends to be smaller when most students have low levels of performance, as is the case in Mexico, but it is more challenging to minimise the impact of family background in countries with higher performance levels, such as Chile.

To measure equity, PISA often compares the variation in student performance between schools with the variation found within schools. The assumption is that larger levels of between school variation reveal larger inequities, because differences in student performance are assumed to be strongly associated with students attending different types of schools and/or schools located in neighbourhoods which differ in family wealth, thus influencing the socio-economic composition of students and resource allocation between schools. Contrary to expectations, this index of inequity developed by PISA shows that in most Latin American countries, between-school variation is considerably smaller than the OECD average (OECD, 2018a). Since PISA has repeatedly shown that messy data should not be allowed to get in the way of a good story, the OECD surprisingly concludes that "the variation is largely due to differences in performance between schools", unlike "comprehensive education systems—those which do not sort students by programme or school based on their ability—which often tend to have small between school variations in performance". It also concludes that the supposedly "large" between-school variation in Latin America is due to the "segregated nature of their societies" (OECD, 2018a). This in sharp contrast to the way this same index is used again and again to conclude that, because between-school variation is low in Spain (as in most Latin

American countries), the education system is equitable. The problem, of course, lies with the index.

The reason why this presumed index of equity gives results which are very different to other measures of equity is that in countries where grade repetition is high (as in Latin America and Spain), there is much greater variation within schools, because a large proportion of fifteen-year-old students surveyed by PISA are one or two grades below their modal grade. In all Latin American countries grade repetition is high, with more than 25% of students in most countries repeating a grade at least once, a figure which increases to over 40% of students in Colombia. Thus, in the context of high rates of grade repetition, this index is not a reliable indicator of levels of equity, whether high or low. In the case of Latin America, detailed analyses in Chile using the results of students from the same grade in national exams show that there is a strong correlation with the area in which schools are located (Fontaine and Urzúa, 2018).

As we have seen, PISA recommends "comprehensive" policies in general, and for Latin America in particular, but it also concludes that grade repetition is "often unfair and always costly" (OECD, 2018a). The problem is that in societies with high levels of economic and social inequity, as shown by the Gini index (World Bank, 2021) and where parents have huge differences in their levels of skills (OECD, 2019e), adopting the recommendation to follow "comprehensive policies" (i.e., no streaming or grouping according to student ability) seems to go hand-in-hand with grade repetition. It seems likely that among societies with high levels of inequity, children begin school with very different starting points in terms of basic skills and receive very different levels of support from their families throughout school. In this context, 'comprehensive' policies which are based on the principle of treating all students equally, probably end up leaving some students so far behind that at some point the only alternative is for them to repeat a grade. As we have seen, experimental studies have shown that when there are major differences between students, streaming may give low performers a much better chance of achieving their potential (Duflo *et al.*, 2011; Kremer *et al.*, 2013). The case of Singapore clearly shows that early tracking is an efficient policy with which to fight early school leaving when rates are high. Even after Singapore became a top performer in

PISA, early tracking in lower-secondary education led to high levels of student performance without compromising equity.

Historically in Latin America, families and students have actively defended education as an engine of social mobility, leading to powerful social movements against private education and in support of free access to university. The student strikes in Chile in 2011 illustrate this point clearly. As a consequence of this huge political pressure, in Latin America government-funded and privately run schools are almost non-existent, except in Chile, where they represent almost half of schools and have played a major role in improving student performance (Fontaine and Urzúa, 2018). These social movements consider the so-called 'comprehensive' policies to be an essential element of equity, very much in line with the recommendations from the OECD. As a consequence, there are no different trajectories until the age of fifteen or sixteen and very few students choose vocational education at upper-secondary level (OECD, 2016b, and 2016c), since families regard university as the only way to ensure a good job for their children.

Latin America is unfortunately the prime example of what goes wrong when education policies that work well in societies that were already egalitarian (such as Nordic countries) are implemented in non-egalitarian societies in the belief that they will achieve similar results in terms of quality and, more importantly, equity. 'Comprehensive' policies in Latin American countries imply a monolithic path that is the only option available to a very diverse student population, creating the illusion that such an education system offers all students the same opportunities to succeed.

Latin America represents the laboratory for investigation into the outcome of such policies in societies with high levels of inequity: high drop-out rates, high rates of grade repetition, an almost non-existent VET system and low standards in order to maximise the number of students progressing through the education system despite their low levels of performance. It is likely that the low quality of teachers makes it even more difficult to achieve good levels of student performance when a diverse student population only has one path and, contrary to expectations, makes equitable outcomes impossible. Such poor outcomes lead to intense levels of frustration even among students who achieve high levels of education attainment formally, since they have low levels of knowledge and skills and therefore do not obtain the expected returns. When education systems offer big promises through high levels of enrolment, but fail to deliver on quality, they breed resentment, which is reflected in the massive student protests that periodically sweep through Latin America. Such a system not only fails those who drop out. It also fails those who remain.

5.3. What Have Countries Learned from the PISA Shock?

From time to time, some countries have worse results than expected in PISA and this generates an intense policy debate about education that puts pressure on governments to implement reforms. This strong reaction to disappointing results in PISA is known as the 'PISA shock'. The better-known cases are Germany, Denmark and Japan, which are often cited as examples of PISA's strong impact on education policy (Baird *et al.*, 2016; Breakspear, 2014; Egelund, 2008; Ertl, 2006; Martens and Niemann, 2010; Martens *et al.*, 2016; Ringarp, 2016; Takayama, 2008; Waldow, 2009).

However, it is striking that after more than twenty years of PISA cycles there are so few countries where PISA results have led to the implementation of education reforms. It is also important to consider whether those education reforms were aligned with the policy recommendations from PISA and, most importantly, whether they improved student performance.

Germany apparently expected to be recognised as a top performer in the first PISA cycle, but ultimately performed below the OECD average and worse than many European countries (OECD, 2001). PISA data also showed that student socio-economic background and immigrant status had a large impact on student outcomes, raising concerns of low levels of equity in the German education system. The fact that these poor results were a shock is remarkable and highlights an important feature of the impact strategy developed by PISA. From the beginning, PISA has developed a very proactive communications strategy that targets media in all participating countries and provides them in advance (under embargo) with data, as well as the most important policy messages it is developing for each country. This collaboration with the media also includes interviews with OECD staff by major media, targeting those countries where the impact is greatest. The media effort is such that PISA has developed launches at different levels: global, regional, and national launches. In relation to the latter, it works closely with governments to prepare joint launches at press conferences once the main conclusions have been discussed. The public presentation of results hand-in-hand with governments all over the world greatly facilitates the internal policy discussions that PISA intends to promote within countries, since it places current governments at the centre of the debate and elevates the OECD to the role of honest broker.

As a result, its impact is achieved mainly through the media, who give greater salience to the findings by highlighting poor results. This explains at least partly what happened in Germany when the results of PISA 2000 were launched, since the low levels of performance could not possibly have come as a surprise to policymakers, who already knew that the results of Germany in TIMSS 1995 (Harmon *et al.*, 1997) were very poor and that the data available from other international surveys showed that student performance in Germany was already below most other European countries in 1975, and continued to decline further until 2000 (Hanushek and Woessmann, 2015; Martens and Niemann, 2010). But the results of previous international surveys did not have a similar impact on the media and were therefore not widely known. By generating a media scandal, PISA does attract the attention of the public and other stakeholders, which may put pressure on governments to take action.

In an OECD report which claims that PISA was the trigger in Germany for a package of reforms that led to rapid improvement in student performance, the fact that this approach aimed to create a significant media impact is openly acknowledged as the following quotes show:

> Whilst the TIMSS results had hardly been reported, major newspapers ran four, five and six-page special sections on the PISA results. The news and discussions of the results were all over the radio and television. The news about Germany's poor results got far more coverage in Germany than the surprise news that Finland had topped the PISA league tables got in Finland [...] Each (political) side had been effectively blocked by the other for years, producing gridlock on educational policy change. But the "PISA shock" changed all that. Now, for the first time in years real change was possible on a surprisingly large scale. The uproar in the

press reflected a very strong reaction to the PISA results from the public. Politicians who ignored it risked their careers. (OECD, 2011)

These quotes also reflect a unique attribute among international surveys that PISA proudly emphasises: by amplifying poor results in the press, it intensifies the pressure from the public and stakeholders such that governments end up caught between a rock and a hard place. As a consequence, they need to be seen to act swiftly. Although PISA also claims that it facilitates governments' jobs by providing the right solutions, this is an overstatement to say the least. In any case, it seems contradictory that PISA boasts about the costs it inflicts on governments to the extent of claiming that policymakers may risk their careers, since it is those same governments who have decided, funded and implemented the participation in PISA. Furthermore, forcing governments to respond quickly to public outcry does not seem the best strategy to ensure an in-depth analysis and the search for appropriate policy solutions that each country needs. On the one hand, this 'awe and shock' strategy is likely to prompt the wrong quick-fix response in governments. On the other hand, it does not seem appropriate for a member-led organisation like the OECD to play this name-and-shame game against its own members.

The same OECD report cites Edelgard Bulmahn, who was the German Minister for Education at the time, claiming that:

> the tripartite system of secondary schools was a mirror image of the feudal system, a system that only needed a small number with high qualifications, a few with the middle range of education and the rest with only a basic education. (OECD, 2011)

Andreas Schleicher (widely recognised as the father of PISA) has always supported this view, but in this report he goes further and states that after the fall of the Berlin Wall,

> the West German system was implemented in the East. Lost to East Germany was their more equitable, de-tracked education system along with their excellent early childhood system (OECD, 2011)

Here, Schleicher clearly highlights the contrast between what he calls "feudal" and real "communist" education systems and shows a clear ideological preference for the latter in a misguided interpretation of "equity", despite the clamorous failure of the Soviet Union (OECD, 2011).

While in the case of Finland, PISA developed its policy recommendations gradually after the results of the first cycle, in the case of Germany the conclusion that the most pernicious element of its education system was early tracking and the co-existence of at least three tracks from lower-secondary education was adopted immediately. The fact that Andreas Schleicher is German may have contributed in a positive and a negative way, through a better understanding of the education system and perhaps the prejudices commonly associated with personal, direct experience.

Whatever the reasons, PISA attributed both the low levels of student performance and the low levels of equity to early tracking and a well-developed vocational education and training system which attracts a significant proportion of students (OECD, 2011). The contrast between Finland's unexpected success and Germany's unexpected failure was used to create a strong narrative that remains powerful today: comprehensive policies in Finland were associated with high levels of equity, which led in turn to high levels of quality, while early tracking in Germany was linked to low levels of student performance and large inequalities. But this strong recommendation was never followed by Germany, nor by other European countries with early tracking such as Switzerland and the Netherlands.

Germany is a federal republic with sixteen states (*Länder*) which have full responsibility over education and coordinate their activities through the Standing Conference of the Ministers of Education (*Kultusministerkonferenz*, KMK). The 'PISA shock' generated an intense policy debate in Germany that led to important reforms. These included the establishment of national educational standards in 2004 that defined curricular elements for core subjects, as well as common objectives for all states; each state is then required to develop a full compulsory curriculum which is aligned with these objectives (Ertl, 2006; OECD, 2011; Tarelli *et al.*, 2012). The reforms also led to the creation of the Institute for Educational Quality Improvement in 2003, which evaluates whether advances are being made towards these standards.

In June 2006, the Standing Conference of the Ministers of Education adopted a strategy for educational monitoring which included national student assessments, designed independently by the Institute for Educational Quality Improvement, as well as participation in international comparative surveys. Teacher unions ensured that student performance in the new exams would not be linked to teachers' pay or influence their promotion or retention (OECD, 2011).

Since Germany has not followed the consistent and generalised recommendation from PISA to delay vocational education and training until upper-secondary level, early tracking remains today, as well as several differentiated academic and vocational tracks (Tarelli et al., 2012).

Thus, in lower-secondary schoolchildren are assigned to different tracks according to their ability level. States differ in the age at which children are assigned to different tracks (which varies from ten to twelve years) and in the options that they offer, although the three traditional tracks are the most common: *Hauptschulbildungsgang* which allows students to proceed to vocational training, *Realschulbildungsgang* which leads to vocationally oriented upper-secondary school and *Gymnasialer Bildungsgang* which allows students to obtain the *Abitur*, which qualifies them for university. These secondary school tracks may be offered by different types of schools known as *Hauptschule*, *Realschule* and *Gymnasium*.

In the 2012–2013 academic year, about 14% of German students in eighth grade attended a *Hauptschule*, about 23% attended a *Realschule*, and about 36% attended a *Gymnasium* (Tarelli et al., 2012). An increasing number of schools offer several of these tracks and some states have re-designed the offer so that schools combine at least two tracks (*Gesamtschule*).

Upper-secondary education offers different pathways that cover a broad range from full-time general education to dual vocational education and training, which integrates on-the-job-learning (Tarelli et al., 2012). Since more students are attracted to vocational education and training than in most other European countries, a lower proportion of students attend university, a feature that has been repeatedly criticised by the OECD (OECD, 2020d).

Despite the decision by Germany to maintain early tracking, according to PISA equity improved from 2000 to 2015 (OECD, 2018c). The impact of socio-economic background on student performance is slightly higher than the OECD average, but much lower than the same impact in some countries with no early tracking, such as France. Furthermore, 32% of disadvantaged students in Germany perform at high levels of proficiency, which is higher than the OECD average (25%) and higher than most European countries. Thus, although family background has a stronger impact, it is also true that a much larger proportion of disadvantaged students reach high levels of performance.

These findings suggest that early tracking *per se* does not necessarily have a negative impact on quality or equity, but it depends entirely on whether students in each track acquire a good level of knowledge and skills, whether the assignment of students to tracks is based on a fair assessment of student ability rather than personal factors that may lead to discrimination (such as family socio-economic background or immigrant status), whether there is flexibility to move between tracks when levels of performance change and whether mobility between each track to higher levels of education is allowed. Other examples in Europe include Switzerland and the Netherlands and we have already discussed Singapore, a top performer with early tracking. Furthermore, the development of vocational education and training, its attractiveness to students and its close links to firms (through on-the-job training), has led to high rates of youth employment in Germany during economic crises compared to other countries in Europe, since many VET students get jobs that require middle and high levels of skills (OECD, 2020d and 2020e).

In the European context, Germany has received many refugees and migrants, particularly as a consequence of the Syrian crisis in 2014 and 2015, and it has granted asylum to the largest number of applicants of any European country. Consequently, a large number of children and teenagers have arrived in Germany who do not speak the language. The proportion of immigrant students increased from 18% in 2009 to 22% in 2018 (OECD, 2019d and 2020c). In order to facilitate these students' integration, several measures have been implemented to support immigrants, including basic programmes to learn German (Bergseng *et al.*, 2019; Fazekas and Field, 2013; OECD, 2020f). However, this has proven difficult, as illustrated by the fact that the performance of foreign-born students deteriorated from 2009 to 2018, and that they face higher rates of early school leaving (OECD 2020f). In this particular case, VET has proven to be a pathway that allows immigrant students to acquire strong foundation and practical skills more rapidly, thus facilitating their entry to the labour market (Bergsen *et al.*, 2019; Fazekas and Field, 2013; OECD, 2020f).

Undoubtedly the most important question is: was the 'PISA shock' effective in promoting reforms that led to enhanced student performance? Although PISA widely claims that this is the case, in our view data from PISA and other international surveys show that it is debatable (see Martens and Niemann, 2010; Martens *et al.*, 2016). According to PISA, while the performance of fifteen-year-olds in reading improved slowly and gradually until 2012, it has remained at levels around the OECD average since then. German students had better starting points in mathematics (OECD, 2004) and science (OECD, 2007), which remained more or less stable until 2012 and declined thereafter.

Other international surveys show that, among primary students, performance in reading was lower than that of other European countries and remained stable from 2001 until 2016 (Mullis *et al.*, 2017), while performance in science and mathematics remained stable from 2007 onwards and was also lower than the performance of students in many European countries (Mullis *et al.*, 2020). Thus, the data from international surveys do not show significant improvements over time, although the large increases in the share of immigrant students may have contributed to the declines observed in recent years.

If we analyse other countries which experienced the so-called 'PISA shock', we realise that the policy reactions are quite different, but none of them have had a significant impact on student performance (Niemann and Martens, 2018). Denmark was also shocked by its first PISA results, which were not only worse than expected but also below the performance level of its Scandinavian neighbors, particularly Finland (OECD, 2001). This was surprising in a country with high levels of investment in education.

However, the government did not implement reforms until an in-depth international review was able to analyse in detail the strengths and weaknesses of the education system, and policy recommendations were developed on the basis of several studies (Breakspear, 2014; Egelund, 2008). The recommendations included developing student assessments, improving teacher pre-service training, which was perceived as too generalist in its approach, and taking advantage of the high levels of investment to develop in-service training for teachers. Most of the reforms in Denmark aimed at implementing national assessments and providing support for disadvantaged students (Egelund, 2008). Despite this more elaborate approach, the performance of fifteen-year-old Danish students has not improved significantly over time according to PISA (2000–2018) (OECD, 2019f). Their performance in reading and science has followed a flat trajectory, with scores similar to the OECD average, while their performance in mathematics declined until 2012 and then returned back to the levels observed in the first cycles.

Data from TIMSS and PIRLS support the conclusion that Denmark has not improved over time, in this case by looking at the performance of primary students: no significant changes have been observed between 2007 and 2019 in mathematics and science, and no changes have taken place in reading between 2006 and 2016 (Mullis *et al.*, 2017 and 2020). In all domains, Danish students continue to be outperformed by Norway, Finland and Sweden, providing additional support to the idea that investment *per se* is not a guarantee of better student outcomes.

Japan is also often cited as an example of PISA shock, but in this case it seems to be the reaction of a top-performer to a slight decline in the performance in reading in PISA 2003. Japan had been a top performer since at least 1975 according to previous international surveys, and it continued to improve until the year 2000 (Hanushek and Woessmann, 2015). When the first PISA cycle took place in 2000, all of the media attention focused on Finland, which became the top performer in reading (the main domain in the initial cycle), while Japan, the top performer in mathematics and "joint top-performer in science" with Korea (OECD, 2001), generated no interest.

It has been argued that biased media reporting on PISA results in 2003 was used as an opportunity by the government to halt an unpopular curriculum reform known as *yutori* (Takayama, 2008). Once again, according to PISA no major changes have been observed in the performance of Japanese students from 2000 until 2015, and over this period the country has remained a top performer particularly in science and mathematics (OECD, 2019g). The results from other international surveys are more positive, and show that, despite being a top performer, Japanese students continued to improve in mathematics and science both in fourth grade and eighth grade (although no significant changes were observed between 1995 and 2011) (Mullis *et al.*, 2020). Thus, improvements occurred well after the PISA shock and are unlikely to be related to reforms implemented as a reaction to it.

The evidence shows that the first reaction to PISA results consists mainly of media outrage, which supposedly serves as a wake-up call for governments to act. The fact that the media act as a mediator in creating a narrative around the PISA results is a direct consequence of the effort that PISA makes to engage with media all over the world. Although PISA boasts that this forces governments to react, this strategy involves huge risks. The most important is that even when governments do respond to the pressure by hastily implementing reforms, the evidence shows that it has had no impact on student performance. This may be either because (a) governments do follow policy recommendations which happen to be wrong, (b) governments use additional data and analyses to deal with weaknesses that PISA data do not identify and therefore implement reforms which are not aligned with PISA recommendations and have an impact on variables not captured by PISA, or (c) stakeholders with vested interests take advantage of the media uproar and escalate the pressure on governments to implement policies that are beneficial to them but not necessarily to students.

5.4. What Can We Learn from Countries that Improve in Europe?

In the European context, there is a different group of countries which have improved rapidly over time. As is the case with top-performing countries in Asia, such improvements seem mostly unrelated to PISA policy recommendations. We will analyse which policies have proven successful, the extent to which they are aligned with PISA policy recommendations and the extent to which PISA has learned from them.

Poland

Poland joined PISA in the first cycle (2000) and performed below the OECD average in reading, mathematics and science. Student performance improved rapidly to the extent that Poland became a top-performing country within Europe in 2012, but then declined in 2015 (OECD, 2019h). Data from TIMSS broadly support these findings since the performance of primary students in Poland improved from 2011 until 2015 and declined in 2019 (Mullis *et al.*, 2020). In addition, data from PIRLS show that primary students had high levels of performance in 2016 (Mullis *et al.*, 2017).

After the collapse of the communist system in 1989, Poland experienced a rapid transition to a Western-style parliamentary democracy and a fast-growing market economy. The first changes in education were focused on eliminating the indoctrination that the communist regime had introduced in textbooks and curricula. It took almost a decade to prepare for major structural reforms of the education system. The series of reforms started in 1999 with a structural reform, followed by a curriculum and evaluation reform in 2007 and an early education reform which was gradually implemented from 2009 until 2015 (Jakubowski, 2021). Despite their positive impact on student performance, these reforms were largely reversed in 2016 following the arrival to power of right-wing populists, the PiS (Law and Justice) party.

The structural reform of 1999 was very ambitious since it introduced several major changes into the education system at the same time: it extended compulsory education by one year, by replacing eight years of basic primary education with nine years of comprehensive education, which was divided into two stages: six years of primary education and three years of lower-secondary education. The creation of a new school level (lower-secondary) was the most dramatic structural change, which was aligned with the implementation of a new curriculum and opened up the possibility of hiring teachers specialised in particular subjects. Thus, all students had access to one additional year of compulsory education which delayed the beginning of upper-secondary education by one year; the byproduct of these major changes was that the differentiation between academic and vocational tracks in upper-secondary education was delayed by one year until the age of sixteen. In upper-secondary education, students could choose between the *lyceum* (academic, three years), technical school (four years) or vocational school (two to three years).

An important aspect of the reform was to improve teachers' professional development. The Ministry organised a new programme,

"New School" (*Nowa Szkola*) to train a large number of coaches who then provided professional development programmes for teachers, which included changes in the curriculum, capacity building to assume new responsibilities as a consequence of enhanced school autonomy, the establishment of school assessments, and preparation for external examinations (Wisniewski and Zahorska, 2020). Approximately 70% of all Polish teachers participated in these programmes.

The reform also introduced standardised external national exams, which were implemented in 2002 at the end of every educational stage. The results were evaluated centrally to ensure the same standards. They were available to students and teachers and had academic consequences. The results at the school level were made public based on measures of student progress. The impact on student performance was particularly positive for students lagging behind. Additional measures included changes in governance towards the decentralisation of the education system, which increased school autonomy, and changes in funding, which made the system more efficient (Jakubowski, 2021).

Later in 2008, the curricular reform designed a consistent curriculum from preschool all the way to upper-secondary level, defined learning outcomes as targets for each educational stage, and strengthened the core subjects in vocational schools. Students who followed vocational degrees improved their employability substantially. Finally, the reform of early education which started in 2005 expanded compulsory education by another year by advancing the starting age to five years. Thus, all in all these reforms extended the duration of compulsory education by two years.

This complex package of reforms was aligned with the rapid changes that were taking place in the economy and was successful in achieving the goals that had been defined. A growing number of students enrolled in upper-secondary (either academic or vocational) education, which provides access to tertiary education. As a consequence, Poland experienced one of the largest increases in the proportion of students with a tertiary degree in Europe.

But the most convincing evaluation of the success of such reforms was the drastic improvement in the performance of fifteen-year-olds revealed by PISA. Despite the sheer complexity and magnitude of the reform package, the conclusions that PISA extracted from the improvement in Poland focused almost exclusively on the fact that vocational education and training was delayed by one year (OECD, 2011). Other authors have placed greater emphasis on the extension of compulsory education by one year to all students, which involved the creation of new lower-secondary schools with new curricula and more autonomy, as well as greater emphasis on core subjects in vocational education (Wisniewski and Zahorska, 2020).

The effort made by the government was huge since the education reform was implemented in parallel with reforms on pensions, health and public administration. The political cost was enormous, partly because the implementation of so many structural reforms simultaneously was a mammoth task, and partly because the reduction of years in primary school, the closure of small rural schools, and higher requirements (university degrees) for teachers of the new lower-secondary level all led to some teachers losing their jobs. In addition, the new professional development framework linked participation to promotion and salary increases.

Some of the reasons behind the rejection and reversal of the reforms are a good example of the extent to which cultural factors can play a key role, and of the low impact of international evidence when it clashes with values held by societies, or segments of them. The fact that school became compulsory for six-year-olds and pre-school for five-year-olds was used to criticise government for supposedly taking young children away from their families, a concern which was stronger among rural families (Wisniewski and Zahorska, 2020). As a consequence, a grassroots social protest movement was organised under the slogan "Save the Toddlers". Although there is plenty of evidence that early childhood education and care is the best tool enabling children from disadvantaged backgrounds to catch up with others before they start school (OECD, 2015d), once these fears were triggered the policy was rejected and the compulsory school starting age was raised to seven years.

The political cost of implementing such an ambitious package of reforms meant that the government collapsed shortly after, and some elements of the reform were never implemented by succeeding governments (for example, an obligatory standardised mathematics exam at the end of upper-secondary school was postponed for nearly ten years) (Jakubowski, 2021). The high political cost and the fact that such reforms were implemented despite strong rejection from the unions may have contributed to the popular support for reversing the reforms in 2016 (Jakubowski, 2021). It is uncertain whether such an ambitious package of reforms could have achieved consensus without major concessions and delays; some have argued that this is highly unlikely (Jakubowski, 2021).

Portugal

In the first PISA cycle (2000) Portuguese students performed well below the OECD average and near the bottom of the ranking (OECD, 2001). This generated no shock, since Portugal had already performed poorly in TIMSS 1995 (Harmon et al., 1997) and it was not afflicted by the superiority complex that other countries shaken by PISA results seemingly were. Quite the opposite: universal access to education, length of compulsory education and completion rates had traditionally lagged behind other European countries, so Portugal did not have high expectations (Crato, 2021). As an example, let us just mention that compulsory schooling was extended from three to four years in 1956 for boys and in 1960 for girls, to six years in 1967, to ninth grade in 1986 and to twelfth grade as recently as 2012 (Crato, 2021).

Despite this unpromising start, Portugal's performance in PISA improved up until 2015, and it is the only OECD country that has shown a positive trend in all three domains (OECD, 2019i; Maroco, 2021). Such progress means that fifteen-year-old students in Portugal have evolved from performing at the equivalent of one school year behind the OECD average, to performing at the same level as the OECD average. This improvement has occurred due to the combination of two positive trends: the proportion of low-performing students has decreased, while the proportion of high-performing students has increased (OECD, 2015; Maroco, 2021). This shows that reforms can improve the quality and equity of education systems simultaneously, by supporting struggling students and developing the potential of top performers (OECD, 2016b; Maroco, 2021).

However, in PISA 2018 Portugal's performance declined, which could be due to the methodological issues that plague the results from this cycle, or to changes in policy. Data from other international surveys which assessed students in primary education also show rapid improvements from 1995 until 2015, and a drop or stagnation in 2019 in mathematics and science (Mullis *et al.*, 2020), suggesting that policy changes may be responsible for the declines.

The steepest increase in PISA results took place from 2006 to 2009, just after the introduction of standardised ninth grade exams for mathematics and Portuguese in 2005, leading to the conclusion that high-stakes assessment was probably the policy with the single largest impact on student performance (Bergbauer *et al.*, 2018; Maroco, 2021). The fact that several consecutive governments gave continuity to the reforms initiated by previous ones is key to Portugal's success. Further improvements in student performance were achieved despite the deep financial crisis, which led to the international bailout of Portugal from 2010 until 2014. This period was marked by an intense austerity policy, and a significant decrease in the level of investment in education (which reduced from 4.8% invested in education in relation to GDP in 2000 to 3.6% in 2018) (Maroco, 2021).

The education minister, Nuno Crato (2011–2015), implemented a package of reforms which ensured that improvements in student performance continued. These include defining learning targets in the curriculum, reinforcing core subjects and implementing new high-stakes exams (Crato, 2021; Maroco, 2021). The leadership of school principals was strengthened and major reforms were introduced to enhance the quality of the teaching profession. These included higher academic requirements to enter educational programmes, stronger content of STEM subjects in teacher training, improved pre-service training, more demanding selection procedures to enter the profession, evaluation of teachers, and a new framework for teachers' professional development (OECD, 2020g). An important aim was to decrease high rates of grade repetition and associated high rates of early school leaving. The policies included the modernisation and development of two differentiated tracks of vocational education and training in upper-secondary level, including stronger links with industry and more on-the-job-training, as well as the introduction of vocational courses in lower-secondary starting at the age of thirteen (Crato, 2021).

The positive impact of these policies was clear: dropout rates decreased from 43.6% in 2000 to 28.3% in 2010 and 13.7% in 2015. To this day Nuno Crato claims (pers. comm.) that one of the key elements of the success of such reforms was to increase expectations for disadvantaged students through more demanding assessments and aligned curricular content, instead of lowering standards to make it easier for students with low levels of performance to obtain educational degrees (Crato, 2020). However, student performance dropped after 2016 when the national high-stakes exams for fourth and sixth grades were substituted for diagnostic tests that covered only a sample of students and had no academic consequences; teacher evaluations were also abolished (Crato, 2021; Maroco, 2021).

In conclusion, both in Poland and Portugal, education reforms began before the first PISA cycle and were therefore not the result of PISA policy recommendations. More worryingly, such reforms were undone after PISA data demonstrated that improvements in student performance were substantial. Thus, the evidence from PISA was not used to design the reforms and was not enough to prevent the reversal of successful policies.

Estonia

This is how Estonian education expert Gunda Tire describes the impact of the launch of PISA 2018 results in Estonia:

> PISA 2018 data was released on December 3, 2019 and it turned out to be almost like a national holiday. The press conference led by the minister of education and research was streamed online, all the main media channels were present, and the news spread fast—according to PISA 2018, Estonian education system is the best in Europe and among the best performing systems in the world! The evening news on national TV devoted more than 10 min to covering PISA results, journalists had interviewed students and teachers from different urban and rural schools, and everybody felt that they had personally contributed and were very proud of their achievement. (Tire, 2021)

Estonia joined PISA in 2006 with levels of student performance similar to the OECD average in reading, slightly above the OECD average in mathematics, and considerably better than it in science (OECD, 2019j). Since then, performance in reading has improved steadily, surpassing the OECD average in 2012 and continuing to improve in successive cycles, while improvements in mathematics have been smaller, and science has shown no improvement from 2006 until 2018. Despite small or no improvements in the latter two domains, student performance has remained well above the OECD average in science and mathematics. It is revealing that PISA elevated Estonia to the status of "PISA star" in 2018, although Estonia did not perform better in all domains in that cycle. In fact, it was in PISA 2012 when the country achieved its steepest improvements and highest levels of performance: a peak in science (which declined thereafter), as well as in mathematics (which remained unchanged in the following cycles), and the largest improvement in reading (which continued to increase slightly).

This points to the importance of the country rankings for PISA conclusions and policy recommendations: Estonia reached its highest levels of performance in science and mathematics in 2012, but in this PISA cycle it performed below other European countries such as Finland, Switzerland or the Netherlands (OECD, 2014c). Although its performance in science declined in 2018, and remained unchanged in mathematics and reading, the fact that it became the top-performing country in Europe in all domains and, in particular, the fact that it outperformed Finland in reading, was used to elevate it for the first time into a success story. This decision was questionable, since Estonia was already performing better than the OECD average in two domains since joining PISA in 2006.

This early success is supported by data from TIMSS: in 2003 Estonia was *the* top performer among European countries in science (performing only below East Asian Countries) and one of the top performers in mathematics (Mullis *et al.*, 2017). Data from the survey of adults (PIAAC) paints a similar picture since Estonia ranks among the top ten participating countries in literacy and only slightly lower in numeracy (OECD, 2019e). The improvement in the level of basic skills acquired by the adult population took place some time ago, since the survey conducted in 2011 shows that the youngest cohort (sixteen to twenty-four years old) has a level of numeracy and literacy which is very similar to that of older cohorts (twenty-five to thirty-four and thirty-five to forty-four years old), and only moderately above the oldest cohorts (forty-five to fifty-four and fifty-five to sixty-five) (OECD, 2019l). This in stark contrast with countries whose education systems have improved in the last decades, such as Singapore, where younger cohorts have acquired much higher levels of basic skills than older cohorts (OECD, 2019l). Thus, as appealing as it may be to be proclaimed the winner of the European gold medal, the nice story built around Estonia's surprising success in 2018 is misleading, because the roots of the country's success can be found much earlier.

One of the main messages from PISA was that Estonia had achieved the status of top performer despite the fact that it invested 30% less than the OECD average on education, thus making it a prime example of efficient investment (OECD, 2019c and 2019d; Tire, 2021). However, if we take into account that the number of students in Estonia has decreased dramatically over the last years (40% decrease in the last fifteen years) due to emigration and low birth rates (OECD, 2019k), public spending per student as a percentage of GDP per capita in 2015 was similar in Estonia to that in Canada and higher than that in Australia, Germany or the Netherlands (Goss and Cowgill, 2019; OECD, 2020d).

What factors have led to the high level of performance of students in Estonia? According to the Vice-Minister of Education and Research, Mart Laidmets, who was asked this question in an interview after the launch of PISA 2018,

> the three pillars of the Estonian education system are the national curriculum, the second is the teachers who are highly qualified—holding master's degrees" and "the third important aspect is parents. It is important that parents recognise that education gives people the chance to move forward and to reach their potential. (*TES Estonia*: "PISA's European success story", John Roberts, 3 December 2019)

As is the case in Finland, teachers in Estonia have played a significant role in its history and in the creation of a national identity since the nineteenth century. Estonia first became an independent state in 1918 and introduced free, compulsory and public education for all, but in 1940 it was occupied by the Soviet Union. A few years before Estonia regained independence, teachers became particularly vocal in their defence of a curriculum free from communist indoctrination.

Estonia regained independence in 1991 and used this opportunity to implement an ambitious reform of the whole education system. Due to its geographical proximity and cultural and linguistic similarities to Finland, the redesign of the education system borrowed many elements from Finland. Some have argued that the cultural similarities between the two in fact go much further, since both countries share a history of high levels of literacy. In the second half of the seventeenth century, the Church played a major role in teaching peasant children to read by providing education in the native language, and in 1897 literacy levels among Estonians (80%) were the highest in the Tsardom of Russia (Lees, 2016). In 1920, six grades of education were compulsory, and this was extended to eight grades between 1959 and 1963, and then to nine grades between 1968 and 1988 (Lees, 2016).

After Estonia regained independence, a national education system was created and several laws were adopted during the 1990s to provide the legal framework. The national curriculum implemented in 1996 lays out the learning outcomes that students should achieve at different stages and has been praised for its quality and coherence (Oates, 2010). Thus, the first opportunity that Estonia had to compare itself on the international stage and measure the impact of this new curriculum was six to ten years later, when it joined first TIMSS and then PISA.

During the 1990s, schools were decentralised, transferring more responsibilities to local municipalities and giving more autonomy to principals (who could select teachers and manage the budget) and teachers (who could choose learning materials). In the mid-1990s Estonia started to develop centrally administered assessments and evaluations (Lees, 2016). In 1997 an external evaluation system was implemented to evaluate the extent to which students had achieved the learning goals set in the curriculum (Tire, 2021). At the end of compulsory education (lower-secondary level) and at the end of upper-secondary education, exit exams were introduced for all students. These are centrally designed and are required to enter tertiary education.

As a country, Estonia made a commitment to become a digital economy and society and this has been incredibly successful. Internet voting is used by almost half of the population and 99% of public services are available online (E-estonia, 2019b; OECD, 2020a). Digitalisation also had a big influence in the education sector, since the "Tiger Leap" (a reference to the successful economies in East Asia) programme, initiated in the 1990s, which was developed to ensure Internet connectivity in schools, access to computers for all students, and IT training for teachers (Laanpere, 2002). All schools in Estonia use "e-school solutions", which is an online school-management and communication system for pupils, teachers, parents and government bodies (E-estonia, 2019a and 2019b), the "e-schoolbag", which is an online portal that provides digital learning materials for all education levels (E-estonia, 2019b) and the Examination Information System, which is a tool to carry out and evaluate examinations and assessments (Innove, 2019).

The Estonian Education Information System is a particularly powerful tool. It is a database that collects data on students, schools, examinations and curricula, among other things. It allows the tracking of each student´s development over time, including teachers´ assessments, grades, state exam results and any cases requiring special support. Individuals have access to their own personal data, schools to their own information, aggregated data are available to the public, and parents can advise their children on career decisions since information on employment rates and average income for vocational training courses and university degrees is available. Finally, policymakers make decisions based on these data. This is in our view fundamental, since evidence-based policymaking requires reliable data, which are rarely available. However, the link between this unique asset and high student performance has not been investigated so far.

As part of the general reforms, teachers were required to obtain a master´s degree (Tire, 2021). In 2013, professional standards were defined to assess potential candidates who wished to become teachers, and a programme of teacher professional development was designed (Lees, 2016). However, teachers in Estonia follow a so-called teacher-centred approach, which is considered traditional (Tire, 2021). Despite the excellent student outcomes achieved through this approach, the recent Estonian Lifelong Learning Strategy 2020 has outlined its goal to move to a so-called 'student-centred approach'.

The education system has high levels of equity, with few differences in student outcomes due to family socio-economic background and only minor gaps between rural and urban areas. However, a major divide seems to persist between students attending Estonian schools and those attending Russian schools, with the latter lagging behind by the equivalent of a year of schooling in reading and science (Tire, 2021). It would be important to analyse the extent to which changes in reading performance in PISA are related to the existence of an education system with two languages taught in different schools.

Finally, the importance that parents place on education is reflected in the high rates of pre-school education, with 91 % of four-year-olds and 87% of three-year-olds enrolled in early-childhood and care institutions, which is well above the OECD average (Lees, 2016). While attending kindergartens before they join school at the age of seven, children follow the national curriculum and learn to read and write.

Despite all these reforms, some have argued that the success of the education system in Estonia is to a larger extent the result of cultural and historical factors. Marc Tucker has stated:

> So the fact that Estonia is among the top ten performers on PISA worldwide does not appear to be the result of education policies pursued since Estonia gained its independence, as much as it is the result of hundreds of years of political, social and educational development which ended up supporting a strong, deep and widespread commitment to education as well as a tradition of very high education standards, a very demanding curriculum matched to the standards, high quality examinations built directly on that curriculum, highly educated teachers with masters degrees from research universities, a well designed qualifications system, a strong system of support for families with young children, and most of the other drivers of high performing national education systems that we had found over the years in such systems. (Tucker, 2015)

The quote seems a bit misleading since it refutes the role of education policies in the first sentence and then goes on to identify a number of education policies which are key to Estonia's success. In any case, Estonia has often been used as an example of a country where history, culture and the value placed on education by families, all play a much greater role than specific education policies (*The Economist*: "PISA results can lead policymakers astray—the parable of Finland", 7 December 2019). Whether this is true or not, it raises important issues: to what extent does PISA measure what happens in school or elsewhere? If the latter, to what extent can policymakers improve education systems in cultures where education is not highly valued?

5.5. What Can We Learn from Countries where PISA Has a Huge Media Impact but No Policy Reactions?

Spain has a unique relationship with PISA: the media impact in Spain is much greater than in most other countries (Martens and Niemann, 2010), but the policy reactions have been scarce. Contrary to what happened in countries such as Germany, where the contrast between high expectations and poor results led to media outrage (the so-called PISA shock) and put pressure on policy makers to initiate a number of reforms, in Spain there is no discrepancy between the level of expectations (low) and the results (mediocre). The good adjustment between expectations and actual levels of performance is a trap that has prevented most policymakers from reacting to PISA findings and reveals a clear lack of ambition as a country or, in other words, a lack of trust in the power of education to transform lives, societies and economies. The only consolation which has become a sort of mantra is the argument that Spain has prioritised equity over excellence, a misleading message that has been reinforced by PISA (Gomendio, 2021).

So why does PISA have such a media impact if no one cares? The most likely explanation is that Spain does not have national assessments, nor regional evaluations with common standards. Thus, PISA scores represent the only information available to compare regions using the same metric and to evaluate trends over time. The first issue attracts a lot of attention since there are major differences in performance between regions that give rise to intense political bickering about the causes, which inevitably ends up escalating into conflicts on the mechanisms by which central government transfers funds to regions for education, health and social matters (Gomendio, 2021; Wert, 2019). It seems fair to say that in Spain, PISA is not as valuable as an international benchmark as it is in other countries, since the country (but not all regions) seems resigned to its fate as a mediocre performer. Instead, it is a powerful weapon in the invariably heated political debate surrounding education.

The picture that different ILSAs paint about the performance of Spanish students is consistent in terms of relative performance when compared to other countries, but not in their assessment of trends over time. The three major surveys show that Spain performs below around twenty OECD countries and much lower than top performers in East Asia. Spain joined PISA in its first cycle (2000) and scored below the OECD average until 2015, when it finally reached OECD average levels (the OECD initially withdrew the results for Spain in the launch of PISA 2018 due to their unreliability, and published them months later warning that they are not comparable to previous cycles, as we have discussed before). Spanish students exhibit particularly bad level of performance in mathematics when compared to other OECD countries, mainly due to the substantially low proportion of top-performing students (Gomendio, 2021; Wert, 2019). Thus, one of the weaknesses of the education system in Spain is that it does not allow top-performing students to develop their potential. The evidence from PIRLS and TIMSS is broadly similar for primary school students: Spanish students perform slightly below the OECD average in science and reading, and much lower than it in mathematics.

But ILSAs draw different conclusions when trends are analysed over time: according to PISA, student performance remained stagnant from 2000 until 2015, while PIRLS and TIMSS show greater improvements. In mathematics and science, Spain improved from 2011 until 2015 and experienced a clear improvement in reading in 2016, after a lack of any progression between 2006 and 2011 (Gomendio 2021; Wert 2019).

In terms of equity, from its very first cycle, PISA identified Spain as a champion of equity, a conclusion that successive cycles have strengthened (OECD, 2001). This conclusion is based on one of the measures which PISA often uses to evaluate equity: the variance explained by between- and within-school variation. PISA assumes that large between-school variation is a reliable indicator of inequity because it reflects the extent to which differences in student performance arise from attendance at different types of schools, either due to early tracking (academic versus vocational schools, which happens in very few countries when students are fifteen years of age), major differences in wealth between neighbourhoods, or different admission policies by schools. Spain consistently ranks as having one of the lowest levels of between-school variation, since most of its variance is explained by within-school variation. An early OECD report investigating levels of equity in the Spanish education system reinforced this conclusion: "the Spanish results point to a low level of inequity that is more centred on differences within the institutions than between institutions" (Calero, 2005). Unfortunately, the conclusion by PISA is wrong on two counts: first, the variable used as an indicator of inequity is not appropriate, and second, there are many other variables that show high levels of inequity which PISA either does not measure or chooses to ignore.

As we have discussed in the case of Latin America, the reason why most of the variance is explained by within-school variation is that rates of grade repetition are high in Spain (from 2000 until 2011 it was almost 40%, three times that of the OECD average). Since PISA assesses fifteen-year-olds irrespective of the grade in which they study, the survey does identify and quantify this problem, showing that 67.9% of fifteen-year-olds were in tenth grade, 23.4% were one year behind and 8.6% were two years behind in 2015 (OECD, 2016b and 2016c). PISA data clearly show that students who repeat a grade score much lower than those who do not. Hence, it is clear that having fifteen-year-old students in the same school performing at such different levels overrides any differences that may exist between schools.[1]

The relevance of this issue goes far beyond the flaws in the use and interpretation of this variable in the context of equity, because PISA fails to recognise both the causes and consequences of grade repetition. The conclusion that PISA draws is oversimplistic: since grade repetition is associated with lower levels of performance, it systematically recommends avoiding this practice. The problem, of course, is that some education systems use grade repetition as a last resort when students are lagging so far behind that they can hardly follow what is being taught in the classroom and the magnitude of the delay is such that it prevents any learning progress.

Thus, grade repetition is a symptom rather than a cause of severe underperformance. It reveals the inability of the education system to allow struggling students to catch up at earlier stages. It also has dire consequences for students, since grade repetition is a reliable proxy of early school leaving, which is an endemic problem in Spain. The level of early school leaving remained incredibly high for decades (around 30%) with many of these students dropping out of school without even a lower-secondary diploma (Gomendio, 2021; Wert, 2019). Most early school leavers come from disadvantaged and migrant backgrounds. Thus, an education system which has been praised by PISA as being a model of equity actually leads to the worst type of inequity: the expulsion of disadvantaged students who have not acquired the most basic levels of knowledge and skills from an education system which

---

1   Actually, in the case of Spain in PISA 2015, students who had not repeated any grade scored ninety points above those who had repeated one or two grades (OECD, 2016a).

basically gave up on them from the very beginning. But PISA seems blind to this kind of inequity.

Huge regional differences are another major source of inequity. In PISA 2015, the difference between the top-performing region and the bottom-performing region was equivalent to almost two years of schooling. Among the seventeen regions, the variation was such that, if they were to be sorted with national entities in PISA rankings, some would be considered top performers (Castille and León and Madrid have similar levels of performance to some East Asian countries such as Hong-Kong and South Korea), while others perform well below the OECD average. Huge regional disparities in levels of student performance (as measured by PISA among fifteen-year-olds) have a huge impact on their lives: students in regions with lower levels of performance overall suffer higher rates of grade repetition, which lead to high rates of early school leaving and very high rates of youth unemployment (Gomendio, 2021; Wert, 2019).

The fact that the Spanish education system generates such terrible outcomes in terms of equity represents a big failure of the education models (explicitly designed to achieve high levels of equity) which have been implemented there during the last decades. So why this profound contradiction between aims and outcomes?

The evaluation of the outcomes leaves only one plausible explanation: despite all of the good intentions, the policies which were implemented were wrong. This is relevant for many other countries, because some of these policies have been associated with equity elsewhere, but they did not work in the Spanish context. We will review the major education policies in Spain, their impact, and the reaction by PISA in the following chapter.

5.6 Conclusions

It seems reasonable to argue that robust, reliable and objective evidence about which education policies lead to better student performance should guide policymakers and help them overcome any divisive ideological issues or strong conflicts of interest. Most of the information available comes from ILSAs and, since PISA from its inception adopted a policy advisor role, it boasts about the impact of its policy recommendations on governments and the reforms that they implement. However, when we look at the impact of PISA on actual education reforms, the evidence suggests that this is small.

There is much consistency between ILSAs in terms of the levels of student performance attributed to countries, and how they compare to each other. Thus, the rankings do provide important and reliable information about which countries should be analysed in order to understand which education policies lead to outstanding levels of student performance, and which should be analysed to understand which combination of policies leads to poor levels of student performance. Over time, more countries have become participants of ILSAs, so care must be taken to understand the precise contexts in which countries are labelled as "top" or "low" performers in different cycles.

A detailed review of top performers reveals that Finland became *the* legend after the first PISA cycle, when it was the top performer in reading (but not in science or mathematics). In this same cycle, Germany experienced the so-called 'PISA shock', owing to the huge mismatch between expectations and results, which led to media outrage followed by a number of reforms. Since this was the very first cycle, PISA had not developed any policy recommendations. In our view, the vivid contrast between the unexpected success of a small and humble European nation like Finland and the wounded pride of powerful Germany was crucial to the creation of a narrative which remains almost intact and very influential today. In 2000, the education system in Finland was described as comprehensive (no early tracking), having a high-quality teaching force, high levels of school autonomy and being equitable. In contrast, Germany had early streaming of students into vocational and academic tracks at the age of ten years and a greater impact of family socio-economic background and immigrant status on student performance.

As with all influential narratives, the one that emerged from this comparison was rather simplistic: education reforms should address inequalities before student excellence can be achieved, and the way to do this is by designing comprehensive systems which do not segregate students into academic vs vocational tracks, ability grouping, or different types of schools (e.g. charter vs public). High levels of school autonomy and good-quality teachers were combined in a conclusion which proved to be far-reaching: teachers should be trusted. Eventually this concept got lost in translation and unions all over the world argued that PISA demonstrated that teachers should not be evaluated, should not be asked to follow a pre-defined curriculum, and should be allowed to innovate. PISA has contributed to this narrative, arguing that teachers should own their profession, establish their own standards and design education reforms.

As this narrative crystalised and became more popular, the data collected over successive cycles clearly challenged some of its conclusions. First, the initial success of Finland was followed by a decline in student performance over time. This suggests that while Finland was basking in the glory of its success it failed to recognise the need for reforms. Thus, PISA may be as influential in promoting reforms as it is in preventing them, a potential role that has been largely ignored. Second, it has been argued that the high performance of fifteen-year-olds in the year 2000 is related to the education system that was in place before then, which was more centralised and gave less autonomy to schools. This suggests that some of the causal relationships established are wrong, because this time lag has not been taken into account. Similarly, a high-quality teaching force had been the focus of much attention long before PISA. Third, there is also plenty of evidence that in Finland reading literacy had historically been high, and society and families contribute substantially to early learning before students start school. This is a good example of the extent to which PISA outcomes may be the result of what happens outside of school. While this is something that PISA recognises, it does not seem to accept the limitations of policy recommendations which address the education system.

In the small group of countries that experienced the PISA shock, such as Germany, the findings of successive cycles also challenge the view that PISA has played a major role in supporting these countries to improve student performance. Such countries, like Germany, did implement reforms, but none of them improved student outcomes substantially over time. Thus, the impact of PISA was obvious in terms of media visibility, the main variable which it uses to evaluate its influence, but unclear in terms of the positive impact on student performance.

The real education superpowers, the countries which have shown outstanding levels of performance and which continue to improve over time, are countries in East Asia. Despite this indisputable success, no narrative has been developed around them. These countries were top performers from their very first participation in ILSAs, and their journey towards peak performance started decades before, so it cannot be argued that they improved due to PISA's policy recommendations. Perhaps the idea that students perform better because of the pressures that families exert on their children had led to the mistaken conclusion that not much could be learned by education systems in other parts of the world where education is not as highly valued. It is also possible that the fact that some of the policies implemented by these countries clearly contradict the dichotomous narrative (comprehensive vs segregation, trust vs mistrust on teachers) mentioned above has downplayed any lessons than can be learned.

Countries like South Korea and Singapore demonstrate that major improvements can take place much more rapidly than previously assumed. In a few decades, they have evolved from illiterate societies into the best-performing education systems in the world, but this requires long-term vision and consistency. The evolution of these education systems over time clearly shows that a trade-off between teacher quality and class size has been made, and that this delivers excellent results. This has been possible because unions do not have the power to block reforms, so admission processes for university degrees are highly selective, training is of a high standard, entry into the profession is based on merit and highly competitive, teacher professional development is well-structured, and teachers are evaluated on the basis of the performance of their students. Teachers are valued and enjoy high prestige, but the misleading concept of trust does not apply: high curricular standards as well as student assessments are defined centrally, and schools do not enjoy high levels of autonomy. Even more challenging to the dominant narrative is the fact that, by implementing tracking as early as at primary level, Singapore successfully lowered high rates of early school leaving and, in clear opposition to comprehensive policies, has kept early tracking at lower-secondary level to this day. This model does not prevent all students from achieving their full potential and the different pathways represent an efficient way for teachers to successfully manage student diversity.

The region which represents the biggest divergence from East Asia in terms of developing its human potential is Latin America. Despite a better starting point around fifty years ago, at present the performance of its fifteen-year-olds is many years of schooling behind countries in East Asia and well below the OECD average. In a nutshell, the policies implemented are in many ways the opposite of those which have succeeded in East Asia. The effort in terms of increased access to education and higher rates of enrolment in higher levels of educational attainment has been huge, but the returns in terms of the knowledge and skills acquired have been very low. Much investment has gone into decreasing class size, which is supported by unions and parents alike, but does not have any positive impact on student performance. The power of unions in the region is unparalleled, and they have forcefully rejected attempts to improve teacher quality, systematically opposing teacher (and student) evaluations and higher standards. Most education systems are comprehensive, with no early tracking and few students choosing VET. This is probably the result of the hopes that families in societies with high levels of inequity place on education as an engine of social mobility, of the pressures by strong social movements in the region, and of policymakers' desire to be seen as facilitating such aspirations. But these policies have failed.

Obviously good student outcomes cannot be achieved by teachers with low levels of skills, no matter how small the classes are. In addition, in societies with high levels of inequity, education systems need to deal with a very diverse student population. The comprehensive policies, which may work in egalitarian societies with high levels of skills, have proven unable to deal with high levels of diversity in the classroom, leaving those students with difficult starting points without the differentiated support they need, which leads to high rates of grade repetition and early school leaving. In the context of large inequity and diversity, the outcome of comprehensive policies is to expel students who are struggling. This seems the worst form of segregation.

Those countries which have improved after participating in ILSAs may give better insights into which policies contributed to success, even if most of them also started their reforms well before joining ILSAs. These are all European countries which followed (in slightly different ways and at different times) what seem to us elementary good practices:

improve teacher quality, define a coherent curriculum with high standards, implement student assessments which are well-aligned with the curriculum, modernise and develop VET, and give more autonomy to schools in exchange for accountability. While ILSAs have played a crucial role in showing positive trends in student performance over time, this evidence has not prevented most of these reforms from being reversed after they have proven to be successful.

Finally, Spain is another sad case of successful evidence-based reforms followed by reversals. Despite major budget cuts since 2009 due to the financial crisis, in 2015 and 2016 improvements were detected by PISA and to a larger extent by TIMSS and PIRLS among primary students, the educational stage where implementation started.

We believe that is important to emphasise that the Spanish case reveals some important weaknesses of PISA. First, PISA defines the two dimensions which matter in education systems (quality and equity), but while quality is measured straightforwardly (via student outcomes), equity is measured in many different ways, because no single variable can capture all of the layers of this complex dimension. Second, some of the most commonly-used variables developed by PISA as indicators of equity are misleading or interpreted in the wrong way. For example, it is a mistake to use small between-school variation in Spain to conclude that the system is equitable, because high rates of grade repetition make intra-school variation much higher than in other education systems. Third, variables which are either ignored or not measured by PISA clearly show that the Spanish education system suffers from high levels of inequity, because high rates of grade repetition lead to high rates of early school leaving, to the extent that one in every four students is expelled from the education system. Most dropouts are disadvantaged students.

The legend that the Spanish system has prioritised equity over excellence has helped policymakers disguise the system's poor quality and has justified the lack of reforms over decades, which has led to stagnation in student outcomes. Since PISA has supported this mistaken conclusion, it should take responsibility for the stagnation of student performance in Spain. Finally, PISA has refused to give any detailed or convincing explanation for the initial withdrawal and later publication of unreliable results for Spain in 2018, which were used for political purposes. PISA is a high-stakes exam for policymakers, of the kind it no longer supports for students, but it should be held accountable if it wishes to be regarded as a trusted source of data.

6. Spain

An Inside Story

In this chapter, we wish to provide a different perspective which we hope will complement what the data and the literature tell us. After much thought, we have decided to try to provide an insider's view of what we experienced when we accepted the task of designing and implementing an education reform in our own country. Our personal experiences will undoubtedly be narrower and we obviously run the risk of inadvertently including some biases, but we hope to shed some new light on the nature and magnitude of the political costs that education reforms face. As we shall see, many of the real obstacles in the process of reform remain hidden from the general public and even from academics who tend to gain access only to official documents, media articles and, in some cases, a limited number of interviews.

6.1. A Rough Start

We both joined the Spanish Government after the conservative party Partido Popular (PP) won the general election in November 2011. The severe impact of the financial crisis was by then highly visible. In fact, opinion polls show that PP's outright parliamentary majority was mainly rooted in widespread public dissatisfaction with how the previous (socialist) government had managed the financial crisis. However, as the new government took office it became apparent that the magnitude of the fiscal crisis was much greater than anticipated. Thus, the main focus was on the economy and fiscal issues. The fundamental aim was to avert the risk of being 'rescued', i.e. of receiving critical financial aid from the European Union, the European Central Bank and the International

Monetary Fund. This entailed accepting the imposition of severe cuts to pensions and other public expenses (Wert, 2020). Furthermore, during the first months of government the main concern was how to prevent economic collapse.

The urgency of addressing these immediate problems did not prevent the government from looking at the medium and long term. It was clear that the reason why the financial crisis had a much greater impact in Spain than in other European countries was that it suffered from deep structural problems that had to be addressed in order to overcome this shock, as well as any future ones. Thus, the government decided to implement an ambitious package of reforms in many sectors, such as the economy, labour and education. At the same time, budget cuts had to be implemented in order to reduce the deficit. We were all aware that it was a toxic combination. But we were also aware that there was no choice.

The unavoidable target of decreasing the deficit (which was at 10% of GDP in 2011) could only be achieved by individual regions. Most—over 85%—of the public funding allocated to education, health and social affairs is managed by regional governments. Thus, the first hurdle was to work out how to empower regions to make the necessary decisions.

A brief historical overview will suffice to explain the governance arrangements implemented after a long process of decentralisation. After the transition from the Franco dictatorship to democracy, which was rightly hailed as an example of peaceful transition in which all parties involved had agreed to put their differences aside to reach a consensus, a new constitution was drafted and approved by referendum in 1978.

It defined asymmetric governance arrangements, granting special treatment to regions with strong nationalistic movements (such as the Basque Country and Catalonia) which included the 'devolution' of decision-making power and favourable fiscal arrangements. It also involved the upfront transfer of the management of education, health and social affairs. This asymmetric treatment of regions was regarded as unfair and soon created political tensions, eventually leading to the transfer of education, health and social affairs to all seventeen regions, a process which lasted from 1980 until 1999.

Thus, the main reason for transferring decision-making power and funds to regions was a vain political attempt to appease the centrifugal forces of nationalist movements. Since the main objective of decentralisation was not improving efficacy or outcomes, central government agreed not to implement accountability mechanisms and accepted the role of raising most of the funds through taxes before transferring them to regions. Such governance arrangements would prove inadequate because efficiency did not improve. In addition, they led to never-ending political tensions between central government and regions, with the latter demanding greater decision-making power and more funds. Attempts to appease nationalist movements failed since education proved to be a very powerful tool in creating national identities, so some of these regions (in particular Catalonia) in practice took over control of education.

In the context of this quasi-federal governance model, the first issue that central government needed to solve was how to allow regions more flexibility to reduce public spending. Even after the risk of a 'rescue' was averted, stringent measures to control the deficit had to be implemented under fiscal euro area rules. Since central government is responsible for basic law which defines the ranges for a number of dimensions with a big impact on investment levels (such as student-teacher ratios, hours of teaching, replacement of teachers on leave, and so on) it had to modify the limits.

All teams at different ministries spent the first months estimating the impact of different measures on levels of investment and whether they were likely to affect outcomes. At the Ministry of Education, we worked tirelessly to analyse all the different options, which proved to be a very depressing start. Just a few months after coming into power the government approved a royal decree which allowed regions to increase student-teacher ratios by 20%, and to increase the hours of teaching, as well as a whole package of measures to reduce spending. It was up to regions to decide what the right balance was for spending in education vs health and social services and, within each of these sectors, which measures from a broad spectrum of options to implement.

To cut a long story short, on the whole, regions decided to implement larger budget cuts in education than in health. Since student-teacher ratios were already low in Spain compared to other European and OECD countries, the small increases implemented led to student-teacher ratios that were still below the OECD average. Actually, after the implementation of those increases in 2014, the student-teacher ratio in secondary education was 11:1 in Spain vs the OECD average of 13:1 (OECD 2016a). Thus, in educational metrics such as these, there was room for improvement in the efficiency of investments.

Opposition political parties and unions were quick to build a very strong narrative denouncing the 'budget cuts' and the supposed damage they inflicted on public education; this causal link was taken for granted despite the lack of evidence. Central government was blamed and strong opposition to these measures was mounted, as regions watched on in relief. The political costs were so great that the education reform that we later designed at the Ministry of Education was met with fierce resistance because, among all the confusion caused by the blame games, people had been led to believe that the reform (which was not approved until late 2013 and did not address any of these issues) was responsible for the budget cuts (implemented by regions in 2012). The power of this narrative proved lethal to the education reform before it was even born.

The fact that a conservative government started with 'budget cuts' had far more damaging consequences than we could foresee in those difficult months. The government was blamed for using the financial crisis as an excuse to dismantle the welfare state. In the midst of a terrible financial crisis which led to very high rates of unemployment (which peaked at 26% in the first quarter of 2013, the highest rate in history), this idea proved so powerful that some years later it led to the emergence of populist movements on the radical left for the first time in Spanish history (Wert, 2020). But that is a different story. Let us get back to education.

6.2. Laws, Laws, Laws .... Are They Any Good?

One of the most damaging mantras about the Spanish education system is that it has suffered from the instability generated by too many laws, implemented by the two main political parties (socialist and conservative) when in power, for no other reason than to pursue their ideological agendas. Contrary to widespread belief, the Spanish education system had not undergone many changes after the transition to democracy. Quite the opposite: it has followed one basic model, approved by a socialist government, which has generated very poor outcomes. On the one hand, Spain has high rates of early school leaving (around 30%) which have led to high rates of NEETs and youth unemployment; these were exacerbated during the financial crisis, which created astronomic levels of youth unemployment (65% at the peak of the crisis). On the other hand, student outcomes are mediocre (below the OECD average) and have stagnated for over two decades (Gomendio, 2021). These deficiencies together have resulted in Spain having an adult population with one of the lowest levels of basic skills among European countries (OECD, 2019l).

Since the 1990s, when a major education reform (*Ley Orgánica General del Sistema Educativo* or LOGSE) was approved by a socialist government with a parliamentary majority, Spain had implemented a very rigid form of comprehensive system. Following the steps taken much earlier by social democrats in some European countries, and particularly Nordic countries, the 1990s education reforms adopted a comprehensive model. This law, which was complemented by other laws approved by socialist governments during the following years, developed quite a radical and unique version of comprehensive education on the assumption that it would lead to higher levels of equity and thus contribute to the creation of a more egalitarian society.

This logic was based on the often-cited link between comprehensive education and equity in Nordic countries. It is based on the assumption that comprehensive education models generate egalitarian societies, rather than the opposite, i.e. that comprehensive education models can only work in societies that have achieved certain levels of equity (such as Nordic countries). The architecture and rules of the game of a 'radical comprehensive' system remained in place until 2013, when we designed a partial reform of the education basic law approved by parliament (LOMCE, 2013). Thus, in twenty-three years there was plenty of time to evaluate the impact of this model. But this was never done. The system lacked any means to evaluate the impact of the policies implemented. Good-natured intentions based on an ill-defined concept of equity seemed enough.

The LOGSE extended compulsory education to the age of sixteen and increased the number of teachers by 35%, which led to a marked decrease in class size. This is a constant demand from unions which the left has appropriated as a flag mistakenly assumed to signal good quality. This required a substantial increase in education investment, which continued to grow until 2009, when the financial crisis led to the first budget cuts for education.

The extension of compulsory education had the immediate consequence of delaying the start of upper-secondary education by two years. Since a fully comprehensive model was implemented for all years of compulsory education, the start of academic and vocational tracks was delayed by two years (to sixteen years of age). Previously, at the age of fourteen, students could follow either an academic track or a two-year first vocational track. The sudden disappearance of the option to choose a vocational track at the age of fourteen, and the prospect of remaining on the academic track for two additional years led to a steep increase in early school leaving (30% of students), which remained at high levels for decades. This negative impact has been documented by research:

> Results show [...] that elimination of FP1 [first level of vocational education] for the youth 14 to 16 which took place after the enforcement of LOGSE had a negative impact on the will to pursue education among males (Felgueroso et al., 2013)

After 1990, a progressive decrease in VET enrolment took place: in the academic year 1999–2000, with the new system fully operational, less than 150,000 students were enrolled in secondary VET, while the general programme (*Bachillerato*) enrolled over half a million students.[1] In tertiary education the imbalance was much bigger: almost 1.6 million students were enrolled in Spanish universities in the academic year 1999–2000, while tertiary VET enrolment was less than 150,000, i.e. less than 10% of total tertiary enrolment. At the same time, youth unemployment, early school leaving and NEETs (not in employment, education or training) were on the rise.

Since the main (if not only) explicitly stated goal was to achieve equity, the comprehensive model went far beyond delaying tracking. Any measure that could be regarded as leading to segregation was eliminated: students could not be grouped according to their ability (either within or between classes), students could not receive differential treatment according to their level of performance, and during compulsory education almost no subject choices were available.

---

1 Both programmes are two years long.

In other words, all students had to follow the same curriculum, in the same classroom, at the same pace.

The lack of national (and standardised regional) evaluations was regarded as a key element to avoid segregation and stress among students, so no national (or regional) standardised student assessments at the end of educational stages were implemented. As a consequence, students who were struggling in primary school could not be identified early enough and did not receive the additional support that they needed; they lagged further and further behind as they grew older until they started repeating grades when they became unable to learn what was being taught. As soon as they reached the age of sixteen (when compulsory education ends), they abandoned a system which had failed them well before they were legally entitled to leave. In addition, schools, teachers and families all felt the lack of the clear signaling system that national exit exams provide, since they set the standards that all students need to achieve to obtain a national degree. Finally, students who had the potential to become top performers were not given the opportunity to do so. The fact that the education system was rigid and blind to the performance and needs of a diverse student population led to the emergence of the two main deficiencies of the Spanish education system: a high rate of grade repetition, which was linked to a high rate of early school leaving among disadvantaged students and migrants.

According to PISA, the system remained flat: a small proportion of top-performing students and a similar proportion of low performers to the OECD average led to overall mediocre results (Gomendio, 2021). Levels of student performance were particularly poor for mathematics. Student outcomes also stagnated, with no improvements observed between 2000 (first PISA cycle) and 2012. But what PISA failed to interpret correctly was the association between the high rate of grade repetition in Spain at age fifteen (around 40% from 2000 until 2011) and the high rate of early school leaving (26% in 2011), which it consistently ignores, despite the obvious connections between the two that most analyses highlight. Thus, PISA has concluded from the very first cycle that the Spanish education system is equitable, contributing to the myth that it has prioritised equity over quality. In fact, it has led to the worst type of inequality: one in every four students is excluded from the education system because they have been lagging behind for years and have lost any motivation or hope that it has anything to offer them. These students leave with such low levels of knowledge and skills that they face high levels of unemployment during their lifetimes and are very reluctant to engage in any form of adult learning (Gomendio, 2021; Wert, 2019).

How is it possible that an education system designed to avoid segregation and discrimination and to promote equity has ended up generating the worst kind of inequity? The explanation is complex and involves many factors. Compared to Nordic countries, Spain is not an egalitarian society. This is reflected not only in differences in wealth and income, but also in major differences in the skills of the adult population. While in Nordic countries most adults have high levels of skills, in Spain older generations, who have had fewer years of schooling, and a substantial proportion of those in younger cohorts who have dropped out of school do not reach the most basic levels of literacy and numeracy (OECD, 2016e).

In fact, the first round of the survey of adults' skills (PIAAC) revealed that Spain was the participating country with the lowest level of skills (along with Italy) in 2011. This was a shockingly poor result. If we look at progress over time, by comparing different age cohorts, we find that in Spain the level of skills of the older cohort (aged between fifty-five and sixty-four) is very low compared to other countries, but the levels of skills have improved as a larger proportion of the population gained access to education and remained in school at least until the end of compulsory education (forty-five to fifty-four-year-olds). Below this age range, the levels of skills stagnated. Thus, the skills of the sixteen to twenty-four cohort are similar to those of previous cohorts (twenty-five to thirty-four and thirty-five to forty-four), which means that no further progress has been made in over twenty years. This stagnation happened despite the fact that access to higher levels of education, particularly university, increased very rapidly in the last decades. Thus, a huge effort to expand access to university had very poor returns in terms of actual skills, due to the poor quality of the education system as a whole.

The lack of improvement in the acquisition of skills after universal access to education was achieved clearly shows that the quality of the system did not improve over time, which is consistent with PISA findings. Since differences in family socio-economic background and parental levels of educational attainment are linked to major differences in the parental level of skills, these are likely to have a major impact on the development of cognitive skills during early years, on the support that parents can provide to their school-aged children, and on the expectations that parents have and how much they value education. This implies that the student population is more diverse than in egalitarian societies. Thus, when students join school, they have very different starting points which require a more flexible system able to adapt to their different needs. When rigidity and uniformity is misunderstood as equity, students with difficult starting points have no alternative way of catching up. In addition, students with different levels of skills learn at different paces and, when the degree of variation in the classroom is high, those lagging behind are likely to suffer the most. As we have seen, one of the main challenges that teachers face is dealing with student diversity within the classroom.

This seems to be a key factor, since international surveys show that teachers in Spain have relatively low levels of skills (Tatto, 2014). This is because students studying for degrees in education obtain low grades on university entrance exams, the training they receive at university is weak on subject content and strong on pedagogy, selection procedures to enter the profession give more weight to seniority (number of years on temporary contracts) than to merit, and there is poor professional development. Teachers with low levels of skills are less likely to be able to achieve learning gains from a diverse group of students, since they are unable to cater for their different needs. The combination of a low-quality teaching force, a diverse student population, the education system's lack of flexibility to adapt to different needs, and the absence of common standards ends up generating the very same issue that it sought to avoid: the expulsion of the most disadvantaged students, who cannot adapt to such a rigid model.

6.3. An Education Reform in the Middle of a Storm

A legitimate question which crops up again and again is whether the peak of the financial crisis and the difficult political context of 2012 was the right context for an education reform. It is often argued that education reforms should be carried out during less stressful times when politics are less polarised, social tensions less intense and, therefore, consensus and social acceptance may be within easier reach. At the time, we decided that the education reform could not wait any longer because a low-quality education system was a major part of the problem. The poor development of human capital made it very difficult to transform the economy, which was still too reliant on low-skilled jobs in the construction sector and services, into a knowledge economy, let alone a digital economy. But this transformation had become more urgent in 2012 because the construction sector collapsed and, in order to prosper again, Spain needed to free itself from the low-skills trap: an education system which does not equip students with high levels of skills aligns well with an economy that does not demand high levels of skills.

We became acutely aware from the very beginning that consensus was not possible. It is well-known that in politics what is discussed at private meetings is very different from the public narrative which is carefully crafted to ensure key elements that will prompt rejection or support among certain sectors of public opinion. But we were not prepared for the abysmal gap between the resources that most stakeholders demanded in exchange for their support and the extremely antagonistic public narrative, which distorted the reform to the extent that it targeted elements which were not even part of it. In other words, with professional backgrounds in evidence-based sectors, we were prepared to defend the policies that we proposed against counter-arguments. But we did not expect opponents of the reform to send us a Trojan horse.

At the political level, we were informed in early private meetings that the socialist party would not support *any* reform by a conservative government, even before we had designed it. A 'socialist model' had prevailed for decades, and the left regarded education as their own territory. Thus, there was no room for any negotiation. The unions asked for the kind of compensation package that they had received as part of the negotiations to gain their support for previous reforms: further increases in teacher salaries and decreases in student-teacher ratios. They knew that we could not afford such measures under such strong fiscal constraints, but they expected some gains. We could not offer anything in exchange. Since the management of education was transferred to regional governments, central government's budget for education was almost entirely devoted to studentships for disadvantaged students.

Most unions joined political parties on the left in denouncing our supposed intentions to 'privatise' education. There was never any element in the reform that would have justified such a criticism, but it worked. It fitted nicely alongside the scary story of a conservative government dismantling the welfare state built by the socialist party when in power. Neither narrative was true, but families were suffering the consequences of the economic crisis, mainly because of growing unemployment, and people were deeply concerned, so any argument suggesting that the safety nets of a welfare state would be removed under such terrible circumstances could light a fire that would soon grow out of control.

Most critics argue that policymakers are so short-sighted that they are prone to impose reforms when governments enjoy a majority in parliament, without taking into account the fact that reforms that lack consensus tend to be short-lived. This is oversimplistic and unfair. Most education ministers with whom we have discussed this issue were painfully aware of it when they decided to push ahead with a reform under such circumstances. They decided to proceed not because they were unwilling to negotiate or make concessions. Rather, they were aware that consensus was not possible, because they could not accept the demands of different stakeholders in exchange for their support. In countries where education is a highly polarised issue, consensus is difficult; the fact that it is more common in countries with rules that have historically promoted consensus (consociationalism) does not mean that it should be the norm for all countries. The mantra that consensus should guide all education reforms would lead in many countries to reforms which follow the minimum common denominator, or to no reforms at all. These critics fail to acknowledge that defending the need to reach a consensus is a formidable weapon for those opposing a reform (Allègre, 2000). It is also a great excuse for stakeholders who wish to gain more resources; a huge amount of investment goes into education systems, which rely on a vast number of teachers and other stakeholders who receive direct financial gains. Rent-seeking behaviour by some (or most) of the beneficiaries is often part of the reason why education reforms are derailed and in this context calls for consensus are just a means of disguising the underlying conflicts of interest.

We were among those who decided to go ahead with a reform despite becoming deeply aware after negotiations that consensus was not possible. We were also aware that this threatened the continuity of the reforms, since the socialist party openly declared that no matter what reform was eventually approved by parliament, they would reverse it by approving a new reform as soon as they regained power. In fact, in Spain all major education reforms until then had been approved by governments which enjoyed a parliamentary majority (socialist). History showed that consensus was difficult in our country, but that did not stop us from trying.

With hindsight, we believe that our mistake was to trust that an evidence-based reform would help us to overcome the polarisation and that the positive impact we expected to achieve would be enough to preserve those policies which had proven to be effective. This turned out to be wrong on many counts. The fact that the reform was based on international evidence, as well as a deep analysis of the national and regional data, did not make any difference: some contested the evidence, claiming—without grounds—that it was biased, while others simply refused to take it into consideration. The conflicts of interest were too deep for any robust evidence to have an impact: political games and vested interests combined to form a coalition against the reform which used very basic levers to create a narrative which proved a fatal blow: budget cuts and the fear of privatisation took over any rational argument.

We did try hard to explain the real aims of the reform, but we refused to denounce in public what we were told in private so that people could be aware of the real motivations behind the rejection of the reform. We were concerned that, if we did, any trust between us and stakeholders would be destroyed and the public debate would escalate even further. We pinned all our hopes on the evaluation of the reform's impact. Although improvements could be objectively assessed in many areas, the most visible metric for the media (PISA) failed too.

6.4. Aims, Policies and Impact of the Education Reform

To address the deficiencies of our education system, we worked with our teams of experts from different sectors at the Ministry of Education, as well as groups of teachers, to design an education reform which was approved by parliament on 9 December 2013. The new law, *Ley Orgánica para la Mejora de la Calidad Educativa*, or LOMCE (Law for the Improvement of Quality in Education), consisted of amendments to around one third of the provisions of the *Ley Orgánica de Educación*, LOE, which had been passed in 2006. These amendments basically aimed to address the main weaknesses of the system (high early school leaving and low VET enrolment) and were supported by strong international evidence.

The law explicitly used PISA data to justify the need for improvement and we (the authors) are responsible for that, but it did not follow all (or even most) PISA recommendations, and we are also responsible for that. The reason for this much-criticised approach is that while PISA data clearly showed that Spanish students had low levels of performance and that no improvement had taken place for over a decade, we believe that PISA failed to identify major deficiencies and gave recommendations which did not apply to the Spanish context. But this is very far from manipulating PISA to justify enforcing reforms which were part of an ideological agenda, as some critics have argued in the Spanish case and others (e.g., Choi and Jerrim, 2015; Fischman *et al.*, 2018).

The reform was ambitious. It introduced national assessments to signal common evaluation standards at the end of each educational stage, to identify struggling students early enough and provide them with additional support, to overcome major regional disparities and to evaluate the impact of education policies. It gave more autonomy to schools and strengthened the leadership of principals. It developed and modernised vocational education and training in order to offer an alternative pathway to those students who were dropping out of school, as well as those who wished for more direct access to the labour market and higher employability levels than universities were achieving. It also modernised the curricula, introduced evaluation standards and re-defined the responsibilities of the state and the regions.

Shortly after implementation started, these changes in educational polices led to clear and rapid improvements in some areas: the proportion of students enrolled in vocational education and training at upper-secondary level increased dramatically, leading to a historic decline in the rate of early school leaving between 2011 and 2015 (down from 26.3% to 20.0%) and a marked decrease in the rate of grade repetition (Gomendio, 2021; Wert, 2019). Most of these variables remain outside the scope of what PISA measures and taking them into consideration radically changes the overall perception of levels of quality, equity and progress over time.

However, the national evaluations were never fully implemented due to the intensity of political pressures against them. They had not been designed as high-stakes exams, in the sense that the final grade was a combination of the result of the end-of-stage assessment and of the grades that teachers had given to students as part of the school's internal assessments.[2] But all main stakeholders formed a strong coalition against them: some regional governments and nationalist political parties opposed them because they regarded them as a form of re-centralisation; unions rejected them outright because they regarded them as an indirect means of assessing teachers; and parties on the left rejected them because they refused to support any change to the prevailing, radically comprehensive socialist model.

While it is easy to understand what kind of vested interests facilitated this 'coalition of the unwilling', all of the stakeholders created a common narrative which disguised the underlying conflicts of interest. This narrative attributed intentions to national exams which were completely false, such as excluding underprivileged students from university. They were re-labelled with an old nickname (*reválidas*) which had a huge impact, since the name itself resuscitated in the collective imaginary vivid memories of exams which had been implemented a long time ago and which acted as bottlenecks at a time when access to university was quite limited. As we explained many times in parliament, at meetings with regional ministers, with unions, at press conferences and media interviews, all of the evidence from international surveys clearly showed that exit exams had a positive impact on student performance,

---

2   The relative weight of marks given internally by teachers, 60%, was actually larger than the weighting of the exam (40%) in the final grade.

particularly on the performance of those students who were struggling, but the impact of such evidence was null in the face of such strong conflicts of interest, because this was not the real issue at stake.

In relation to the curriculum, the modernisation of the content, the establishment of evaluation standards, and the development of a more schematic curriculum which gave greater freedom to schools to complement the basic content, did not generate strong reactions. Our role was to provide guidelines, such as moving away from a system which was almost exclusively based on memorisation to one in which the acquisition of knowledge remained important, but the development of more complex tasks such as teamwork or problem solving were also required. The actual work was carried out by experienced teams of teachers under our guidance. It really was a massive enterprise to coordinate all of them. These curricular changes were implemented in primary schools and were associated with improvements in mathematics and science among primary-level students (TIMSS) and even more substantial improvements in reading (PIRLS) (Gomendio, 2021). More subtle improvements were detected in PISA 2015, as would be expected given that the implementation calendar was designed so that changes in lower-secondary education would take place later (after changes to primary education).

What did cause a strong negative reaction at the political level was the change in how responsibilities were shared between central and regional governments. The previous model adopted the solution proposed by King Solomon when faced with two women claiming to be the mother of the same baby: splitting the curriculum in every subject. In those regions with an official vernacular tongue (Catalonia, Basque Country, Galicia, Balearic Islands and Valencia) the national government defined 55% of the subject (the so-called 'minimal content') while the regional government defined the remaining 45%. In all other regions, the national government defined 65% of the content and the regional government defined the remaining 35%. This led to difficulties in deciding which metrics were used to measure such percentages, and misalignments between the curricular content defined by central government and that defined by regions.

To solve these problems, we used a different approach and defined three different categories of subjects. For the subjects we labelled as 'core subjects' (equivalent to foundation skills at every stage, including reading, mathematics, Spanish, English and History) the national government defined the content, the assessment criteria and the standards to achieve. These subjects would account for at least 50% of teaching time. For those other subjects we labelled as 'specific subjects', the national government decided only on evaluation standards and assessment criteria, but the regional government defined the content. Finally, a third group of subjects that we labelled as 'free subjects' were entirely defined by regional governments. This new arrangement faced strong opposition from nationalist parties, who found it easier to have control over subjects which had proven instrumental in creating a new national identity, such as history and geography, thanks to the previous 'unmeasurable' percentages. Thus, the changes were labelled as 're-centralisation', a term coined to create the false impression that central government had a hidden agenda to regain control of education.

At this point, we wish to explain perhaps the most 'political'—and one of the costliest—decisions that we made. As we have explained, the decentralisation process in Spain led to some sort of quasi-federal asymmetric distribution of powers, by which some regions (Catalonia, Basque Country and Galicia) were able to seize more political power from the outset, including in education. As a result, the regional governments of those regions have had a lot of leeway to define substantial aspects of their education systems. In all three regions, co-official vernacular languages (Catalan, Basque and Galician) were given the status of learning languages, together with Spanish (Castilian, the common language). In most of these regions a system developed which integrated Spanish, English and the co-official language.

The exception was Catalonia, where Spanish had in practice been eliminated as a language for teaching and learning. Even when some families in Catalonia asked for bilingual teaching and learning in Spanish and Catalan, the regional education authority systematically applied the principle of "linguistic immersion", meaning that all teaching (except of Spanish as a subject) takes place in the vernacular language, Catalan. We introduced in LOMCE some mechanisms to allow families to exert their right to choose a mix of both Spanish and Catalan as teaching and learning languages. However, the Constitutional Court dismissed it on the grounds—debatable in our opinion—that this was beyond the role on education assigned by the constitution to the national government. Consequently, until 2020, families in Catalonia were denied the right to choose a combination of Spanish and Catalan for their children´s education. This highly contentious issue was solved in theory by a ruling of the *Tribunal Superior de Justicia de Cataluña*—the highest court at the regional level—in 2020, which finally established that at least 25% of the teaching in primary and secondary education must take place in Spanish. In practice, this means that on top of Spanish as a subject, another "relevant" subject has to be taught in Spanish. There is widespread skepticism about the extent to which this ruling will be effectively enforced, given the permanent reluctance of Catalan education authorities to abide with laws or court rulings on this matter.

In contrast, the policy which was supported by the strongest international evidence, but which proved futile, was granting more autonomy to schools in exchange for accountability through national standardised exams. In this case, all regions reacted in the same way: they offered their full support to a measure which involved transferring decision-making power away from central government, but during the implementation phase they hijacked those powers. As a result, schools did not enjoy greater autonomy because regions seized the opportunity to gain more power leaving virtually no room to school autonomy.

Since national standardised exams were never implemented, regions are not held accountable for their results. As we have seen, divergence between regions is such that at the age of fifteen the difference in student performance between the best- and worst-performing regions is equivalent to more than one year of schooling. Despite clear regional differences, all Spanish students receive the same educational degree from the Ministry of Education given that there are no national evaluations (or regional evaluations with common standards) at the end of educational stages. Perhaps counterintuitively, in regions which are top performers according to PISA, students have lower grades in the university entrance exam, the only evaluation which is similar at the national level and in which secondary schoolteachers participate in deciding the grades (Wert, 2019). This finding strongly suggests that the level of demand that teachers place on students differs widely between regions. All these factors may generate large regional disparities in terms of student performance (as measured by PISA among fifteen-year-olds) which will have a huge impact on their lives: students in regions with lower levels of overall performance suffer higher rates of grade repetition, which lead to high rates of early school leaving and very high rates of youth unemployment (Gomendio, 2021; Wert, 2019).

A major pillar of the reform was the development and modernisation of VET. The reforms we undertook first in 2012, by developing a legal framework for Dual VET, and then in 2013 with the new Education Act (LOMCE), had a twofold aim: to attract more students to VET in order to decrease early school leaving by encouraging progress towards upper-secondary education among those more interested in applied subjects and to offer an alternative with better employability prospects for those who regarded university as the default option. However, there was strong opposition to the fact that we introduced curricular optionality for specific subjects (applied and academic options) gradually in eighth grade and more resolutely in ninth grade, at the end of compulsory secondary education. Together, these reforms produced a very swift improvement in an area where results were particularly poor: enrolment in VET grew at an unprecedented pace, with a 40% increase between 2010 and 2015. But thereafter, as the practical implementation of the new act stalled, growth in VET enrolment, though still significant, slowed down, with only an 18% increase between 2015 and 2020 (Ministerio de Educación y Formación Profesional, 2020).

The main and most powerful argument against our efforts to make VET a more attractive option was that it was a secondary pathway designed to prevent disadvantaged students from attending university. In addition, the introduction of a modified version of a Dual VET system, which established closer links to a labour market which was undergoing major disruption by introducing on-the-job-training, was criticised on the grounds that it represented 'cheap labour' for employers. We emphasised that in the Spanish case the *real* problems that we needed to tackle were that one in four students were dropping out of school, while access to university for those who continued into upper-secondary education was not an issue since Spain had one of the highest rates of access in Europe, and that university graduates had much lower employability levels than in other European countries (Wert, 2019). But we discovered that the narrative depicting the reform as one intended to make it more difficult for economically disadvantaged students to go to university—which was neither the aim nor the result—was more powerful than reality. Time and again opposition parties, unions of teachers and students used imaginary narratives like, for instance, the tale of the grand-daughter of the illiterate peasant who had been able to make it to university and become a doctor, a vivid example of social mobility which opponents argued could no longer take place due to the reform. Scary tales became more compelling than reality.

Here are a few examples taken from the parliamentary hearings in the education committee. First, this was the statement given by the PSOE spokesperson at the Education Committee of Spanish Congress:

> [T]his law, Mrs Secretary of State, represents more obstacles in the path of disadvantaged students, because as we have stated repeatedly, underperforming students can either receive help or they can be expelled, and you have decided to expel them just in case they reach university if they get any help. Thus, you have designed an obstacle course and you have searched for sewers like VET. (Education Committee Spanish Congress, 26 June 2013)

Or, in the words of the spokesperson for the Catalan Nationalist Party:

> [Y]ou have presented many data, but we are talking about people, education, feelings, personal relationships […] many variables which these data fail to take into account properly; so you just propose copying and copying when we have enough people in our country to be creative and design our own education system […] You just want external evaluations to centralise, to impose, to decide how to homogenise all students in the Spanish state. (Education Committee Spanish Congress, 26 June 2013)

Or, for a taste of the unions' perspective, these excerpts from statements made by Comisiones Obreras (the main Teachers' Union) on evaluations:

> [E]xit exams are based on the atrocious belief that any improvement in education will be the result of the pressure exerted by the results of students […] they classify students into those that are successful (because they pass) and those which are not (because they fail) which is the most repugnant aspect of this reform […] teachers feel that this is a challenge to their professional competence. This is because they are losing control over what they teach and how they wish to evaluate it. (Milán and Recio, 2013)

Eventually the implementation of national exams was halted by the very same conservative government—we had quit government a few months before—that proposed it as a concession to facilitate a national consensus on education. But no progress was made for years.

6.5. Back to the Future

As we explained before, the impact of the financial crisis and the budget cuts led to a political tsunami of a magnitude that we failed to recognise when it began. A mostly bi-partisan system was replaced with a very fragmented landscape in which new populist parties on the radical left emerged with unexpected energy. Later on, populist parties on the radical right also emerged, probably due to concerns about the power gained by nationalist movements with the next government.

By mid-2018 a vote of no confidence ousted the conservative government, and a minority socialist government took office. It was short-lived, since it did not get the 2019 budget approved and was forced to call an early election. In late 2019 a new government was formed, a coalition between the socialist party and a new far-left party (Podemos). Since the coalition does not have a parliamentary majority it relies on the support of other parties, such as nationalist parties, to approve budgets and legislation. Under these conditions, a new education reform has been approved in exchange for budget approval support, which has required many concessions (LOMLOE, 2020). The latest reform not only returns to the failed model which had been prevalent for over two decades. It actually goes even further: national standardised evaluations at the end of lower- and upper-secondary education for all students have been replaced with so-called 'general evaluations of the education system' which include only a sample of students and take place once every three years. Regional governments can implement diagnostic evaluations, but these cannot take place at the end of educational stages, and no common standards between regions are agreed. In an unexpected move, students who are failed by their teachers (according to the teachers' own standards) will be promoted to the next grade (since grade repetition has been almost forbidden) and can eventually obtain a national degree. In addition, students who fail several subjects at the end of upper-secondary level can still take the university entrance exam. The current government has argued that these policies follow OECD recommendations since all students will advance irrespective of their performance, in order to avoid grade repetition (Gomendio, 2020a). The logic here seems perverse: grade repetition is avoided, not because all students achieve pre-defined levels of performance at the end of each grade, but rather because performance no longer matters.

The government has defended these measures on the grounds that they promote equity. All students will advance and obtain degrees irrespective of their levels of performance, therefore eliminating the impact of family socio-economic background and migrant status, but also of effort and ability. In our view, the approval of this education reform represents an open capitulation by central government of the responsibility to implement policies to improve student performance and, in particular, mechanisms to allow disadvantaged students to perform well.

Central government has given up on evaluations, curricula and any aspiration to improve quality. Instead, it has created a complete disconnect between levels of student performance and educational degrees, by eliminating reliable ways to assess the former. This will devalue degrees and de-incentivise effort. No education system has improved under these circumstances. It is just a mirage to pretend that equity can be achieved when those who learn are treated exactly the same as those who do not. A system which intends not to leave anyone behind will ultimately leave everyone behind.

In contrast, the current government has maintained most of the elements of our reform (LOMCE) which made VET (and Dual VET) an attractive option for an increasing number of students. Given that in Spain rates of early school leaving and youth unemployment remain high when compared to other European countries, the current government seems to have taken a more practical approach and buried all the ideological arguments against the first steps taken by our reform. This is a very revealing case of a political party (in this case the socialist PSOE) imposing very high political costs on its main opponent (the conservative PP) on ideological grounds and then reaping the benefits of the very policies that it deemed unacceptable once they have been implemented and they hold power.

The rationale for relaxing the requirements for grade promotion and for obtaining degrees is probably the same as the rationale for keeping changes already implemented in VET. This seemingly contradictory combination will improve the statistics to which the EU pays attention: early school leaving and grade repetition will decrease, as will youth unemployment. But these statistics will be a mirage because they will provide no information in relation to the performance of students, which is likely to suffer.

In response to pressures from nationalist political parties, the new reform transfers more control over the curriculum to regional governments and completely eliminates the obligation to use Spanish (along with the co-official language) in schools. The reform also limits parental choice and implements rules of admission by schools which represent a threat to government-funded, privately run schools; this is a concession to the radical-left populist (Podemos) partner in government, which proposes eliminating these schools to ensure that all children attend public schools thus eliminating any privilege. The current education minister has repeatedly stated that the latest reform follows OECD recommendations to avoid segregation and inequality by eliminating standardised assessments, allowing students to make progress and obtain degrees irrespective of their level of performance and decreasing the role of government-funded, privately run schools.

6.6. What Has Been the Role of PISA?

In recent years, successive education reforms at the opposite end of the spectrum in terms of aims and policies (LOMCE and LOMLOE) have argued that they use PISA data and policy recommendations. Thus, it seems fair to ask: what position has been defended by the OECD?

In short, it has supported both sides, as well as a long and futile pause to find consensus. Andreas Schleicher (widely recognised as the father of PISA) is highly respected in Spain, so he has been invited to parliamentary commissions and other relevant committees. He has been granted an influential role.

In the 2013 parliamentary Education Committee hearings which discussed the LOMCE prior to its approval by parliament, his statements included:

> [T]here are systems which work well from the point of view of equity but not quality, which is the case in Spain [...] to use evaluation to improve quality, accountability and evaluate the improvement in student performance [...] is one of the areas in which the reform [LOMCE] is trying to improve education in Spain [...] It is very important that school autonomy and accountability go hand in hand [...] Student performance

improves when there are standardised student assessments [...] I do not think that it is correct to argue that the reform implements early tracking and therefore segregation, because both options are offered when most countries do. (Education Committee, 15 July 2013)

Four years later, in 2017, his statements for the same Education Committee included:

PISA data do not show major regional differences [...] Teachers need to play a relevant role in the design of education reforms [...] Modern curricula need to be designed by teachers [...] Evaluation is key because you cannot improve what you don´t measure, but I don´t see a relationship with accountability [...] Some countries do not share the results of student assessments with anybody [...] because if teachers feel that they are being evaluated from the outside [...] it is possible that they will withdraw and there will be no benefit because they may feel judged (Education Committee, 13 September 2017)

There were no hearings in parliament to discuss the most recently approved education reform (LOMLOE). In fact, no debates took place despite the governments´ claims about ongoing negotiations and the search for consensus. Instead, the channel through which Andreas Schleicher expressed full support for this reform was a recent interview in the leading Spanish newspaper, in which he stated:

To memorise content about physics or chemistry is not useful. The real issue is: can students think like a scientist and design an experiment? [...] The same happens with history. To remember facts does not help. [...] Successful schools are those which equip students with strategies to learn and unlearn and relearn as the context changes (*El País*, 2021)

We assume that this means that it is not important to memorise facts, and from this mistaken premise it follows that the acquisition of knowledge should not be evaluated. It seems contradictory that the person who is responsible for PISA would support a lack of evaluations at the national level, because evaluating student performance in different countries is precisely what PISA does.

The personal support that Schleicher has lent to the latest reform has led some education experts to criticise OECD support of education policies which disguise the poor quality of the Spanish education system with good intentions based on a misleading concept of equity (Luri, 2021).

It is difficult to understand why PISA has supported successive reforms in Spain each representing such different approaches, but this is probably the result of a willingness to be seen as having influence in the policy arena. More importantly, PISA values its huge media impact in Spain highly, since it uses this variable as the main measure of its own success. Finally, it needs to ensure that Spain continues to make the massive financial contribution that an extended sample of all seventeen of its regions represents. Spain is one of the countries which provides the largest amount of funding to PISA, so its participation is key to PISA's survival. In other words, PISA also has vested interests to defend in Spain, even at the expense of clear contradictions.

Perhaps the greatest incongruity has been the publication of the PISA 2018 results after they were withdrawn a few months earlier at the official global launch due to inconsistencies and unreliability. Apparently, the same results (with no corrections to or explanations about the inconsistencies detected) were published at the request of the current Minister of Education, who wished to use the alleged decline in performance to justify a new education reform and to point fingers at those regions governed by other political parties which supposedly had worse results (Gomendio, 2020b). The education reform was approved a few months later with no consensus at the national level but with the support of PISA. In the controversy surrounding this reform, no one seemed to notice that the OECD had published the results but included a warning in small print stating that they were not comparable with those of previous cycles.

PISA's lack of accountability and the inconsistencies shown when supporting reforms which propose completely different policies throw into question its role as an honest broker using objective evidence. It also challenges its self-proclaimed role as an influential player in education policy. Education reforms are crucial, and robust evidence about good practices should guide the decisions of policymakers. To play a role in the education policy debate, PISA needs to be consistent about its policy recommendations, should address any concerns that countries may have about the reliability of the data, and should provide solid data and objective advice to reformists willing to pay the heavy price of education reforms.

7. Education Reforms

The Interaction between Ideology, Governance, Conflicts of Interest and Evidence

7.1. Who Cares about Education and Why?

Education reforms matter. They actually matter a great deal, both at the individual and microsocial levels, as well as at the societal level. The reason for this is that good education systems equip individuals with the knowledge and skills required to obtain good-quality jobs, to navigate uncertain and rapidly changing labour markets, to develop innovative ways to deal with new challenges and to integrate fully in complex societies. Over time it has become increasingly clear that it is not just about having an education, but rather about enjoying a good-quality education, as knowledge-based societies and technological change have resulted in dramatic increases in the demand for higher levels of skills that are likely to continue or even accelerate in the future. Well-educated people can take control of their lives and adapt to a changing landscape, while poorly-educated people will struggle. At the aggregate level, high-quality education systems are key for improving human capital, which is the fundamental driver of economic growth and prosperity.

Families care deeply about education because it has a strong influence on the future of their children, but how much education is valued, and the extent to which parents get involved, varies significantly between countries and cultures. Employers also value education highly since it ensures that students acquire the increasingly complex levels of skills that they demand; obviously they care more in societies where advanced economies already demand high levels of skills. Political parties seize the opportunity that educational ideologies provide to feed their electoral bases with educational flags, which seem to have considerable mobilising influence. Governments can exert a strong influence through education: they can boost human capital and economic growth; promote social mobility and equity; instil common values; facilitate integration and social cohesion, thus shaping the fundamentals of their societies, which could result in strengthening citizens' support. Finally, the sheer size and complexity of education systems and the levels of investment that they require imply that there are many stakeholders who receive direct benefits from the education system. The most numerous and politically powerful are teachers, who are expected to share the goal of achieving a high-quality education system in which they will thrive.

In this book, we try to understand the following paradox: everyone seems to agree on the value of high-quality education, and yet education reforms are uniquely difficult to implement. What are the main obstacles and how might they be overcome?

Conventional wisdom has it that governments rarely decide to embark on education reforms because the political costs in the short term are huge, while the benefits are rather diffuse and only become tangible in the long term. While it is obvious that it takes years before an education reform has an impact on all schoolchildren, and even longer before any benefits in adult life can be assessed, we still contest the argument that benefits only happen in the long term. As we have seen, many education reforms do have a positive impact in the short term. Thus, the main issue seems to be understanding the nature of the political costs and whether these can be overcome.

7.2. Ideological Battles: What Are They About?

In most countries, education is a highly polarised issue in the political arena. In this battlefield the quality of the education system as a whole plays a very minor role, partly because for most voters it seems to be a rather vague and wide-ranging concept which bears little relation to their specific needs, interests and values. The most divisive ideological flags focus on two issues.

On the one hand, parental choice is a key component for political parties on the right of the spectrum, and is attractive to parents who wish to have the freedom to choose the school they believe is best for their children in terms of quality, reputation, discipline, specialisation, values and in some cases religious faith. The education system can only allow parents to make meaningful choices if there is a diversity of schools on offer and this is achieved mainly through privately managed, government-funded schools (also known as charter schools). Thus, freedom of choice implies (i) the existence of different types of schools which, in turn, leads to competition to attract students, and (ii) transparency and accountability on the outcomes, so that parents can make informed choices.

On the other hand, equity is the main issue for political parties on the left of the spectrum. In this case, the focus is on public education as a guarantor that all children will have access to the same educational opportunities and the emphasis is on comprehensive policies which ensure that all children are treated equally.

Many education systems show that parental choice and equity are compatible, but ideological battles require much more than the defence of certain principles. The demonisation of the principles defended by one's opponents is just as important. In this rather destructive process, parental choice is portrayed by the left as leading to the privatisation and marketisation of education, promoting segregation between children based on their socio-economic status, taking resources away from the public system and thus overwhelming public schools with disadvantaged students who face greater challenges. In contrast, political parties on the right caricature the pledge for equity as a disguised attempt to conceal the limitations of a public system too weak to deal with any form of competition and too mediocre to generate anything but low standards for all students. As a consequence, the original priorities become blurred and the debate often ends in an oversimplistic and false dichotomy between private versus public education, which are portrayed as serving the interests of the elites or those of the most vulnerable parts of society respectively. These, of course, are strawmen. But they are powerful images that define the coordinates along which the educational debate unfolds in many places.

These basic ideological views have overspill effects that end up influencing political attitudes on many other educational issues. Raising equity to the status of the main, if not the only, goal of the education system, often goes hand-in-hand with supporting the abolition of any measures that are regarded as 'discriminatory' or leading to 'segregation', such as grouping students by their ability so that teachers can achieve greater learning gains with a more homogeneous group of students, or tracking of students into academic and vocational paths before they enter upper-secondary education. Thus, advocates of equity as the main goal of education systems tend to support the implementation of the most radical comprehensive policies, even though the evidence shows that, in societies with high levels of inequality, such education policies can lead to the worst outcomes in terms of equity. In other words, while egalitarian societies have implemented comprehensive policies successfully, in societies with high levels of inequity the levels of student heterogeneity are so high that they require other policies to deal with this major challenge first and foremost.

The trend to avoid any policy which could potentially be linked to some form of discrimination has become so influential in recent years that standardised student assessments are being questioned (or eradicated) because socio-economic status, immigrant status, gender and ethnicity tend to have an impact on the results. It is obvious that this is a symptom of the extent to which the education system has failed to minimise the impact of those factors, not a causal effect. Standardised assessments are just metrics which set common targets and the results reflect the extent to which the education system has enabled all students to achieve such goals. But many now seem to believe that being blind to this reality will make the problem disappear. Ideology is based on beliefs, fears and values, and its links to evidence are tenuous at best.

Those in favour of parental choice also tend to support competition between schools, accountability, transparency and a culture of effort. In other words, diversification and merit rather than uniformity. The risk in this case is that, unless clear rules are established, privately managed, government-funded schools may select students according to their socio-economic status, or discriminate against minorities, leading to social segregation. Furthermore, the main limitation of this ideological position is that, while it defends a parent's right to choose what they regard as best, it does not make clear proposals about the overall education system, thus catering to a very targeted audience. In the worst-case scenario, it could lead to parents choosing a few good schools, while the public system as a whole remains in a poor state. Also, information asymmetry has to be considered in order to achieve a level playing field, since some parents have access to rich information resources on the quality of schools, while others do not.

While these issues seem to constitute the main pillars of the ideological views at opposite ends of the spectrum, in many countries the fiercest battles focus on issues which have less to do with the quality of the education system. In countries where no common narrative of history has prevailed, or where there are strong pro-independence parties in some regions, the curricular content of subjects such as history is the source of constant and bitter disputes. Those issues that are related to strong values and beliefs held by different groups will generate an ongoing conflict as to which will predominate or how they can be reconciled; in addition, as perceptions on culturally sensitive issues (such as abortion, euthanasia or LGBTQ+) evolve over time, the curriculum needs to adapt and the time lag tends to generate constant tensions. One clear example is religious faith: an agreement has to be reached as to whether different schools will adhere to different faiths, whether they will all teach a common subject that will deal with all religions and reflect their differences, or whether religion should remain entirely outside the scope of what schools teach.

Of course, ideological issues will always play a role in education reforms, in one way or another. They can be dealt with in different ways. In many instances, parties will be confrontational. They will claim that they will look for consensus but will do exactly the opposite, defending the radical views of those voters for whom education is a major electoral issue and trying to distance themselves from their opponents. This seems to be the only way in which political parties in most countries may obtain additional votes, by making education a major issue. In contrast, in countries where there is a *consociational* political culture, they will try find common ground and sideline the most divisive issues.

Ideological divides create deep cracks between political parties and between groups of voters that may be difficult to overcome after the elections are over. As a consequence, where those divides are deeper, governments may only dare to embrace an education reform when they enjoy a parliamentary majority. However, as different parties alternate in power over time, a succession of reforms and reversals following different ideological interests is a common and sterile experience. Countries where an agreement can be reached between the main political parties over basic issues linked to improved student performance—and not influenced by ideological views—which will be implemented in the long run, are rare but meaningful exceptions.

The recent trend in the political landscape, which has seen many countries moving away from mostly bipartisan or quasi-bipartisan systems to a much more fragmented political landscape, does not seem to have made things easier for education reforms, since coalitions often avoid divisive political issues.

At the end of the day, what seems to be the most productive strategy—agreement on the basics and *agreeing to disagree* on the rest—is becoming more difficult as polarisation, identity politics and echo chambers are intensifying everywhere. Ideological confrontations on education are here to stay and will continue to obstruct performance-oriented education reforms.

7.3. Reform: Who Decides What, Who Funds, Who Has a Say, Who Has the Power to Block

When governments do decide to engage in an education reform, the governance arrangements in place determine who decides what, who raises and who spends the funding, who is accountable to whom, and the power that stakeholders and groups with vested interests have in supporting or blocking reforms.

Centralised and federal countries represent the two opposite extremes where there is clear definition of responsibilities at different levels: either central government or regions (respectively) hold most decision-making power, as well as the responsibilities for raising and allocating funding. The challenges for these two types of governance systems are very different. Centralised countries need to implement the right mechanisms to deal with the diversity in their countries. On the other hand, federal countries need to find ways to balance regional inequalities to prevent the education system from magnifying them;

this is normally achieved through additional funding provided by central government to compensate for regional disparities in wealth and resources, and by agreeing on common standards for all students to ensure that the education system implements the mechanisms required to avoid regional disparities in student outcomes.

In the last decades, there has been a widespread trend of decentralising education systems and the rationale has been that decision-making should take into account the specificity of regional and local needs, so that greater responsiveness to such needs would make the system more efficient. However, to achieve greater efficiency, several conditions need to be met, such as capacity building, a clear definition of responsibilities, and the implementation of accountability mechanisms, which unfortunately have not always been put in place.

Such decentralised, non-federal systems inhabit a grey area where responsibilities and funding can be shared in many different ways. Generally speaking, central government remains in charge of raising most of the funding through taxes which is then transferred to regional or local authorities, who decide how to spend it. If proper accountability mechanisms are not put in place, the disconnect between the responsibility for fundraising and the capacity to spend funds may lead to overspending and inefficient allocation of resources. It is also common for central government to retain decision-making powers on the general rules and architecture of the education system, as well as the national core curriculum and standardised national assessments, while the management of schools as well as some degree of autonomy in terms of curriculum and assessments, is transferred to regions,.

Among these *de facto* decentralised systems, a large number of actors play a role in education reforms and therefore the degree of complexity is much greater. In particular, central government has responsibility for approving new laws, but regions are key in the implementation of such reforms. Since it is often the case that different political parties hold power in central government and in different regions, political alliances may play a key role in the level of support or rejection that regions voice about specific reforms and, even more importantly, in whether they are willing to implement the reforms approved by the national parliament.

When responsibilities are not well-defined, there is an inevitable tension between regions demanding more resources and power and central government reinforcing accountability mechanisms. Since most education reforms entail major re-distributional effects, regions are likely to react by escalating their demands. In this context, measures which may benefit the education system as a whole may be rejected by regions, either because they interpret them as a form of re-centralisation (e.g. national standardised exams), or because some regions regard themselves as losers in the new configuration (either because they fear receiving fewer resources, losing decision-making power, or being subject to greater control from central government). Although the interests of both central and regional governments are legitimate, central government's role is to improve the whole education system, while the role of regional governments is to ensure local advancement. Thus, the prism is very different and often leads to conflicts. In this context, voters' capacity to understand who is responsible for what, in the face of either improvements or declines, is often limited, particularly when the division of responsibilities is ill-defined.

As education systems have expanded to provide first universal access to education and then an increasing number of years of compulsory education, they have created complex and vast networks of schools which require a substantial amount of public funding. This growth has been accompanied by the surge of an increasing number of stakeholders who play very different roles, have different interests and hold very asymmetric powers. Obviously, policymakers would benefit from involving stakeholders in the design and implementation of education reforms since they can provide useful information, their support will give legitimacy to reforms, ensure their smooth implementation and increase the chances that they will last in the long term. Following this logic, it has become a mantra that reforms should be based on consensus. This seems an idealistic goal since major conflicts of interest often make consensus impossible, forcing governments either to adopt the lowest common denominator or to choose between the interests of powerful stakeholders and those of students. Thus, it seems more realistic to ask to what extent should different stakeholders be involved in the reform process and whether they should have veto powers.

Stakeholders can be categorised in two groups: those who benefit from a quality education system and those who benefit because they obtain resources directly. Clearly, the main beneficiaries of a quality education system are the students. The purpose of education systems is to serve students and therefore their improved performance should be the *raison d'être* of every education reform. However, the influence of parents as stakeholders is very weak, mainly because they are not organised in ways that would make them powerful players, but also because they tend to lack information about the quality and efficiency of the education system as a whole. As stakeholders, parents hold the weakest position in the information chain, and very often they can be misled or confused about the consequences of policy interventions. Generally speaking, parents tend to mobilise when they perceive that their rights are being curtailed, i.e. when their freedom of choice is threatened either due to changes in admission rules, or because privately managed, government-funded schools are at risk. Employers also benefit from good education systems because this ensures that their workers have high levels of skills. However, in most countries employers only become directly involved in vocational education and training by providing on-the-job training, useful information about the needs of the labour market and, in some cases, by setting the standards of apprenticeships.

The education system mobilises a huge amount of public funding which provides resources to many providers, such as the textbook publishing industry, ed-tech companies, transport or school canteen companies. However, the majority of the funding by far is spent on staff (teacher salaries mainly). This means that teachers directly receive most of the funding that is allocated to education and their huge numbers imply that in many countries the public education payroll makes governments the largest employer. A natural consequence of this is that teachers have become organised in unions which defend their interests. During the era of institutional formation (when access to education expands and children spend an increasing number of years in school) there is strong alignment between the interests of governments and teacher unions: the funding goes to building and equipping schools, and mostly to hiring an increasing number of teachers.

However, once this stage is over most governments look for ways to improve the quality and efficiency of the education system. In many countries this involves decentralisation, choice, accountability and, above all, a focus on student performance. This shift inevitably leads to conflicts of interest with unions.

Perhaps the main conflict arises as a consequence of the slowdown in the hiring of new teachers. The power of unions rests with the size of their membership and potential candidates (such as teachers on temporary contracts) expect unions to facilitate their entrance into the profession. Thus, once the stage where the education system is being built is over, unions shift their focus to class size: they demand smaller class sizes in order to ensure that more teachers continue to be hired. Although this is a legitimate defence of their interests, what seems misleading is that they disguise these vested interests as altruistic attempts to improve the quality of teaching.

Here, we have a very telling example of information asymmetry. Parents tend to believe that small class sizes equate to a more personalised, better-quality education, so they tend to actively support this demand. This has led to a widespread trend of gradually decreasing class sizes, despite the well-documented fact that this has no impact on student performance and is very costly. This has created a vicious cycle which has long-term consequences, since an increasing amount of funding goes to the salaries of a growing teaching force, instead of those resources being used to train and select fewer teachers of higher quality.

In many countries, unions have opted to ensure job security and good working conditions for all of their members, which entails a strong defence of similar salaries and job safety for all teachers (irrespective of their performance) and strong opposition to the dismissal of underperforming teachers, performance-linked pay, demanding training for teachers, selective hiring of teachers based on merit, and teacher evaluations. When unions have taken these demands to the extreme and they have enjoyed the political power to force governments to accept them, the result has been entrenched low teacher quality. This leads to a very dangerous loop since, given that the role of unions is to defend the interests of their members, when teacher quality is low unions will regard any accountability measure as a threat to their members. Thus, as governments have shifted the focus from inputs (resources) to outputs (student performance) and have looked for efficiency and accountability, conflicts of interest with the unions have escalated. In those countries where unions have veto powers, they have systematically blocked reforms.

In the case of education reforms, the crux of the matter is that unions and other stakeholders are well-organised and have political power to defend the status quo, while those who would benefit from better outcomes (students and their families) are not.

For this reason, many governments face very difficult choices when they wish to undertake education reforms because they have to confront and deal with such intense conflicts of interest. Imposing an education reform is likely to shorten its life-span, but reaching a consensus often involves capitulating to vested interests and giving up on contentious but necessary policies which are rejected by ideological opponents. As we have seen, PISA claims that the policy recommendations that it provides in practice lower the costs for policymakers who are willing to follow them, because they can justify that reforms are based on evidence and are therefore exempt from ideological biases and free from manipulation by groups with vested interests.

Is the evidence from international surveys robust enough to empower policymakers to the extent that they can overcome conflicts of interest and ideological battles? Our answer is unfortunately not.

7.4. International Evidence versus Conflicts of Interest: Who is David and Who is Goliath?

International surveys have generated a vast amount of data on student performance in different countries which have revealed major differences in quality between countries and allowed comparative analyses to identify which features of education systems are associated with good outcomes. The availability of this information has raised hopes that governments could improve their education systems by using this objective evidence to design their education reforms and policies. In this way policymaking would ensure its success by using rigorous and irrefutable data, rather than partisan wrangling.

For this evidence-based approach to work, several conditions have to be met. The main condition is that the data must be reliable and that robust and solid conclusions can be drawn from it about 'what works' and in which contexts. The second is that all stakeholders (not just policymakers) should agree that whenever there is strong evidence concerning the positive impact of specific policies, this should be enough to overcome underlying conflicts of interest, which should be sacrificed for the sake of improving student performance. Finally, for evidence to become a guiding light, societies should agree on what they wish to achieve through education.

All international surveys measure student outcomes in the same domains: reading, science and mathematics. While PIRLS and TIMSS also examine curricular content to analyse the extent to which students learn what they are taught in school, PISA obtains additional information through questionnaires and claims to measure the extent to which students are able to apply knowledge to solve problems in unfamiliar contexts, irrespective of whether the learning takes place in schools, homes or the social environment. Another relevant difference between these surveys is that while PIRLS and TIMSS assess student performance in specific grades, PISA evaluates the performance of fifteen-year-olds irrespective of grade.

Despite the more tenuous links between school practices and student performance in PISA, this is the only survey that has defined advising governments on good practices as its main priority and boasts about its influential role in education policy. Although the data provided by these surveys are not adequate to draw causal inferences, PISA has become a powerful tool in the political debate. Its influence arises mainly from the emphasis it places on targeting the media in most countries to enhance awareness of the national results and as an effective way to put pressure on governments to follow the policies that PISA recommends. Thus, in a way PISA has become part of the political debate rather than a source of independent evidence to allow governments to steer away from ideological battles.

In order to understand whether PISA policy recommendations are based on robust and solid evidence it is important to explain that they are based almost exclusively on correlations which are included in PISA publications and which follow a very similar pattern cycle after cycle, although the number of participating countries has grown over time. It is well-known that correlations do not allow the establishment of causal relationships, so this is a major weakness of PISA's conclusions. Although more sophisticated analyses have been carried out using the available data from all ILSAs to establish more robust links between education policies and student outcomes, these are often ignored by PISA and instead remain within the academic realm, thus having no substantial impact on the media or policymakers. We therefore need to distinguish between the conclusions drawn from the correlations used by PISA and other, more robust analyses.

There is complete unanimity on one issue: the overall level of investment per student does not have any impact on student performance when it is above a certain threshold. While most OECD countries are above this threshold, many low- and middle-income countries are still below it. This result is robust when comparisons at different levels are made: comparative analyses between countries, as well as between regions within countries (which share the same architecture of the education system and often the same curriculum and assessments, thus eliminating many confounding factors that are present when countries are compared). In addition, when trends over time are analysed, it becomes clear that most countries have increased investment in education substantially over time, with no impact whatsoever on student outcomes.

The evidence that—above a certain threshold—investment *per se* is unrelated to student outcomes is the most solid evidence about what does not work in education. These findings contradict the most widely accepted premise in any debate on education: the higher the input (investment) the better the outcome (student performance). And the reverse: that budget cuts in education will inevitably lead to a decline in student outcomes. Knowing that the assumption is wrong does not seem to have had any impact on the education debate or investment policies. Why?

Since most of the investment in education is allocated to staff, the total amount is largely the product of two factors: the number of teachers and their salaries. In turn, the number of teachers is the result of the number of students and class size. The reason why the level of investment per student is unrelated to student performance is that neither class size nor teacher salaries have a direct impact on student outcomes. But the main driver is class size because it determines to a large extent the number of teachers and therefore has a huge impact on overall levels of investment.

It seems fair to say that this solid conclusion has had no impact at all as it goes against the tide of public conversation. Most countries have continued to substantially increase levels of investment over time, mainly because class size has continued to decrease, but also because teacher salaries have increased. There are several reasons why governments have been oblivious to this finding. The idea that investment is what matters the most in education is so ingrained that the majority of voters tend to agree irrespective of their ideology or political affinity and support growing levels of investment, so political parties in general do not dare question such a crucial matter. In virtually every country the political cost of reducing investment in education is huge, since it is interpreted as an unequivocal sign that a government does not regard education as a priority.

For unions and their allies on the left of the political spectrum, these two variables are the most important by far: decreases in class size require the hiring of more teachers and therefore make unions more powerful, and increases in teacher salaries greatly benefit their members. Thus, unions will go to great lengths to put pressure on governments and political parties to ensure that class size continues to decrease and teacher salaries continue to increase. Often, their support of reforms is contingent on increases in investment which ensure the continuation of these trends. The narrative built to defend these measures has been carefully crafted to avoid mentioning these vested interests and instead focuses on presumed benefits for students.

Despite all the evidence to the contrary, this narrative seems convincing to most families, owing to the widespread belief that smaller class sizes allow individualised teaching, which is assumed to improve quality of teaching. Policy recommendations from PISA have confused matters further: the conclusion in most cycles made it clear that neither investment, nor class size or teacher salaries, had a positive impact on student outcomes, but in the last cycle this stance was changed without any clear empirical evidence.

It seems as if PISA has decided that since the world was paying no attention to its most robust conclusion, it was better to accommodate 'mainstream beliefs' than to be seen as having no influence after two decades. This leaves governments with little support from PISA to defend one of the few policies actually based on strong evidence. This has far-reaching consequences since, in the context of tight budgets, most investment continues to go towards reducing class sizes, rather than measures which would improve teacher quality, such as better teacher training and professional development, or incentives for teachers to perform well.

There is a second group of policy recommendations where PISA deviates from conclusions based on more robust analyses. As we have seen, there is evidence-based consensus that curriculum-based, standardised exit exams improve student performance. The reasons seem obvious: assessments in primary school allow early detection of those students lagging behind at a point when support measures are more likely to work, and assessments at the end of lower- and upper-secondary school are powerful indicators for students and teachers of what is expected and the level of effort required, giving ample opportunity to establish compensatory measures that allow disadvantaged students to achieve those standards, as well as providing guidance for further direction in students' educational pathways. Such assessments also ensure that teachers do not set different standards, and that education systems implement the necessary mechanisms to ensure that students in different regions achieve the same basic standards.

Although PISA did show in its early cycles that student assessments had a positive impact on student performance, it gradually changed its stance, aligning itself with those who believe that assessments are too stressful and could demotivate disadvantaged students who may feel that the standards are unachievable. As a consequence, it started warning against "high-stakes" exams (a negatively-loaded tag) and supporting assessments with no academic consequences, including those which only target a sample of students. At present, there is a tidal wave of rejection of student exams on the grounds that they are discriminatory, because factors such as socio-economic background, gender or migrant status tend to have an impact on the results.

In our view, student assessments are the equivalent of an X-ray which clearly diagnoses the weaknesses which afflict any education system but are not the cause of discrimination. Education systems will only be able to address such problems if they have a clear view, which can only be obtained if all students are assessed using the same metrics. The alternative would be to eliminate exams and therefore make education systems blind to student outcomes, which would lead to governments renouncing their responsibility to minimise the impact of such factors. They would also give up on evaluating the impact of policies and on implementing any sort of accountability mechanisms based on student outcomes.

The repudiation of standardised and external student assessments is also the consequence of the stern defence of vested interests. In countries where teacher quality is poor, unions oppose student assessments because they fear that they will be used as indirect means of teacher evaluation. In such contexts, political parties on the left of the spectrum often decry exams using the argument that the fact that disadvantaged students or migrant students achieve poor results is proof that they have not enjoyed the same opportunities and therefore cannot be evaluated with the same metrics. In addition, in decentralised countries, regions often reject national assessments as a form of 're-centralisation', since they wish to expand their educational autonomy and minimise any form of accountability. In sum, there is a constellation of factors which make the evidence irrelevant despite its robustness.

Most analyses also show that giving more autonomy to schools in exchange for accountability has a positive impact on student outcomes. The reason is that when principals are able to make decisions about their schools, and teachers have the responsibility to choose which approach to use in the classroom, they tend to become more efficient thanks to their knowledge of their students and their needs. It also makes their jobs more stimulating, since they have greater responsibility and freedom to innovate. However, all analyses show that greater autonomy must go hand-in-hand with greater accountability, so that regional and national governments can make sure that the decisions taken by principals and teachers do lead to better student outcomes.

This is perhaps one of the more influential policy recommendations, although transferring greater autonomy to schools enjoys wider support than implementing accountability mechanisms, so the interplay between the two factors is often ignored. Granting more autonomy to schools has become part of PISA's recommended policy package, including for low-performing countries. This is unfortunate, since the evidence clearly shows that school autonomy will only bring benefits when principals and teachers are prepared to use those responsibilities in an effective way. This requires capacity building before responsibilities are transferred, as well as a good-quality education system with highly-skilled principals and teachers. In fact, there is solid evidence that school autonomy has a negative impact on student outcomes in low- and middle-income countries.

Once again, unions fully support school autonomy as part of a more ambitious agenda that revolves around the idea that teachers should be 'trusted', a figure of speech which implies that teachers should have the freedom to choose what they teach and how, without being subject to accountability measures. The attitude of regions in decentralised systems is often contradictory, since they support greater autonomy as a means of further decentralisation, but when central government grants it, they often seize the opportunity to retain the new decision-making powers rather than transferring them to schools. Thus, while increasing school autonomy may be one of the clearest signals of the impact of evidence on education policy, it is often advised in contexts where it has harmful effects and it does not always go hand-in-hand with proper accountability measures.

This is a classic example of the risk of extrapolating practices which work in mature, high-quality education systems, and applying them in low-performing systems which are still not ready to take those steps. Improving education systems requires careful orchestration. School autonomy is one of the last steps in that sequence, because it relies on an established high quality of teaching, and on principals being true leaders. In other words, there is a mistaken logic which assumes that any practices present in top-performing systems will have a positive impact when transplanted into low-performing systems. The reality is much more complex. Only top-performing systems can successfully implement certain practices, such as school autonomy, because many other pieces of the complex puzzle are already in place for that change to have the desired positive impact. Thus, context matters, and most education policies cannot be extrapolated from high-performing systems to low-performing systems. But when vested interests benefit from such policies, this tilts the balance in favour of implementing them. It goes without saying that policy borrowing is not the same as policy learning.

The last policy recommendation on which PISA deviates from other analyses is the issue of school choice and the existence of privately managed, government-funded (charter) schools. A few countries have traditionally developed these schools to allow parents to choose from a diverse offering. From the 1990s, a growing number of countries has introduced reforms to enhance school choice in order to make the education system more sensitive to the increasingly different needs of societies that have become more diverse and plural, and also to enhance quality and stimulate innovation. When addressing this issue, PISA tends to group privately managed, government-funded schools with private schools and directly compares this broad category with public schools. Thus, the analyses are not granular enough to compare the three categories individually and to draw clear conclusions about government-dependent private schools, which are the focus of much controversy. The general conclusion drawn by PISA is that private schools tend to do better, but this advantage disappears when socio-economic background is accounted for and therefore there are no clear benefits that could outweigh the risks associated with potential student segregation.

Thus, PISA seems more concerned about the potential risks of privately managed, government-funded schools leading to the segregation of students, than about any potential benefits. More robust analyses have concluded that privately managed, government-funded schools do generate better student outcomes due to their greater autonomy, which is linked to accountability of results, and to enhanced competition between schools to improve student performance in order to attract new parents. The data also show that government-dependent private schools tend to be much more cost-effective than public schools since they usually provide education at a lower cost per student than the latter. This is the result of a combination of factors: teachers in government-dependent private schools invest more time in teaching, these schools have larger class sizes, and principals have more control over the hiring of teachers.

However, when government-dependent private schools receive too little funding from government, they may not be able to afford to provide free education and instead charge tuition fees or add-on fees for extra-curricular activities. Since this undermines the principle of free-school choice, it is important that enough funding is provided by government and that these schools do not charge additional fees or follow a policy of selective admissions. Regulatory mechanisms should be implemented to prevent government-dependent private schools from targeting families who can afford to pay for their children's education and/or the best-performing students since both would increase inequalities. Thus, PISA warnings against the potential negative impact of school choice seem exaggerated, since the risks can and should be mitigated.

This policy measure is one of the most controversial in the political debate, because political parties on the right strongly support school choice while political parties on the left and unions strongly oppose it. The rationale used by political parties on the right is that school choice is a right that parents have and that privately managed, government-funded schools combine efficiency with quality. In contrast, unions and leftist parties claim that they segregate students according to socio-economic background and detract resources from the public system, which becomes over-burdened with disadvantaged students. Unions also fear that the large degree of autonomy granted to privately managed, government-funded schools and, in particular, the power that principals have to hire and dismiss teachers threaten some of their highly-valued privileges.

While in many countries this has become the most divisive issue, creating a schism between opponents of so-called 'privatisation' and supporters of choice and open competition, a few countries have managed to make it the core of a multi-party agreement. This is the case in the UK, where the main political parties have agreed to support a new type of school—academies—which entailed a major change in governance: the responsibility and funding shifted from local authorities to central government, and new accountability mechanisms based on student outcomes were put in place. Originally, low-performing public schools were converted into academies, but the model has proven so successful that it has grown, thanks to the support of consecutive governments of different ideological affiliations, to the extent that at present nearly 70% of publicly funded secondary schools are academies. It should be noted that agreement across political parties was possible, at least partly, due to the weakened power of unions in the UK.

The third and last group covers PISA policy recommendations not based on robust data or not based on data at all. Unfortunately, these policy recommendations address a major and fundamental dimension of education systems: equity.

There seems to be consensus on the idea that quality and equity are the two main dimensions of the education system. However, while measures of quality are quite straightforward (student performance), equity is multi-dimensional, and the available indicators only capture partial aspects. This leads to a largely unrecognised problem: when complex phenomena are simplified by the use of several indicators, this often gets lost in translation, meaning that one or a few of those narrow indicators is equated with the much broader and complex educational issue that they are meant to measure, i.e. equity. Thus, conclusions about such a multifaceted issue depend to a large extent on which indicator is chosen, and changes in one indicator are often used to draw general conclusions about progress towards educational equity. In short, equating any of these narrow indicators with the complex dimension of equity leads to the wrong conclusions.

PISA uses a large number of indicators to measure equity, such as the variance of student outcomes explained by student socio-economic background, the proportion of students who reach basic levels of proficiency, the variance explained by differences between schools and differences within schools, or the proportion of disadvantaged students that achieve high levels of performance (resilient students). As we will see, each indicator tells a different story and none of them tells the full story.

There is widespread consensus that socio-economic background is the factor with the single largest impact on student outcomes, a fact supported by robust analyses of data from different ILSAs. No education system has been able to completely overcome the influence of family background. While it seems unrealistic to expect that education systems will eliminate such an influential factor, it is important that they try to minimise it. However, good-quality education systems tend to raise the performance of all students, so disadvantaged students in high-quality education systems tend to outperform advantaged students in poor-quality education systems. From these findings, PISA concludes that the world is no longer divided between rich countries where all students perform better and poor countries where student performance is low. But unfortunately it is. Since poor students in Finland are not as poor as those in Colombia, if the wealth of the country is taken into account, it becomes clear that rich students in poor countries do perform worse than poor students in rich countries. This is probably the consequence of systemic deficiencies affecting poorer countries and which parental resources cannot overcome, such as low curricular standards, teachers with low levels of skills and poorly designed assessments.

The broader and most challenging question is to what extent such differences between countries reflect the degree to which societies are egalitarian, or are mainly the result of the implementation of policies which simply minimise the impact of inequity. The evidence shows that the impact of household income upon student performance in countries with high levels of inequity is much greater than in more egalitarian societies. These findings suggest that education systems cannot overcome the impact of profound social and economic inequalities, unless policymakers succumb to the temptation of lowering standards for all students. They question the establishment of causal links between specific education policies and equitable outcomes, when these have been deployed in egalitarian societies. They warn against the risk of assuming that transferring policies which are implemented by egalitarian societies to countries with high levels of inequity will help to reduce inequality in student outcomes. The issue is clearly very complex, but the available evidence suggests that the degree of social and economic equity permeates education systems; as a result, egalitarian societies do not require major interventions against inequity. In contrast, societies with high levels of inequity face very different challenges and require specific policies to minimise the impact of inequity.

For most education systems, finding ways to deal with student heterogeneity is a major challenge, since teachers need to ensure that students with different performance levels continue to learn and achieve similar goals. Clearly, this issue is exacerbated in countries with high levels of inequality, where students have very different starting points, different levels of support at home and different access to resources. All these factors amplify differences in student performance, which become a major obstacle to learning gains. A number of policies have been devised to reduce variation in student ability when it compromises learning gains, but these have generated heated controversy. While supporters claim that teachers will be able to make greater learning progress in a classroom or group where students have similar levels of ability and needs, opponents argue that they will harm low-performing students who will not be allowed to learn from their high-achieving peers, and that this will lead to discrimination and segregation since disadvantaged students will be placed in low-achieving groups/classes/tracks, irrespective of their level of performance.

The recommendations from PISA are consistent with this predominant narrative and do not support practices which aim to reduce student heterogeneity in performance, such as ability grouping, early tracking or grade repetition. However, careful analyses of the data reveal that such conclusions are not supported by robust evidence, so they must be challenged. In addition, the set of equity indicators that PISA uses is rather narrow and therefore fails to detect the harmful effects that supposedly 'egalitarian policies' inflict upon education systems in countries where social and economic inequity is pronounced. Vocational education and training, which PISA seems to abhor, is perhaps the clearest example of a policy conclusion contaminated by ideology and prejudice. One of the strongest policy recommendations from PISA is that VET decreases student performance and therefore should be delayed as much as possible. This is surprising, given that in most countries students cannot choose VET until the age of sixteen and PISA evaluates students at the age of fifteen. Put simply, PISA data cannot evaluate the impact of VET on student performance because there is no sample of students for the vast majority of countries.

In the case of grade repetition, PISA seems to fall into the well-known reverse causality trap: since the performance of students who repeat a grade is lower, then grade repetition lowers performance and should be avoided. This conclusion misses the point entirely because when students repeat a grade it is because their level of performance is so below average that they cannot continue to learn at the pace of their classmates. Grade repetition is a last resort and a second chance for students who have fallen far behind; thus, recommendations to abolish this practice do not address the root of the problem, which is the question of how to implement mechanisms earlier on that will allow students to catch up as soon as they start to struggle. Finally, conclusions regarding ability grouping face a similar issue: a simple correlation will show that this practice is more common when student performance levels are highly varied, as in non-egalitarian societies. The association between these variables cannot be used as proof that ability grouping directly decreases levels of equity.

More importantly, PISA fails to grasp important issues which should be considered in this profoundly ideological debate on equity because it does not take into account any indicators that are not generated by the survey itself. The available evidence shows that practices which aim to reduce student heterogeneity and cater for different needs and interests, such as ability grouping and differentiated academic and VET programmes, do not decrease student performance. Furthermore, it shows that in non-egalitarian societies they tend to benefit low-performing students the most. When PISA recommendations are followed and 'comprehensive' policies borrowed from Nordic countries are implemented in countries with low-quality education systems and high levels of inequality, we see the worst outcomes in terms of equity: high rates of grade repetition, which lead to high rates of early school leaving. Students who drop out of school face high levels of unemployment for the rest of their lives. But PISA seems blind to these atrocious outcomes.

Obviously, we are not denying that any differential treatment of students carries a hidden risk of discrimination. Poorly designed ability grouping could result in students from low socio-economic backgrounds being unfairly assigned to low-performing groups, therefore limiting their chances of making progress. Similarly, old-fashioned VET systems may target students from underprivileged backgrounds and equip them with such a narrow set of skills that they can only aspire to low-skills jobs. The fear that education systems may fall into these traps is seemingly not supported by the evidence. But it is this fear that leads to recommendations to treat all students equally, which is widely regarded as an inclusive strategy. However, the needs of disadvantaged students will not be addressed by them receiving the same treatment as other students, because they require compensatory measures. While inclusive policies may serve as a safeguard against potential discrimination, they are by no means a solution to the very real problems that education systems face. When student heterogeneity becomes an obstacle to learning, reducing differences between students by grouping them according to their ability and offering different pathways grants the education system flexibility to adapt to the diverse needs of its student population.

7.5. The Geography of Education Success

A very consistent picture emerges when ILSA data are used to compare countries in terms of performance: the top performers are countries in East Asia, the low performers are mostly low- and middle-income countries in Latin America, Africa and the Near Middle East and the mid-performers are mostly European and North American countries along with New Zealand and Australia. The international surveys also reveal that in a number of cases differences between regions within countries are larger than differences between countries. Thus, despite their differences, ILSAs seem to be measuring similar features of student performance.

It is shocking that no strong narrative has been developed to explain the indisputable success of countries in East Asia, which are the real education superpowers. These countries have shown outstanding levels of performance from their earliest participation in ILSAs, and continue to improve over time. There is a commonly-held view based on the mistaken idea that students perform better only because of the extreme pressures that families exert on their children and the many hours of rote learning. This has led to the unfortunate conclusion that there is not much to be learned from these East Asian education systems in other parts of the world where education is not valued as highly and parents shy away from putting pressure on their children to perform well.

Instead, we argue that the fact that some of the policies implemented by these countries clearly contradict the dichotomous narrative (comprehensive vs segregation policies, trust in vs mistrust of teachers) that has invaded the ideological debate has downplayed any lessons to be learned.

Countries such as South Korea and Singapore clearly demonstrate that major improvements can take place much faster than is widely assumed, as long as the right policies are implemented and there is continuity over time. Continuity here does not mean preserving the same policies, but rather the opposite, i.e. that changes must take place over time as the quality of the education system improves, but these must be consistent with previous steps. Policymakers in these countries decided that human capital was the best asset, and in a few decades they evolved from illiterate societies to the top-performing education systems in the world. One key element is the trade-off between teacher quality and class size. These countries, like most in East Asia, have opted for very large class sizes, so that investment goes mainly into teacher training and professional development. The excellent quality of the teaching force has yielded outstanding student outcomes. Such policy choices have been possible because unions do not have the power to block reforms, so admission processes both for university and for the teaching profession are highly selective. Teachers spend more hours engaged in professional development of excellent quality than in most other countries and this is linked to promotion and meaningful career choices. Because of the levels of excellence prevalent among teachers, the profession is highly valued and respected. But the misleading concept of trust does not apply: high curricular standards, as well as student assessments, are defined by central government and schools do not enjoy high levels of autonomy.

A key element of Singapore's sucess is the fact that tracking was initially implemented as early as primary level, in order to lower high rates of early school leaving. Given the success of these different tracks which cater to the needs of a diverse student population, Singapore has preserved tracking in lower-secondary education until today, long after it became a top performer. This fact has been conveniently ignored, probably because the success of early tracking contradicts the dominant narrative, which supports comprehensive policies.

In East Asia, consistency has been achieved over time because in some countries political parties adopt a very pragmatic view of education that avoids divisive ideological issues. More troubling, however, is the fact that other countries are semi-democracies (with restricted political competition) and some are outright authoritarian regimes. Recognising that limited political quarrelling and a lack of union veto powers on education policy seem to facilitate educational advancement does not mean that full democracies could not achieve the same results if ideological prejudices and vested interests were kept at bay.

The region which has moved in the opposite direction to East Asia is Latin America. Despite a better starting point around fifty years ago and huge efforts over the last decades to expand access to higher levels of educational attainment, the performance of students is very poor, so the returns in terms of skills are very low. This is mainly because

Latin American countries have implemented the opposite policies to those in East Asia. Investment has grown, but it has been directed mainly towards reducing class sizes, and few efforts to improve teacher quality have been successful. The power of the unions in Latin America is unparalleled, so they have put enormous pressures on governments to decrease class size (a measure that parents also support) and have forcefully rejected attempts to improve teacher quality by introducing selection measures for university degrees in education, training of a higher standard, and more demanding requirements for entering the teaching profession. As a consequence, these countries are locked in a downward spiral: unions defend the interests of a low-quality teaching force, such as lack of student assessments and teacher evaluations. Although class size continues to decrease, it has no impact on student outcomes.

In a region with huge levels of inequity, families, social movements and policymakers have high expectations of education's power as an engine of social mobility. This has led to the adoption of comprehensive policies and the abolition of so-called 'non-inclusive' policies. Thus, there is no ability grouping, no early tracking and VET is poorly developed. The universal aspiration is to access university, which is regarded as the only route to success. But these policies have failed in a big way. Comprehensive policies have not been able to deal with the huge diversity of students who enter school and have blocked any mechanisms which might deal with major differences in performance by providing alternative pathways. Consequently, high levels of grade repetition and early school leaving are prominent features of education systems in Latin America.

Most of the policy recommendations from PISA seem to originate from the contrast between Finland's unexpected success and the shock experienced by Germany in the very first PISA cycle (in 2000, two decades ago). The contrast between the unexpected success of a small and humble nation like Finland and the wounded pride of a powerful country such as Germany was crucial in the formation of a narrative which remains intact and very influential today, despite being—at least, in part—factually wrong. The Finnish education system was regarded as comprehensive (no early tracking), having a high-quality teaching force, high levels of school autonomy and achieving excellence by prioritising equity. In contrast, Germany had early streaming of students into vocational and academic tracks from the age of ten years, and family socio-economic background and immigrant status had a much greater impact on student performance.

As with all influential narratives, this one is rather simplistic: education reforms should address inequalities before student excellence by designing comprehensive systems which do not segregate students into academic vs vocational tracks, ability grouping, or different types of schools (e.g., charter vs public). High levels of school autonomy and good-quality teachers led to what proved to be a far-reaching conclusion: teachers should be trusted. This concept was used by unions all over the world to argue that the evidence showed that teachers should not be evaluated, should not follow a pre-defined curriculum, and should have autonomy to innovate and decide what they teach and how they teach it. Some have taken a step further, arguing that teachers should own their profession and design education reforms, a stance supported by PISA.

But this narrative is not supported by evidence. While Finland became a top performer in reading among a small group of countries, in the following years the performance of its students declined. This suggests that some of the initial conclusions may be wrong. It also shows that success in PISA may impede necessary reforms when countries rely too much on their accomplishments. Alternative explanations for Finnish students' high performance in reading include policies implemented well before PISA 2000 in a much more centralised system where schools did not enjoy high levels of autonomy and teacher excellence was common. The time lag between the year 2000, when fifteen-year-olds were assessed, and the policies in place when they joined schools, is often ignored. In addition, families in Finland play a very important role in developing the reading skills of young children, so this may be an excellent example of PISA not acknowledging causal factors which are most visible outside schools.

In the small group of countries which experienced the so-called PISA-shock, such as Germany, evidence from successive cycles shows that, although in general they did implement reforms, none of these countries improved over time. This has far-reaching implications, since the strategy that PISA has systematically followed, which focuses on targeting the media to put pressure on governments to react, does not seem to have worked, except in the case of PISA's own self-praise. Generating media outrage and placing governments between a rock and a hard place seems an odd strategy for a member-led organisation such as the OECD, where governments decide whether to join PISA and fund their countries' participation in addition to members' contributing to OECD core funding. It may also lead to unintended consequences, since it is possible that under such high pressure some governments may react too hastily and start reforms before they have the time to analyse the pros and cons of different options. Alternatively, since PISA claims to uncover the problems that an education system faces, then promotes a heated public debate and points fingers at governments, and finally claims to have the solutions to the very same issues that it has identified, some governments may end up following policy recommendations that do not apply to their specific contexts.

Those countries which improved after they started participating in ILSAs may provide more reliable insights as to which policies contributed to their success. These are all European countries which followed what seem to us the ABC of good practices: improve teacher quality, define a coherent curriculum with high standards, implement student assessments which are well-aligned with the curriculum, modernise and develop VET and, once a certain quality has been achieved, give more autonomy to schools in exchange for accountability. While ILSAs identified the positive trends in student performance over time in these reformist countries, it is deeply troubling that this evidence has not prevented most of these reforms from being reversed after they had proven to be successful. This fact shows that even when policies work, the evidence of this is not enough to protect them, because of a complete disregard for the objective assessments of policies.

7.6. Is the World a Better Place with Data?

According to PISA, no significant improvements in student performance have taken place almost two decades since the survey started. This is true when trends over time are considered for OECD countries, but also when a much larger group of countries is examined, since very few show improvements over time. This represents a failure of its self-proclaimed mission: to identify good practices, to advise governments on which policies should be implemented and, in this way, to enhance student performance all over the world.

The OECD claims that PISA has helped policymakers lower the costs of implementing education reforms by backing difficult decisions with evidence, and therefore concludes that the lack of progress detected is the result of countries not implementing the right policies, by which it means the policies that the OECD recommends. But putting the blame on governments seems unfair and unsubstantiated.

We have argued in this book that it is more constructive to analyse the interaction between evidence, vested interests and ideology. The picture that emerges is much more complex. We identify three types of evidence depending on how robust the data are: strong, context-dependent, and weak. The first group includes variables related to levels of investment. The evidence from ILSAs is particularly strong regarding the lack of impact of overall investment, and its two main components (class size and teacher salaries), on student performance. But this evidence leads to a head-on clash with the vested interests of teacher unions, which benefit greatly from decreases in class size and increases in teacher salaries, which require higher levels of investment. Thus, when unions are powerful and the evidence generates conflicts with vested interests, the evidence does not play any role.

The second group includes policy recommendations which, based on the evidence provided by ILSAs, are strongly context-dependent: standardised student assessments have a positive influence if well-aligned with a high-quality curriculum; school choice does have a positive impact as long as it does not select students according to socio-economic status or demand fees from parents; school autonomy has a positive impact only among high-quality education systems and when implemented along with accountability mechanisms. Thus, it may be difficult for policymakers to evaluate which policies are required in their specific context.

Finally, the evidence concerning policy recommendations on equity is weak. This is partly because equity is multidimensional so all conclusions are partial and depend on which indicator is used. Furthermore, PISA does not take into account indicators which the survey itself does not generate and therefore misses crucial information by which to assess equity, such as rates of early school leaving. When the evidence is weak, ideology takes over. It is worrying that this does not only happen at the level of political parties. It seems unfortunate that ideology also influences PISA's policy recommendations; in the absence of strong evidence, it seems to embrace the predominant narrative in a questionable effort to be seen as influential.

Despite these shortcomings, the evidence provided by ILSAs has proven very useful in identifying major differences in performance between countries and generated a wealth of data which are being used to decipher what seemed an intractable problem: how can education systems improve? These data represent the only way to understand which policies governments should implement to improve student outcomes in different contexts. But by targeting the media and causing such an uproar in the political debate, PISA has turned itself into a high-stakes exam for policymakers of the kind it no longer supports for students. As a consequence, governments expose themselves to huge media scrutiny, which may have a major influence on the way particular education policies or reforms are perceived by their societies. In exchange, PISA must ensure that its policy recommendations are based on strong evidence and that it is accountable when the reliability of the results generate reasonable doubts, if it wishes to be regarded as a trusted source of data.

Policymakers often face difficult decisions when confronted with a divisive ideological debate and powerful vested interests. It is often assumed that most choose not to act due to fear of political costs, but many may evaluate the situation and realistically conclude that entrenched conflicts of interest with powerful stakeholders make reform attempts unlikely to succeed. The only known fact is that those who do embrace education reforms and are willing to pay the political costs often encounter insurmountable obstacles. Since education systems serve students, progress will only be achieved when families and societies understand which polices benefit them, to the extent that civil society as a whole supports such changes. In the absence of a common understanding, major changes at the systemic level may prove impossible, and in this case the alternative may require taking small steps by implementing pilot studies which will eventually expand if proven to be successful. Small steps may lead to major changes, but it will take time. It remains an open question whether education systems can wait much longer for such change.

References

Abdulkadiroglu, A., Angrist, J., Dynarski, S., Kane, T. and Pathak, P. (2011). "Accountability and Flexibility in Public Schools: Evidence from Boston's Charters and Pilots", *The Quarterly Journal of Economics*, 126, 699–748.

Academy of Singapore Teachers (2012). *Professional Learning Communities*.

Ackerman, B. (1980). *Social Justice in the Liberal State*. New Haven: Yale University Press.

Adamson, F. and Åstrand, B. (2016). "Privatization or Public Investment? A Global Question", in Adamson, F., Åstrand, B. and Darling-Hammond, L., *Global Education Reform. How Privatization and Public Investment Influence Education Outcomes*. New York: Routledge (pp. 1–15).

Adamson, F. and Darling-Hammond, L. (2016a). "The Critical Choice in American Education", in Adamson, F., Åstrand, B. and Darling-Hammond, L. *Global Education Reform. How Privatization and Public Investment Influence Education Outcomes*. New York: Routledge, (pp. 131–168).

—— (2016b). "Privatization and Public Investment. Is the Invisible Hand a Magic Wand?", in Adamson, F., Åstrand, B. and Darling-Hammond, L., *Global Education Reform. How Privatization and Public Investment Influence Education Outcomes*. New York: Routledge (pp. 194–223).

Adonis, A. (2012). *Education, Education, Education. Reforming England's Schools*. London: Biteback Publishing.

—— (2013). *5 Days in May. The Coalition and Beyond*. London: Biteback Publishing.

Ahonen, A.K. (2021). "Finland: Success Through Equity-The Trajectories in PISA Performance", in Crato, N. (ed.), *Improving a Country's Education. PISA 2018 Results in 10 Countries*. Cham: Springer Nature, 121–136, https://doi.org/10.1007/978-3-030-59031-4_6.

Akman, M., Crawfurd, L. and Hares, S. (2019). "Low-Cost Private Schools: What Have We Learned in the Five Years Since the DFID Rigorous Review", *Center for Global Development*, https://www.cgdev.org/blog/low-cost-private-schools-what-have-we-learned-five-years-dfid-rigorous-review.

Allègre, C. (2000). *Toute vérité est bonne à dire*. Paris: Robert Laffont.

Allen, C.S., Chen, Q., Willson, V.L. and Hughes, J.N. (2009). "Quality of Research Design Moderates Effects of Grade Retention on Achievement: A Meta-Analytic, Multilevel Analysis", *Educational Evaluation and Policy Analysis*, 31/4, 480–499, https://doi.org/10.3102/0162373709352239.

Altschuler, G.C. and Blumin, S.M. (2009). *The GI Bill. The New Deal for Veterans*. Oxford: Oxford University Press.

Althusser, L. (1970). "Idéologie et appareil idéologique d'État (AIE). Notes pour une recherche", *La Pensée*, 151, 67–125.

Amjad, R. and MacLeod, G. (2014). "Academic effectiveness of private, public and private — public partnership schools in Pakistan", *International Journal of Educational Development*, 37, 22–31.

Angrist, J., Cohodes, S., Dynarski, S., Pathak P. and Walters, C. (2016). "Stand and Deliver: Effects of Boston's Charter High Schools on College Preparation, Entry, and Choice", *Journal of Labor Economics*, 34, 275–318.

Angrist, J., Dynarski, S., Kane, T., Pathak, P. and Walters, C. (2010). "Inputs and Impacts in Charter Schools: KIPP Lynn" *American Economic Review*, 100/2, 239–243.

Angrist, J., Pathak, P. and Walters, C. (2013). "Explaining Charter School Effectiveness", *American Economic Journal: Applied Economics*, 5, 1–27.

Ansell, B.W. (2008). "University Challenges: Explaining Institutional Change in higher Education", *World Politics*, 60, 189–230.

—— (2010). *From the Ballot to the Blackboard: The Redistributive Political Economy of Education*. Cambridge: Cambridge University Press.

Apple, M.W. (1979). *Ideology and Curriculum*. London: Routledge and Kegan Paul.

—— (1982). *Education and Power*. London: Routledge and Kegan Paul.

Araki T (2002). *Labor and Employment Law in Japan*. Tokyo: The Japan Institute of Labor.

Archer, M. (2013). *Social Origins of Educational Systems*. London: Routledge.

Armstrong, H. (1990). "The British Education Act of 1988: A Critique from the Labour Party", *Journal of Education Finance*, 15/4,, 572–576.

Ashley, L., Mcloughlin C., Aslam M., Engel J., Wales, J., Rawal, S., Batley, R., Kingdon, G, Nicolai, S. and Rose, P. (2014). *The role and impact of private schools in developing countries: A rigorous review of the evidence. Final report*, Education Rigorous Literature Review, Department for International Development, https://assets.publishing.service.gov.uk/government/uploads/system/uploads/attachment_data/file/439702/private-schools-full-report.pdf.

Aspinall, R.W. (2017). "Teachers' Unions in Japan: The Frustration of Permanent Opposition", in Moe, T.M. and Wiborg, S. (eds), *The Comparative Politics of Education*. Cambridge: Cambridge University Press (pp. 192–214).

Atkinson, A., Burgess, S., Croxson, B., Gregg, P., Propper, C., Slater, H. and Wilson, D. (2009). "Evaluating the impact of performance-related pay for teachers in England", *Labour Economics*, 16/3, 251–261.

Aunio, P., Aubrey, C., Godfrey, R., Yuejuan, P. and Liu, Y. (2006). "Children's early numeracy in England, Finland and People's Republic of China", *International Journal of Early Years Education*, 16/3, 203–321.

Baird, J., Johnson, S., Hopfenbeck, T. N., Isaacs, T., Sprague, T., Stobart, G., & Yu, G. (2016). "On the supranational spell of PISA in policy", *Educational Research*, 58/2, 121–138.

Baker, C. (2019). "An Education Promise We Can Keep", *Boston Globe*, 16 September, https://www.bostonglobe.com/opinion/2019/09/16/education-promise-can-keep/cel6buF6CNJNS9e0RQnTFK/story.html.

Baker, E.L. and O'Neil, H.F. (1994). "Performance Assessment and Equity: A view from the USA", *Journal of Assessment in Education*, 1/1, 11–26.

Ball, S. (2013). *The Education Debate* (2nd edition). Bristol: Policy Press.

Barber, M. (2013). *The Good News from Pakistan: How a Revolutionary New Approach to Education Reform in Punjab Shows the Way Forward for Pakistan and Development Aid Everywhere*. London: Reform.

Barber, M. and Mourshed, M. (2007). *How the world's best-performing school systems come out on top*, McKinsey & Company, https://www.mckinsey.com/industries/public-and-social-sector/our-insights/how-the-worlds-best-performing-school-systems-come-out-on-top.

Bascia, N. and Osmond, P. (2012). *Teacher Unions and Educational Reform: A Research Review*. New York: National Education Association.

—— (2013). *Teacher Union Governmental Relations in the Context of Educational Reform*. Brussels: Education International.

Bates, J., Lewis, S. and Pickard, A. (2019). *Education Policy, Practice and the Professional. Second Edition*. London: Bloomsbury.

Bautista, A., Wong, J. and Gopinathan, S. (2015). "Teacher Professional Development in Singapore", *Psychology, Society, & Education*, 7/3, 423–441.

Bergbauer, A., Hanushek E.A. and Woessmann, L. (2019). *Testing*, NBER Working Paper No 24836, http://hanushek.stanford.edu/sites/default/files/publications/BHW%20assessments%20191107.pdf.

Berger, P.L. and Luckmann, N. (1966). *The Social Construction of Reality: A Treatise in the Sociology of Knowledge*. New York: Vintage Books.

Bergseng, B., E. Degler and Lüthi, S. (2019). *Unlocking the Potential of Migrants in Germany*, OECD Reviews of Vocational Education and Training, Paris: OECD Publishing.

Bishop, J.H. (1997). "The effect of national standards and curriculum-based examinations on achievement", *American Economic Review*, 87/2, 260–264.

—— (1999). "Are national exit examinations important for educational efficieny?", *Swedish Economic Policy Review*, 6, 349–398.

—— (2006). "Drinking from the fountain of knowledge: Student incentive to study and learn — Externalities, information problems, and peer pressure", in Hanushek, E.A. and Welch, F., *Handbook of the Economics of Education, Vol. 2*. Amsterdam: North Holland (pp. 909–944).

Blanchenay, P., Burns, T. and Koester, P. (2014). *Shifting Responsibilities: 20 years of Education Devolution in Sweden: A Governing Complex Education Systems Case Study*, OECD Education Working Paper, No. 104, Paris: OECD Publishing, http://dx.doi.org/10.1787/5jz2jg1rqrd7-en.

Blanquer, J.M. (2015). *L´École de demain. Propositions pour une Éducation nationale rénovée*. Paris : Odile Jacob.

Bourdieu, P. and Passeron, J.C. (1970). *La Reproduction. Éléments d'une théorie du système d'enseignement*. Paris : Les Éditions de Minuit.

Bray, M. (2013). "Shadow education: Comparative Perspectives on the Expansion and Implications of Private Supplementary Tutoring", *Procedia. Social and Behavioral Sciences*, 77, 412–420, https://pdf.sciencedirectassets.com/277811/1-s2.0-S1877042813X00096/1-s2.0-S1877042813005338/main.pdf.

Breakspear, S. (2014). *How does PISA shape education policy making? Why how we measure learning determines what counts in education*, Seminar Series Paper No. 240, East Melbourne: Centre for Strategic Education.

Bruneforth, M., Chabera, B., Vogtenhuber. S., and Lassnigg, L. (2015). *OECD Review of Policies to Improve the Effectiveness of Resource Use in Schools. Country Background Report for Austria*. Vienna: Bundesministerium für Bildung und Frauen.

Brunello, G. and Rocco, L. (2017). "The effects of vocational education on adult skills, employment and wages: What can we learn from PIAAC?", *SERIEs*, 8/4, 315–343, http://dx.doi.org/10.1007/s13209-017-0163-z.

Bruns, B., Filmer, D. and Patrinos, H.A. (2011). *Making Schools Work: New Evidence on Accountability Reforms*, Human Development Perspectives. Washington, D.C.: World Bank.

Bruns, B. and Luque, J. (2015). *Great Teachers: How to Raise Student Learning in Latin America and the Caribbean*. Washington, D.C.: World Bank Group.

Bruns, B., Macdonald, I.H. and Schneider, B.R. (2019). "The politics of quality reforms and the challenges for SDGs in education", *World Development*, 118, 27–38, https://doi.org/10.1016/j.worlddev.2019.02.008.

Burnet, J. (1903). *Aristotle on Education. Extract from the Ethics and Politics*. Cambridge: Cambridge University Press.

Burnett, N. and O'Donnell, S. (2016). "Lost in translation? The challenges of education policy borrowing", *Educational Research*, 58/2, 113–120.

Busemeyer, M. (2008). "The impact of fiscal decentralization on education and other types of spending", *Swiss Political Science Review*, 14, 451–481.

—— (2009). "Asset Specificity, Institutional Complementarities and the Varieties of Skills Regimen in Coordinated Market Economis", *Socio-Economic Revew*, 7/3, 375–406.

—— (2015). *Skills and Inequality. Partisan Politics and the Political Economy of Education Reforms in Western Welfare States*. Cambridge: Cambridge University Press.

Busemeyer, M.R., Garritzmann, J.L. and Neimanns, E. (2020). *A Loud but Noisy Signal? Public Opinion and Education Reform in Wwstern Europe*. Cambridge: Cambridge University Press.

Busemeyer, M. and Trampusch, C. (2011). *The Political Economy of Collective Skill Formation*. Oxford: Oxford University Press.

Butler, D. and Stokes, D. (1969). *Political Change in Britain: Forces Shaping Electoral Choice*. London: Macmillan.

Calero, J. (2005). *Equity in Education. Thematic Review: Country Analytical Report — Spain*. Paris: OECD Publishing.

Caplan, B. (2018). *The Case Against Education. Why Education System Is a Waste of Time and Money*. Princeton: Princeton University Press.

Carr, D. (2003). *Making Sense of Education: An Introduction to the Philosophy and History of Education and Teaching*. London: RoutledgeFalmer.

Cedefop (2009). *Using Tax Incentives to Promote Education and Training*, Cedefop Panorama Series. Luxembourg: Office for Official Publications of the European Communities.

Chambers-Ju, C. and Finger, L. (2017). "Teachers' Unions in Mexico: The Politics of Patronage", in Moe, T.M. and Wiborg, S. (eds), *The Comparative Politics of Education: Teacher Union and Education Systems around the World*. Cambridge: Cambridge University Press.

Chapman, C. and Salokangas, M. (2012). "Independent state-funded schools: Some reflections on recent developments", *School Leadership and Management*, 32/5, 473–486, http://dx.doi.org/10.1080/13632434.2012.731329.

Cheshire, P.C., Nathan, M. and Overman H.G. (2014). *Urban Economics and Urban Policy: Challenging Conventional Policy Wisdom*. Cheltenham: Edward Elgar.

Chetty, R., Friedman, J.N. and Rockoff, J. (2014). "Measuring the impact of teachers II: Teacher value-added and the student outcomes in adulthood", *American Economic Review*, 104/9, 2633–2679.

Chingos, M.M. and Peterson, P.E. (2011). "It's easier to pick a good teacher than to train one: Familiar and new results on the correlates of teacher effectiveness", *Economics of Education Review*, 30/3, 449–465.

Chitty, C. (1999). "Sex Education", in Hill, D. and Cole, M. (eds), *Promoting Equality in Secondary Schools*, London: Cassell, pp. 298–318.

Choi, A. and Jerrim, J. (2015). "The Use (and Misuse) of PISA in Guiding Policy Reform: The Case of Spain", *IEB Working Paper*, No. 2015/06, http://dx.doi.org/10.2139/ssrn.2580141.

Christodoulou, D. (2014). *Seven Myths About Education*. London: Routledge.

Clark, G. (2003). "The Great Escape: The Industrial Revolution in Theory and in History", *Working Paper*, University of California at Davis, http://faculty.econ.ucdavis.edu/faculty/gclark/papers/IR2003.pdf.

Clarke, M., Haney, W. and Madaus, G. (2000). "High stakes testing and high school completion", *National Board on Educational Testing and Public Policy Statement*, 1/3, www.bc.edu/research/nbetpp/publications/v1n3.html.

Clarke, M., Shore, A., Rhoades, K., Abrams L., Miao, J. and Li, J. (2003). *Perceived Effects of State-Mandated Testing Programs on Teaching and Learning: Findings from Interviews with Educators in Low-, Medium-, and High-Stakes States*, Lynch School of Education, Boston College, MA: National Board on Educational Testing and Public Policy.

Collins, C.A. and Gan, L. (2013). "Does sorting students improve scores? An analysis of class composition", *NBER Working Paper*, No. 18848, Cambridge, MA: National Bureau of Economic Research, http://dx.doi.org/10.3386/w18848.

Common Core Standards Initiative (2020). "Development Process", http://www.corestandards.org/about-the-standards/development-process/.

Conservative (2019). *Get Brexit Done. Unleash Britain's Potential. The Conservative and Unionist Party Manifesto 2019*. London: Paragon.

Corcoran, S. P., Evans, W.N. and Schwab, R.M. (2004). "Women, the Labor Market, and the Declining Relative Quality of Teachers", *Journal of Policy Analysis and Management*, 23/3, 449–470.

Cordero, J.M., Crespo, E. and Pedraja, F. (2013). "Educational achievement and determinantes in PISA: A review of literature in Spain", *Revista de Educación*, No. 362, 273–297, https://doi.org/10.4438/1988-592X-RE-2011-362-161.

Cordero, J.M., Cristóbal, V. and Santín, D. (2018). "Causal inference on education policies: A survey of empirical studies using PISA, TIMSS and PIRLS", *Journal of Economic Surveys*, 32/3, 878–915.

Corrales, J. (2005). *The State is Not Enough: The Politics of Expanding and Improving Schooling in Developing Countries*. Cambridge, MA: American Academy of Arts and Sciences, https://jcorrales.people.amherst.edu/promise_of_participation/images/corrales_edu%20state_is_not%20enough.pdf.

Crato, N. (2020). "Curriculum and educational reforms in Portugal: An analysis on why and how students' knowledge and skills improved", in Reimers,

F.M. (ed.), *Audacious Education Purposes*, Cham: Springer Open, https://doi.org/10.1007/978-3-030-41882-3 (pp. 209–232).

—— (2021). "Setting up the Scene: Lessons Learned from PISA 2018 Statistics and Other International Student Assessments", in Crato, N. (ed.), *Improving a Country's Education*, Cham: Springer Open, https://doi.org/10.1007/978-3-030-59031-4_1 (pp. 1–23).

Crehan, L. (2016). *Cleverlands. The Secrets behind the Success of the World's Education Superpowers*. London: Unbound.

Dall, A. (2011). "Is PISA counter-productive to building successful educational systems?", *Social Alternatives*, 30/4, 10– 14.

Darder, A., Torres, R. and Baltodano, M. (2017). *The Critical Pedagogy Reader (3rd Edition)*. New York: Routledge.

Darling-Hammond, L. and Rothman, R. (2015). *Teaching in the Flat World. Learning from High Performing Systems*, New York: Teachers College Press, Columbia University.

Davidson, A.L. (1996). *Making and Molding Identity in Schools*. New York: New York State University Press.

Davidson, T. (1892). *Aristotle and Ancient Educational Ideals*. New York: Charles Scribner's Sons

Dee, T.S. and Jacob, B.A. (2006). "Do high school exit exams influence educational attainment or labor market performance?", *NBER Working Paper 12199*, Cambridge: National Bureau of Economic Research, www.nber.org/papers/w12199.

Dee, T.S, and Levine, J. (2004). "The fate of new funding: Evidence from Massachusetts' education finance reforms", *Educational Evaluation and Policy Analysis*, 26/3, 199–215.

Dennison, S. and Pardjis, D. (2016). "The World According to Europe's Insurgent Parties: Putin, Migration and People Power", *Flash Scorecard*, ECFR/181, June.

Dewey, J. (1916). *Democracy and Education. An Introduction to the Philosophy of Education*. New York: Macmillan

Dimmock, C. (2011). "Diversifying schools and leveraging school improvement: A comparative analysis of the English radical, and Singapore conservative, specialist schools' policies", *British Journal of Educational Studies*, 59/4, 439–458, https://doi.org/10.1080/00071005.2011.636732.

Dimmok, C. and Tan, C.Y. (2015). "Explaining the success of the world's leading education systems: the case of Singapore", *British Journal of Educational Studies*, 64/2, 161–184, https://doi.org/10.1080/00071005.2015.1116682.

Dobbie, W. and Fryer, R. (2011). "Are High Quality Schools Enough to Close the Achievement Gap? Evidence from a Social Experiment in Harlem", *American Economic Journal: Applied Economics*, 3/3, 158–187.

—— (2013). "Getting Beneath the Veil of Effective Schools: Evidence from New York City", *American Economic Journal: Applied Economics*, 5/4, 28–60.

—— (2014). "The Medium Term Impacts of High Achieving Charter Schools", *Journal of Political Economy*, 123/5, 985–1037.

Dobbins, M. (2014). "Explaining Change and Inertia in Swedish and French Education: A Tale of two Corporatisms?", *Policy Studies*, 35/3, 282–302, https://doi.org/10.1080/01442872.2013.875149.

—— (2017). "Teacher Unionism in France: Making Fundamental Reform an Impossible Quest?", in *The Comparative Politics of Education: Teacher Unions and Education Systems around the World*, Cambridge: Cambridge University Press (pp. 87–113).

Doraisamy, T. R. (ed.) (1969). *150 Years of Education in Singapore*. Singapore: Teachers' Training College.

Dufaux, S. (2012). "Assessment for qualification and certification in upper secondary education: A review of country practices and research evidence", *OECD Education Working Papers*, No. 83, Paris: OECD Publishing.

Duflo, E., Dupas, P. and Kremer, M. (2015). "School governance, teacher incentives, and pupil–teacher ratios: Experimental evidence from Kenyan primary schools", *Journal of Public Economics*, 123, 92–110.

Edwards, D. (2019). *ISTP Speech 2019*, https://eiie.sharepoint.com/:w:/s/eiwebsite/EeehMpmVSdAjLWkodBuGxoBBKQVYaAFp0wG3DwKOWDNpA?rtime=RNhhqhYw2Ug.

E-estonia (2019a). *Education*, https://e-estonia.com/solutions/education/.

—— (2019b). *We Have Built a Digital Society and So Can You*, https://e-estonia.com/.

Egelund, N. (2008). "The value of international comparative studies of achievement – a Danish perspective", *Assessment in Education: Principles, Policy and Practice*, 15, 245–251.

Ehman, L.H. (1980). "The American School in the Political Socialization Process", *Review of Educational Research*, 50/1, 99–119.

Eide, E.G., Goldhaber, D. and Brewer, D. (2004). "The Teacher Labour Market and Teacher Quality", *Oxford Review of Economic Policy*, 20/2, 230–244.

El Mundo (2019a). "La Comunidad de Madrid pide a la OCDE que retire todo el informe PISA por errores de un calibre considerable: Toda la prueba está contaminada", 29 November, https://www.elmundo.es/espana/2019/11/29/5de108e0fc6c839a2b8b4635.html.

—— (2019b). "Las sombras de PISA: ¿hay que creerse el informe tras los errores detectados?", 2 December, https://www.elmundo.es/espana/2019/12/02/5de25413fdddffbb848b468f.html.

—— (2020). "La OCDE atribuye los errores del PISA a la 'disposición negativa' de los alumnos españoles por coincidir varios exámenes", 23 July, https://www.elmundo.es/espana/2020/07/23/5f187856fdddff27198b4606.html.

El País (2019). "Madrid pide que no se publique ningún dato de PISA porque todo está contaminado", 30 November, https://elpais.com/sociedad/2019/11/28/actualidad/1574976906_857649.html.

—— (2020). "Falta de interés y cansancio en mitad de los exámenes finales: así explica la OCDE las 'anomalías' del informe PISA en España", 23 July, https://elpais.com/educacion/2020-07-23/falta-de-interes-y-cansancio-en-mitad-de-los-examenes-finales-asi-explica-la-ocde-las-anomalias-del-informe-pisa-en-espana.html.

—— (2021) "Entrevista con Andreas Schleicher", 21 June, https://elpais.com/educacion/2021-06-18/el-creador-del-informe-pisa-la-educacion-espanola-prepara-a-los-alumnos-para-un-mundo-que-ya-no-existe.html.

Elacqua, G. (2012). "The impact of school choice and public policy on segregation: Evidence from Chile", *International Journal of Educational Development*, 32/3, 444–453, http://dx.doi.org/10.1016/j.ijedudev.2011.08.003.

Enqvist, I. (2011). *La buena y la mala educación. Ejemplos internacionales*. Madrid: Encuentro.

Epstein, E.H. (2008). "Setting the Normative Boundaries: Crucial Epistemological Benchmarks in Comparative Education", *Comparative Education*, 44/4, 373–386.

Ertl, H. (2006). "Educational standards and the changing discourse on education: The reception and consequences of the PISA study in Germany", *Oxford Review of Education*, 32/5, 619–634.

Eurobarometer (2019). *Standard Eurobarometer 92. Public Opinion in the European Union (Spring 2019). First Results*, https://ec.europa.eu/commfrontoffice/publicopinionmobile/index.cfm/Survey/getSurveyDetail/surveyKy/2255.

European Commission (2011). *The Challenge of Shadow Education. Private Tutoring and its implications for Policy Makers in the European Union*, Report prepared for the European Commission by the NESSE network of experts, http://www.nesse.fr/nesse/activities/reports/the-challenge-of-shadow-education-1.

European Training Foundation (2018). *Support VET Financing Policy guidance note: Financial incentives for companies*, European Training Foundation, https://www.etf.europa.eu/sites/default/files/2018-11/Policy%20guidance%20note_Financial%20incentives.pdf.

Eyles, A. and Machin S. (2019). "The Introduction of Academy Schools to England's Education", *Journal of the European Economic Association*, 17/4, 1107–1146, https://doi.org/10.1093/jeea/jvy021.

Faas, D. (2010). *Negotiating Political Identities: Multiethnic Schools and Youth in Europe*. Farnham: Ashgate.

Fazekas, M. and Field, S. (2013). *A Skills beyond School Review of Germany, OECD Reviews of Vocational Education and Training*. Paris: OECD Publishing, http://dx.doi.org/10.1787/9789264202146-en.

Felgueroso, F., Gutiérrez-Domènech, M. and Jiménez-Martín, S. (2013). "¿Por qué el abandono escolar se ha mantenido tan elevado en España las últimas dos décadas? El papel de la Ley de Educación (LOGSE)", in Cabrales, A. and Ciccone, A. (eds), *La educación en España. Una visión académica*, Madrid: Fedea (pp. 180–220).

Field, S., Kuczera, M. and Pont, B. (2007). *No More Failures: Ten Steps to Equity in Education*. Paris: OECD Publishing, https://www.oecd.org/education/school/45179151.pdf.

Fischman, G.E., Topper, A.M., Silova, I., Goebel, J. and Holloway, J.L. (2018). "Examining the influence of international large-scale assessments on national education policies", *Journal of Education Policy*, 34/2, https://doi.org/10.1080/02680939.2018.1460493.

Fontaine, A. and Urzúa S. (2018). *Educación con patines*. Santiago de Chile: El Mercurio.

Forster, A., Bol, T. and van de Werfhorst, H. (2016). "Vocational Education and Employment over the Life Cycle", *Sociological Science*, 3, 473–494, http://dx.doi.org/10.15195/v3.a21.

Frassinelli, L. (2006). *Educational Reform in Finland*. East Lansing: Michigan State University.

Fredriksson, P., and Ockert, B. (2007). "The Supply of Skills to the Teacher Profession", Uppsala University, Uppsala, https://www.researchgate.net/profile/Bjoern-Oeckert/publication/228433008_The_Supply_of_Skills_to_the_Teacher_Profession/links/02bfe510c15d20b945000000/The-Supply-of-Skills-to-the-Teacher-Profession.pdf.

Frey, C.B. (2019). *The Technology Trap. Capital, Labor, and Power in the Age of Automation*. Princeton, NJ: Princeton University Press.

Fuchs, T. and Woessmann, L. (2007). "What accounts for international differences in student performance? A re-examination using PISA data", *Empirical Economics*, 32, 433–464, https://doi.org/10.1007/s00181-006-0087-0.

Fukuyama, F. (1992). *The End of History and the Last Man*. New York: Free Press.

Garelick, B. (2013). "Let's go back to grouping students by ability", *The Atlantic Monthly*, 26 March 2007, http://www.theatlantic.com/national/archive/2013/03/lets-go-back-to-grouping-students-by-ability/274362.

Gibb, N. (2017). *England's Education Reforms*. Speech delivered at the Centre for Independent Studies, 11 April 2017, https://www.gov.uk/government/speeches/nick-gibb-englands-education-reforms.

Gift, T. and Wibbles, E. (2014). "Reading, Writing, and the Regrettable Status of Education Research in Comparative Politics", *Annual Review of Political*

Science, 17, 291–312, https://www.annualreviews.org/doi/abs/10.1146/annurev-polisci-080911-131426.

Gillard D. (1988). *The National Curriculum and the Role of the Primary Teacher in Curriculum Development*, www.educationengland.org.uk/articles/07ncteacher.html.

—— (2018). *Education in England: A History*, www.educationengland.org.uk/history.

Giroux, H.A. and Giroux, S.S. (2006). "Challenging Neoliberalism's New World Order: The Promise of Critical Pedagogy", *Cultural Studies ←→ Critical Methodologies*, 6/1, 21–32.

Glewwe, P., Hanushek, E.A., Humpage, S.D. and Ravina, R. (2014). "School resources and educational outcomes in developing countries: A review of the literature from 1990 to 2010", in Glewwe, P. (ed.), *Education Policy in Developing Countries*, Chicago: University of Chicago Press (pp. 13–64).

Goldin, C. and Katz, L.R. (2009). *The Race Between Education and Technology*. Cambridge, MA: Harvard University Press.

Goldoni, M. and Wilkinson, M.A. (2018). "The Material Constitution", *Modern Law Review*, 81/4, 567–597.

Gomendio, M. (2017). *Empowering and Enabling Teachers to Improve Equity and Outcomes for All, International Summit of the Teaching Profession*. Paris: OECD Publishing.

—— (2020a). "La educación a subasta", *El Mundo*, 26 November.

—— (2020b). "PISA y España: ¿Se ha roto el termómetro?", *El Mundo*, 8 August.

—— (2021). "Spain: The Evidence Provided by International Large-Scale Assessments About the Spanish Education System: Why Nobody Listens Despite All the Noise", in Crato, N. (ed.), *Improving a Country's Education*, Cham: Springer Open, https://doi.org/10.1007/978-3-030-59031-4_1.

Gopinathan, S. and Deng, Z. (2006). "Fostering school-based curriculum development in the context of new educational initiatives in Singapore", *Planning and Changing*, 37/1–2, 93–110.

Gorard, S., & Smith, E. (2004). "An international comparison of equity in education systems", *Comparative Education*, 40/1, 15–28.

Goss, P. and Cowgill, M. (2019). "Estonia didn´t deliver its PISA results on the cheap, and neither will Australia", *The Conversation*, 8 December 2019.

Graham, A.R. and Husted, T. (1993). "Understanding state variation in SAT scores", *Economics of Education Review*, 12/3, 197–202.

Gran, G. and Copeland, G. (2014). "School Board Elections: Theory Meets Reality", *Journal of School Leadership*, 24/1, 4–30.

Green, A. (2013). *Education and State Formation: Europe, East Asia and the USA*. Houndmills: Palgrave Macmillan.

Grindle, M.S. (2004). *Despite the Odds. The Contentious Politics of Education Reform*. Princeton, NJ: Princeton University Press.

Grubb, N., Jahr, H.M., Neumüller, J. and Field, S. (2005). *Finland. Country Note. Equity in Education Thematic Review*. Paris: OECD Publishing.

Gruber, K.H. (2006). "The German 'PISA-Shock': Some aspects of the extraordinary impact of the OECD's PISA study on the German education system", in Ertl, H. (ed.), *Cross-National Attraction in Education: accounts from England and Germany*, Oxford: Symposium Books (pp. 195–208).

Grundgesetz (1949). *Grundgesetz für die Bundesrepublik Deutschland (Constitution of the Federal Republic of Germany)*, 23 May 1949, Bonn: Bundesgesetzblatt, http://perma.cc/3VDB-NJW4; http://perma.cc/DEF5-A57P.

Gustafsson, J.E. and Rosen, M.R. (2014). "Quality and credibility of international studies", in Strietholt, R., Bos, W., Gustafsson, J.E., and Rosen, M. (eds), *Educational Policy Evaluation through International Comparative Assessments*, Münster: Waxmann (pp. 19–49).

Gutmann, A. (1999). *Democratic Education*. Princeton, NJ: Princeton University Press.

Gutmann, A. and Ben-Porath, S. (2015). "Democratic Education", in Gibbons, M. (ed.), *The Encyclopedia of Political Thought*, Hoboken, NJ: John Wiley and Sons (pp. 863–875).

Hall, P.A. and Soskice, D. (2001). "An Introduction to Varieties of Capitalism", in Hall, P.A. and Soskice, D. (eds), *Varieties of Capitalism. The Institutional Foundations of Comparative Advantage*, Oxford: Oxford University Press (pp. 1–68).

Hans, N. (1964). Comparative Education. *A Study of Educational Factors and Traditions*. London: Routledge and Kegan Paul.

Hanson, M. (2018). "Teaching is on the road to hell-the story of the national curriculum proves it", *The Guardian*, 12 February 2018, https://www.theguardian.com/lifeandstyle/2018/feb/12/teaching-is-on-the-road-to-hell-the-story-of-the-national-curriculum-proves-it.

Hanushek, E.A. (1992). "The trade-off between Child Quantity and Quality", *Journal of Political Economy*, 100/1, 84–117.

—— (2003). "The failure of input-based schooling policies", *The Economic Journal*, 113/485, 64–98.

—— (2009). "Teacher Deselection", in Goldhaber, D. and Hannaway, J. (eds), *Creating a New Teaching Profession*. Washington, D.C.: Urban Institute Press (pp. 163–180).

—— (2021). "United States: The Uphill Schools' Struggle", in Crato, N. (ed.), *Improving a Country's Education. PISA 2018 Results in 10 Countries*, Cham: Springer Nature (pp. 227–247).

Hanushek, E.A., Link, S., and Woessmann, L. (2013). "Does school autonomy make sense everywhere? Panel estimates from PISA", *Journal of Development Economics*, 104, 212–232.

Hanushek, E.A., Peterson, P.E. and Woessmann, L. (2013). *Endangering Prosperity: A Global View of the American School*. Washington, D.C.: Brookings Press.

Hanushek, E.A., Piopiunik, M. and Widerhold, S. (2019). "The Value of Smarter Teachers. International Evidence on teacher Cognitive Skills and Student Performance", *The Journal of Human Resources*, 54, 857–899.

Hanushek, E.A. and Rivkin, S.G. (2006). "Teacher quality", in Hanushek, E.A. and Welch, F., *Handbook of the Economics of Education*, Amsterdam: North Holland (pp. 1051–1078).

—— (2010). "Generalizations about using value-added measures of teacher quality", *American Economic Review*, 100/2, 267–271.

—— (2012). "The distribution of teacher quality and implications for policy", *Annual Review of Economics*, 4, 131–157.

Hanushek, E.A., Schwerdt, G., Woessmann, L. and Zhang, L. (2017). "General Education, Vocational Education, and Labor-Market Outcomes over the Lifecycle", *Journal of Human Resources*, 52/1, 49–88.

Hanushek, E.A. and Woessmann, L. (2011). "The economics of international differences in educational achievement", in Hanushek, E.A., Machin, S. and Woessmann, L. (eds), *Handbook of the Economics of Education Vol. 3.*, Amsterdam: North Holland (pp. 89–200).

—— (2014). "Institutional structures of the education system and student achievement: a review of cross-country economic research", in Strietholt, R., Bos, W., Gustafsson J.E. and Rosen, M. (eds), *Educational Policy Evaluation through International Comparative Assessments*. Münster: Waxmann (pp. 145–175).

—— (2015). *The Knowledge Capital of Nations. Education and the Economics of Growth*. London: The MIT Press.

—— (2020). "A quantitative look at the economic impact of the European Union's educational goals", *Education Economics*, 28/3, 225–244.

Hanushek, E.A., Woessmann, L. and Zhang, L. (2011). *General Education, Vocational Education, and Labor-Market Outcomes over the Life-Cycle*. Cambridge (MA): National Bureau of Economic Research, http://dx.doi.org/10.3368/jhr.52.1.0415-7074R.

Harju-Luukkainen, H. and McElvany, N. (2018). "Immigrant student achievement and education policy in Finland", in Volante L. *et al.* (eds),

Immigrant Student Achievement and Education Policy. Springer International Publishing AG (pp. 87–102), https://doi.org/10.1007/978-3-319-74063-8_687.

Harmon, M., Smith, T.A., Martin, M.O., Kelly, D.L., Beaton, A.E., Mullis, I.V.S., González, E.J. and Orpwood, G. (1997). *Performance Assessment in IEA's Third International Mathematics and Science Study (TIMSS)*. Boston: TIMSS International Study Center, Boston College.

Harris, D.N. and Sass, T.R. (2011). "Teacher training, teacher quality and student achievement", *Journal of Public Economics*, 95/7–8, 798–812.

Henriques, R., Nunes, L. Reis, A. and Seabra, M.C. (2018). "Vocational education: coursetaking choice and impact on dropout and college enrollment rates", *Investigaciones de Economía de la Educación*, 13, 37–53.

Hernani-Limarino, W. (2005). "Are Teachers Well Paid in Latin America and the Caribbean? Relative Wage and Structure of Returns of Teachers", in Vegas, E. (ed.), *Incentives to Improve Teaching: Lessons from Latin America*, Washington, DC: World Bank (pp. 63–99).

Hippe, R., Jakubowski, A. and Araújo, L. (2018). *Regional inequalities in PISA: the case of Italy and Spain*. Luxembourg: Publications Office of the European Union, https://doi.org/10.2760/495702.

Hodges, C., Moore, S, Lockee, B., Trust, T. and Bond, A. (2020). "The Difference Between Emergency Remote Teaching and Online Learning", *EDUCAUSE Review*, 27 March, https://er.educause.edu/articles/2020/3/the-difference-between-emergency-remote-teaching-and-online-learning.

Hooge, E., Burns, T. and Wilkoszewski, H. (2012). "Looking Beyond the Numbers: Stakeholders and Multiple School Accountability", OECD Education Working Papers, No. 85, Paris: OECD Publishing.

Hopfenbeck, T.N., Lenkeit, J., El Masri, Y., Cantrell, K., Ryan J. and Baird J.A. (2018). "Lessons Learned from PISA: A Systematic Review of Peer-Reviewed Articles on the Programme for International Student Assessment", *Scandinavian Journal of Educational Research*, 62/3, 333–353.

Howell, W.G. and Peterson, P.E. (2002). *The Education Gap: Vouchers and Urban Schools*. Washington DC: Brookings Institution Press.

Hoxby, C.M. (1996). "How teachers' unions affect education production", *The Quarterly Journal of Economics*, 111, 671–718, https://doi.org/10.2307/2946669.

Hoxby, C. M., and Leigh, A. (2004). "Pulled Away or Pushed Out? Explaining the Decline of Teacher Aptitude in the United States", *American Economic Review*, 94/2, 236–240.

Hoxby, C, Murarka, S. and Kang, J. (2009). *How New York City's Charter Schools Affect Achievement*. Cambridge, MA: New York City Charter Schools Evaluation Project.

Hunt, T. (2005). *Building Jerusalem. The Rise and Fall of the Victorian City*. London: Hachette UK.

IEA (2020). *Mission and Strategy*, https://www.iea.nl/about/org/mission.

IFAU (2014). *Decentralisering, skolval och fristående skolor: resultat och likvärdighet i svensk skola, IFAU Report 5*, https://www.ifau.se/globalassets/pdf/se/2014/r-2014-25-decentralisering-skolval-och-friskolor.pdf.

Ikeda, M. and García, E. (2014). "Grade repetition: A comparative study of academic and non-academic consequences", *OECD Journal: Economic Studies*, 2013/1, http://dx.doi.org/10.1787/eco_studies-2013-5k3w65mx3hnx.

Jacob, B. (2005). "Accountability, Incentives and Behavior: The Impact of High-Stakes Testing in Chicago Public Schools", *Journal of Public Economics*, 89/5-6, 761–796.

—— (2012). "Teacher Labor Markets: Current Evidence and Continuing Questions", Presentation at Latin American Economics Association Meetings in Lima, Peru, November 2012.

Jacob, B. A., and Lefgren, L. (2008). "Can Principals Identify Effective Teachers? Evidence on Subjective Performance Evaluation in Education", *Journal of Labor Economics*, 26/1, 101–136.

Jacob, B., and Levitt, S. (2003). "Rotten Apples: An Investigation of the Prevalence and Predictors of Teacher Cheating", *Quarterly Journal of Economics*, 118/3, 843–877.

Jakoby, A.P., Martens, K. and Wolf, K.D. (eds) (2010). *Education in Political Science: Discovering a Neglected Field*. London: Routledge.

Jakubowski M. (2021). "Poland: Polish Education Reforms and Evidence from International Assessments", in Crato, N. (ed.), *Improving a Country's Education*, Cham: Springer, https://doi.org/10.1007/978-3-030-59031-4_7.

Jerrim, J. (2021). "PISA 2018 in England, Northern Ireland, Scotland and Wales: Is the data really representative of all four corners of the UK?" *Review of Education*, 9: e3270, https://doi.org/10.1002/rev3.3270.

Jiménez, E. and Paqueo, V. (1996). "Do local contributions affect the efficiency of public primary schools?" *Economics of Education Review*, 15/4, 377–386, http://dx.doi.org/10.1016/S0272-7757(96)00029-5.

Johansson, S. (2016). "International large-scale assessments: what uses, what consequences?", *Educational Research*, 58, 139–157, https://doi.org/10.1080/00131881.2016.1165559

Hussar, B., Zhang, J., Hein, S., Wang, K., Roberts, A., Cui, J., Smith, M., Bullock Mann, F., Barmer, A., and Dilig, R. (2020). *The Condition of Education 2020*. Washington, DC: National Center for Education Statistics, https://nces.ed.gov/pubsearch/pubsinfo.asp?pubid=2020144.

Innove (2019). *About Innove*, https://www.innove.ee/en/about-innove/.

Iversen, T. and Stephens, J.D. (2008). "Partisan Politics, the Welfare State and Three Worlds of Human Capital Formation", *Comparative Political Studies*, 41/4–5, 600–637.

Kamens, D.H. and McNeely, C.L. (2010). "Globalization and the Growth of International Educational Testing and National Assessment", *Comparative Education Review*, 54/1, 5–25, https://doi.org/10.1086/648471.

Kang, N., and Hong, M. (2008). "Achieving excellence in teacher workforce and equity in learning opportunities in South Korea", *Educational Researcher*, No. 37, 200–207.

Kaufman, R. and Nelson, J. (2004). "The politics of education sector reform: Cross- national comparisons", in Kaufman, R. and Nelson, J. (eds), *Crucial Needs, Weak Incentives*. Baltimore: Johns Hopkins University Press (pp. 249–270).

Kenworthy, L. (2003). "Quantitative indicators of corporatism", *International Journal of Sociology*, 33, 10–44.

Kim, S. and Lee, J.H. (2001). *Demand for Education and Developmental State: Private Tutoring in South Korea*, Social Science Research Papers Collection, http://dx.doi.org/10.2139/ssrn.268284.

—— (2010). "Private tutoring and demand for education in South Korea", *Economic Development and Cultural Change*, 58/2, 259–296.

Klieme, E. (2013). "The role of large-scale assessments in research on educational effectiveness and school development", in von Davier, M., Gonzalez, E., Kirsch, I. and Yamamoto, K. (eds), *The Role of International Large-Scale Assessments: Perspectives from Technology, Economy, and Educational Research*. Dordrecht: Springer (pp. 115–147).

—— (2016). *TIMSS 2015 and PISA 2015 How Are They Related on the Country Level?* DIPF Working Paper, December 2016, http://eng.kedi.re.kr/khome/eng/education/genernalInfo.do.

Korea Institute for Curriculum and Evaluation (KICE) (2012). *Education in Korea: Research report*. Seoul: KICE.

Korean Educational Development Institute (KEDI) (2015). *Education for the Future: Korean Educational Policy Development*. Seoul: Korean Education Development Institute.

Koretz, D. (2005). *Alignment, High Stakes, and the Inflation of Test Scores*. Los Angeles: University of California, National Center for Research on Evaluation, Standards, and Student Testing (CRESST).

Koretz, D., Linn, R.L., Dunbar, S.B. and Shepard, L.A. (1991). "The effects of high-stakes testing on achievement: Preliminary findings about generalization across tests", Paper presented at the Annual Meeting of the American Educational Research Association (AERA), Chicago, 11 April 1991.

Kosack, S. (2012). *The Education of Nations: How the Political Organization of the Poor, Not Democracy, Led Governments to Invest in Mass Education*. New York: Oxford University Press.

Kreising, M. (2001). "Vocational education in the United States: Reforms and results", *European Journal of Vocational Training*, 23, 27–35.

Kremer, M., Brannen, C. and Glennerster, R. (2013). "The challenge of education and learning in the developing world", *Science*, 13 April, 297–300, https://doi.org/10.1126/science.1235350.

Kuczera, M. (2017). *Incentives for Apprenticeship*, OECD Education Working Papers, No. 152, Paris: OECD Publishing.

Kulik, J. (1998). "Curricular tracks and high school vocational education", in Gamoran, A. (ed.), *The Quality of Vocational Education: Background Papers from the 1994 National Assessment of Vocational Education*, Washington DC: US Department of Education (pp. 65–132).

Laanpere, M. (2002). "Tiger Leap Plus — an ICT Strategy for Estonian Schools, 2001–2005", *Baltic IT&T Review*, No. 24, 67–69, http://www.ebaltics.com/doc_upl/Laanpere.pdf.

Labour (2019). *Labour Manifesto 2019. Rebuild our Public Services*, https://labour.org.uk/manifesto/rebuild-our-public-services/.

Ladd, H. and Walsh, R. (2002). "Implementing Value-Added Measures of School Effectiveness: Getting the Incentives Right", *Economics of Education Review*, 21/1, 1–17.

Lähdemäki, J. (2019). "Case Study: The Finnish National Curriculum 2016—A Co-created National Education Policy", in Cook, J. (ed.), *Sustainability, Human Well-Being, and the Future of Education*. Cham: Palgrave Macmillan (pp. 397–422), https://doi.org/10.1007/978-3-319-78580-6_13.

Lakoff, G. (2004). *Don't Think of an Elephant! Know Your Values and Frame the Debate*. Vermont: Chelsea Green Publishing.

Lee, S. K., Goh, C.B. and Fredriksen, B. (2008). *Toward a Better Future: Education and Training for Economic Development in Singapore since 1965*. Washington, DC: The World Bank.

Lees, M. (2016). *Estonian Education System 1990–2016: Reforms and Their Impact*, https://4liberty.eu/wp-content/uploads/2016/08/Estonian-Education-System_1990-2016.pdf.

Levin, B. (2003). *Approaches to Equity in Policy for Lifelong Learning*, OECD Working Paper, https://www.oecd.org/education/school/38692676.pdf.

Levin, H.M., Cornelisz, I. and Hanisch-Cerda, B. (2013). "Does educational privatisation promote social justice?", *Oxford Review of Education*, 39/4, 514–532, http://dx.doi.org/10.1080/03054985.2013.825983.

Lijphart, A. (1969). "Consociational Democracy", *World Politics*, 21/2, 207–225.

—— (1977). *Democracy in Plural Societies: A Comparative Exploration*. New Haven, CT: Yale University Press.

Lindblad, S., Pettersson, D., & Popkewitz, T. S. (2015). *International Comparisons of School Results: A Systematic Review of Research on Large Scale Assessments in Education*. Stockholm: Swedish Research Council.

Linz, J.J. and Stepan, A. (1996). "Toward Consolidated Democracies", *Journal of Democracy*, 7/2, 14–33.

Locke, J. (1693). *Some Thoughts Concerning Education*. Edinburgh: J. Brown.

Lockheed, M.E. and Wagemaker, H. (2013). "International large-scale assessments: thermometers, whips or useful policy tools?", *Research in Comparative and International Education*, 8/3, 296–306, doi.org/10.2304/rcie.2013.8.3.296.

Loh, J. and Hu, G. (2019). "Teacher education in Singapore", in *Oxford Research Encyclopedia of Education*. Oxford: Oxford University Press, https://www.polyu.edu.hk/fh/research/research-output/others/teacher-education-in-singapore/.

LOMCE (2013). *Ley Orgánica para la Mejora de la Calidad de la Educación* (Act for the Improvement of Quality in Education, a Partial Amendment of the General Education Act of 2006), approved on 9 December 2013, https://www.boe.es/eli/es/lo/2013/12/09/8/con.

LOMLOE (2020). *Proyecto de Ley por el que se modifica la Ley Orgánica de Educación* (Draft of the Law That Modifies the Basic Education Act), https://www.educacionyfp.gob.es/dam/jcr:1ef5d4e5-a41b-40a3-867b-e3b320dc48be/03-loe-con-lomloe-web-2020-03-03.pdf

Loveless, T. (2013a). "PISA's China Problem" *The Brown Center Chalkboard*, Brookings Institution, 9 October, https://www.brookings.edu/research/attention-oecd-pisa-your-silence-on-china-is-wrong/.

—— (2013b). "Attention OECD-PISA: Your Silence on China is Wrong", *The Brown Center Chalkboard*, Brookings Institution, 11 December, https://www.brookings.edu/research/attention-oecd-pisa-your-silence-on-china-is-wrong/.)

—— (2014). "PISA's China Problem Continues: A Response to Schleicher, Zhang, and Tucker", *The Brown Center Chalkboard*, Brookings Institution, 8 January, https://www.brookings.edu/research/pisas-china-problem-continues-a-response-to-schleicher-zhang-and-tucker/.

—— (2019). "The children PISA ignores in China", *The Brown Center Chalkboard*, Brookings Institution, 19 December, https://www.brookings.edu/blog/brown-center-chalkboard/2019/12/19/the-children-pisa-ignores-in-china/.

Lüdemann, E. (2011). *Schooling and the Formation of Cognitive and Non-cognitive Outcomes*, ifo Beiträge zur Wirtschaftsforschung. Munich: ifo Institut.

Luri, G. (2021). "La Lomloe o la exaltación de la mediocridad", *El Mundo*, 30 March 2021, https://www.elmundo.es/opinion/2021/03/30/6061b71421efa 00d5a8b463b.html.

Lynch, K. (1987). "Dominant Ideologies in Irish Educational Thought: Consensualism, Essentialism and Meritocratic Individualism", *The Economic and Social Review*, 18/2, 101–122.

Machiavelli, N. (1960). *Il Principe e Discorsi sopra la Prima Deca di Tito Livio*. Milan: Feltrinelli.

Manzon, M. (2011). *Comparative Education. The Construction of a Field*. Dordrecht: Springer.

—— (2018). "Comparative education histories: a postscript", *Comparative Education*, 54/1, 94–107.

Maroco, J. (2021). "Portugal: The PISA Effects on Education", in Crato, N. (ed.), *Improving a Country's Education*. Cham: Springer Open (pp. 159–174), https://doi.org/10.1007/978-3-030-59031-4_6.

Martens, K. and Nienmann, D. (2010). "Governance by comparison: How ratings and rankings impact national policy-making in education", *TransState Working Papers*, No. 139.

Martens, K., Niemann, D. and Teltemann, J. (2016). "Effects of international assessments in education — a multidisciplinary review", *European Educational Research Journal*, 15/5, 516–522.

Martin, M.O., Mullis, I.V.S., Foy, P. and Hooper, M. (2016). *TIMSS 2015 International Results in Science*. Boston: Boston College.

Martínez, J. S. (2017). *La equidad y la educación*. Madrid: Los Libros de la Catarata.

McArthur, D.L. (1987). "Educational Assessment: A Brief History", in McArthur, D.L. (ed.), *Alternative Approaches to the Assessment of Achievement*. Boston: Kluwer (pp. 1–20).

McCulloch, G. (2000). "The Politics of the Secret Garden: Teachers and the School Curriculum in England and Wales", in Day, C., Fernandez, A., Hauge, T.E. and Möller, J., *The Life and Work of Teachers. International Perspectives in Changing Times*. London: Falmer Press (pp. 26–37).

Milán, M. and Recio, M. (2013). "LOMCE: 8 puntos para entender sus consecuencias", *T.E.* (*Trabajadores de la Enseñanza*), 344, 9–17, https://hemerotecate.fe.ccoo.es/assets/te-2013.06.pdf.

Mill, J. S. (1848). *Principles of Political Economy*. London: John W. Parker.

—— (1859). *On Liberty*. London: John W. Parker and Son.

—— (1869). *The Subjection of Women*. London: Longmans, Green, Reader and Dyer.

—— (1873). *Autobiography*. London: Longmans, Green and Co.

—— (1981). *The Collected Works of John Stuart Mill. Volume I — Autobiography and Literary Essays*. London: Routledge and Kegan Paul.

—— (2008). *On Liberty and Other Essays*, Oxford: Oxford University Press.

Ministerio de Educación y Formación Profesional (2020). *Datos y Cifras. Curso Escolar 2020–2021*, Madrid: Ministerio de Educación y Formación Profesional.

Ministry of Education (2017). *Globalization of Korean Education — Education in Korea, 2017*. Sejong: Publishing Institution_Ministry of Education, pp. 48–53, http://english.moe.go.kr/boardCnts/view.do?boardID=282&boardSeq=72461&lev=0&searchType=null&statusYN=C&page=1&s=english&m=0303&opType=N.

Ministry of Education (2020). *Education in Korea 2020*. Sejong: Publishing Institution Ministry of Education, http://english.moe.go.kr/boardCnts/view.do?boardID=282&boardSeq=83771&lev=0&searchType=null&statusYN=W&page=1&s=english&m=0303&opType=N.

Moe T.M. (2005). "Teacher unions and school board elections", in Howell, W.J. (ed.), *Besieged. School Boards and the Future of Education Politics*. Washington D.C.: Brookings Institution Press (pp. 254–287).

—— (2006). "A Union by Any Other Name", in Peterson, P.E. (ed.), *Choice and Competition in American Education*. Lanham, MD: Rowman and Littlefield Publishers (pp. 123–135).

—— (2011). *Special Interest. Teachers Unions and American Schools*. Washington D.C.: Brookings Institution Press.

—— (2017a). "Teacher Unions in the United States: The Politics of Blocking", in Moe, T.M. and Wiborg, S. (eds), *The Comparative Politics of Education: Teacher Unions and Education Systems Around the World*. Cambridge: Cambridge University Press (pp. 24–55).

—— (2017b). "The Comparative Politics of Education: Teachers Unions and Education Systems Around the World", in Moe, T.M. and Wiborg, S. (eds), *The Comparative Politics of Education: Teacher Unions and Education Systems Around the World*. Cambridge: Cambridge University Press (pp. 269–324).

—— (2019). *The Politics of Institutional Reform. Katrina, Education and the Second Face of Power*. Cambridge: Cambridge University Press.

Moe, T.M. and Wiborg, S. (2017). *The Comparative Politics of Education. Teacher Unions and Education Systems Around the World*. Cambridge: Cambridge University Press.

—— (2017b). "Introduction", in *The Comparative Politics of Education: Teacher Unions and Education Systems Around the World*. Cambridge: Cambridge University Press (pp. 1–23).

Mounk, Y. (2018). *The People vs. Democracy. Why Our Freedom Is in Danger and How to Save It*. Cambridge, MA: Harvard University Press.

Mourshed, M., Chijioke, C. and Barber, M. (2010). *How the World's Most Improved School Systems Keep Getting Better*. McKinsey & Company, https://www.mckinsey.com/industries/social-sector/our-insights/how-the-worlds-most-improved-school-systems-keep-getting-better.

Mullis, I.V.S., Martin, M.O., González, E.J., Gregory, K.D., Garden, R.A., O'Connor, K.M., Chrostowski, S.J. and Smith, T.A. (2000). *TIMSS 1999 International Mathematics Report*. Boston: Boston College.

Mullis, I.V.S., Martin, M.O., Foy, P. and Hooper, M. (2016). *TIMSS 2015 International Results in Mathematics*. Boston: Boston College.

—— (2017). *PIRLS 2016 International Results in Reading*. Boston: Boston College.

Mullis, I.V.S., Martin, M.O., Foy, P., Kelly, D.L. and Fishbein, B. (2020). *TIMSS 2019. International results in Mathematics and Science*. Boston: Boston College

NAE (2009). *What Influences Educational Achievement in Swedish Schools? A Systematic Review and Summary Analysis*. Stockholm: NAE.

Nagel, A.K. (2010). "International networks in education politics", in Jakoby, A.P., Martens, K. and Wolf, K.D. (eds), *Education in Political Science: Discovering a Neglected Field*. London: Routledge (pp. 156–174).

Norrudin, N. (2018). *Ministry of Education*, SingaporeInfopedia, https://eresources.nlb.gov.sg/infopedia/articles/SIP_2018-01-17_103146.html.

Nusche, D., Miron, G., Santiago, P., Teese, R. (2015). *OECD Reviews of School Resources: Flemish Community of Belgium 2015*. Paris: OECD Publishing.

Nusche, D., Radinger, T., Busemeyer, M.R. and Theisens, H. (2016). *OECD Reviews of School Resources: Austria 2016*. Paris: OECD Publishing

Nozick, R. (1974). *Anarchy, State, and Utopia*. New York: Basic Books.

Oates, T. (2010). "Could do better: Using international comparisons to refine the National Curriculum in England, *The Curriculum Journal*, 22/2, 121–150, https://doi.org/10.1080/09585176.2011.578098.

—— (2015). *Finnish Fairy Stories*. Cambridge: Cambridge University Press.

OECD (2001). *Knowledge and Skills for Life. First Results from the OECD Programme for International Student Assessment (PISA) 2000*. Paris: OECD Publishing.

—— (2004). *Learning for Tomorrow's World. First Results from PISA 2003*. Paris: OECD Publishing.

—— (2007). *PISA 2006 Science Competencies for Tomorrow's World (Volume I)*. Paris: OECD Publishing.

—— (2010a). *PISA 2009 Results: What Students Know and Can Do — Student Performance in Reading, Mathematics and Science (Volume I)*. Paris: OECD Publishing.

—— (2010b). *PISA 2009 Results: What Makes a School Successful? — Resources, Policies and Practices (Volume IV)*. Paris: OECD Publishing.

—— (2011). *Lessons from PISA for the United States. Strong Performers and Successful Reformers in Education.* Paris: OECD Publishing.

—— (2012). *Equity and Quality in Education: Supporting Disadvantaged Students and Schools.* Paris: OECD Publishing.

—— (2013a). *PISA 2012 Results: What Makes Schools Successful? (Volume IV) Resources, Policies and Practices.* Paris: OECD Publishing.

—— (2013b). *Synergies for Better Learning. An International Perspective on Evaluation and Assessment.* Paris: OECD Publishing.

—— (2014a). *Education at a Glance 2014.* Paris: OECD Publishing.

—— (2014b). TALIS 2013 Results: An International perspective on Teaching and Learning. Paris: OECD Publishing.

—— (2014c). *PISA 2012 Results: What Students Know and Can Do — Student Performance in Mathematics, Reading and Science (Volume I, Revised edition, February 2014), PISA.* Paris: OECD Publishing.

—— (2015a). *Improving Schools in Sweden: An OECD perspective.* Paris: OECD Publishing.

—— (2015b). *Education Policy Outlook. Making Reforms Happen.* Paris: OECD Publishing.

—— (2015c). *OECD Skills Strategy Diagnostic Report Spain.* Paris: OECD Publishing.

—— (2016a). *PISA 2015 Results (Volume I): Excellence and equity in education.* Paris: OECD Publishing.

—— (2016b). *PISA 2015 Results. Policies and Practices for Successful Schools. Volume II.* Paris: OECD Publishing.

—— (2016c). *PISA 2015 Results (Volume II): Policies and practices for successful schools.* Paris: OECD Publishing.

—— (2016d). *Education at a Glance 2016.* Paris: OECD Publishing.

—— (2016e). *Skills Matter: Further Results from the Survey of Adult Skills*, OECD Skills Studies. Paris: OECD Publishing.

—— (2017a). *The Funding of School Education: Connecting Resources and Learning*, OECD Reviews of School Resources. Paris: OECD Publishing.

—— (2017b). *OECD Skills Strategy Diagnostic Report Italy.* Paris: OECD Publishing.

—— (2017c). *PISA for Development Assessment and Analytical Framework: Reading, Mathematics and Science.* Paris: OECD Publishing.

—— (2017d). *Education Policy in Greece. A Preliminary Assessment.* Paris: OECD Publishing.

—— (2017e). *School Choice and School Vouchers: An OECD Perspective*. Paris: OECD Publishing.

—— (2018a). *Skills in Ibero-America. Insights from PISA 2015*. Paris: OECD Publishing.

—— (2018b). *Seven Questions about Apprenticeships. Answers from International Experience*. Paris: OECD Publishing.

—— (2018c). *PISA: Equity in Education: Breaking Down Barriers to Social Mobility. Germany. Country Note*. Paris: OECD Publishing.

—— (2019a). *Education at a Glance 2019. OECD Indicators*. Paris: OECD Publishing.

—— (2019b). *OECD Skills Outlook 2019: Thriving in a Digital World*. Paris: OECD Publishing.

—— (2019c). *OECD Skills Strategy 2019: Skills to Shape a Better Future*. Paris OECD Publishing.

—— (2019d). *PISA 2018 Results (Volume I): What Students Know and Can Do*. Paris: OECD Publishing.

—— (2019e). *PISA 2018 Results (Volume II): Where All Students Can Succeed*. Paris: OECD Publishing.

—— (2019f). *Denmark-Country Note-PISA 2018 Results*. Paris: OECD Publishing.

—— (2019g). *Japan-Country Note-PISA 2018 Results*. Paris: OECD Publishing.

—— (2019h). *Poland-Country Note-PISA 2018 Results*. Paris: OECD Publishing.

—— (2019i). *Portugal-Country Note-PISA 2018 Results*. Paris: OECD Publishing.

—— (2019j). *Estonia-Country Note-PISA 2018 Results*. Paris: OECD Publishing.

—— (2019k). *OECD Economic Surveys: Estonia 2019*. Paris: OECD Publishing.

—— (2019l). *Skills Matter: Additional Results from the Survey of Adult Skills*, OECD Skills Studies. Paris: OECD Publishing.

—— (2020a). *Strengthening the Governance of Skills Systems: Lessons from Six OECD Countries*. Paris: OECD Publishing.

—— (2020b). *TALIS 2018 Results (Volume II): Teachers and School Leaders as Valued Professionals*. Paris: OECD Publishing.

—— (2020c). *PISA 2018 Results (Volume V): Effective Policies, Successful Schools*. Paris: OECD Publishing.

—— (2020d). *Education at a Glance 2020: OECD Indicators*. Paris: OECD Publishing.

—— (2020e). *OECD Employment Outlook 2020: Worker Security and the COVID-19 Crisis*. Paris: OECD Publishing.

—— (2020f). *Education Policy Outlook: Germany, Education Policy Perspectives*. Paris: OECD Publishing.

—— (2020g). *Education Policy Outlook in Portugal, OECD Education Policy Perspectives*. Paris: OECD Publishing,

—— (2021a). *Positive, High-achieving Students?: What Schools and Teachers Can Do*. TALIS, Paris: OECD Publishing.

—— (2021b). *Who We Are*, https://www.oecd.org/about/.

Olson, M. (1965). *The Logic of Collective Action: Public Goods and the Theory of Groups*. New York: Schocken Books.

Opfer, D. (2016). "Conditions and Practices Associated with Teacher Professional Development and Its Impact on Instruction in TALIS 2013", *OECD Education Working Papers*, No. 138, Paris: OECD Publishing.

Ornelas, C. (2003). "The bases of federalism and decentralization in education", *Revista Electrónica de Investigación Educativa*, 5/1, http://redie.uabc.mx/vol5no1/contents-ornelas.html.

Ozga, J. (2012). "Introduction. Assessing PISA", *European Educational Research Journal*, 11/2, 166–171.

Palamidessi, M. and Legarralde, M. (2006). "Teacher's Unions, Governments and Education Reforms in Latin America and the Caribbean: Conditions to Dialogue", *IDB Working Paper 14978*, Washington DC: Inter-American Development Bank, https://publications.iadb.org/en/teachers-unions-governments-and-education-reforms-latin-america-and-caribbean-conditions-dialogue.

Papay, J.P., Murnane, R.J. and Willett, J.B. (2008). "The consequences of high school exit examinations for struggling low-income urban students: Evidence from Massachusetts", *NBER Working Paper 14186*, Cambridge, MA: National Bureau of Economic Research, www.nber.org/papers/w14186.

Park, Y. and Jang, M.H. (eds) (2014). *The Present and Future of Secondary Vocational Education in Korea*, Sejog-si: Korea Research Institute for Vocational Education and Training (KRIVET), http://eng.krivet.re.kr/ eu/ec/prg.euCDAVw.jsp?gn=M06-M060000064.

Parkyn, G.W. (1969). "Structure and function in education systems", *Prospects: Quarterly review of Education*, UNESCO, 1: 8–12, https://unesdoc.unesco.org/ark:/48223/pf0000262088.

Pasias, G. and Roussakis, Y. (2009). "Towards The European Panopticon: EU Discourses and Policies in Education and Training", in Cowen and Kazamias (eds), *International Handbook of Comparative Education*. London: Springer (pp. 479–498).

Patel, D. and Sandefur, J. (2020). "A Rosetta Stone for Human Capital", *Working Paper 550*, Washington, DC: Center for Global Development, https://www.cgdev.org/publication/rosetta-stone-human-capital.

Patrinos, H.A. (2011). *School Choice in The Netherlands*. CESifo DICE Report 9, pp. 55–59.

Pellegrino, J.W. (2004). *The Evolution of Educational Assessment. Considering the Past and Imagining the Future*. Princeton: Educational Testing Service.

Pew Research Center (2019). *Public's 2019 Priorities*, https://www.pewresearch.org/politics/2019/01/24/publics-2019-priorities-economy-health-care-education-and-security-all-near-top-of-list/.

Piopiunik, M., Schwerdt, G. and Woessmann, L. (2012). "Central School Exit Exams and Labor-Market Outcomes", *IZA discussion paper No. 68889* (September 2012).

Pistone, M. and Horn, M.B. (2016). *Disrupting Law School: How Disruptive Innovation Will Revolutionize the Legal World*, Clayton Christensen Institute for Disruptive Innovation, https://files.eric.ed.gov/fulltext/ED568678.pdf.

Podgursky, M.J. and Springer, M.G. (2007). "Teacher performance-pay: A review", *Journal of Policy Analysis and Management*, 26/4, 909–949.

Popham, W.J. (2001). "Teaching to the Test?", *Educational Leadership*, 58/6, 16–20.

PP (2019). *Elecciones Generales 2019. Programa Electoral*, http://www.pp.es/sites/default/files/documentos/programa-electoral-elecciones-generales-2019.pdf

Priestley, M., Biesta, G. and Robinson, S. (2015). *Teacher Agency. An Ecological Approach*. London: Bloomsbury Publishing.

PSOE (2019). *Programa Electoral PSOE. Elecciones 2019*, https://www.psoe.es/media-content/2019/04/PSOE-programa-electoral-elecciones-generales-28-de-abril-de-2019.pdf

Puelles, M. (2010). *Educación e ideología en la España contemporánea*. Madrid: Tecnos.

Quinn, R. (2012). "The Future Development of Education in Ireland", *Studies: An Irish Quarterly Review*, 101/402, 123–138.

Radio Sweden (2013). "Sweden slides down international education table. PISA Report 2012 — Sweden Worst in Class", 3 December 2013, https://sverigesradio.se/artikel/5722237.

Ramirez, F. and Boli, J. (1987). "The Political Construction of Mass Schooling: European Origins and Worldwide Institutionalization", *Sociology of Education*, 60/1, 2–17.

Rautalin, M. (2018). "PISA and the criticism of Finnish education: justifications used in the national media debate", *Studies in Higher Education*, 43/10, https://doi.org/10.1080/03075079.2018.1526773.

Rautalin, M. and Pertti, A. (2007). "The curse of success: The impact of the OECD´s Programme for International Student Assessment on the Discourse of the Teaching Profession in Finland", *European Educational Research Journal*, 6/4, 348–363.

Rawls, J. (1971). *A Theory of Justice*. Cambridge, MA: Harvard University Press.

Rechnungshof (2011). *Report of the Court of Audit: Controlling in the Federal Schools Sector, Vol. 2011/1*. Vienna:_Austrian Court of Audit.

Rechnungshof (2012). *Report of the Court of Audit: Financing Provincial Teachers, Vol. 2012/4*. Vienna: Austrian Court of Audit.

Reimers, F.M. (2020). "Thinking Multidimensionally About Ambitious Educational Change", in Reimers, F.M. (ed.), *Audacious Education Purposes. How Governments Transform the Goals of Education System*. Springer Open (pp. 1–46).

Reisner, E.H. (1922). *Nationalism and Education: Since 1789, a Social and Political History of Modern Education*. London: Macmillan.

—— (2008). *Nationalism and Education Since 1789: A Social and Political History of Modern Education*. London: Forgotten Books.

Renehan, C. and Williams, K. (2015). "Religion, education and conflict in the Republic of Ireland", *Ricerche di pedagogia e didattica. Journal of Theories and Research in Education*, 10/1, 67–87, https://doi.org/10.6092/issn.1970-2221/4684.

Renzulli, L.A. and Evans, L. (2005). "School choice, charter schools, and white flight", *Social Problems*, 52/3, 398–418, www.jstor.org/stable/10.1525/sp.2005.52.3.398.

Richards, S. (2017). *The Rise of Outsiders: How Mainstream Politics Lost its Way*. London: Atlantic Books.

Ringarp, J. (2016). "PISA lends legitimacy: A study of education policy changes in Germany and Sweden after 2000", *European Educational Research Journal*, 15/4, 447–461.

Ripley, A. (2013). *The Smartest Kids in the World*. New York: Simon & Schuster.

Rivkin, S.G., Hanushek, E.A. and Kain, J.F. (2005). "Teachers, schools, and academic achievement", *Econometrica*, 73/2, 417–458.

Roberts, D. (2013). "Chinese Education: The Truth Behind the Boasts", *Businessweek*, 4 April.

Robitzsch, A., Lüdtke, O., Goldhammer, F., Kroehne, U. and Köller, O. (2020). "Reanalysis of the German PISA Data: A Comparison of Different Approaches for Trend Estimation With a Particular Emphasis on Mode Effects", *Frontiers in Psychology*, 26 May 2020, https://doi.org/10.3389/fpsyg.2020.00884.

Roche, P. and Léon, A. (2018). *Histoire de l'enseignement en France*. Paris : Que Sais-Je ?

Rockoff, J.E. (2004). "The impact of individual teachers on student achievement: Evidence from panel data", *American Economic Review*, 94/2, 247–252.

Rodríguez Ramírez, C.A. (2015). "El Derecho a la Educación en Costa Rica: entre la realidad y la utopía", *Revista Calidad en la Educación Superior*, 6/1, 249–268.

Roldán, T. and Cabrales, A. (2020). "Dos acuerdos educativos para la legislatura: una propuesta transversal", *ESADE-EcPol*, Policy Briefing 1, https://www.esade.edu/itemsweb/wi/research/ecpol/EsadeEcPol_policybrief1.pdf.

Ross, E.W. and Vinson, K. (2014). "Dangerous Citizenship", in Ross, E.W. (ed.), *The Social Studies Curriculum. Purposes, Problems, and Possibilities*, Albany: State University of New York Press (pp. 93–125).

Rousseau, J.J. (1762). *Émile ou de l'Éducation*. Paris: La Librairie.

Rowe, C. (2016). "Massachusetts is a lot like us, so why are its schools so much better?", *The Seattle Times*, 19 March, https://www.seattletimes.com/education-lab/massachusetts-is-a-lot-like-us-so-why-are-its-schools-so-much-better/.

Rözer, J. and Bol, T. (2019). "Labour Market Effects of General and Vocational Education over the Life-Cycle and across Time: Accounting for Age, Period, and Cohort Effects", *European Sociological Review*, 35/5, 701–717, http://dx.doi.org/10.1093/esr/jcz031.

Rumberger, R.W. and Lim, S.A. (2008). *Why Students Drop Out of School: A Review of 25 Years of Research*. Santa Barbara (CA): California Dropout Research Project, http://lmri.ucsb.edu/dropouts/pubs_reports.htm#15.

Sahlberg, P. (2006). "Education Reform for Raising Economic Competitiveness", *Journal of Educational Change*, 7/4, 259–287.

—— (2016). "The Finnish Paradox. Equitable Public Education Within a Competitive Market Economy", in Adamson, F., Åstrand, B. and Darling-Hammond, L., *Global Education Reform. How Privatization and Public Investment Influence Education Outcomes*. New York: Routledge (pp. 110–130).

—— (2021). *Finnish Lessons 3.0. What Can the World Learn from Educational Change in Finland*. New York: Teachers College Press.

Sahlgren, G.H. (2015). *Real Finnish Lessons. The True Story of an Education Superpower*. Surrey: Centre for Policy Studies.

Sandel, M. (2020). *The Tyranny of Merit. What's Become of the Public Good*. New York: Farrar, Strauss and Giroux.

Saporito, S. (2003). "Private choices, public consequences: Magnet school choice and segregation by race and poverty", *Social Problems*, 50/2, 181–203, http://dx.doi.org/10.1525/sp.2003.50.2.181.

Schleicher, A. (2011). *Building a High-Quality teaching Profession: Lessons from around the World*. Paris: OECD Publishing.

—— (2015). *Schools for 21st-Century Learners: Strong Leaders, Confident Teachers. Innovative Approaches, International Summit on the Teaching Profession*. Paris: OECD Publishing.

—— (2018). *World Class. How to Build a 21st-century School System*. Paris: OECD Publishing.

—— (2020). *The Secret to Finnish Education: Trust*. Paris: OECD Publishing.

Scott, T. (2004). "Teaching the Ideology of Assessment", *Radical Teacher*, 71, 30–37, http://www.jstor.com/stable/20710280?seq=1&cid=pdf-reference#references_tab_contents.

Shepherd, J. (2009). "Prescriptive national curriculum restricts teachers", *The Guardian*, 13 April, http://www.ascd.org/publications/newsletters/policy-priorities/vol15/issue2/England's-National-Curriculum,-20-Years-On@-A-Teacher's-Viewpoint.aspx.

Simola, H. (2005). "The Finnish miracle of PISA: historical and sociological remarks on teaching and teacher education", *Comparative Education*, 41/4, 455–470.

Simon, B. and Rubenstein D. (1969). *The Evolution of the Comprehensive School*. New York: Routledge and Kegan Paul.

Sireci, S. (2015). "Beyond ranking of nations: Innovative research on PISA", *Teachers College Record*, 117/1, 1–8.

Smith, K.B. (2003). *Ideology and Education. The Commonwealth, the Market and American Schools*. Albany: State University of New York Press.

Soon, T.W. (1988). *Singapore's New Education System: Education Reform forNational Development*. Singapore: Institute of Southeast Asian Studies.

Sorensen, C.W. (1994). "Success and Education in South Korea", *Comparative Education Review*, 38/1, 10–35.

SOU (2014). *The Government Must Not Abdicate (Staten får inte abdikera)*. Stockholm: Statents Offentliga Utredningar, https://www.regeringen.se/rattsliga-dokument/statens-offentliga-utredningar/2014/02/sou-20145/.

Spring, J. (2015). *Globalization of Education. An Introduction* (2nd edition). New York: Routledge.

Steiner-Khamsi, G. (2003). "The Politics of League Tables", *Journal of Social Sciences Education*, 2/1, 1–6.

Striethold, R., Bos, W., Gustafsson, J.E., Rosen, M. (eds) (2014). *Educational Policy Evaluation through International Comparative Assessments*. Münster: Waxmann.

Swift, M. (2009). "England's National Curriculum 20 Years On: A Teacher's Viewpoint", *Infobrief*, 15/2, http://www.ascd.org/publications/newsletters/policy-priorities/vol15/issue2/England's-National-Curriculum,-20-Years-On@-A-Teacher's-Viewpoint.aspx.

Takayama, K. (2008). "The politics of international league tables: PISA in Japan´s achievement crisis debate", *Comparative Education*, 44, 387 – 407.

—— (2017). "Imagining East Asian education otherwise: neither caricature, nor scandalization", *Asia Pacific Journal of Education*, 37/2, 262–274, http://dx.doi.org/10.1080/02188791.2017.1310697.

Tan, J. (1997). "Church, State and Education: Catholic Education in Hong Kong during the Political Transition", *Comparative Education*, 33/2, 211–232, http://www.jstor.org/stable/3099890.

Tan, Y. K., Chow, H. K. and Goh, C. (2008). *Examinations in Singapore: Change and Continuity (1891–2007)*. Singapore: World Scientific Publishing.

Tao, L., Zhen, L., Kardaszewicz, K. and Liljert, M. (2013). *They Are Also Parents: A Study on Migrant Workers with Left-behind Children in China*. Beijing: Center for Child Rights and Corporate Social Responsibility.

Tarelli, I., Bos. W., and Bremerich-Vos, A. (2012). "Germany", in Mullis, I.V.S., Martin, M.O., Minnich, C.A., Stanco, G.M., Arora, A., Centurino, V.A.S. and Castle, C.E. (eds), *PIRLS 2011 Encyclopedia: Education Policy and Curriculum in Reading*, Chestnut Hill, MA: TIMSS & PIRLS International Study Center, Boston College (pp. 313–340).

Tatto, M. (2014). "Teacher Education Development Study-Mathematics (TEDS-M)", in Lerman, S. (ed.), *Encyclopedia of Mathematics Education*. Dordrecht: Springer (pp. 828–834), https://doi.org/10.1007/978-94-007-4978-8_151.

Tatto, M.T., Schwille, J., Senk, S.L., Ingvarson, L., Rowley, G., Peck, R., Bankov, K., Rodríguez, M. and Reckase, M. (2012). *Policy, Practice, and Readiness to Teach Primary and Secondary Mathematics in 17 Countries. Findings from the IEA Teacher Education and Development Study in Mathematics (TEDS-M)*. Amsterdam: International Association for the Evaluation of Educational Achievement.

The Economist (2014). "Education in Mexico: Phantom Teachers", 7 April, https://www.economist.com/americas-view/2014/04/07/phantom-teachers.

—— (2015). "China's left-behind", 17 October, https://www.economist.com/briefing/2015/10/17/little-match-children.

—— (2021). "The plight of China's 'left-behind' children", 10 April, https://www.economist.com/china/2021/04/08/the-plight-of-chinas-left-behind-children

—— (2021). "PISA results can lead policymakers astray — the parable of Finland", 7 December, https://www.economist.com/international/2019/12/05/pisa-results-can-lead-policymakers-astray.

Thelen, K. (2004). *How Institutions Evolve: The Political Economy of Skills in Germany, Britain, the United States, and Japan*. Cambridge: Cambridge University Press.

Tillmann, K.J., Dedering, K., Kneuper D., Kuhlmann, C. and Nessel, I. (2008). *PISA als bildungspolitisches Ereignis: Fallstudien in vier Bundesländern*, Wiesbaden: VS Verlag für Sozialwissenschaften.

Tire, G. (2021). "Estonia: A positive PISA experience", in Crato, N. (ed.), *Improving a Country's Education*. Cham: Springer Open (pp. 101–119), https://doi.org/10.1007/978-3-030-59031-4_1.

Thomas, W.I. and Thomas, D.S. (1928). *The Child in America. Behavior Problems and Programs*. New York: Knopf.

Thompson, C. and Cunningham, E. (2000). "Retention and Social Promotion: Research and Implications for Policy", *ERIC Digest No. 161*, New York: ERIC Clearinghouse on Urban Education, Teachers College, Columbia University.

Tucker, M. (2019). *Leading High-Performance School Systems: Lessons from the World's Best*. Alexandria, VA: ASCD.

Turnbull, C. M. (2009). *A History of Modern Singapore, 1819–2005*. Singapore: NUS Press.

Valijarvi, J., Linnakyla, P., Kupari, P., Reinkainen, P. and Arffman, I. (2002). *The Finnish Success in PISA — and Some Reasons Behind It*. Jyväskylä: Institute for Educational Research, University of Jyväskylä.

Van der Berg, S., Van Wyk, C., Burger, R., Kotzé, J., Piek, M. and Rich, K. (2017). "The Performance of Low Fee Independent Schools in South Africa — What Can Available Data Tell?" *Stellenbosch Economic Working Papers*, No. 1/2017, Stellenbosch.

Van Leeuwen, F. (2017). *International Summit on the Teaching Profession 2017. A Briefing by Education International*, https://download.ei-ie.org/Docs/WebDepot/EI_ISTP_Summit_2017_final.pdf.

Vedder, R. and Gallaway L. (1991). "The War between the Rent Seekers", *Public Choice*, 68/1–3, 283–289.

Verkaik, R. (2019). "Labour is right to target private school privilege but abolition isn't the right answer", *The Guardian*, 24 September 2019, https://www.theguardian.com/commentisfree/2019/sep/24/labour-class-war-private-schools-inequality.

Viet Nam News (2019). "VN gets high scores but not named in PISA 2018 rankings", 6 December.

Wahlström N. (2018). "Where is 'the political' in curriculum research?", *Journal of Curriculum Studies*, 50/6, 711–723.

Waldow, F. (2009). "What PISA did and did not do: Germany after the 'PISA-shock'", *European Educational Research Journal*, 8/3, https://doi.org/10.2304/eerj.2009.8.3.476.

Wert, J.I. (2019). *La Educación en España. Asignatura Pendiente*. Córdoba: Almuzara.

—— (2020). *Los Años de Rajoy. La política de la crisis y la crisis de la política*. Córdoba: Almuzara.

West, M.R. (2012). *Is Retaining Students in the Early Grades Self-Defeating?*, CCF Brief No. 4, Washington DC: Center on Children and Families at Brookings Institution.

West, M.R. and Woessmann, L. (2010). "Every Catholic child in a Catholic school: Historical resistance to state schooling, contemporary private competition and student achievement across countries", *Economic Journal*, 120, 229–255.

Wiborg, S. (2009). *Education and Social Integration. Comprehensive Schooling in Europe*. New York: Palgrave Macmillan.

—— (2017a). "Teacher Unions in England: The End is Nigh?" in Moe, T.M. and Wiborg, S. (editors), *The Comparative Politics of Education: Teacher Unions and Education Systems Around the World*. Cambridge: Cambridge University Press (pp. 56–83).

—— (2017b). "Teacher Unions in the Nordic Countries: Solidarity and the Politics of Self-Interest", in Moe, T.M. and Wiborg, S. (eds), *The Comparative Politics of Education: Teacher Unions and Education Systems Around the World*. Cambridge: Cambridge University Press (pp. 144–191).

Wiborg, S. and Larsen, K.R. (2017). "Why School Choice Reforms in Denmark Fail: the blocking power of the teacher union", *European Journal of Education*, 52, 92–103, https://doi.org/10.1111/ejed.12203.

Willets, D. (2017). *A University Education*. Oxford: Oxford University Press.

Wilson, H. E. (1978). Singapore: Singapore University Press.

Wisniewski, J. and Zahorska, M. (2020). "Reforming Education in Poland", in Reimers, F.M. (ed.), *Audacious Education Purposes*. Cham: Springer Open (pp. 181–208), https://doi.org/10.1007/978-3-030-41882-3.

Woessmann, L. (2007a). "International evidence on expenditure and class size: A review", *Brookings Papers on Education Policy*, 2006/2007, Washington DC: Brookings Institution (pp. 245–272).

—— (2007b). "International evidence on school competition, autonomy and accountability: A review", *Peabody Journal of Education*, 82/2–3, 473–497.

—— (2009). "International Evidence on School Tracking: A Review", *CESifo DICE*, Report 1, http://www.cesifo.de/DocDL/dicereport109.

—— (2011). "Cross-country evidence on teacher performance pay", *Economics of Education Review*, 30/3, 404–418.

Woessmann, L., Luedemann, E., Schuetz, G. and West, M.R. (2009). *School Accountability, Autonomy and Choice around the World*. Cheltenham: Edward Elgar.

Woessmann, L. and West, M.R. (2006). "Class-size effects in school systems around the world: Evidence form between-grade variation in TIMSS", *European Economic Review*, 50/3, 695–736.

Wooldridge, A. (2021). *The Aristocracy of Talent*. New York: Skyhorse Publishing.

Wong, K.K., Knüpling, F., Kölling, M. and Chebenova, D. (2017). "Federalism and Education: Cross-National Lessons on Governance, Standards and Accountability for the 21st Century", *Forum of Federations*, Occasional Papers Series No. 22, http://www.forumfed.org/wp-content/uploads/2014/01/OC_22_Forumfed.pdf.

Woodward, B. (2001). "What's new?", *The Guardian*, 16 October, https://www.theguardian.com/education/2001/oct/16/schools.uk.

Worcester, R.M. (1983). *Political Opinion Polling. An International Review*. London: Macmillan.

World Bank (2021). *Gini Index (World Bank estimate)*, https://data.worldbank.org/indicator/SI.POV.GINI?locations=ZJ).

Wu, M. (2010). *Comparing the Similarities and Differences of PISA 2003 and TIMSS*, OECD Education Working Papers, No. 32, Paris: OECD Publishing, http://dx.doi.org/10.1787/5km4psnm13nx-en.

Yew, L.K. (2000). *From Third World to First: The Singapore Story 1965–2000*. New York: HarperCollins.

Zimmer, R. (2003). "A new twist in the educational tracking debate", *Economics of Education Review*, 22/3, 307–315, http://dx.doi.org/10.1016/s0272-7757(02)00055-9.

Index

ability grouping xvi, 38, 161–164, 168–171, 183–185, 196, 201, 238, 290–291, 294–295
academic training xii, 8, 16, 38, 41–43, 60, 96, 106, 108, 110, 113, 146–148, 161–162, 165, 169–176, 182–184, 194–196, 201, 218, 223–224, 227–228, 235, 238, 250, 262, 272, 281, 283, 291, 295
academies 26–27, 70, 76–77, 154, 156, 194, 199, 287
accountability xiv–xv, 3–4, 8–9, 18, 30, 58–61, 65, 75, 77, 84, 87–88, 90–93, 95, 98, 100–101, 104–105, 114–116, 121, 133, 143, 147, 150, 154–156, 158, 180–182, 186, 189–192, 199, 208, 242–243, 247, 261, 266–268, 271–272, 274–278, 284–287, 296–298
Ackerman, Bruce 25
Adams, John Quincy 22
Adonis, Andrew 27–28, 70, 76–77
Africa 125, 159, 177, 292
Althusser, Louis 48
Ancient Greece 21
Apple, Michael W. 48
apprenticeships xiv, 109–112, 162, 171, 174, 199, 277
Argentina 102, 210
Aristotle 21
Armstrong, Hillary 50
Asia xvi, 13, 69, 76, 108, 122–126, 137, 144–146, 165, 177, 179, 187, 192–195, 198, 200–202, 206–208, 210, 222, 229, 231, 234, 237, 239–241, 292–294
assessment xiii–xiv, 4, 20, 36, 39–40, 45–46, 55–62, 65, 70, 91–93, 100, 106, 119–120, 126, 130–133, 140, 142, 146–147, 149–150, 158–159, 168, 176, 179–181, 183, 186, 191, 197, 199–201, 203–204, 209, 218–221, 224, 227–228, 231–232, 234, 240–241, 251, 256–258, 260, 266–267, 270, 272, 275, 281, 283–284, 289, 293–297
Australia xvii, 44, 81, 125, 130, 137, 140, 164, 177, 230, 292
Austria 90, 108–109, 171, 173–174, 176

Baker, Kenneth 50, 52
Balearic Islands 259
Ball, Stephen 30
Basque Country 246, 259–260
Belgium 78, 81, 146, 153–154, 171, 174
Bergbauer, Annika 61
Berger, Peter 48
Björklund, Jan 88
Blair, Tony 27–28, 154
Bourdieu, Pierre 48
Bray, Mark 36
Brazil 101–102, 124, 144, 160, 208, 210
Brown, Gordon 28
Bulmahn, Edelgard 216
Busemeyer, Marius 107
Bush, George W. 20
Butler, David 19

Callagham, James 50
Canada 81, 83, 90, 127, 136–137, 143, 147, 230
Caplan, Bryan 65
Catalonia 53, 55, 86, 246–247, 259–261, 263
central government. *See* government: central government
centralisation xiii, 8, 27, 54, 74, 81–83, 86–87, 89, 93, 95, 105, 115, 191, 198, 239, 258, 260, 274, 276, 284, 295

charter schools. *See* schools: charter schools
Chile 10, 26, 34, 101, 124–125, 130, 140, 142, 153, 163–164, 167, 207, 210–213
China, People's Republic of 56, 69, 123–124, 133, 136, 144, 153, 192–193, 195, 201–206
choice 4, 23, 25–28, 30, 32, 38, 41–43, 53, 60, 65, 67, 75–76, 86–87, 89, 94, 96–97, 112, 141, 151, 153–157, 162, 171–172, 174, 179, 181–182, 184, 186, 195, 210, 213, 223, 231, 246, 250–251, 260–261, 266, 271–272, 276–277, 279, 284–287, 290, 293, 297–298. *See also* parents: parental choice
church 2, 154, 231
class size xv–xvii, 4, 47, 64–65, 68, 97, 139, 144–146, 156, 170, 178–179, 186, 197, 209–210, 240–241, 250, 278, 281–283, 286, 293–294, 297
colleges 13, 54, 112
Colombia 26, 102, 159–160, 164–165, 167, 207, 210, 212, 289
competition 4, 8, 28, 30, 32, 58, 76, 112, 114, 155–156, 182, 190, 193, 199, 271–272, 286–287, 293
comprehensive policies. *See* policy: comprehensive policies
conflicts of interest xii, xvii, 2–3, 11, 75, 79, 84, 86, 98–99, 109, 111, 179, 209, 237, 256, 258–259, 269, 276, 278–280, 298
consensus xiii, 19–20, 31, 34, 38, 55, 63, 69–70, 78–79, 105, 112, 179, 193, 226, 246, 254–256, 264, 266–268, 273, 276, 279, 283, 288
consociationalism 31, 78, 255, 273
corporatism 105
correlation 125, 134, 141, 143–146, 155, 159, 166, 186, 212, 280–281, 290
Costa Rica 26, 63, 210
COVID-19 16, 64
Crato, Nuno 95, 227–228
Cuba 210
curriculum xiii–xiv, 4, 20, 29, 40–42, 47–51, 53–55, 57–58, 60, 62, 70, 77, 80, 84–88, 91–93, 97, 111–112, 119–120, 125, 134, 142, 147, 150, 157–158, 166, 168, 177, 181, 183, 191, 195, 197–201, 217, 221, 223–225, 227–228, 230–233, 239–242, 251, 257, 259, 262, 265–267, 273, 275, 280–281, 283, 286, 289, 293, 295–297
Czech Republic 173

data xi–xii, 1, 4, 29–30, 101–103, 112, 127–129, 131–132, 134–135, 138, 141, 143, 145, 155–159, 164, 173, 175–176, 179–180, 182, 184, 186, 190–191, 193, 198, 201–202, 205, 211, 214–215, 220–223, 226, 228–229, 232, 236, 239, 243, 245, 256–257, 263, 266–268, 279–281, 286–288, 290, 292, 296–298
decentralisation xiii–xiv, 8, 55, 74–75, 81–87, 89–93, 95, 105, 115, 126, 146–147, 224, 231, 246–247, 260, 275, 277, 284–285
decision making xiii, 11, 46, 55, 59, 73, 75, 78–79, 81–84, 86–87, 89–90, 93–95, 97, 105, 114, 116–117, 133–134, 147, 149–150, 152, 181, 194, 198, 232, 246–247, 260–261, 268, 274–276, 284–285, 297–298
demographic trends 14, 75, 78
Denmark 67, 141, 165, 167, 214, 220–221
Dewey, John 22, 24–25
Democracy and Education 24
digitalisation 13–14, 16, 78, 231
discrimination xvi, 56, 59, 149, 162, 165, 168, 180, 184–185, 219, 252, 272, 283, 290–291
diversification 39, 41, 161, 189, 272
diversity 24, 37–38, 46, 85, 127, 135, 161, 163, 168, 171, 181, 240–241, 253, 271, 274, 294
Dominican Republic 125, 131, 144, 207, 210
Dual VET. *See* Vocational Education and Training (VET): Dual VET

early school leaving 11, 38, 41–43, 53, 92–93, 113–114, 127, 148, 167, 169, 176, 185, 212, 219, 227, 236–237,

240–242, 249–251, 257–258, 262, 265, 291, 293–294, 298
early tracking. *See* tracking: early tracking
East Asia xvi, 69, 76, 122–126, 137, 144–146, 165, 177, 179, 192–193, 195, 198, 200–202, 206–208, 210, 229, 231, 234, 237, 239–241, 292–294
Ecuador 207, 209–210
education xi–xvii, 1–57, 59–71, 73–88, 90–101, 103–117, 121–122, 125–126, 132–142, 144, 146–163, 165–169, 171–183, 185–204, 206–220, 223–242, 245–299
 education policy xi–xiii, xvi, 1, 5, 12–13, 19–20, 29–31, 38–39, 43, 47, 55, 57, 68–69, 71, 81, 84, 90, 103, 106, 114, 121, 133–134, 158, 160, 172, 177, 183, 197, 213–215, 233, 237–238, 257, 267–268, 272, 280–281, 285, 289, 293, 298. *See also* policy
 education providers 3, 20, 21, 23, 25, 27–29, 32, 44, 66, 116. *See also* state provision
 education reforms xi–xiii, 1, 3, 8–11, 17–19, 26, 30–31, 33–34, 45–47, 52–53, 60, 64, 67–69, 71, 76, 79–80, 83–84, 86, 95, 97, 103–105, 113–117, 132–134, 176, 189, 193, 195, 214, 223, 225, 228, 238–239, 245, 248–249, 254–257, 264–270, 273–277, 279, 295, 297–298. *See also* reforms
  lower-secondary education 43, 113, 122, 144, 161, 171–172, 196–198, 201, 213, 217–218, 223, 225, 227, 231, 236, 240, 259, 293
  primary education 13, 74, 144, 165, 168, 170, 195–196, 201, 223, 225, 227, 235, 240, 251, 259, 283, 293
  upper-secondary education 38, 92–93, 107, 146, 162, 168, 171–172, 174–175, 197, 207, 213, 218, 223–225, 227, 231, 250, 258, 262, 264, 272, 283
Education International (EI) 47, 99–101
Edwards, David 99
efficiency xiv, 3–4, 8–9, 12, 14, 32, 56, 58, 65, 75, 81, 84, 87, 90, 92, 94–95,
102–103, 126, 133, 155, 162, 175, 181–182, 184, 189, 194, 196, 201, 212, 224, 230, 240, 247–248, 275, 277–278, 284, 287
egalitarianism xvi, 33, 38–39, 137, 160–161, 182–184, 186, 190, 213, 241, 249, 252–253, 272, 289–291
Ekström, Anna 88
employers xiv, 74, 78–79, 84, 97, 108–111, 117, 262, 269, 277
England 28, 50–51, 125–126, 161, 171, 195, 260
equity xv–xvi, 4, 5, 7, 20, 27, 29, 32–41, 43, 47, 50, 56, 65, 68, 80, 87, 90, 92–93, 116–117, 133, 149, 155, 158–161, 168–169, 182–183, 188, 190, 192, 201–203, 205, 211–214, 216–219, 226, 232, 234–238, 242, 249–253, 258, 265–267, 270–272, 288–291, 295, 297–298. *See also* inequity
Estonia 137, 145, 165, 167, 228–233, 317
Europe xvii, 2, 6–7, 9–10, 13, 23, 36, 44, 56, 67, 74, 77–78, 80, 87, 94–95, 108–110, 125–127, 137, 148, 167, 173, 177, 188, 191, 194, 207, 214–215, 217–220, 222–224, 226, 228–230, 238, 241, 245–247, 249, 262, 265, 292, 296, 313
evaluation 4, 8, 20, 29, 43, 56, 58–60, 62, 82, 86–88, 93, 98, 100, 103, 105–106, 133, 146–149, 158, 168, 177, 189, 200, 206, 208–209, 223–224, 227–228, 231, 234, 237, 239–241, 251, 256–261, 263–267, 278, 284, 294–295
evidence xi–xvii, 1, 4–5, 18–19, 25, 27, 29–30, 36, 38, 43, 47, 53, 58–66, 68, 71, 82, 89, 95, 99–101, 108, 115, 130, 133–135, 138–139, 143–144, 147–148, 150–151, 155, 161, 163, 174, 176, 179–182, 184–185, 190–191, 205, 210, 222, 225, 228, 232, 235, 237–239, 242, 248, 254, 256–259, 261, 268, 272, 279–285, 289–291, 295–298
evidence-based policies. *See* policy: evidence-based policies
Eyzaguirre, Nicolás 34, 37

federalism xiii, 6, 10, 20, 42, 44, 48–49, 55, 73, 81–84, 86, 90–91, 112, 115, 209, 217, 247, 260, 274–275
Ferry, Jules 105
Field, Simon 34
Finland 30–31, 85, 99–101, 141–143, 145, 150–151, 159–160, 164–165, 187–193, 195, 200–202, 215, 217, 220–221, 229–230, 233, 238–239, 288, 294–295
fiscal policy 8, 67, 90, 245–247, 254. *See also* policy
France 6, 41, 74, 81, 83, 104–105, 219
Franco, Francisco 62, 148, 246
free schools. *See* schools: free schools
Fukuyama, Francis 69
funding xiii–xiv, 1–4, 8, 18, 20, 22, 24, 26–27, 32, 37, 63–66, 70, 73, 77, 80, 82–83, 87, 89–95, 98, 103, 105, 108, 114, 116–117, 137, 139, 152–155, 157, 181–182, 195, 213, 216, 224, 234, 246–247, 266, 268, 271–272, 274–278, 286–287, 296

Galicia 126, 259–260
Georgia 173
Germany 7, 10, 49, 74, 81, 84, 90–91, 107–109, 130, 136, 146–147, 171, 173–174, 176, 214–220, 230, 234, 238–239, 294–295
Gift, Thomas 5
globalisation 8, 14, 30, 58, 61, 75, 78, 80
Goldin, Claudia 12
governance xii–xiii, xv, 8–10, 27, 31–32, 73, 82–85, 87, 89, 92, 106–111, 114–115, 117, 154, 156, 224, 246–247, 269, 274, 287
government xi–xv, xvii, 1–3, 5, 7–9, 11, 18, 20, 23–24, 26–32, 36, 45–47, 49–53, 55, 67, 69–70, 73–95, 97, 103, 105–106, 108–111, 114–117, 121, 128, 130, 132–134, 137, 144–146, 149–150, 152–157, 178, 181–182, 193–195, 197–200, 208–210, 213–216, 220–222, 225, 227, 232, 234, 238, 245–249, 254–256, 258–261, 263–266, 270–272, 274–280, 282, 284–287, 293–294, 296–298

central government xiii–xiv, 49–50, 75, 77, 81, 83–90, 92–95, 97, 105, 115, 137, 146, 154, 234, 247–248, 255, 259–261, 265, 274–276, 285, 287, 293
grade repetition 53, 120, 125, 127, 162–169, 183–184, 201, 212–213, 227, 236–237, 241–242, 251, 258, 262, 264–265, 290–291, 294
Greece 10, 21, 36, 142, 145, 148, 151, 207
Grindle, Merilee 8–9, 75
Guatemala 160
Gutmann, Amy 51–52

Hall, Peter 107
Hanushek, Eric 61
Hong Kong 26, 36, 123–124, 133, 150, 153–154, 164, 192, 194, 201, 237
Hungary 10
Hunt, Tristram 37

Iceland 165, 167
ideology xi, xiii, xv–xvii, 3–6, 11, 18–21, 25, 29–34, 38–41, 43–44, 47–48, 51, 53–55, 57, 59–60, 62–64, 68–71, 76–78, 80, 106, 114, 148, 182, 190, 193–194, 206, 216, 237, 248, 257, 265, 269–274, 279–280, 282, 287, 290–293, 297–298
implementation xi–xiv, xvi–xvii, 1, 8–10, 18, 28, 38–39, 42, 47, 49–51, 58, 67–68, 70, 73–76, 78–80, 82–83, 85, 87–89, 91–95, 103, 106, 112, 114–115, 121, 128, 130, 133–134, 142, 148–150, 155, 157–158, 161–163, 167–169, 178–180, 182, 186, 189–190, 192, 195–196, 199, 202, 208–209, 213–214, 216, 219–227, 230–231, 237–242, 245–251, 258–259, 261–265, 270, 272, 274–276, 283–285, 287, 289–299
inclusivity xvi, 28, 37, 162, 184–185, 291, 294
Indonesia 26, 124
inequity 148, 160, 162–163, 168, 182–185, 211–213, 235–237, 241–242, 252, 272, 289–290, 294. *See also* equity
International Association for the Evaluation of Educational

Achievement (IEA) 61, 69, 119–120, 134
International Large-Scale Assessments (ILSAs) xiv, 4, 60–62, 66, 119–122, 125, 128, 133–135, 140, 145, 165, 176–178, 180, 182, 186–187, 192–193, 196, 206, 234–235, 237–238, 240–242, 281, 288, 292, 296–298
international surveys xii–xiii, xv, xvii, 1, 4, 82–83, 93, 103, 119–122, 128, 137, 140, 177–178, 180, 197, 215–216, 220–221, 226, 253, 258, 279–280, 292
  high performers 101, 131, 136, 156, 187, 207, 209, 226, 233, 239, 285, 295
  low performers xii, xvi, 10, 41, 65, 70, 91, 98, 101–102, 113, 122, 124, 126–128, 131, 144–145, 147, 150–152, 154, 158, 162, 168–170, 172, 177, 184–185, 187, 196, 201, 203, 207–208, 210, 212, 226, 251, 284–285, 287, 290–292
  top performers 38, 82, 99–100, 102–103, 121–125, 127–128, 131, 133, 136–137, 140, 142, 144–145, 151, 161, 164, 169, 177, 183, 187, 192–193, 196–198, 200–203, 205, 207–208, 210, 212, 214, 219, 221–223, 226, 229–230, 234–235, 237–238, 240, 251, 261, 285, 292–293, 295
investment xiv–xvii, 2, 4, 8, 13, 25, 32, 35–37, 64–65, 67, 75, 82–83, 88, 93–94, 96–97, 116, 121, 124, 126, 135–138, 144, 156, 160, 177–179, 186, 188–190, 195, 199, 210, 220–221, 227, 230, 241, 247–248, 250, 255, 270, 281–283, 286, 293, 297
Ireland 26, 70, 140, 153–154, 173
Italy 64, 101–102, 126–127, 142, 164, 173, 252

Jakoby, Anja 5
Japan 81, 101–102, 123–124, 130, 140, 143–144, 153, 165, 167, 173, 187–188, 192, 198, 200–201, 214, 221
Johnson, Boris 27

Kamens, David 61
Katz, Larry 12

Kazakhstan 131
Kenya 145, 170
Kosovo 124
Kremer, Michael 145
Kuczera, Malgorzata 34

labour market 2, 12–13, 17, 75, 82, 96, 109–110, 113, 117, 126, 171, 175–176, 220, 257, 262, 269, 277
Laidmets, Mart 230
Lakoff, George 62
Latin America xvi, 13, 44, 104, 124–125, 136, 140, 149, 159–160, 163, 165, 173, 177, 179, 206–214, 235, 240, 292–294, 314
Lebanon 26, 124
Levin, Ben 33
Lewin, Leif 89
Ley Orgánica de Educación (LOE) 43, 67, 257
Ley Orgánica de Modificación de la LOE (LOMLOE) 264, 266–267
Ley Orgánica General del Sistema Educativo (LOGSE) 42, 67, 249–250
Ley Orgánica para la Mejora de la Calidad Educativa (LOMCE) 43, 52–53, 62, 70, 86, 93, 97, 113, 249, 257, 260, 262, 265–266
lifelong learning 15–16, 110, 112, 175, 196, 232
Linz, Juan 69
literacy xvi, 6, 30, 63, 110, 119, 128, 180, 191, 195, 197, 200, 207, 229, 231, 239, 240, 252, 263, 293. See also reading
Lithuania 130
local authorities xiii, 27, 32, 50, 70, 75, 77, 81, 91, 154, 275, 287
Locke, John 21–22
  Some Thoughts Concerning Education 21
Löfven, Stefan 88
López Obrador, Andrés Manuel 45
lower-secondary education. See education: lower-secondary education
Luckmann, Thomas 48
Luxembourg 137, 172–174

Macao 26, 124, 144, 153
Malaysia 101, 124
marketisation 27, 32, 60, 80, 271
mass schooling 2, 6–7, 24, 74, 115
mathematics 43, 100, 110, 119–120, 123–126, 128–130, 138, 140, 177, 187, 192, 203–204, 220–222, 225, 227–229, 235, 238, 251, 259–260, 280
May, Theresa 27
McArthur, David 55
McNeely, Connie 61
Mexico 10, 45, 102, 104, 124, 140, 143–144, 151, 188, 207, 209–211
Middle East 125, 177, 292
Mill, John Stuart 22–25
  On Liberty 23–24
Moe, Terry 5, 66, 75, 106
Moldova 145
Morocco 124, 165

Netherlands, the 26, 78, 81, 85, 133, 150, 153–154, 171, 174, 217, 219, 229–230
New Zealand xvii, 125, 137, 154, 177, 292
non-profit organisations 79, 153
Nordic countries 39, 78–79, 105, 125–126, 158, 165, 213, 249, 252, 291
North America xvii, 125, 177, 194, 292
Norway 160, 221
Not in Employment Education or Training (NEET) 93, 127, 249–250
numeracy 6, 30, 63, 170, 180, 207, 229, 252
Nuño, Aurelio 45

Olson, Mancur 9
Organisation for Economic Cooperation and Development (OECD) xii, xvi, 10, 15, 26, 34, 36, 61, 64, 69, 94, 99–101, 103, 119–120, 123–125, 127, 129, 131–135, 137–140, 143–146, 150, 153, 159, 165, 169, 171–173, 175, 177, 179, 187–190, 192–193, 197, 199–207, 210–223, 225–231, 233–237, 241, 248–249, 251–252, 264, 266–268, 281, 296–297

Panama 145, 210

Paraguay 210
parents xiv, 4, 23, 25–27, 35–37, 39, 46, 52, 66, 77, 96, 104, 153–154, 156–157, 160, 171, 179, 181, 183, 185, 209–210, 212, 230, 232–233, 241, 253, 266, 269, 271–273, 277–278, 286–287, 289, 292, 294, 297
  parental choice 4, 26, 181, 266, 271, 272. *See also* choice
Passeron, Jean-Claude 48
Peña Nieto, Enrique 45
Peru 26, 124, 207, 209–210
Philippines, the 124, 140, 145
PIAAC (Survey of Adult Skills) 141–142, 180, 193, 207, 229, 252
Poland 11, 222–225, 228
policy xi–xiii, xv–xvii, 5, 7–9, 12, 19–20, 29, 31, 33, 38–39, 43, 47, 57, 65, 68–71, 73, 80–81, 83–84, 88, 90, 103, 105–106, 112, 115, 120–121, 133–135, 141–147, 150–151, 156, 172, 177–178, 180, 189, 212, 214–217, 220, 222, 225–229, 233–234, 237–240, 261, 266, 268, 272, 277, 279–280, 283–290, 293–294, 296–298. *See also* education: education policy; *See also* fiscal policy
  comprehensive policies xvi, 38, 189, 192, 202, 212, 217, 240–241, 271–272, 293–294
  evidence-based policies xii, 30
  policy borrowing xvi, 285
  policy recommendations xi–xii, xv–xvii, 5, 134–135, 143–146, 150–151, 178, 180, 214, 217, 220, 222, 228–229, 237–240, 266, 268, 279–280, 282–285, 287–288, 290, 294, 296–298
policymakers xi–xii, xv, 5, 18, 33–34, 39, 41, 44–46, 48, 79, 94, 114, 121, 128, 134, 147, 162, 178, 183, 185–187, 196, 215–216, 232–234, 237, 241–242, 255, 268, 276, 279–281, 289, 294, 297–298
politics xiii, 27, 54, 57, 66, 71, 78, 108, 254, 274
  political costs xii, xvii, 11, 18, 94–95, 130, 133, 179, 210, 225, 245, 248, 265, 270, 282, 298

political economy xiii, 8, 64, 107, 114
political parties xi–xiv, 4, 11, 18, 20–21, 45, 64, 76, 78, 80, 84, 104, 106, 108, 114, 128, 193, 208, 248, 255, 258, 265–266, 268, 270–271, 273–275, 282, 284, 287, 293, 298
Pont, Beatriz 34
Popham, William J. 60
Portugal 11, 95, 133, 136, 164–165, 167, 207, 226–228
power xi–xiv, xvi, 3–4, 7, 9, 11–12, 27, 31, 33, 44–46, 48, 50, 52–53, 55–56, 61–62, 66–67, 73, 75–76, 78–84, 86, 88–90, 93, 95, 97–99, 103–106, 115–116, 121, 135, 147, 151–152, 158–159, 179, 181–182, 190, 193–194, 198, 208–209, 213, 217, 223, 232, 234, 238, 240–241, 246–248, 255–256, 260–265, 270–271, 274–280, 282–283, 285, 287, 293–294, 297–298
primary education. *See* education: primary education
privatisation 28, 32, 68, 255–256, 271, 287
privileged students. *See* students: privileged students
professional development xvi, 45–46, 80, 82, 139–140, 145, 179, 188, 196–198, 200, 210, 223–225, 227, 232, 240, 253, 283, 293
Programme for International Student Assessment (PISA) 1, 10–11, 25–26, 29, 87–89, 99–103, 119–139, 141, 143–146, 149–150, 152, 155, 157–159, 162–163, 165–169, 172–174, 177–182, 184–192, 201–207, 210–218, 220–222, 224, 226–240, 242, 251, 253, 256–259, 261, 266–268, 279–288, 290–291, 294–298
    PISA shock 10, 214–215, 217, 220–222, 234, 238–239, 295
Progress in International Reading Literacy Study (PIRLS) 11, 119–120, 126, 128–129, 138, 159, 177, 221, 223, 235, 242, 259, 280
public debate xii, 51–54, 65, 256, 296
public opinion 9–10, 19, 47, 62, 67, 79, 134, 254

public schools. *See* schools: public schools
Puerto Rico 128

Qatar 143
quality xiv–xvii, 3–4, 8, 11, 14, 17–18, 29, 32, 36–38, 40, 45, 56, 64–65, 68, 75, 82–83, 86–87, 91–93, 96, 100, 108, 113, 116, 121–122, 125–126, 133, 136, 139–142, 145–146, 148–151, 153–154, 157–158, 161, 173, 175–176, 178–182, 186, 188–189, 196, 198–200, 206–210, 213–214, 217, 219, 226–227, 231, 233, 238–242, 250–254, 258, 265–267, 269–271, 273, 276–279, 282–288, 291–297. *See also* teachers: teacher quality
Quinn, Ruairy 70

Rawls, John 33
reading 119–120, 126, 129, 131–132, 138, 170, 177, 187, 191–192, 204, 220–222, 228–229, 232, 235, 238–239, 259–260, 280, 295. *See also* literacy
reformers 8, 28, 46, 79, 99
reforms xi–xiv, xvi–xvii, 1, 3–4, 6, 8–11, 17–19, 26–27, 30–31, 33–34, 45–47, 52–54, 60–64, 66–71, 73–80, 82–84, 86–89, 93, 95–99, 103–106, 113–117, 132–134, 143, 154–155, 176, 185, 189–191, 193–195, 199, 209, 214–215, 217, 220–228, 230, 232–234, 238–242, 245–246, 248–249, 254–257, 262–270, 273–277, 279, 282, 286, 293, 295–298. *See also* education: education reforms
regions xii–xiv, xvi, 13, 28, 32, 49–50, 53, 55, 67, 69, 75–76, 81–86, 89–95, 102, 109–111, 115–116, 119, 122–124, 126–127, 132, 137–138, 145–147, 149–150, 159, 167–168, 177–178, 180, 192, 203–211, 215, 234, 237, 240–241, 246–248, 251, 255–262, 264, 266–268, 273–276, 281, 283–285, 292–294
Reimers, Fernando 22
reskilling 15, 110, 200
resources xiv–xv, 3, 9, 18, 24–26, 35–37, 63, 65, 67–68, 73–75, 79, 86–87, 90, 92, 94–97, 99–101, 104, 114–116, 121,

136, 138–139, 144–145, 150–151, 155, 159, 164, 170, 178–179, 182–183, 185, 188–189, 192, 197–198, 201, 203, 210–211, 254–255, 271, 273, 275–278, 287, 289
reverse causality 166, 173, 184, 290
Ricci, Matteo 56
Rousseau, Jean-Jacques 21–22
 Émile ou de l'Éducation 21
Russia 203, 231–232

Sahlberg, Pasi 30, 60, 80
Schleicher, Andreas 133, 189, 216–217, 266–267
schools xiii, xv, 2, 4, 7–9, 11, 13–14, 16–17, 22–29, 31–32, 35–44, 46, 49–55, 57–61, 63, 65–67, 70, 74, 76–77, 81, 83–85, 87–93, 95–105, 111–114, 119–120, 122, 125–127, 131, 133–134, 136, 139, 142, 144–145, 147–157, 159, 163, 165, 167–171, 175–178, 180–182, 185–186, 188, 190–191, 193–199, 201–206, 208, 210–213, 216, 218–219, 223–228, 231–233, 235–242, 249–253, 257–259, 261–262, 265–267, 271–273, 275–277, 280, 283–288, 291, 293–298
 charter schools 26, 32, 96, 152–153, 156, 190, 271
 free schools 27, 77
 lower-secondary schools. *See* education: lower-secondary education
 primary schools. *See* education: primary education
 public schools 24–28, 32, 35–36, 66, 77, 91, 144, 152–157, 181–182, 266, 271, 286–287
 school autonomy xv, 149–151, 180–181, 186, 188, 201–202, 224, 238, 261, 266, 275, 284–287, 293, 295–297
 upper-secondary schools. *See* education: upper-secondary education
science 5–6, 22, 57, 100, 110, 119–120, 123, 125–129, 138, 177, 187, 192, 204, 220–222, 227–229, 232, 235, 238, 259, 280

Scotland 26, 100
Scott, Tony 57
segregation 25–26, 39, 41, 43, 62, 89, 108, 148–149, 155, 161–162, 168, 184, 189, 211, 238, 240–241, 250–252, 266–267, 271–272, 286–287, 290, 292, 295
Singapore 13, 76, 82, 102, 108, 123–125, 140, 142, 164–165, 171, 173, 192–196, 198, 200–202, 207, 212, 219, 229, 240, 292–293
skills xii, 1–2, 6, 11–17, 39, 43, 57, 59–60, 63, 70, 82, 91, 96, 98, 108–114, 120, 122, 126, 128, 131, 140–143, 146–147, 149–151, 157, 160, 163–164, 166, 169–171, 174–177, 180–181, 183, 185, 188, 191, 193, 197, 200–201, 204, 206–208, 212, 214, 219–220, 229–230, 236, 241, 249, 252–254, 260, 269–270, 277, 285, 289, 291, 294–295. *See also* reskilling; *See also* upskilling
Smith, Kevin 29–30
socio-economic background 59, 89, 147–149, 156–159, 161–162, 165, 167–169, 171–172, 182, 184–185, 190, 202–204, 211, 214, 218–219, 232, 238, 253, 265, 283, 286–288, 291, 295
Soskice, David 107
South America 149
South Korea 13, 102, 123–124, 130–131, 142, 187–188, 192–195, 197–201, 221, 237, 240, 292
Soviet Union 217, 230
Spain ix, xi, xii, 6, 11, 20, 27–28, 42, 49, 52–53, 55, 64, 67–68, 70, 81, 85–86, 92, 94–95, 101, 112, 126–127, 130–132, 137–138, 148–149, 154, 164–165, 167–169, 173, 176, 188, 204, 211–212, 233–237, 242, 245–254, 256–257, 260–263, 265–268
stakeholders xi–xv, 2–3, 8–9, 11, 18, 46, 51, 64, 73–76, 78–80, 83, 96–97, 103, 106, 110–111, 114–117, 189, 208, 210, 215–216, 222, 254–256, 258, 270, 274, 276–277, 279, 298
state provision 2, 4, 20–25, 27–29, 32, 44, 51, 56, 64, 70, 73, 77, 79, 88, 91,

191, 204, 257. *See also* education: education providers
Stepan, Alfred 69
Stokes, Donald 19
students xii–xvii, 1, 3–4, 7–12, 14–18, 20, 25–26, 29, 32, 35, 37–43, 46–48, 50, 52–63, 65–66, 69, 71, 74–75, 80–81, 85, 87–89, 91–94, 96–106, 112–114, 116–117, 119–153, 155–215, 217–232, 234–243, 247–255, 257–259, 261–267, 269, 271–272, 274–298. *See also* Vocational Education and Training (VET): VET students
privileged students 157–158, 182
student outcomes xiv–xv, 4, 8, 11, 18, 29, 48, 53, 61, 69, 75, 80, 88, 98–102, 105–106, 114, 116, 120–121, 126–127, 134–135, 137–144, 146, 149, 151, 156–157, 159–161, 177–180, 183, 190, 193, 195, 210, 214, 221, 232, 239, 241–242, 249, 251, 275, 280–282, 284–289, 293–294, 298
student performance xii–xiii, xv–xvi, 1, 3–4, 10, 59, 69, 75, 80, 87–89, 93, 101–102, 104, 106, 114, 116, 120–122, 125–131, 134–148, 150–152, 155–158, 160, 163, 165–166, 169–174, 176–184, 186–189, 191–193, 198, 201–202, 206–207, 209–211, 213–215, 217–218, 220, 222–224, 227–229, 232, 235, 237–239, 241–242, 251, 258, 261, 265–267, 274, 278–281, 283, 286, 288–292, 295–297
underprivileged students 40, 157–158, 258
Sweden 10, 87–89, 108, 136, 142, 165, 167, 176, 221, 304
Switzerland 90, 108–109, 140, 171, 173–174, 176, 217, 219, 229
Syria 219

Taipei 26, 123–124, 144
Taiwan 123, 192, 194, 201
taxes xiii, 65, 87, 89–92, 94, 110, 247, 275
teachers xii–xv, xvii, 2–3, 8–9, 17–18, 20, 27, 29, 40, 43–47, 51, 57–64, 66–68, 71, 74–77, 79, 82–84, 94–95, 97–106, 114–117, 136, 139–152, 156, 158, 162–168, 170–171, 178–184, 188–189, 191–193, 195–202, 207–210, 213, 218, 221, 223–225, 227–228, 230–233, 238–241, 247, 249, 251, 253, 255, 257–259, 261, 263–264, 267, 270, 272, 277–278, 281–287, 289, 292–293, 295
teacher quality xvi–xvii, 29, 56, 82–83, 100, 139, 149, 151, 179, 181, 186, 188–189, 196, 207, 209, 213, 240–241, 278, 282–285, 293–294, 296
teachers' salaries xiv–xv, 4, 64, 68, 97, 105, 139, 142–144, 179, 186, 188, 208, 254, 277, 281–282, 297
teachers' unions. *See* unions
Teaching and Learning International Survey (TALIS) 101–103, 140–141
Thailand 124, 136
Thatcher, Margaret 50
Thelen, Kathleen 107
Tire, Gunda 228
tracking xvi, 7, 34, 38, 41–43, 47, 106, 112–113, 139, 161–163, 168, 170, 172, 175, 183–184, 189, 195–199, 201–202, 212–213, 216–219, 223, 227, 232, 235, 238, 240–241, 250, 267, 272, 290, 293–295
early tracking xvi, 38, 41, 163, 168, 184, 201–202, 212–213, 217–219, 235, 238, 240–241, 267, 290, 293–295
trade-offs xvi–xvii, 55, 109, 145, 161, 178–179, 197, 210, 240, 293
Trends in International Mathematics and Science Study (TIMSS) 11, 119–120, 123–126, 129–130, 138, 159, 177, 196, 215, 221, 223, 226, 229, 231, 235, 242, 259, 280
Tucker, Mark 198, 233
Tunisia 164
Turkey 10, 145, 151

underprivileged students. *See* students: underprivileged students
unions xiv–xvi, 3–4, 9, 43–47, 51, 58, 62, 64, 66–68, 76, 79, 83–84, 97–106, 108–111, 114–117, 179, 187–190, 193–194, 199–200, 208–210, 218, 226, 239–241, 248, 250, 254–255, 258, 263,

277–279, 282, 284–285, 287, 293–295, 297
United Arab Emirates 26, 102, 143
United Kingdom xvii, 6, 23, 26–28, 30–31, 35, 41, 44, 50, 52, 64, 70, 76–77, 81, 102, 133, 137, 153–154, 156, 164, 287
United States of America 2, 6–7, 10, 13, 20, 22, 24, 26, 42, 44, 46, 48–49, 64–66, 70, 74, 81, 83, 91, 98, 104–105, 107, 112, 127, 130, 133, 136–138, 146–147, 154, 198
universities xvi, 5, 14–16, 36, 62, 77, 108, 112–113, 139–142, 148, 171, 175–176, 180, 188, 194, 196, 198–200, 208, 213, 218, 225, 232–233, 240, 250, 252–253, 257–258, 261–264, 293–294
upper-secondary education. *See* education: upper-secondary education
upskilling 15, 140, 200
Uruguay 164, 167, 207, 210

Valencia 259
van Leeuwen, Fred 47, 100
vested interests xiii, xv, 3–5, 8, 63–64, 66–67, 76, 79–80, 96, 98, 116, 189, 193, 222, 256, 258, 268, 274, 278–279, 282, 284–285, 293, 297–298
Vietnam 130, 133, 136, 159, 202, 205
Vocational Education and Training (VET) xiv, 11, 38, 41, 43, 53, 67, 84, 96, 106–114, 117, 162, 171–176, 183–185, 199, 213, 217–219, 223, 225, 227, 238, 241–242, 250, 257–258, 262–263, 265, 272, 277, 290–291, 294–296
  Dual VET 84, 108–110, 113, 262, 265
  VET students 172, 174–176, 219

Wales 50
Wibbels, Erik 5
Wiborg, Susan 75
Wiborg, Susanne 5, 23, 66
Woessmann, Ludwig 61, 313
Worcester, Robert 9

About the Team

Alessandra Tosi was the managing editor for this book.

Melissa Purkiss performed the copy-editing, proofreading and indexing.

Jeevanjot Kaur Nagpal designed the cover. The cover was produced in InDesign using the Fontin font.

Luca Baffa typeset the book in InDesign and produced the paperback and hardback editions. The text font is Tex Gyre Pagella; the heading font is Californian FB.

Luca produced the EPUB, AZW3, PDF, HTML, and XML editions — the conversion is performed with open source software such as pandoc (https://pandoc.org/) created by John MacFarlane and other tools freely available on our GitHub page (https://github.com/OpenBookPublishers).

This book need not end here...

Share

All our books — including the one you have just read — are free to access online so that students, researchers and members of the public who can't afford a printed edition will have access to the same ideas. This title will be accessed online by hundreds of readers each month across the globe: why not share the link so that someone you know is one of them?

This book and additional content is available at:

https://doi.org/10.11647/OBP.0332

Donate

Open Book Publishers is an award-winning, scholar-led, not-for-profit press making knowledge freely available one book at a time. We don't charge authors to publish with us: instead, our work is supported by our library members and by donations from people who believe that research shouldn't be locked behind paywalls.

Why not join them in freeing knowledge by supporting us: https://www.openbookpublishers.com/support-us

Follow @OpenBookPublish

Read more at the Open Book Publishers BLOG

You may also be interested in:

Learning, Marginalization, and Improving the Quality of Education in Low-income Countries
Daniel A. Wagner, Nathan M. Castillo and Suzanne Grant Lewis (eds.)

https://doi.org/10.11647/OBP.0256

Open Education
International Perspectives in Higher Education
Patrick Blessinger and TJ Bliss (eds.)

https://doi.org/10.11647/OBP.0103

The Power of Music
An Exploration of the Evidence
Susan Hallam and Evangelos Himonides

https://doi.org/10.11647/OBP.0292

www.ingramcontent.com/pod-product-compliance
Lightning Source LLC
Chambersburg PA
CBHW061249230426
43663CB00022B/2951